FEMINISM SPOKEN HERE

FROMSITE TOVISION

PACIFIC STANDARD TIME: ART IN L.A. 1945–1980 | An initiative of the Getty with arts institutions across Southern California.

Presenting Sponsors | The Getty | **Bank of America**

 Otis College of Art and Design

Doin' It in Public: Feminism and Art at the Woman's Building
is made possible by a generous grant from the Getty Foundation with additional funding provided by the Andy Warhol Foundation for the Visual Arts, Henry Luce Foundation, Department of Cultural Affairs of the City of Los Angeles, and the Barbara Lee Family Foundation.

This book is published with the assistance of the Getty Foundation as part of a two-volume set in conjunction with the exhibition **Doin' It in Public: Feminism and Art at the Woman's Building**, October 1, 2011–January 28, 2012, organized by the Ben Maltz Gallery at Otis College of Art and Design. This project is part of the Getty's initiative Pacific Standard Time: Art in L.A. 1945–1980.

Doin' It in Public: Feminism and Art at the Woman's Building
ISBN 0-930209-22-2
Copyright © 2011 Ben Maltz Gallery, Otis College of Art and Design

From Site to Vision: the Woman's Building in Contemporary Culture
ISBN 0-930209-23-0
Copyright © 2011 Ben Maltz Gallery, Otis College of Art and Design and the Woman's Building

Otis College of Art and Design
9045 Lincoln Boulevard, Los Angeles, CA 90045
www.otis.edu/benmaltzgallery; galleryinfo@otis.edu; 310. 665. 6905

Ben Maltz Gallery is grateful to all those who gave their generous permission to reproduce the publications' images. Every effort has been made to contact the owners and photographers of objects reproduced and to secure all permissions and we apologize for any inadvertent errors or omissions. Anyone having further information concerning copyright holders is asked to contact Otis College of Art and Design so this information can be included in future printings.

Editors: Sondra Hale and Terry Wolverton
Production Editors: Meg Linton, Sue Maberry, Elizabeth Pulsinelli
Design: Susan Silton
Production assistance: Kevin Wong
Printer: CS Graphics, Singapore
Edition: 2,000

Cover: **Founders of the Woman's Building: Judy Chicago (L), Sheila Levrant de Bretteville (M), Arlene Raven (R)**, circa 1973. Photographer unknown. Woman's Building Image Archive, Otis College of Art and Design. Flyleaf: **Feminist Art Workers, *This Ain't No Heavy Breathing***, 1978. Publicity still. Pictured Laurel Klick (L), Nancy Angelo (M), and Cheri Gaulke (R). Photograph by E.K. Waller. © Feminist Art Workers.

FROMSITE TOVISION

THE WOMAN'S BUILDING
IN CONTEMPORARY CULTURE

Ben Maltz Gallery
Otis College of Art and Design

Editors
Sondra Hale
Terry Wolverton

OTIS Otis College of Art and Design
the Woman's Building

TABLE OF CONTENTS

10   **Foreword**
Going Around in Circles
Lucy Lippard

18   **Introduction**
Terry Wolverton

38   **Power and Space: Feminist Culture and the Los Angeles Woman's Building, a Context**
Sondra Hale

84   **The Woman's Building and Los Angeles' Leading Role in the Feminist Art Movement**
Laura Meyer

118   **Looking Through a New Lens: An Interview with Arlene Raven**
Terry Wolverton

140   **Feminist Art Education at the Los Angeles Woman's Building**
Betty Ann Brown

162   **"At Home" at the Woman's Building (But Who Gets a Room of her Own?): Women of Color and Community**
Michelle Moravec and Sondra Hale

192   **The Ritual Body as Pedagogical Tool: The Performance Art of the Woman's Building**
Jennie Klein

230   **The Community of Design/The Design of Community: An E-Mail Dialogue**
Sheila Levrant de Bretteville and Bia Lowe

266   **Books in a New Language**
Kathleen Walkup

302   **Stories from a Generation: Video Art at the Woman's Building**
Cecilia Dougherty

328   **Words, Writers, Women**
Michele Kort

352   **Lesbian Art: A Partial Inventory**
Terry Wolverton

386   **Unburying Histories: the future(s) of feminist art**
Theresa Chavez

414   **Author Biographies**

417   **Acknowledgments**

Maria Karras, Woman's Building–Grandview location.
1973. Image shot for the first Feminist Studio Workshop
brochure. © Maria Karras.

WANTS/NEEDS

SPACE FOR Intellect disc.

IDEA EXCHANGE

MORE EXT courses ✳
(FREE)

Space to Sharing Work ✳✳✳

STUDIO Space ✳✳✳✳

CRITIQUE ✳✳✳✳

~~building space Planning~~

STUDENT MTG.

Relationship of FSW
to building
(Finances, Board of Directors)

SKILL EXCHANGE

Journal Class

STUDENT CRIT

FOCUS on Process ~~Product~~

~~Sharing of Responsibility~~

~~plus~~ PLANNING

Bulletin Board (communication) FSW

Bldg Relationship to Community

Define FSW (to DR)

~~DR~~

LESBIAN Support Group

OPEN FORUM: Sexuality

Continues evaluation

~~NOT HIRING OF MEN~~

Supplies Equipment ETC.

~~EST Analyzed~~

~~FSW relation to CAA~~

ASSURE COLLECTIVE

DISPLAY WORK

Curriculum Committee

VISUAL ARTISTS on STAFF

PROFESSIONAL Orientation

COMMUNITI

1. C.A.A. Co

2. DEFINE F

a. relation
b. finance
c. Board of

BLDG TO

10

FOREWORD
GOING AROUND IN CIRCLES

Lucy R. Lippard

My own memories of the Woman's Building mainly are exhilarating. On my first visit, in 1974, I was impressed and moved deeply that a bunch of women could claim space on such a scale—that they could renovate a big building (with pink tools), then furnish it with daring new art and ideas. I was dazzled by the school, design program, graphics center, women-owned and women-run galleries, bookstore, thrift shop, theater, coffeehouse, and eventually the video center and various offices, including the magazine *Chrysalis*. I later described my experience as "immediate intimacy with women who were—but were not—strangers." It seemed, as Sondra Hale puts it, "a house large enough for everyone."

And I was envious. There was nothing like this full-fledged woman's community in New York, where our branch of the feminist art movement was too often preoccupied with fending off or competing with the male-dominated mainstream art scene. Los Angeles, by virtue of its relative isolation at the time, was freer to innovate than we were in the art capital. For almost two decades, I kept up with many of the participants and activities, visited, wrote about and for the Building, spoke at the 1992 Vesta Awards, and was probably more influenced by West Coast feminism than most of my East Coast sisters (thanks in part to a friendship with Judy Chicago that goes back to the fifties). But the day-to-day workings of this elaborately participatory institution were distant. The essays in this volume—mostly by insiders, by women with profound connections to the space, the place, the principles, and the people—reveal that while externally the Building epitomized separatism, internally it was varied and contested. The honesty and from-the-gut analysis of their recollections is all the more compelling today, when such straight talk is in short supply.

The Woman's Building was the capital of cultural feminism, where the spiritual and the political met and rowdily merged. It was an off-center center, defying the marginalization of women's lives and arts. In 1973, when it was founded, a women's community was something new and very appealing. To visit the Woman's Building then was like vacationing at a wonderful, healing resort. To live there was obviously a lot more demanding. (Bernice Reagon of Sweet Honey in the Rock once observed, "If you're in a coalition and you're comfortable, your coalition isn't big enough."[1]) It provided not a room of one's own but of our own, and sharing did not always come easily to all the fledgling egos occupying it. As the Building became "home," the community was also "family"—a situation that was at once comforting and threatening. Leaders— though there weren't supposed to be any, and no one wanted to replicate the psychological tensions of the mother/daughter relationship—encouraged ego-expanding ambition along with community, and the two were not always compatible.

For artists in particular, collisions of self and community could be wrenching. (Having organized politically with artists most of my life, I recognize the often painful push/pull from studio to organizing and back again.) It was also obvious that just as there were different kinds of feminism, there were different kinds of communities, and most women belonged to several simultaneously. As Theresa Chavez writes in her essay in this volume, "Unburying Histories: the future(s) of feminist art," "I am someone who is connected to and surrounded by many histories, all of which are buried, misunderstood, or romanticized."

From an East Coast vantage point, Los Angeles women sometimes seemed more outspoken, more soul-searching (embarrassingly so for a Yankee), and less conventionally "intellectual" than New Yorkers. "High theory" was seen as linear, male, and elite; many of us aspired to the circular, female, and egalitarian. I recognized my own brand of "organic intellectual"—a reaction against what Griselda Pollock has called "the structural sexism of most academic disciplines."[2] As on the Left, the theory being created on the ground from practice was mostly disregarded in the ivory towers, which led to a kind of mutual distancing by the eighties. As Hale notes in her essay herein, the notion of women's culture—"one of the most potentially dynamic concepts within feminism, faltered from theoretical neglect."

On the other hand, the C-R (consciousness-raising), the crit-self-crit (criticism/self criticism), the warmth and curiosity, the ideology tempered by humor and intelligence, and the impassioned debates were all very familiar from my New York feminist world, based in the Heresies collective and journal. Collectivity defined feminism for me, and for many others. Art was important because, as one of the editors of this volume declares, "Women could represent themselves through their creative work." The Woman's Building's focus on an independent pedagogy rooted in dialogical process was unique and changed the lives of many participants. Taboos such as incest, rape, menstruation, and sexuality were blown into the public eye. Each of the Woman's Building's founders—Judy Chicago, Sheila Levrant de Bretteville, and Arlene Raven—had a somewhat different vision for the building, but they managed, for the most part, to weave their goals into a singularly effective feminist institution.

While artist Chicago's and art historian Raven's work at the Feminist Studio Workshop has received more attention, de Bretteville's design program was equally significant—the source of many pioneering concepts (paralleling what Susana Torre and others were doing for architecture on the East Coast). Called "Pinkie" by her students because she took up the challenge of re-investing that much-maligned color with a new strength and social significance in the famous, gridded *Pink* poster (1975), de Bretteville was determined to create a political and cultural bridge or a fluid membrane between public and private spheres. Space itself was a "precious commodity" in an era when alternative institutions were every activist's goals. It is no coincidence that performance art—action within and transforming space, and by extension, society—was the favored medium of the Woman's Building and the core of student-then-teacher Suzanne Lacy's ongoing innovations in the field. As essayist Sondra Hale writes in this volume, "Space is not a given. It is not a container or a void that is filled up; it is created just as gender is created, as part of culture."

Media art, rarely perceived as a feminist forte, and experimental video were also explored early in this context. (In her essay, "Stories from a Generation: Video Art at the Woman's Building," Cecilia Dougherty points out that the mainstream obsession with individual artists precluded attention to feminist collaborative enterprises.) Similarly, much mainstream art and theory based on body and desire, touted as "new" in the Postmodern period, is clearly the offspring of feminist art from the seventies, when a threatened public was forced to confront notions of the cunt itself as space. By 1980, we knew the body as agency, beyond narcissism ("Your body is a battleground," à la Barbara Kruger), but the reception of Chicago's *The Dinner Party* in 1979 proved that female genitalia, even offered as metaphor, remained beyond the pale, outside of history.

It is often said that feminist art is about content and communication. Lived experience and autobiography, which are not same thing, were at the core of that content, which arrived at the gates of the art world during a period when American Art critic Clement Greenberg was still railing against "literary art." Feminism gave all artists permission to consider what Cheri Gaulke called in her interview with Betty Ann Brown, included in Brown's essay in this volume, "Feminist Art Education at the Los Angeles Woman's Building," the "unleashing of self," as a preface to social change. Reading the unflinching essays that make up this book, I regained my admiration for the truism that opened so many eyes: "The personal is political." This modest phrase was the baseline for "cultural," "radical" and "socialist" feminisms, with emphases differently placed in each branch. It remains a living and dynamic proposition, a brilliant way to translate lived experience—positive and negative—into political action.

"The political is personal" is not the opposite of "the personal is political," but its other half. When we understand who we are in a historical sense we are better able to understand what other cultural groups are experiencing within a time and place we all share. Given the fact that many of us came from the factionalized Left, women's groups had to simultaneously transcend and reinvent our own experiences of political organizing. The egalitarian, anti-hierarchal, often anarchic spirit of seventies and eighties feminism sometimes descended into chaos, while those who accepted community leadership were often disgruntled by their own lack of power.

One of the most engrossing aspects of the Woman's Building's history is the evolution of the lesbian community and its art. Terry Wolverton's exhilarating description of the Natalie Barney Collective, the Lesbian Art Project (LAP), and the "Great American Lesbian Art Show" (GALAS, 1980) conveys the wacky and indomitable spirit of the early years. It also exposes the familiar contradictions of exclusion and outreach that plagued the initially white women's movement. Ethnic, class, and sexual differences loomed large in feminist lives in the seventies and eighties, as we struggled with ourselves and others to be as just, tolerant, fair, and revolutionary as our ideals. Identity politics did not turn out to be a unifying force. In her e-mail exchange with founder de Bretteville, captured herein, Bia Lowe remarks on "an American rage for identity that seems nearly nonexistent elsewhere. U.S. feminism seems narcissistic, while elsewhere in the world it is real." The token integration of women of color into largely white feminist organizations did not go well on either coast. ("Add a woman of color and stir," commented one sarcastic critic of tokenism.) This remains the great failure of "second-wave feminism." Good intentions were rampant, but so was ignorance and sometimes arrogance. Despite a lot of hard work (but too little, too late), conscious and unconscious racism plagued the Woman's Building as it did virtually every other American feminist organization.

Today the notion of feminist community is far less powerful, more splintered—in part because of right-wing ascendancies, in part because postcolonial theory has highlighted the weaknesses of earlier "multiculturalism," and in part because the women's movement did succeed in integrating women artists into the mainstream, a double-edged sword evident in the reactionary eighties, when populist activism was overwhelmed by less accessible (and less dangerous) theory. The Woman's Building came to be seen as the proud epitome of dreaded "essentialism." Yet even today, I suspect that few women, no matter how "post-feminist," no matter how emancipated from "old-fashioned women's liberation," would deny that women's experiences—social, sexual, biological—differ from those of men, though debates continue about their social and/or innate construction. Some of us struggled to maintain a balance of power. Believing that feminism should eschew "either/or," I wrote optimistically about "Both Sides Now."

The utopian foundations of the Woman's Building, its conscious and strategic marginalization from the mainstream, and its valorization of femaleness in the face of overwhelming odds have met with backlash and disdain in the intervening decades. But it was necessary at the time and may well be necessary soon again. If the first wave of feminism in the United States was the early twentieth-century suffrage movement, and the second wave was the Women's Liberation Movement from the late sixties, where are we now? Are we sunk in a trough? Should we be looking forward to a third wave? (It has been almost forty years.) Despite cultural amnesia and the fear of erasure common to all progressive movements, the exuberant optimism of vintage feminist art is attracting more attention these days. A symposium on feminist art at the Museum of Modern Art, New York (in early 2007) was sold out months ahead of time. Chicago's *Dinner Party* has found a permanent home at the Brooklyn Museum. We are still asking, as essayist Michele Kort recalls: "What do you want to say? What's the form that will hold it?" And we are still advising each other, "Don't be limited by the forms [or institutions] that exist." And we are also seeing new ramifications in past work, realizing that, as essayist Jennie Klein argues, "the meaning of the image often exceeds the stated intentions of its maker…."

In this book, Brown quotes Chicago remarking (with a certain amazement) that as one goes around the circle "one discovers that the strangest people know the 'right' answer." As we recall these histories, we are still going around in circles—an image not of futility but of a future in which the work we have done will be useful for the next generations of women, providing a scaffolding for the next Woman's Building. This book is one of the tools with which it will be built—perhaps virtually, perhaps once again in real space.

Notes

1. Bernice Johnson Reagon, "Coalition Politics: Turning the Century," in Barbara Smith, ed., *Home Girls* (New York: Kitchen Table Press, 1983), 358.

2. Griselda Pollock, "Screening the Seventies: Sexuality and Representation in Feminist Practice—a Brechtian Perspective," in Amelia Jones, ed., *The Feminism and Visual Culture Reader* (New York: Routledge, 2004), 80.

Sandy Orgel, *Linen Closet*, 1972. Installation. *Womanhouse*,
Los Angeles, CA; © California Institute of the Arts Archives.

INTRODUCTION

Terry Wolverton

The founding of the Woman's Building in Los Angeles in 1973 was the culmination of several years of activity by women artists who were energized by the feminist movement in the United States.[1] The Woman's Building was a concrete realization of the dreams of women artists to find "a room of one's own"—a room they could not find in the mainstream art world at that time.[2]

To understand the origins of the feminist art movement in the United States, one must look to the foment of the sixties and early seventies, to the swarm of rebellions and leaps in consciousness that redefined American culture. In 1955, a seamstress named Rosa Parks refused to give up her seat on a Montgomery, Alabama, bus and thus gave rise to the Civil Rights Movement, which ignited a host of struggles for social liberation waged by women, African Americans, Chicanos, Native Americans, gays and lesbians, and others. These movements not only demanded more equitable distribution of power and resources, but also raised profound questions about the meaning assigned to these identities and the cultural representations of these groups.

Opposition to the United States' involvement in Vietnam stoked an unprecedented youth movement that, in addition to the politics of protest, embraced "sex, drugs, and rock 'n' roll." This fueled a thriving counterculture determined to forge alternatives to the economic, social, and moral structures of the mainstream.

Within the art world, too, began a challenge to the hegemony of formalism that had dominated the fifties and sixties, in which any concern for content in art was disregarded or disdained. Questions of cultural identity incited a push for the democratization of art, a demand for greater inclusiveness with regard to both who could make images and who had access to them. Disenfranchised artists also began to create alternative institutions—later to be called artists' organizations—that would better represent them.

In 1970, women artists in Los Angeles mobilized. The impetus was "Art and Technology," an exhibition at the Los Angeles County Museum of Art (LACMA) in which no women artists were included. Upon further investigation, it was found that of eighty-one one-person exhibitions at LACMA over a ten-year period, only one had featured the work of a woman artist.

Women began to meet together to protest their exclusion from the LACMA show; to share the difficulties they faced in getting their work shown, reviewed, purchased, or even regarded seriously; to discuss the concerns they as women wanted to express in their artwork; and to create strategies for what to do next.

Finding the gallery and museum system generally closed to most of them, women artists in Southern California decided to launch their own gallery: Womanspace. Opened in an old laundromat in Culver City in early 1973, Womanspace was dedicated to showing and documenting women's artwork. It quickly garnered a membership of a thousand artists and supporters.

Meanwhile, several women artists teaching in college and university programs felt the need to provide new models for the next generation of women artists and pioneered the concept of feminist art education. Painter Judy Chicago started the Feminist Art Program, the first of its kind, at California State University, Fresno.

That first year, Chicago's visionary Feminist Art Program[3] drew fifteen women students, many of whom were new to both feminism and art making. It was from the work of this initial group of participants that many of the core principles of feminist art education evolved. These concepts would guide Chicago and her colleagues when they established the Feminist Studio Workshop in Los Angeles three years later.

It was in the Fresno program that women first employed the process of consciousness-raising in the classroom, both to understand more deeply their position as women and to generate material for their art.[4] This strategy flew in the face of the art establishment; in 1970, women's experience was considered trivial and frivolous, unsuitable as subject matter for creative work. Indeed, since the end of World War II, narrative content had become taboo in the New York art world; formalist concerns dominated the critical discourse. Serious art was, by definition, the province of men, and if a woman hoped to pass into this hallowed terrain, she could only do so by making herself as much like a man as possible. The rare female art student who called attention to her gender by daring to create a work about menstruation, marriage, motherhood, or household drudgery could fully expect to be criticized or mocked by her male instructors.

Feminist Studio Workshop (FSW): First day of the FSW's second year, 1974. Photograph by Sheila Ruth, Woman's Building Image Archive, Otis College of Art and Design.

In order to create an environment in which women could explore their lives through art, participants in the Fresno program insisted upon a separate classroom environment for female art students, one in which women could create the context and control what happened there. Such separation would provide not only protection from corrosive or undermining feedback, but also would allow women to bond with one another and to define for themselves their paths as artists. Additionally, the women of the Fresno program asserted the importance of female role models, both in being instructed by women and in studying the long-buried history of women's art. Finally, Chicago and her students openly challenged the notion of art as a work of individual genius by engaging in collaborative creations.

In 1971, Chicago moved the Fresno program to California Institute of the Arts (CalArts). With the school still under construction, the twenty-five students of the Feminist Art Program launched a large-scale, site-based, collaborative project, called *Womanhouse*, spearheaded by Chicago and her colleague, artist Miriam Schapiro. Working together, they transformed the rooms of a slated-for-demolition Hollywood mansion into art environments that eloquently protested the domestic servitude of women's lives. In *Breast Kitchen*, for example, the all-pink walls and ceiling were affixed with fried eggs—sunny side up—that gradually morphed into women's breasts, a trenchant comment on women's role as nurturers. *Fear Bathroom* contained the plaster figure of a woman in the tub, frozen up to the neck in cement, and addressed the

21

Artist and cofounder of the Woman's Building, Judy Chicago, speaking at Womanspace Gallery, 1973. Woman's Building Image Archive, Otis College of Art and Design.

state of confinement and paralysis felt by women. *Linen Closet* displayed the torso of a female mannequin segmented by the closet shelves. This latter image was reproduced in *Time* magazine, which ran a story on the project. It galvanized me, and I sped around for the next week, showing the magazine to everyone at school. *Womanhouse* was, without question, the most publicly visible work of feminist art to date.

Art historian Arlene Raven had joined the faculty of the CalArts Feminist Art Program, and graphic designer Sheila Levrant de Bretteville established the Women's Design Program at CalArts. In conversations with Chicago, they shared their frustrations about working within a male-dominated institution. Separate classes for feminist students could only be so effective, they observed; what went on in those classrooms was too easily dwarfed by the larger context. They would routinely spend their class sessions building up the confidence of women students, encouraging them to take risks, only to see those same students' works disparaged or dismissed by male instructors.

In 1973, frustrated with the limitations of working to educate women art students within the confines of a male institution, Chicago, de Bretteville, and Raven left CalArts to found an independent school for women artists: the Feminist Studio Workshop (FSW).[5] The FSW focused not only on the development of art-making skills (in visual arts, writing, performance art, video, design, and the printing arts), but also on the development of women's identities and sensibilities, and feminist practices of art-making, and the translation of these elements into their art.

Central to the founders' vision was the notion that the arts should not be separated from other activities of the burgeoning women's community, and the three looked for a space that could be shared with other organizations and enterprises. The FSW opened in September. Initial class sessions were held in de Bretteville's living room, but by the end of November, the FSW was installed in the building that had once housed the old Chouinard Art Institute on Grandview Boulevard in the Wilshire District of Los Angeles. In November 1973, the Woman's Building opened its doors.

Eighty years earlier, another Woman's Building had existed in Chicago, Illinois. Designed by architect Sophia Hayden, that Woman's Building was part of the World's Columbian Exposition of 1893 and housed exhibitions of artistic and cultural works by women. After the exposition, the building was demolished; little documentation remains. The founders of the Los Angeles Woman's Building wanted to resurrect the lost memory of its predecessor and also create a public center where the current artistic and cultural accomplishments of women could be presented and appreciated.

Before the Chouinard building could be opened to the public, massive renovation was required. Hundreds of women, men, and children worked together to build walls, scrape and paint ceilings, sand floors, move furniture and printing presses, paint signage, and generally prepare the space to welcome the community. For many of the newly recruited FSW students, their initial introduction to feminist arts education involved getting dirty and learning to use tools.

In addition to the FSW, the Woman's Building was shared by a number of other women's cultural groups. Womanspace moved from Culver City to join the Building, and a cooperative gallery, Grandview, took over two skylighted rooms to show members' work. A third gallery, 707, also opened its doors in the Woman's Building. Sisterhood Bookstore sold feminist and non-sexist literature and music, and three women's theater groups—L.A. Feminist Theater, Women's Improvisational Theater, and the Women's Performance Project—used the auditorium for performances. Over the next two years, the Woman's Building also housed an office of the National Organization for Women, a coffeehouse, and Womantours, a feminist travel agency.

Womanspace was forced to close in 1974 due to financial difficulties, but the FSW absorbed its gallery and events program under the aegis of the Woman's Building, which became a producing entity as well as the name of a physical structure.

In 1975, a series of conferences brought nationally renowned women working in a variety of media to the Woman's Building. Women in Design included the participation of Ellen Perry Berkeley, Jane Thompson, Claire Forrest, Denise Scott Brown, Susana Torre, and Ethel Kramer. This conference was scheduled to coincide with a retrospective exhibition of the works of British architect Eileen Grey, curated by de Bretteville. Women's Words featured writers Kate Millett, Jill Johnston, Meridel Le Seuer, Kathleen Fraser, and Barbara Myerhoff. Personal and Public Issues: Women in Performance Art involved Eleanor Antin, Pauline Oliveros, Helen Harrison, and Barbara Smith. The Feminist Eye honored women in film and video, and Lady Fingers/Mother Earth was a tribute to women in ceramics.

These conferences were to be a sort of "last hurrah" at the old Chouinard building, which was sold in 1975. Once again, an army of volunteer painters, builders, and movers worked to renovate the new Woman's Building, at 12 North Spring Street in an industrial section of downtown Los Angeles. Funds still needed to be raised to open the new building, and an extraordinary concert, called "Building Women," was produced. Featured entertainers read like a Who's Who in women's culture at the time, including actress Lily Tomlin, and musicians Holly Near, Cris Williamson, Margie Adam, Meg Christian, and the New Miss Alice Stone Ladies Society Orchestra.

Many of the organizations and businesses that occupied the Chouinard space did not move to North Spring Street, and, over time, the full eighteen thousand square feet were taken up by the FSW, the Extension Program (which offered classes in everything from journal writing to self-defense, and was designed to accommodate the schedules of women who could not enroll in the fulltime FSW program), and other activities generated by women of the Woman's Building. These included a full-scale gallery program, the annual Women's Writers Series, the Women's Graphic Center, the L.A. Women's Video Center, the Center for Art Historical Research, screenings of film and video, lectures by activists and theorists such as Bernadette Devlin and Mary Daly, slide presentations by artists and art historians, musical and dance events, and gala fundraisers.

Above: **The courtyard of the first location of the Woman's Building on Grandview Boulevard**, 1973. Woman's Building Image Archive, Otis College of Art and Design.

Right: **Detail of a panel showing the Court of Honor on display at the "Woman's Building 1893 Historical Handicrafts Exhibition,"** March–May 1976. Woman's Building Image Archive, Otis College of Art and Design.

Far right: **Scraping the ceiling of the new Woman's Building on Spring Street**, 1975. Woman's Building Image Archive, Otis College of Art and Design.

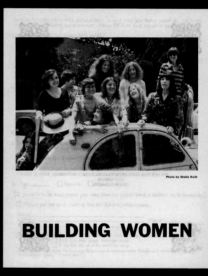

BUILDING WOMEN

Chrysalis

a magazine of woman's culture

announces an incomparable evening of poetry, thought, and inspiration with

Mary Daly

Mary Daly, author of The Church and the Second Sex, and Beyond God the Father, will talk about the ideas in her recently published new book, Gyn/Ecology: The Metaethics of Radical Feminism.

and

Adrienne Rich

Adrienne Rich, author of nine books of poetry and the prose work, Of Woman Born, will read new poems and selections from her latest book, The Dream of a Common Language.

together

January 10

Wednesday, at 8:00 p.m.
Admission—$4.00
Signed books will be available for purchase.

1727 North Spring Street, Los Angeles, CA 90012. tel. (213) 221-6161

at the Woman's Building

a public center of woman's culture

Clockwise from top: **Sheila Levrant de Bretteville, Women in Design: A Conference**, 1975. Diazo blueprint, 21" x 15 ³/₁₆". Woman's Building Image Archive, Otis College of Art and Design.

Building Women Concert, 1975. Program brochure for a fundraiser featuring women's music and comedy by Margie Adam, Meg Christian, Holly Near, Miss Alice Stone's Ladies Society Orchestra, Lily Tomlin and Cris Williamson. Photograph by Sheila Ruth. Woman's Building Image Archive, Otis College of Art and Design.

Chrysalis **magazine poster announcing readings by Mary Daly and Adrienne Rich at the Woman's Building**, 1978. Woman's Building Image Archive, Otis College of Art and Design.

Sisterhood Bookstore at the Woman's Building, 1975. Woman's Building Image Archive, Otis College of Art and Design.

Clockwise from top: **The Woman's Building, second location on North Spring Street**, 1975. Woman's Building Image Archive, Otis College of Art and Design.

Susan King (upper left) teaching at the Women's Graphic Center, 1981. Woman's Building Image Archive, Otis College of Art and Design.

Cover of *Spinning Off*, announcing fundraiser at the home of Sheldon Andelson featuring Lily Tomlin and the Waitresses, 1980. Woman's Building Image Archive, Otis College of Art and Design.

At various times the Woman's Building housed a bookstore; a thrift store (The Store, created by artist Nancy Fried in 1977); the Identified Woman Café; Val's Café; Inanna, a women's arts and crafts store; and the offices of both *Chrysalis* magazine and Women Against Violence Against Women (WAVAW). From 1978 through 1981, the Woman's Building published a monthly newsletter, *Spinning Off*, which included news of cultural, political, and social events in the community and was distributed free.

A large number of collaborative projects and art-making groups emerged from the Woman's Building, due both to the proximity of artists working in diverse media but also to a philosophy that encouraged cooperation over competition. Performance art groups such as Mother Art, Feminist Art Workers, The Waitresses, and Sisters Of Survival originated at the Woman's Building. Ariadne: A Social Art Network and the Lesbian Art Project both began as programs of the Feminist Studio Workshop.

As other feminist organizations burst on the scene and flared out, the Woman's Building went on to celebrate its fifth anniversary in 1978, with the hoisting of a giant Naked Lady sculpture, by Kate Millett, to the roof of the building. (An image was reproduced on the front page of the *Los Angeles Times*.) A gala birthday party included the Feminist Art Workers' performance "To Love, Honor, Cherish . . ." Other fifth anniversary activities included the exhibition "Posters, Postcards, and Books by Women," the Family of Women Dance, and the children's play, *Why Can't a TV Cook a Potato?* by Leslie Belt.

Great challenges lay ahead. In 1981, the Woman's Building underwent major organizational change and redefinition, as a profound sea change was occurring within the social, political, and economic climates of the United States. As demand for alternative education ebbed, the Feminist Studio Workshop closed its doors. The educational programs of the Woman's Building were restructured to better accommodate the needs of working women.

The Woman's Building also founded two profit-making enterprises to strengthen its financial base: the rental of artists' studio space, and a design and typesetting business, Women's Graphic Center, Inc. In addition, in 1982 the organization launched an annual awards event and fundraiser, the Vesta Awards, honoring women artists in a variety of disciplines.

In the eighties, the Woman's Building needed to re-envision itself, to forge new purpose and programs that would serve the needs of our audience and at the same time prove able to attract funding support. And we needed to redefine and broaden that constituency, to serve more women.

We wanted to continue to present women's art in various forms—visual, performance, literary, video. But we needed to ask ourselves what services we were providing to those artists: a place to show, an audience to view it, the potential for sales, the possibility of critical review, a catalog to document it? A decade after the women's art movement had begun in Los Angeles, we could no longer assume that a woman artist

The Waitresses, Easy Three-Step Guide to Food Protection in the Event of Nuclear Attack, 1982–1983.
Performance created as part of "Target LA Fallout Fashion Show." Pictured L to R: Denise Yarfitz Pierre, Chutney
Berry, Anne Gauldin, (also performed by Anne Mavor). Photograph by Joyce Dallal. © The Waitresses: Jerri Allyn
and Anne Gauldin.

Great Lady Rising event as part of the 5th Anniversary Celebration of the Woman's Building. 1978. Kate Millet's sculpture beginning her ascent. Woman's Building Image Archive. Otis College of Art and Design.

would be grateful just to have a wall on which to hang her work. In some ways our movement had succeeded; women artists were in galleries all over town. What could we offer? The art scene in Los Angeles was developing, and most women artists were working toward carving a place for themselves within it.

In its founding, the Woman's Building had sought to step outside the discourse of the mainstream art world from which women were largely excluded. Now we needed to rejoin the conversation. In the seventies, we had been a women's organization about art; in the eighties we became an arts organization about women.

The content of feminist art was changing too, no longer exclusively concentrated on women's conditions. As the political landscape became more conservative, artists turned activists for a variety of causes—the increased threat of nuclear war, United States intervention in Central America, the environment, gay and lesbian rights. Our understanding of oppression grew more sophisticated as we began to perceive patterns and linkages between women, people of color, political exiles, immigrants, poor people, gays and lesbians. Whereas once we might have believed that ending sexism would transform the world, we now saw oppression as a web with many strands that would require alliance, not separatism, to untangle.

We rented an office in the Woman's Building to the Committee in Solidarity with the People of El Salvador (CISPES) and were placed under FBI surveillance. We also became a sponsor of Target L. A., a citywide anti-nuclear arts festival. My own 1984 performance, "Me and My Shadow," addressed racism from a feminist perspective. When an official in the Reagan Administration was quoted as saying that all we needed to survive nuclear war was "enough shovels to go around" (presumably because we could dig shelters), the political cartoonist Paul Conrad published a cartoon in the *Los Angeles Times* that depicted a graveyard, the crosses made of shovels. Artist Marguerite Elliott, a former member of the FSW, recreated Conrad's shovel graveyard on the lawn of City Hall to demonstrate the threat posed by the administration's dangerous policies. A group of performance artists from the Woman's Building, including Sue Maberry, Cheri Gaulke, and Nancy Angelo, constituted themselves as the Sisters Of Survival; dressed in nun's habits in the colors of the rainbow (nuns were often used as a metaphor for sisterhood), they staged a performance in Elliott's environment, and later carried their anti-nuclear art activism to Europe.

We also set out to feature a more culturally diverse community of artists, and our audiences began to reflect this as well. The Woman's Building secured funding to commission artists to produce new works. The first such project, "Madre Tierra," supported twelve Chicana artists and writers, under the direction of artist Linda Vallejo, to produce broadsides that were printed in the Women's Graphic Center studio. In a 1983 project, "Private Conversations/Public Announcements," ten artists—including Betye Saar, Alexis Smith, and Qris Yamashita—were chosen to produce a limited edition print reflecting their personal connection to a public site in Los Angeles. This theme—

the links between personal and public life and women's relationship to each sphere—had been an important source of exploration since the early days of the Woman's Building. The prints were exhibited at the Bridge Gallery in Los Angeles City Hall.

Throughout the eighties, we remained committed to projects that encouraged the production of new works of art. In 1986, the project "Cross Pollination" commissioned twenty-two artists to produce posters addressing issues of their cultural heritage. Artist Patssi Valdez created a glorious tribute to Latinas in her photographic portrait of writer Sylvia Delgado, ringed by gladiolus blossoms. Artist Cyndi Kahn and poet Michelle T. Clinton created and illustrated a tapestry exploring the state of relations between the Jewish and African-American communities. Suzan Ocona combined image and text in a moving statement about her own experience of homelessness. As part of the commitment to help artists expand their audiences, complete sets of posters were distributed, free, to eighty arts and community organizations across the United States, along with information about how to purchase posters from the artists.

The Woman's Building also embarked upon literary publication projects, including *Manteniendo El Espiritu*, edited by Aleida Rodríguez, and *Women for All Seasons*, edited by Wanda Coleman and Joanne Leedom-Ackerman. In 1987, we launched a show on local public access cable stations, "The Woman's Building Presents," which screened women's video art, both those tapes created by artists directly connected to the Woman's Building, and other tapes submitted to us by artists. In order to engage in the critical dialogue about art, the Woman's Building also sponsored two conferences, "The Way We Look/The Way We See: Art Criticism for Women in the Nineties," which explored the various critical theories being utilized at the time (1988) and their implications for women's art. In 1989, "Three Generations of Black Women Writers," presented the evolution of concerns and literary styles in the work of African-American women writers. Both projects were co-sponsored with other institutions in an effort to broaden their impact.

Co-founder Sheila de Bretteville had always envisioned the Woman's Building as a crossroads, a place in which women from different sectors of society could gather and meet—heterosexual and lesbian, trust-fund babies and welfare mothers, academics and politicos and artists. Ironically, perhaps it was in the eighties that this vision came closest to being fulfilled. Hmong weavers were exhibiting in the gallery, while poet-in-residence Gloria Alvarez coaxed Central American refugee women to write their stories in their native language. Later that night, a champagne donor reception would fill the potholed Aurora Street with Porsches and BMWs. And no, these groups did not necessarily rub elbows in the small café, or chat while standing in line for the bathroom, but they did walk through a common door, and stand under the same roof.

When, in 1991, the Woman's Building closed its doors, there were many reasons. The vision of feminism had shifted so drastically. The funding climate for the arts had grown brutal. The revolution in personal computers had sunk the typesetting

"REMEMBER YOUR HUMANITY" BERTRAND RUSSELL

"MEMORU VIAN HOMECON"

Right: **Morgan Thomas,** *Remember Your Humanity*, 1985. From "Current Wave" poster show, curated by Lucy Lippard. Woman's Building Image Archive, Otis College of Art and Design.

Below: **1st Annual Vesta Award Winners**, 1982. Pictured L to R: (back row) Helene Rosenbluth, Deena Metzger, Josine Ianco Starrels, Cynthia Marsh; (middle row) Suzanne Lacy, Judy Baca, Betye Saar, June Wayne; (front row) Mitsuye Yamada, Arlene Raven, Sheila Levrant de Bretteville, Eloise Klein Healy. Woman's Building Image Archive, Otis College of Art and Design.

Above: *Shovel Defense*, **public performance by Sisters Of Survival and Marguerite Elliot, staged for the media, Los Angeles City Hall**, 1982. Photograph by Sheila Ruth. © Sisters Of Survival and Marguerite Elliot.

Left: Yriena Cervantes, *Dedicated to My Home Girls*, 1982. Madre Tierra Press, print from portfolio. Woman's Building Archives, Otis College of Art and Design.

Clockwise from top: ***Me and My Shadow***, 1984. Performance by Terry Wolverton. Photograph by Theresa Chavez. © Theresa Chavez.

Artist in *Textiles as Text* exhibition of Hmong textiles, Dec. 1986. Curated by Amy Catlin. © Woman's Building Image Archive, Otis College of Art and Design.

Michelle Clinton, *The Jewish Palm/The Black Fist*, 1986. Poster from "Cross Pollination," a commissioned poster project exhibited at Bridge Gallery, Los Angeles City Hall, 22" x 17". Woman's Building Image Archive, Otis College of Art and Design.

business. And the women who did put so much hard work and passion into the organization for nearly two decades needed to direct their energies elsewhere: their careers as artists, their families, their individual lives. Yet each of them has carried the vision and the skills learned from their time in the feminist art movement into other arenas: as teachers, as activists, as artists, as parents. The vision of the Woman's Building, the processes and practices and philosophies of the feminist art movement, have exploded beyond the walls of brick and mortar, have entered the very DNA of the future.

The essays that follow attempt to analyze the legacy of this eighteen-year experiment. The writings of Sondra Hale, Laura Meyer, Arlene Raven, Betty Ann Brown, and Michelle Moravec (with Sondra Hale) explore the theoretical foundations of feminist art as promoted at the Woman's Building. The essays of Cecilia Dougherty, Jennie Klein, Sheila de Bretteville and Bia Lowe, Michele Kort, Kathleen Walkup, and myself address specific art forms and specific art communities (respectively, video, performance art, design, creative writing, book arts, and lesbian art) that were shaped or influenced by the practice of artists at the Woman's Building. A final essay by Theresa Chavez examines the consciousness and beliefs about art and feminism as expressed by a group of young women art students at CalArts from 2001 to 2007.

The editors wish to thank each of the contributors who so generously devoted themselves to the research and articulation of these histories and interpretations, so that artists and researchers of subsequent generations might continue to learn about the legacy of the Woman's Building.

Notes

1. Much of the historical information in this introduction draws heavily from three previously published works, each authored by me: *The First Decade and Sweet Fifteen*, two booklets written to commemorate the Woman's Building's tenth and fifteenth anniversaries, respectively, and *Insurgent Muse: Life and Art at the Woman's Building* (San Francisco: City Lights, 2003). I spent thirteen years—from 1976 to 1989—at the Woman's Building, beginning as a student in the FSW, then becoming a teacher, program director, exhibiting artist, publicist, typesetter, newsletter editor, grantwriter, board member development director, and eventually, executive director.

2. Reference to Virginia Woolf's *A Room of One's Own* (London: The Hogarth Press, 1929).

3. I am indebted to Faith Wilding's *By Our Own Hands* (Santa Monica, CA: Double X, 1977) for this history of the early feminist art movement in California.

4. Consciousness-raising, or C-R, is a communication process in which women sit in a circle and each takes equal time to speak, uninterrupted, about her experience while the others listen attentively. C-R sessions are usually directed to a specific topic, such as body image, mothers, etc. The practice allows an individual to validate her experiences and to probe their meanings; it also encourages women to see the commonality of their experiences, to realize that some problems have social, not personal, causes. The slogan "The personal is political" is rooted in the C-R process. It is crucial to remember that in the early days of feminism, most women rarely considered the events of their lives to be worth mentioning, to have any significance at all. C-R was adapted by North American feminists from a practice called "speaking bitterness," used by women in revolutionary China.

5. In addition to the three founders, other early FSW instructors included Edie Folbe, Ruth Iskin, Suzanne Lacy, Deena Metzger, and Helen Alm Roth.

Woman's Building on Grandview Boulevard, first location at the start of construction, September 1973. Woman's Building Image Archive, Otis College of Art and Design.

Founders of the Woman's Building: Sheila Levrant de Bretteville (L), Arlene Raven (M), Judy Chicago (R), circa 1973. Photographer unknown. Woman's Building Image Archive, Otis College of Art and Design.

POWER AND SPACE: FEMINIST CULTURE AND THE LOS ANGELES WOMAN'S BUILDING, A CONTEXT

Sondra Hale

It was a house large enough for everyone, all women, we claimed. It was Womanspace, *Womanhouse*, and the House of Women, "At Home," Everywoman's space, and Femme/ Maison. It was female space, safe space, sacred space, contested space, occupied space, appropriated space, and transformed space. It was revolution and revelation. We were squatters and proprietors, renegades and healers; we dichotomized and fused. We had one commonality: we were convinced that we were transforming culture by offering alternatives, as women, not only in the arts and culture, but also in the way we used space and conducted politics in that space.

In its theory and praxis, the Los Angeles Woman's Building, a material site for nearly two decades, appeared to epitomize much of what is sometimes referred to as "second-wave feminism." However, because of the totalizing claim and limited reality of the concept, I have problematized the term "second-wave feminism" throughout this essay. The term gives the impression of a beginning and an end when, in actuality, activism on behalf of women has been ongoing. It also suggests one movement where there were many. Conventionally, it refers to a series of organizations—both mainstream and radical—that were dominated by white women; the considerable activism on the part of women of color is glossed over and made invisible.

The Los Angeles Woman's Building, by most outside accounts, may be considered part of "second-wave feminism," but the sharp break with the ideas and strategies of "first-wave feminism" (primarily the Suffrage Movement, but including settlement house movements, early experiments in collective living, and other experiments) and the utopian nature of the cultural feminism that was the Woman's Building's linchpin, justify an argument to the contrary, i.e., that cultural feminism was a thing apart. Certainly core activists in the Woman's Building did not describe themselves as part of "second-wave feminism." Surely any community that sees itself as creating an entirely new culture for the future that is based on egalitarian, collective/communal, nonhierarchical, noncompetitive, and, perhaps, gender transcendent principles transcends the notions of democratic ideals espoused by first- and second-wave feminists.

Regardless of its place within the categories of feminism, its niche in the politics of space is, however, unarguable; the Woman's Building was an enduring institution by the longevity standards of the times. But how secure is its place in feminist art history and in social and cultural history, in general? Are the trends that Woman's Building-associated artists and activists originated, developed, transformed, and presaged acknowledged as important to the politics and culture of today? Or is the historical demise of the Woman's Building one more example of the invisibility of women's work: an "anonymous" contribution to feminist art historical and cultural studies?

The Woman's Building of Los Angeles was the first independent feminist cultural institution in the world. Founded in 1973, by artist Judy Chicago, graphic designer Sheila Levrant de Bretteville, and the late art historian Arlene Raven, the Woman's Building drew together talented women of many artistic disciplines from across the United States and around the world to pioneer new modes of art making and arts education within the context of a supportive feminist community. In its eighteen-year history (1973–1991), thousands of artists created and or presented new work, gained new skills, and made bold statements within the context of this vital organization.

In this volume, we bring together a group of writers, artists, and academics (and combinations thereof)—some formerly associated with the Woman's Building and others representing newer generations of feminists—to explore the history and accomplishments of the Woman's Building. Our contributions focus on analyses, art practices, and feminist processes pioneered during the organization's history that continue to have an impact on contemporary culture. The purpose of this combination of reconstruction/recuperation and visionary essays is not only to keep alive the history of this organization and to analyze the impact of its contributions on current art and feminist practices, but also to gain insight into contemporary culture.

This overview frames the phenomenon of the Woman's Building within the social, political, and philosophical atmosphere of late twentieth-century social thought, social movements, and feminisms. The Woman's Building and the ideas that undergirded its founding and continued existence are Modernist; behind the goals and ambitions of the founders and participants was an emancipatory narrative, a liberation theme that typified Modernism.

Although the phenomenon is Modernist, nonetheless, we can also see Woman's

Building origins that are pre-Renaissance—the rise of the concept of "museum" as a place that houses and organizes the cultural resources of a community.[1] Such a facility/ construction of a concept or site as the museum may come about from a crisis of knowl- edge that the fabrication of a building is trying to solve.[2] In the case of the Woman's Building this would refer to feminism and the appropriation of space to address the conditions of women's lives in the midst of an androcentric culture. Women had reached a point where they were no longer able to negotiate, adjust to, and deny an- drocentrism; thus a crisis of knowledge and identity emerged.

Yet, in many ways a museum is also a metaphor for community house, one whose visual, spatial and cultural aspects are able to bridge public and private space,[3] much as the creators and art producers of the Woman's Building saw themselves doing. Another idea that emanates from the original museum concept is that the Woman's Building is "a room of muses."[4]

Still, for all of its pre-Modernist and Modernist roots and manifestations, many of the forms of feminism that permeated the Woman's Building and its rarified environments also straddled Postmodernism, with its insistence on ambiguity; break- ing down of dichotomies; questioning of authority and the authorial figure (traditional male subject and the male artist as romantic hero); the deconstruction of language— both visual and literate; and its undermining of the privileging of sight, of linear thinking, and of conventional definitions of "art."[5] In this way and in many others, the history of the Woman's Building is complex and multilayered. The Woman's Building was always contested space. Nonetheless, while recognizing many feminists' ambiva- lence toward Modernism, the organization's stated goals emanated from many of the goals of Modernist "second-wave feminism." Here I explore some of the most promi- nent themes, privileging two main concepts: *culture* and *space*—their "contents" and points of convergence.

Culture and Space

Among the most prevalent themes of contemporary feminisms are women's need for space ("A Room of One's Own" reaching cliché status by the eighties[6]), and an encour- agement and exploration of the culture that occupied that space. Reaching manifesto status was the linked set of ideas that, if women were to do their best work (defined broadly), they would need an unadulterated space, that they would produce out of their *own experience*, and that the work done in that space would constitute "women's cul- ture." An aspect of the demand for space was the owning and controlling of the space and the *body* that occupies it.

A 1983 symposium on women's culture, The House of Women: Art and Cul- ture in the 1980s,[7] addressed issues under the rubric of "women's culture," at the time one of the more controversial and elusive formulations within communities of women and feminists—scholars, activists, and artists—primarily because of the implications

41

Linda Nishio, *Ghost in the Machine*, 1983. Multimedia performance at the Woman's Building. Photograph by Sheila Ruth. © Linda Nishio.

of *essentialism* and separatism. In many ways the site of the symposium—the Greater Los Angeles/Long Beach area—was perfect for such a gathering because of the proximity of several vital women's communities, research and teaching centers, and perhaps most significantly, a dynamic feminist art community, symbolized by the Woman's Building.

The House of Women, which featured over a dozen Woman's Building practitioners and founders, was held in conjunction with the "At Home" art exhibit at the Long Beach Museum of Art, a celebration of ten years of feminist art in the area.[8] Art historian and Woman's Building co-founder the late Arlene Raven was guest curator of the show. She gathered people to discuss the artistic and sociopolitical themes of "At Home," with an eye toward an analysis of the changes in feminist ideas since *Womanhouse* of ten years before. Toward that end, artists, academicians, and community/movement people were congregated in the same room (house) for an exploration of the changes in how we relate to the house/home environment and for an investigation of the development of the "women's culture" concept.

The House of Women participants recognized that we were both the heirs and progenitors of two significant manifestations of "women's culture"—*Womanhouse* of 1973 and "At Home" of 1983—major feminist environmental and performance art projects.[9] The latter, an homage to the former, expressed and recognized the special relationship feminist art has had to the themes of house and home.[10] Like *Womanhouse* before it, "At Home" recreated the house as environmental art and traced the relationship among women, space, and culture—both abstract and material. The metaphor of the *house* seemed especially appropriate, as it suggests both material (the physical structure of the house) and myth/imagination (refuge, psychological shelter, "home"). Also, if women were the first to seek out and build shelters, then *house* is an important focus in the history of women's material culture.[11]

The "Women's Culture" Concept

By the seventies, feminist scholars, artists, and architects had begun to develop some of the earlier formulations about "women's culture" as an important and self-conscious concept to use aesthetically and programmatically in response to the oppression of women.[12] In 1980, *Feminist Studies*, then only in its sixth year, published a debate about "women's culture" as a problematic concept. Ellen DuBois defined "women's culture" as it is used by U.S. historians: "the broad-based commonality of values, institutions, relationships and methods of communication, focused on domesticity and morality and particular to late eighteenth-and-nineteenth-century women."[13] Others raised questions about "cultural feminism," arguably equated with "women's culture," and its role in the women's movement and the analytical and political distinction between "women's culture" and "feminism," a distinction that also became salient in the House of Women symposium. In a sense, the distinction revealed a tension between "cultural feminists" and "political/materialist/socialist feminists," but that distinction is too facile, just as the stereotype of the Woman's Building as comprised entirely of "cultural feminists" was too totalizing.

In the seventies and eighties, the heyday of the Woman's Building, feminists saw an explosion of works on women's art and art history, feminist literary criticism, and feminist responses to negative images in film and popular culture.[14] However, the concept "women's culture," an important centerpiece concept undergirding the Woman's Building, remained under the skin and was not often explicitly theorized. Therefore, one could say that one of the most potentially dynamic concepts within feminism faltered from theoretical neglect. Partially the neglect was a result of early feminism's distrust of academic "High Theory." The distrust was based on the notion that "High Theory" is male and that men used theories as tools to dominate women and others, primarily by writing women out of history and culture. Women, it was argued by many feminists, were theorized out. Also, "High Theory" was considered a privilege of the elite and a manifestation of elitism, which feminists claimed to eschew.[15]

This is not to erase the fact that theory was being produced by feminists at sites other than academic institutions and being disseminated in ways other than by mainstream publishing houses. Feminists at the Woman's Building, for example, were producing theories about the qualities of a utopian society, the nature of art, power relationships (gender, race and class) and sexuality. In 1992, Beatriz Colomina published a book on sexuality and space,[16] utilizing concepts such as domestic voyeurism, the female spectator and the lesbian specter, and perverse space. Twenty years earlier, performance and other art productions had forwarded theories about sexuality and space, e.g. *Womanhouse*, and a bit later, the Lesbian Art Project at the Woman's Building.

At any rate, the distrust of "High Theory" by most feminists and of academic theorizing by feminist community activists and artists thwarted attempts to define "women's culture" intellectually and rigorously. Likewise theorizing women's culture was often confounded by ideological debates within feminisms. These debates were often framed in the very dichotomies we professed to avoid, e.g. intellect/intuition, academy/community, and separatist or alternative/mainstream.

The lack of intellectual rigor may also be attributed to early second-wave feminism's common professional/intellectual isolationism. One rarely saw the integration of studies in nonverbal communication; gender spatial relationships; landscapes of the home, neighborhood, and city; gender roles and domesticity; material culture and environment; the psychosexual dynamics of interior and exterior; and folklore with art criticism and art historical studies. Artists seldom referenced these works.[17] In other words, in those years we were only gendering certain aspects of society and culture. It worked both ways: academic feminists ignored theories that were being produced in the community; the notion of the "organic intellectual" was rarely ever acknowledged. With distrust on one side and elitism on the other, the possibility for integrated theories of empowerment and the transformation of culture were curtailed, as was the integration of various intellectual communities with the Woman's Building.

One community of feminist scholars/practitioners was developing integrated theories: architects, designers, urban planners, and preservationists such as Gwendolyn Wright, Ann Markusen, Gerda Wekerle and Dolores Hayden. They pointed out the relationship between the way houses, neighborhoods, and cities have been designed and socially sanctioned ideas about gender roles and domesticity.[18] For example, Hayden described the ideas and concrete projects of early material feminists who forged the beginnings of a socialist feminist material culture and environment. She singled out the Woman's Building in a section on "Creating Innovative Institutions to Link Private Life and Public Space," that is, "domesticating urban space."[19] Hayden, whose ideas were greatly influenced by Woman's Building co-founder, Sheila de Bretteville, was at the time one of the few academics to put the Woman's Building on the cultural map and to recognize its importance as a site. Hayden argued:

> In the process of domesticating public space, cultural institutions
> that exist somewhere between the private domain and the public
> domain play a key role.... One such institution is the Los Angeles

> Woman's Building, a public center for women's culture ... [that] serves
> as a gathering place for painters, graphic designers, video artists,
> performance artists, novelists, and playwrights. It includes gallery
> space, artists' studio space, performance space, and offices. The
> Woman's Building was designed to create a political and cultural
> bridge between public and private life. The group encourages mem-
> bers to make public art about their lives.[20]

Hayden singles out a Los Angeles project of de Bretteville's, "Public Announcements/
Private Conversations," the goals of which were to create works about public places
with personal meaning. Hayden also cites Suzanne Lacy, a performance artist associated with the Woman's Building, for her public performances such as *Three Weeks in
May*. Coordinated with Leslie Labowitz, *Three Weeks in May* dealt with the very private/
public themes of rape and violence against women.

By placing their art productions intentionally "midway between the home and the
street," the Woman's Building artists and cultural workers create[d] a "homelike world."[21]

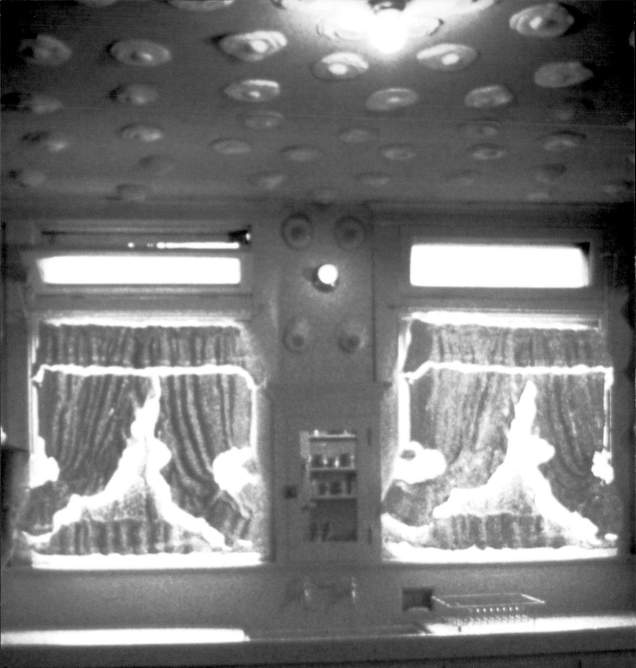

The Experiences Within—Interior and Exterior Space

Although the validity of the dichotomous model of private and public is constantly being challenged, especially as it is associated with gender relationships, nonetheless, it may not have totally exhausted its analytical utility. In order to analyze the interiors of the mind and house and to suggest the reappropriation or redefinition of andro-centers, it may still be helpful to conceive of female and male space, i.e., gendered space.[22]

In *The Poetics of Space*, existentialist Gaston Bachelard comments on the in interior landscape:

> A house that shines from the care it receives appears to have been rebuilt from the inside; it is as though it were new inside. In the inti-mate harmony of walls and furniture, it may be said that we become conscious of a house that is built by women, since men only know how to build a house from the outside.[23]

Bachelard's notion of interior landscape resonates with Violette Leduc's house of women, where the house is space, lineage, material, and myth.[24] The boundaries that separate the interior and the exterior may be the same boundaries thought to separate mind and body. The courtyard of a Northern Sudanese house, where I spent countless hours over decades, may, in material reality, separate the physical spheres of men and women and epitomize the effects of the gender division of labor on the cultural land-scape and built environment.[25] Moreover, metaphorically (in Western literature), the interior separation of male and female in the Arab house may stand for the repression of female sexuality. Nonetheless, although women can be seen as culturally alienated within their own interior space, women's culture that emerges in the seclusion of the courtyard is the transformation of that alienation. Mary Ellen Mazey and David Lee use the ideas of Leila Ahmed to argue that the detached, isolated, single-family house (especially in North America) is more alienating of North American women than is the Arab house of Arab women. In the latter, the combination of the extended family, with its communal advantages, and the harem (women's quarters) allow for sisterhood and collectivity. The harem, then, while suggesting to Westerners a system of sexual access for males, is also a system whereby women have living space (culture) beyond the patriarchy. This merging and alienation, explicit in Leduc, is one of many aspects of the dialectics of interior/exterior space, women, and culture.[26]

Women, original designers of shelter, are said to have lost their architectural roles to men,[27] retreating/escaping, perhaps, into the personal landscape of the gar-den, "a medium for her creative idiosyncrasies and aesthetic sensitivities,"[28] a land-scape of her mind. Thus, the North American, suburban, single-family dwelling—one of the most notable forms of isolation and alienation for women—is also where women

47

transform that alienation through a personal aesthetic, perhaps metaphysically recapturing or reappropriating the lost agricultural fields.

In both the installation *Womanhouse* and the Woman's Building, feminists built the house from the inside.[29] Both projects involved the invention of spaces that covered all and revealed all. In the same way that the "little white apron" of the working-class servant in Leduc's novel signified the repression of women's sexuality by covering the belly and the genitals,[30] *Womanhouse* concealed and revealed the horrors and repression within the domestic interior. Likewise, the woman-made quilt, an interior narrative, a shelter built by women, covered all and revealed all: class, repression, and resistance. The same irony prevailed at the Woman's Building, where often the art revealed the house as the domestic site of repression of female sexuality while, simultaneously, the Woman's Building was offering shelter (a house) for women.

A consideration of our interior landscapes in relation to our material and unconscious culture facilitates an understanding of the importance of the Woman's Building as cultural site. Seeing women's culture as counter hegemonic to patriarchal culture is, perhaps, only part of the story, and we are still only in the fundamental stages of considering the material bases of some of the more elusive concepts within feminist theories, such as patriarchy.[31] Patriarchy's loose counterpart, "women's culture," is also usually analyzed apart from its material base. As a consequence, the analyses are spatially, temporally, and culturally truncated (or, uprooted, to continue the biological metaphor). I argue that had the concept of "women's culture" had more theoretical salience and, had the material bases (including space and house) of both women's culture and patriarchy been more commonly explored, the phenomenon of the existence of the Woman's Building could not have been ignored in both feminist thought and in social history.[32]

The Metaphors of Women's Culture

Explorations of "women's culture" have been of at least two kinds: (1) descriptions of material culture produced by women (these have generally been ethnographic studies); and (2) descriptions of superstructure devoid of consideration of the material base (these are most often feminist studies of North America). These are very limited approaches. We have failed to ask: When women have made vessels or quilts, how have they altered the material environment, and how have these producers themselves been altered? How have women *experienced* their production and reproduction, and how have the people around them changed as part of the interaction? Mainly we have lacked the methods for such analyses; even materialist interpretations have fallen short.

The concept of *space* has potential as a methodological "bridge." Space (ranging from a quilt, a white apron, and a building to a city) is culturally constructed and may be seen as material and myth/metaphor, therefore as both an aspect of material culture and as an element in superstructure (or the ideational level), but also as both production and social reproduction. In these respects, one can certainly see the Woman's Building as multilayered space.

Some feminists have studied or participated in the process of women appropriating space (e.g. squatting) and transforming that space.[33] The creation of women's culture (feminist culture?) can be seen, then, as one of the strategies for transforming male-dominated space. The last Woman's Building site was a 1920s building in a warehouse district—a formerly male space that was filled with "things" that were male associated. It is not an illusion to see this space as transformed by feminist architects, designers, artists and visionaries, re-made from top to bottom, and occupied by metaphoric squatters along the railroad tracks.

In the feminist thought of the seventies and eighties, the separation of men's and women's spheres was a dominant idea. Not until the late eighties did a notion of gender as a system begin to take shape and prevail. If women's culture is a valid concept, what are the metaphors with which it is expressed? Are there spaces generated by that culture? Are they "female cultural spaces"?

Space is not a given. It is not a container or a void that is filled up; it is created just as gender is created, as part of culture. The dialectical process of the generation of space must be considered when looking at all cultural forms. One school of thought expounds that capitalist-patriarchy is a process that generates a particular kind of consumer space. The results of this process may be seen, then, as androcenters, or male spaces. Therefore, it is argued that one can look upon our urban spaces as capitalist-generated male cultural centers.

Following the same argument, would we say that just as there may be male and female methods (processes) for creating and relating to culture, there may be male and female principles in creating and relating to space? Are these principles necessarily liberating? When women and men occupy space are they also occupied by that space? In this essay I have automatically raised questions about space, culture, and freedom, which in turn provokes the question of how dreams, quilts and resistance are related to space, how these are related to alienation, and if culture is liberating or inhibiting. For our purposes here, we might ask if it was liberating for the women of the Woman's Building to have a site, a container, a culture of "their own."

If, as some feminist planners and architects have argued, men and women use different cultural metaphors in relating to their environments, is it valid to speak of female and male space (or androcenters) in analyzing the interiors of the mind and house, and in illuminating the structure of the city? Margrit Kennedy once delineated nine categories where men and women apply different principles of design. She argued that the "female principles" of design are more user-oriented, ergonomic, functional, flexible, organically ordered, holistic, complex, socially oriented, and slowly growing. Respectively, male principles are more designer-oriented, large-scale/monumental, formal, fixed, abstractly systematized, specialized, one-dimensional, profit-oriented, and quickly constructed.[34] Although Kennedy's model is intended as a continuum rather than exclusive or absolute categories, it still raises a central problematic: Is "women's culture" merely or simply the flip side of "men's culture"?

Borrowing from an Adrienne Rich poem, can one speak of the "obscure underside [of women's] imagination?"[35] Gerda Wekerle, Rebecca Peterson, and David Morley refer to women's "distinctive 'underside' experience" as providing the basis for a different institutional style that leads to the development of environments based on a new set of principles.[36] They set up a model for the gender contrasts in institutional metaphors. Male institutional metaphors were individualist, centralized, displayed stratified/hierarchical organization, had a center-periphery relationship with environments, viewed change in terms of technological innovation, used productivity/growth models of change, used rational decision-making processes, and rewarded individuals for leadership. The female metaphors, respectively, were communal, decentralized, engaged in informal networking as organization, had a localist/participatory relationship with environments, viewed change in terms of social innovation, used conserver models of change, used decision-making processes that involved sentiment, emotions, and instinct, and rewarded the individual for service to others.[37] Many of these metaphors of female institutional and organizational behavior also characterized the Woman's Building during its existence as a site.

Rather than interpret "women's culture" as the obscure underbelly of culture, one might instead follow the metaphors, and see women, feminists, and Woman's Building art workers as rebuilding a house from the inside. These "houses" are the institutions of women's culture, which we have built (rather than *re*built), perhaps using "feminist process" and education to develop out from the center. The houses are often referred to as "alternative feminist organizations," those fluid, egalitarian, informal, unstructured nebulae of our imaginations. These are laboratories where women can apply their dreams and metaphors, and recreate themselves in a concrete environment, spinning out redemptive culture-in-formation.

The Work Space—Pedagogy and Process

The "alternative feminist organizations" have been, perhaps, most striking in their attempts to develop new ways of relating in the work environment. Karl Marx and Marxists have written a great deal about the relations of production, but until very recently such labors as art were seldom analyzed in these terms. Artists at California Institute of the Arts in the Miriam Schapiro/Judy Chicago seventies era of the Feminist Studio Workshop, at *Womanhouse*, and at the Woman's Building, among many other art/work places, tried to analyze and change the relations of production.

One of the most important attributes of the Woman's Building was its process and its related *pedagogy*. Community organizations such as the Woman's Building were significant influences on the educational processes in various institutions of learning.

Teachers and students, likewise, in "alternative" feminist university departments (i.e., early, grassroots-oriented, community-oriented women's studies programs) attempted to analyze the relations of production and to develop a process for exploring those relations.[38] Some have referred to "feminist process" as the *practice* of women's studies. Ideally, that means that "content" emanates not only from a person designated as instructor/professor, but also from those designated as students. That means that the teacher learns from the students, as well. The classroom, altered in its structure, is student-oriented. The structure is symbolized, most often, by the circle. Each member of the circle is equal to any other and, consequently, is given equal time and space. Space is, again, a relevant concept—taking, owning, occupying, and controlling space. All experience is valid, and everyone is validated. The person designated instructor (facilitator) may be more experienced in certain areas of curriculum content, but this formal knowledge is not to be mystified and there should be no hidden agenda in that sense or in any other. What takes place is a constant process of consciousness-raising through revelation and sharing and through the politicizing of the personal. The ideal was to make decisions through consensus and to work collectively on projects. The women in the circle were constantly self-evaluating (criticism/self-criticism). This process—a self-empowering, consciousness-raising, action-oriented mode of interaction—is integrally linked to feminist pedagogy.

Such pedagogy and process were at the core of feminist education at the Woman's Building: in the classes, the performances, the organization of the artwork, and in the administrative functioning. For many years, "alternative institutions" were the heart of second-wave feminism and space was a precious commodity.[39]

Are these "alternative" institutions the "flip side" of patriarchal culture/androcenters? Although the form(s) may be different, the *raisons d'être*, goals, functions and processes may be much the same as the quilting bee of an earlier period in North America or the *zaar* of Sudan (a ritualized self-help, therapeutic gathering on behalf of a "sister" in crisis). If these are a "flip side," are they unconscious in their construction and, in that sense, do they involve prefeminist consciousness or "female consciousness"?[40] Or, were all alternative institutions constructed through feminist consciousness?

When the variables of different disciplines are assembled that are said to signal differing principles for the use of space by women and men, differing gender metaphors for the creation of institutions, and a process for the creation of new modes of relationships in the work environment, a women's culture concept begins to develop that moves beyond the descriptive and definitional and into the conceptual.

To summarize, the space (both material and metaphorical) into which women/feminists pour their culture is user-oriented, ergonomic, functional, flexible, organic, holistic, complex, social, slowly growing, communal, decentralized, informal, localist, participatory, conservationist, emotional, affective, instinctual, nurturing, experiential, nonhierarchical, fluid, reflective (self-critical), egalitarian, and collaborative. The way in which we build a house is as important, if not more so, than the house itself. At the Woman's Building, the way the house was run and the relations of production that were developed were as significant as the content of the house, i.e., the art that was produced.[41]

Space, Culture, and Freedom: Revolutionary Feminist Art

What is the possibility for women's culture to transform space radically and, therefore, to transform culture? In other words, does women's culture have revolutionary potential? Is women's art (which so often embodies many of the principles, metaphors, and processes of women's culture) revolutionary? I consider revolutionary art to be that which (1) has a profound relationship to material conditions (i.e., art which is not isolated or isolating and is not alienated from the material world, the producer or the audience); (2) is relatively unbounded or has flexible boundaries; (3) is collective; (4) is egalitarian; (5) is active (especially in the sense of demanding social change); (6) is transcultural (while sometimes using our ethnicities to arrive at that point); (7) is disruptive of the dichotomy between subject and object or any other dichotomy. The act or *process* of creating the art is revolutionary, rather than the actual form or even the content. (This idea is borrowed and altered from John Berger.[42]) More importantly, the revolutionary aspect of the art is in the interaction process of the creators. In this way culture, as it is articulated through art production, is simultaneously theory and practice. That is, through culture, the person is in a state of constant revolt in which she simultaneously fulfills and creates her own values. The revolt is not an intellectual invention, but is based upon human experience and action toward change.[43] In this way, the art form is one around which women can mobilize or organize and build institutions of change. It is, in fact, political organization itself.

To many theorists and activists, performance art was the quintessential revolutionary art. The art form was at its most political when it produced an intersection of space, culture, and freedom. Performance art, especially as we knew it among feminist art producers in the Greater Los Angeles area, was a feminist art of and for the era. It was oftentimes also the epitome of the expression of sexuality and space.

A number of the performance pieces of the era exhibited many of the "principles," "institutional metaphors," and processes explored above: fluidity, egalitarianism, communalism, and informality. The initiator of a massive public performance piece is a self-conscious actor, but the people drawn into it, immersed in the piece sometimes by accident, may take on their own dynamic and are changed and, in turn, change their environment. Whether or not the performances followed the original design of their initiator, they created a political and cultural bridge between public and private life (to which Sheila de Bretteville's design projects also speak so eloquently). There is a great deal in feminist public performance art that emanates from the people themselves, is spontaneous, and is localist/participatory. It is, in that sense, ideal

Take Back the Night, **performance by Leslie Labowitz and Suzanne Lacy**, 1978, San Francisco. Photograph by Rob Blalack. © Leslie Labowitz and Suzanne Lacy.

feminist process. Many of the women passersby who participate are not doing so self-consciously but rather may be responding to their own needs (material or social conditions) or identifying with a particular form of oppression/repression. They may be part of the same community or network in which there are shared institutions, values, relationships, norms, organizations, arts, methods of communication, and history. If only temporarily, they act together to change their environment (space).

It is significant to the theorizing of space, sexuality, and politics that this art was focused as much at the Woman's Building as at any other one site. Performance art workers appropriated space and filled it with autobiography, theater, mysticism, sexuality, and politics to produce compelling invitations to deal with our personal/political selves. Some works by the Feminist Art Workers, Mother Art, Double X (XX), Ariadne: A Social Art Network, The Waitresses, Sisters Of Survival, and others also used collective action to bring about change, to subvert the public/private dichotomy, and to engage in praxis.[44]

In the late seventies, especially in the work of Suzanne Lacy and Leslie Labowitz, performance art as media event, as spectacle, reached its peak. Large, politically conscious action groups were coordinated, appropriating urban space, mapping women's oppression, and using performativity, feminist theory, community organization, media analysis, and ideas from Conceptual art for change.

Change through irony was one of the unstated goals of some performance. One of the best examples of ironic performance was the Feminist Art Workers' *This Ain't No Heavy Breathing* (1978), in which the group selected women's names at random from the phone book, called them, and instead of making lewd comments, affirmed and validated them. Other performances involved juxtaposing opposing groups of people in the same space to cooperate toward one goal and in this way synthesizing structure and method. In these public art events, it was ambiguous who was the audience and who was the "performer"; all became cultural workers who may have been altering space and body within that space. Likewise, it was unclear where the "piece" began and where it ended; such terminology is, in fact, not appropriate. Dialogue, protest, confrontation, and celebration are all human behaviors simultaneously recreating culture and changing the cultural space.

Art Critical Theories and Feminism

Most feminist art of the seventies[45] was political art in many senses, just as feminist art criticism was political criticism, whether critiquing feminist art or conventional/mainstream/patriarchal art. Lillian Robinson, literary critic, referred to feminist art criticism as *engaged* criticism, Lucy Lippard as *advocacy* criticism: It should be just as engaged as the art itself.[46]

For many cultural feminists, it is arguable to posit that the feminist art movement of the seventies emanated from "second-wave feminism," because of the utopian nature of much of feminist art. Nonetheless, both cultural feminists and other "second-wave feminists" were responding to the abysmal material conditions of most women's lives; to the secondary nature of women's lives, so poignantly narrated by Simone de Beauvoir; and to the "problem that had no name" of Friedan's "feminine mystique" (among other things, the boredom and lack of fulfillment of the middle-class [white] housewife).[47] The movements were also a reaction to the fact that existed then and still exists today: more women are killed and maimed by the men in their lives (often in their own homes) than in any other way.

From this knot of facts, and from where most feminists chose to position the site of the struggle at that time, emerged the most famous slogan of the era: "The personal is political." This slogan/theory/praxis/mode of relating to the world was a cardinal belief of most feminists and was to transform many women's lives, the nature of feminism, and the content and practice of feminist art.

"Feminism" itself was/is many things: an academic and theoretical point-of-view, a didactic stance, a political agenda, an ideological and/or philosophical perspective, and a *program* to change the conditions of women's lives. There are many definitions of "feminism" and many different perspectives; each one may be said to contain a cultural component and the seeds of a cultural movement. Not only is feminism not monolithic, no one person fits neatly into one category of feminism. This was, apparently, a difficult idea for the many factions of feminists to grasp and hold onto all of the time. Feminists and their critics also had difficulty or refused to fathom the idea that feminism is dynamic. Therefore, what was true of feminism in the seventies may not be true of feminism in the early twenty-first century.

Second-wave feminism was characterized by an emphasis on consciousness-raising about women's or one's status and identity. It was an exploration and exposé of the socialization processes that were said to account for women's status. In art, literature, and even in academic writings there was an emphasis on images and self-images: challenging, creating, subverting, and valorizing them.

What set "second-wave" feminism off from "first-wave" was the former's emphasis on the spiritual and cultural and on image and imagery. And connected, almost mystically, was the notion that there is a unified subject, a biological femaleness. We were all women after all. Such ideas were theorized by Mary Daly and Susan Griffin, and poeticized through some of the early works of Adrienne Rich, especially *The Dream of a Common Language*, which included "Transcendental Etude," an anthem to women's culture and a call for the invention of a women's history. Some of these pioneers of the women's culture movement presented valorized and "fixed" ideas about the "nature" of women and of women together.[48]

The women's cultural movement has been a very important element in U.S. feminism, and has been especially prominent on the West Coast.[49] Women began to believe that they had to change culture—language, history, philosophy, the arts—to achieve equality and liberation. Just as women had been cut off from their history, they had been cut off from their culture. I argue that there is no better way to dominate a group of people than to withhold, make invisible, or distort their history or culture. To the activists in the women's cultural movement this had to be addressed. The process for addressing it was dialectical; the strategy was twofold. That is, although feminists delegated themselves to change the culture, it was argued by some that women could also use that same culture to accomplish the transformation. A debate over whether or not we can use the "Master's tools to dismantle the Master's house" still rages.[50]

The cultural movement is also a reaction to the condition of women in the arts, including how they have been portrayed in art and how they have been treated as artists, e.g., how their labor has been devalued and the products of their work trivialized or marginalized. That had to be changed. But how would women artists come into their own without knowledge of their role in the history of art?

Therefore, an important goal within the women's cultural movement has been the rewriting of art history to reflect more accurately the contribution of women, but also to assess the negative impact of the traditional depiction of women in art. Although some have called for a rewriting of art history, others such as Griselda Pollock have suggested, instead, "feminist interventions in art history."[51]

Perhaps it is too obvious to say that Western art was the domain of men because art is one of the highest expressions of culture, and therefore, was coveted and protected by men—like a grand copyright. Art in most societies is also the expression of the ideas of a particular class. Within Western capitalist society, this took particular forms. Before the twentieth century, the images of women were patriarchal types. Alexandra Comini referred to "vampires, virgins and voyeurs" and Carol Duncan and others to Madonna, Eve, and Venus (and sometimes Salome). It is among the middle and upper classes where we can trace the ideas that Duncan has referred to as "virility and domination," the pervading themes of Modernism (the Fauves, Cubists, German Expressionists, and other "vanguard" artists). But no salacious or pristine image can compete in ferocity and brutishness with twentieth century Modernist themes.[52]

Modernism and the avant-garde schools were quite different. They asserted,

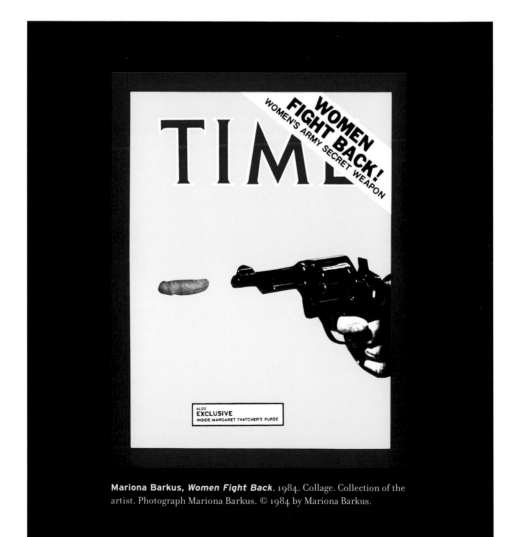

Mariona Barkus, *Women Fight Back*, 1984. Collage. Collection of the artist. Photograph Mariona Barkus. © 1984 by Mariona Barkus.

sometimes in manifestos, the virile, vigorous, and uninhibited sexual appetite of the artist; male artists celebrated the male erotic experience. Modernism was/is voyeuristic in that the woman's body—in the form of the nude—was laid out for the male gaze. She/it is fragmented, objectified, commoditized, passive, vulnerable, and submissive to the male artist. Her blank gaze tells us little about her. She/it is devalued.[53]

Clearly feminist artists and critics had their work cut out for them.

Art and Resistance

The much overworked themes of oppression and resistance characterized a great deal of feminist arts of the seventies; these themes were always visible in differing degrees at the Woman's Building: (1) Woman as oppressed, but with her anger about that oppression turned inward. This was often literature that included ironic or self-mocking acts of degradation, self-hatred, and self-destruction, often directed at the artist's own body. We see this in the poetry of Sylvia Plath and Anne Sexton.[54] (2) Woman as oppressed, but with her anger aimed outward, usually at men, patriarchy, or male-dominated society. Or, in the art by women of color, the anger might be directed at whites of both genders. Action might take the form of talking or fighting back. The early poetry of Ntozake Shange is a good example.[55] (3) Affirmation, validation, or celebration of womanhood and of women being together, or in the case of women of color, of the race and women of the race, bonding.[56] No literature was as validating of women than the poetry of Adrienne Rich, especially in *The Dream of a Common Language*.[57] Celebration of womanhood is the salient theme in Judy Chicago's *The Dinner Party*. In *The Great Wall* and other works, muralist Judy Baca included strong Latinas, alongside Latinos, forging United States history.

Because the structures of domination remain in place no matter how much women celebrated their attributes, the themes above may not have been the most effective methods for achieving the stated goals of the period, which amounted to nothing less than a social revolution. Even if these goals were not achievable, the significant act was to intervene in social history in order to unsettle and subvert the hegemonic process. In the area of art history and art, in general, a lot of feminist intervention had to happen.

Clearly, feminists felt a need to correct the vilification of women in life and in art, starting by pointing out the negative images and then subverting, replacing, or negating them. Second, there was an expressed need to make women visible—in the past (restoration, resuscitation, resurrection, redemption, and recuperation) and in the present. Third, feminists had to address the mistakes and fill in the gaps. Fourth, feminists saw an effective method in turning things on their heads, or turning the tables, for example, rescuing taboos and appropriating them, and in the process, imbuing them with power. Fifth, feminists also saw a need to present new, strong, positive images and heroic narratives to replace the negative images. This often involved valorizing women, making women the narrators of their own lives and the curators of their own culture. Sixth, because women had been deprived of much of their past, feminists aimed at continuity with the past. In art, this often entailed rescuing a "traditional" motif, such as quilting, and giving it meaning in contemporary life (e.g. the art of Faith Ringgold and Miriam Schapiro). Last, and perhaps the most controversial, feminists aimed to find the "Truth" (placing them in the heart of Modernism) that emerged in the form of a unified subject. Many feminists of the seventies took the position that women were more unified by the fact of being "woman" than by the specifics of race, class, sexuality, region, material conditions, religion, and culture.

The last goal mentioned above is controversial because it has been perceived as essentialist by feminist critics, critics of feminism, and by women of color inside and outside of those first two categories. Women of color often did not see themselves in the picture, asserting that by "woman," that unified and totalized subject, the "knowers" (the gatekeepers in the art world and in academia) really were referring to white, middle-class, Western women.[58]

In a way, the splits that were a result of "identity politics" are ironic because, if there is some commonality between the work of women of color and white feminist women, identity politics is one. Yet, it was not *identity politics* that unified women in the seventies and eighties. Quite the contrary. For all of the attempts at spinning and weaving, things spun out of control. The Woman's Building is no exception to the strife that consumed so much of the feminisms of the era. The predominantly white feminists at the Woman's Building were never really able to recover from the charge by women artists, critics, and art historians of color that the agenda was set, and only as an afterthought were women of color invited to the tea party. Internal and external criticisms that the Woman's Building did not have "enough diversity" were mollified by an "add a woman of color and stir" strategy.[59] For women artists of color, the strategy of building a house from within did not, it seemed, resemble moving from the margins to the center (within).

When women artists of color did address some of the themes delineated above, they did it with a twist. For one thing, there was often less emphasis on the individual artist as subject and a greater tendency to talk about one's own group, e.g., African Americans. By depicting the stereotypic Black maid with a gun in *The Liberation of Aunt Jemima*, Betye Saar was appropriating a negative image and imbuing it with power. Thus, although Saar might have been including herself in the general image-making, the comment was broader and served as a reminder to middle-class white women that Black women still occupy the lower rungs of the workforce. White feminist academics and artists devoted a great deal of energy to a characterization of all women as exploited through domestic labor; this piece of Saar's served as a reminder of who is more exploited.

Betye Saar, *The Liberation of Aunt Jemima*, 1972. Mixed media assemblage, 11 ¾" x 8" x 2 ¾". Collection of University of California, Berkeley Art Museum, purchased with the aid of funds from the National Endowment for the Arts. Photograph courtesy of Michael Rosenfeld Gallery, LLC, New York.

The All City Waitress Marching Band, 1979. Performance by The Waitresses, created by Jerri Allyn, Leslie Belt, Chutney Berry (pictured in front with baton), Anne Mavor and 35 waitresses. The DooDah Parade, Pasadena, CA. Performed by: Nancy Angelo, Elizabeth Blouser, Terry Bleecher, Diane Diplata, Laurine DiRicco, Anne Gauldin, Cheri Gaulke, Leibe Gray, Anita Green, Maisha Green, Vanalyn Green, Annette Hunt, Elizabeth Irons, Julie James, Maria Karras, Laurel Klick, Sue Maberry, Anne Phillips, Linda Preuss, Arlene Raven, Maureen Renville, Rita Rodriquez, Jeanne Shanin, Barbara Stopha, Cheryl Swannack, Sue, Talbot, Rina Viezel, Lynne Warshafsky, Christine Wong. Photograph by Mary McNally. © The Waitresses: Jerri Allyn and Anne Gauldin.

The art by women of color added many other themes to the lexicon, however, ones generally not dealt with by white feminist artists. Following Lippard in *Mixed Blessings*, one could characterize the art by women of color as dealing with the various themes of telling, mapping, naming, landing, remembering, longing, dreaming, resisting, and appropriating. Memory and loss are very powerful themes in the art by American Indians/Native Americans and Asian Americans. Telling, naming, and resisting seem very important among African American artists; mapping, *re*appropriating, and resisting are salient themes among Chicanas and Latinas. Certainly, the relationship to land is very significant: no land, stolen land, remembered land, and dual lands or identity.[60] It is this last set of themes that resonate with feminist concern for space, house, and home. White feminists, however, rarely dealt with land. Their art was more insular, closer to home than to faraway lands, closer to the house than to the fields.[61]

Feminist Art Strategies in the 1970s

In its leadership role in the arts communities, the feminist art of the Woman's Building in the seventies and into the eighties was often in the genre of biography or autobiography and was also multiple, layered in time, and non-linear. In tone, its critics said that it was humorless, or "dead serious," and that feminist art dealt primarily with oppression, trivialization, and the brutalization of women. This is reductive, however, because, although it is true that these were some of the prevalent themes of *Womanhouse*, feminist art at the Woman's Building was also about *survivors*, not victims, and it was often very funny.[62]

Some of the art used biting comedy or satire—even about such serious themes as the exploitation and the sexualization of women's labor. The Waitresses, for example, was a Woman's Building-associated performance group that staged events in restaurants throughout the city, appropriating and altering space. They did comical renditions of sexual harassment and exploitation of labor. Arguing that feminist art is "too serious" also overlooks the guerilla theater / performance group Guerrilla Girls, who stage comical public demonstrations and events (in disguise) to protest discrimination against women's art and women artists, and whose publications are equally humorous.[63]

Furthermore, the parallel woman-as-hero theme was also prevalent in seventies feminist art. Linear, heroic narratives were prominent strategies in the construction of a new mythology and cosmology (e.g., Judy Baca's early paintings and murals and Yolanda Lopez's work). In fact, the linear narrative depicting women's lives was a popular feminist strategy for more accurately representing women in art and academic research, and it resulted in the collection of life-histories or personal narratives. Although Baca created strong graphic narratives that are emancipatory in theme, others used oral histories and personal stories to represent "ordinary" women in an attempt to show that no woman is ordinary.

The personal art of quilt making manifests many of the themes I have mentioned. Quilts are, of course, important as examples in feminist art histories of restoring and resurrecting art forms by women that have been trivialized and marginalized (in fact, not even considered "art"). Moreover, by examining quilts in women's history, feminists illuminated issues of work, of community collaboration, personal and family history, ritual, multi-layered history, commemoration, and the importance of decoration. Quilts are also reflections of race, ethnicity, class, and regional diversity. Quilt makers are, indeed, cultural workers. Their work covers and reveals.

Sheila de Bretteville created *Pink* in 1974. She invited women from the Feminist Studio Workshop (FSW) to create page art about the color pink. Some of the squares are text only; some are images. Then she "quilted" the responses together, pinned them to the wall, and photographed the ensemble. From the photograph, she created one poster that is really the patchwork/quilting of twenty-nine women.

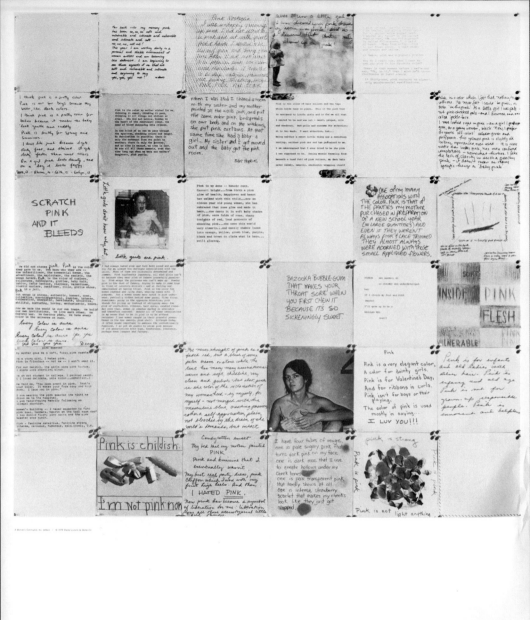

Sheila de Bretteville, *Pink*. 1974. Two color offset poster, edition of 500, printing by Helen Alm Roth. 20½″ x 20″.
© Women's Community Inc., 1974.

In fact, for many feminists, quilts have been used in book and essay titles as metaphors for weaving women's lives together, for particular kinds of labor, for collaborative work, for the layered history of women's lives, and the like. Two striking examples of literary metaphors are Shirley Lim's "A Dazzling Quilt" and Bettina Aptheker's *Tapestries of Life*.[64] In looking at the process of quilting, feminists can see the metaphors of finishing each other's stitches; collaborative work; linking women, families, and generations; the labor of love; and the valuing of women's labor, including art.

The visualization of this process of quilting and the resurrection of needle-work as art were important in the works of at least four prominent artists: Faith Ringgold, with her quilt series depicting African American lives; Miriam Schapiro, who combined the quilt motif with the central core imagery (e.g., "The Poet," "The House That Miriam Built," and "Wonderland"); Faith Wilding, whose scrapbooks, scriptoriums, and *Womb Room*(s) crocheted her environment; and Judy Chicago, whose *Dinner Party* rescued china painting and needle art and who also produced dramatic needle works herself (e.g., "The Birth Project"). The last three artists were closely affiliated with the Woman's Building.

As we can see from the example of *Pink*, it was not only forms and motifs that were rescued from trivialization, but colors as well. De Bretteville appropriated the color pink, the dreaded, super-feminine, and most trivial of colors associated with the construction of femininity. In *Pink*, FSW participants were asked to address a wide range of topics, using only pink. The page art dealt with image and text, the personal and political, and formed an integrated poster. The poster, an art medium that was a salient feature of Woman's Building art, provided a way of appropriating public space to make private communications, which was a trademark of de Bretteville's art (e.g., her 1979 "The Personal Voice in Public Communication").

It is no accident that a poster designed in 1998 by a new generation of feminists at California Institute of the Arts (CalArts), who were intent on reclaiming their feminist history from obscurity, was also predominantly pink! The poster advertised a conference entitled The F Word: Contemporary Feminisms and the Legacy of the Los Angeles Feminist Art Movement.

The tactile and narrative works mentioned above evoked the house and home, domesticity as an extraordinary/ordinary existence, the private and public, and space.

The Body as a Site of Resistance

Another central credo of feminism is that there is nothing more authentic than the self and speaking from that self. Therefore, using the self as subject (as in autobiography and memoir, for example) has been a primary strategy of feminist expression, including much academic writing. Nowhere has this been more striking, however, than in the use of the body, especially the artist's own body, in feminist art, which has resulted in setting up the paradox of the artist as subject and object. The body has been delineated as both the site of oppression and the site of resistance. Using the self as space for art (sometimes as a canvas) became one of the most common strategies of feminist art and writing and a mainstay of the kinds of performance art associated with the West Coast and with the Woman's Building. Part of the legacy is extant in later, "transgressive art" (e.g., Annie Sprinkle).

In our concern for space, and the control and ownership of space, feminists have tried to locate these sites of oppression and sites of resistance. It was clear to seventies feminist artists how much women's bodies are a focus of contestation, and how much this contested terrain of women's bodies is a central theme in feminist theories and in art. As Barbara Kruger asserts: "Your body is a battleground."[65] It is also narrative, discourse, primordial Truth, spectacle, nature, and masquerade.[66]

Use of the body, especially inscribing the body, was a multifaceted strategy. The artists could challenge conventional/historical representation of women's bodies (e.g., Carolee Schneemann's take off on Édouard Manet's *Olympia* [1863] in *Site* [1964], or Hung Liu's version of *Olympia*, with its double pun [1992]); they could appropriate taboos by depicting them (e.g., blood and vagina in Shigeko Kubota's *Vagina Painting* [1965], or Schneemann's *Interior Scroll* [1975], or Chicago's *Menstruation Bathroom* for *Womanhouse* [1972], or later, *The Dinner Party*); they could express the body as perverse space/site (e.g., Schneemann's *Site*) or express site as body (as in Faith Wilding's *Womb Room* [1972] in *Womanhouse*). They could even mock the essentialism of a woman's body as representing her essence, her perfection (or lack of), as in Martha Rosler's video *Vital Statistics of a Citizen, Simply Obtained* (1977), in which she stands in a room where a team of "authorities" measures every crucial inch of her body and announces its findings of her "assets" or "liabilities" to the assembled, who assess if her measurements measure up to the "standard." Or, an artist could use her body to make a commentary on other "historical bodies" (e.g., Cheri Gaulke's Christ/Eve-like persona, who both eats an apple and lounges on the cross in *This Is My Body* and *This Is My Body Illuminated* [both works, 1985]). Feminist artists could use metaphors connected with food, eating, plates, and dinner parties to display vaginas (perhaps as "butterflies"). They could give the body, especially the vagina, texture—crocheting the womb (e.g. Wilding) and quilting that "central cavity" (e.g., Schapiro's quilt motifs).

Perhaps the most common image of feminist art in the seventies, and the most graphic site of resistance, was the vaginal image, or central cavity, mentioned above, or what some refer to as "cunt art." The central cavity image challenged the male view of the woman as "just a hole" or the phallic lack, to use Jane Gallop's terminology.[67] At the time, the mere representation of the vagina was itself a powerful consciousness-raiser.

By using space (including central space), nature, the body, and taboo sites of resistance, a new cosmology was developing—a new mythology with a reservoir of earthy images and an emphasis on female power (for example, Mary Beth Edelson's

Ana Mendieta, *Silueta Works in Mexico*, August 1973/1991. Estate color photograph, one from a series of twelve, 20" x 16". Courtesy Galerie LeLong, New York. © The Estate of Ana Mendieta Collection.

This is My Body, performance by Cheri Gaulke, 1982. ESpace DBD, Los Angeles. Photograph by Sheila Ruth. © Cheri Gaulke.

portrayals of female spiritual power). In order not to be left out of history and culture, women's bodies were inserted/planted in the earth (or emerged from the earth or through a flower). Ana Mendieta's earthy, erotic pieces were carved or burned into nature. In *Excavations* (1985), a lesbian performance work by Terry Wolverton, bodies/beings unearthed themselves (a metaphor for lesbian self-discovery). These art motifs that placed women close to the earth or "blossoming" in the midst of a negative world, such as Leslie Labowitz's *It's Sproutime* (1983) in the "At Home" show, both re-flected and influenced the ecofeminist movement.

However, many of these motifs invited criticisms from a number of different directions. For example, the explicit display of the body was seen as narcissistic. Some said that the genital image, signifying woman, was *essentialist*, that it fed into stereotypes, was ultimately impersonal, and was outside of history.[68] The nature theme was also criticized as essentialist and as romanticizing/exoticizing women's bodies and lives and, thereby nurturing the "man of culture and woman of nature" formula.

However, not all body art, or the use of one's body to convey the theme, seems to have lent itself to "essentialist" interpretations.[69] A number of artists in the seventies and later performed or depicted the idea of women as socially constructed beings/ bodies, sometimes racialized, sometimes biomedically constructed. Among the examples are Cindy Sherman's ongoing series of untitled photographs, which are supposedly of subjects in different time periods, ways of life, and themes. Sherman, indelibly inscribing herself into history and culture, appears as the central figure in all of the photos: Hollywood star; battered woman; dissipated, fearful victim; and corpse[70]— not quite types, but evocative of women we remember. They remind us of something/ someone. Other examples are Martha Rosler's *Vital Statistics* performance and video mentioned above; Hannah Wilke's photographic series that captures the stages of her physical degeneration as she is dying from cancer on a hospital bed (*Intra-Venus*, 1992–93), exhibited in the group show "Sexual Politics," curated by Amelia Jones in 1996; Eleanor Antin's multiple, constructed characters that are either photographed or performed (e.g., the ballerina); and Terry Wolverton's *Me and My Shadow* (1984), a performance at the Woman's Building that addressed racism. These were all far from essentialism and romanticization.

Sometimes using the body as central image has involved re-readings of Freud and the depiction of male sexuality or of human sexuality in general, as in the work of Mira Schor (e.g., *Cunt* and *Penis* of 1993), or Hannah Wilke's *Venus Envy* (1980).[71] These are hard-edged works that lacked sentimentality, romance, or nostalgia.

In the same time period a number of male artists were also using their bodies as subject, as conveyors of meaning. But they were doing "body art" quite differently. For the most part, the violent and hard-edged work of such artists as Vito Acconci and Chris Burden may have transgressed social norms, but in most cases, not the norms of masculinity, which may account for why the reaction to their work was different. Not that what they were performing or depicting did not challenge masculinity, but they were within the range of outrageous, masculinist behavior. Their work was rarely ever deemed narcissistic or self-indulgent. Lippard makes the contrast in commenting on the uproar over Linda Benglis's infamous advertisement in which she wears a giant dildo in *Artforum* (1974).

> The uproar that this last image created proved conclusively that there are still things that women may not do. The notion of sexual transfor-mation has, after all, been around for some time. No such clamor arose in 1970 when Vito Acconci burned hair from this chest, "pulling at it, making it supple, flexible—an attempt to develop a female breast," then tucked his penis between his legs to "extend the sex change," and finally "acquired a female form" by having a woman kneel behind him with his penis "disappearing" in her mouth (*Avalanche*, Fall 1972). Nor was there any hullabaloo when Scott Burton promenaded 14th Street in drag for a 1969 Street Work, or when he flaunted a giant black phallus in a static performance in 1973; or when William Wegman made his amusing trompe-l'oeil

66

Lynda Benglis, *SELF* (*Artforum* Advertisement, November 1974), various dates 1970–76. Portfolio of 9 pigment prints, 34" x 23", edition of 25. Image courtesy of Cheim & Read, New York.

"breast" piece ... or when Lucas Samaras played with himself in front of his Polaroid camera.[72]

Rebecca Schneider claimed, "Nudity was not the problem. Sexual display was not the problem. *The agency of the body displayed, the authority* of the agent—that was the problem with women's work."[73]

Transgressing social norms, especially sexual mores, was a trademark of seventies art. The daring body and performance art of Woman's Building art workers such as Cheri Gaulke, with pieces such as *This Is My Body*, clearly presaged later works represented in both the "Bad Girls" and "Bad Girls West" shows (1994), and in "Sexual Politics."[74] Linda Goode Bryant defines "transgressive" art as "works which speak to a female identity that exists outside conventional feminine traits, aspirations and decorum."[75] That much of feminist art still claims to be transgressive is an homage to much of the art of the Woman's Building.[76] Following in the tradition of such first generation transgressive performance and multimedia artists as Schneemann, we see Karen Finley, Sandra Bernhard, and Annie Sprinkle use primitivism in performance to mock commodity fetishism and pornography, transgressing feminine decorum. The 1990s misappropriation of the concept of transgressive art by curators of "naughty" and titillating art is, however, a contributor to the erasure of the Woman's Building legacy and is discussed below.

Written Out of History: The Woman's Building in Feminist Art and Social History

Can one say about the Woman's Building the same thing that Amelia Jones said about the position of *The Dinner Party*?

> At the same time it has not been incorporated in any satisfactory way into histories and theories of feminism or contemporary art; it seems that the very contentiousness of the piece has precluded the thoughtful examination of its effects.[77]

I contend that the "bookends theory" of feminist art history in Los Angeles and at the Woman's Building, while attempting to argue from a point of strength, instead disables a broader view of the contribution of the art of the Woman's Building.

By "bookends theory" of Los Angeles feminist art, I am referring to the starting point and ending point of discussions about seventies feminist art in this region—the work of Judy Chicago. In this model, the foundation of the Woman's Building is subsumed by the power of Chicago's art, from *Womanhouse* to *The Dinner Party*. An example of this approach to social history is the 1996 "Sexual Politics" show that used *The Dinner Party* as the essence of feminist art, as a bookend for an era. If one wanted

Susan Silton, cover design for the exhibition catalog *Sexual Politics*, ed. Amelia Jones (Los Angeles: UCLA Hammer Museum, and Berkeley: University of California Press, 1996). Cover photograph by Jennifer Cheung and Steve Nilsson, styling by Terry Wolverton. Cover image courtesy Susan Silton.

to create a bookends model, one could just as appropriately select *Womanhouse* and "At Home," which were a decade apart and encompass the major themes of Southern California feminist art. Or, if not restricted to California, one might have begun with Louise Bourgeois's Femme/Maison series and ended with "At Home." I am arguing for the importance of the appropriation of space to feminist art, centering the Woman's Building as the pinnacle of ownership and control of female space.

This is not in any way to denigrate the significance of Chicago's work. In many ways, the content of *The Dinner Party* (that is, the ideas the work chose to carry forward and the form/structure of the work) and the various critiques of it contained most of the guiding methods and ideas of "second-wave" and cultural feminism. In that sense, we could say that it was an attempted hegemonic cultural construct for women on the West Coast and contained in it, dialectically, counter hegemonic detractions and movements (especially as forwarded by women of color).

If one accepts the above "bookends" model of feminist art in Greater Los Angeles or Southern California, one is expected to see the acknowledged and unacknowledged role of a central site, i.e., the Los Angeles Woman's Building. Most of the artists and critics who produced and critiqued art in conjunction with or inspired by this era were also associated in some way with the Woman's Building, e.g., exhibiting in the Woman's Building gallery and offering workshops. Yet, the essays in the "Sexual Politics" catalog barely acknowledged the Woman's Building, virtually erasing the site, perhaps in the name of a cosmopolitanism, which, ironically, could not be achieved in the show because of the very bookends approach. After all, "cosmopolitanism," in the provincial and parochial manner of U.S. social thought, often simply refers to including both East and West Coast contributions.

There is no doubt that the fame and notoriety of Chicago's work, especially *The Dinner Party*, is power in itself, attracting attention to an otherwise "esoteric" segment of the art world. Although a major influence on a segment of feminist artists, the type of attention that the work drew was also a distraction from some of the equally and more profound achievements of some of the other artists.

How do we account for the writing of the Woman's Building out of history? Is it what I have suggested above: the distortion of one artist's importance? Or, has the distancing of the three co-founders contributed to this: de Bretteville leaving Los Angeles to chair Yale's Design Department; Chicago removing herself to New Mexico; Raven moving to New York? All three stayed in touch, but their influence became less local and localized. On the other hand, we could just as easily see this as a possibility for the dissemination of Woman's Building influence. Many other well-known Woman's Building-associated artists have left Los Angeles, e.g., Nancy Buchanan, for a time, and Faith Wilding.

However, attributing the erasure of an institution's viability in historical memory to the presence or absence of particular actors is a weak explanation. In fact, the transfer of power and direction to a second generation can be strength. There are more significant reasons associated with ideas, with changes in mores and in the political climate (i.e., the backlash of the Reagan/Bush years), and with the power of the organization to rub against the grain of society. After all, the Woman's Building represents, as a response to both external and internalized oppression, a conscious and willful attempt on the part of a segment of the feminist community to set itself apart from conventional/mainstream society. This conscious marginalization was both strategic and adaptive, and unlike some other feminist institutions, it was not easily co-opted. It was easier to erase. Certainly, academic feminists who internalized mainstream criticisms made a contribution to that erasure.

Furthermore, one cannot overlook the homophobia that was eventually to produce unprecedented numbers of hate crimes; the cooptation of the hard edge of lesbianism and lesbian ideas by "queer theory"; the softening of the marginalization through popularizing (e.g., the television program "Ellen"); and the dismantling of women's separate spheres through processes such as the preference for "gender studies" over "women's studies" in most elite academic circles.

The importance and preponderance of lesbian art making and community formation at the Woman's Building, and the effect that those processes have had on social ideas, is not neutral. Lesbian art making dealt with the difficult-to-digest themes of incest, violence against women, autoeroticism, and compulsory heterosexuality. It was, however, the profoundly political *ideas* behind this socially conscious cultural work that were threatening: the goal of creating an entirely new culture and community. Whether or not this was achievable is irrelevant to the threat that such ideas posed.

Furthermore, the utopian ideas of much of the art and methods of collaborating on that art were based on the idea of an affirmative women's culture, a celebration of femaleness, the offer of a counter canon. This counter canon is a self-conscious, liberatory women's culture.

The United States is a society that has mastered the art of depoliticization: in the courts, media, schools, and social institutions. Media all too prematurely herald the "post-" of a movement. "Postfeminists" proclaim that they are feminists without the anger and polemics. They are feminists with a sense of humor, or what *Esquire* magazine dubbed the "Do-Me Feminists."

By the 1990s, funny bad girls were appropriating ideas from seventies feminist art. For example, the statements by the curators of the sister shows, "Bad Girls" and "Bad Girls West," in 1994, are a harbinger of ill will toward the Woman's Building, or an index of faulty memory. To Marcia Tucker, curator of the New York show, the "Bad Girls" show exhibited women artists and others "defying the conventions and proprieties of traditional femininity to define themselves according to their own terms, their own pleasures, their own interests, in their own way. But they're doing it by using a delicious and outrageous sense of humor...."[78]

Marcia Tanner, curator of "Bad Girls West," the West Coast version of "Bad Girls," referred to the exhibition as "iconoclastic" art by "outlaws." She differentiates "Bad Girl" art from feminist art of the seventies and eighties: "It's irreverent, anti-ideological, non-doctrinaire, non-didactic, unpolemical and thoroughly unladylike."[79] She, too, stresses sense of humor.

Tanner describes the art of the "Bad Girls West" show as tackling "body-self-image; sexuality and eroticism; gender roles, relationships, and behavior; fashion, make-up, and consumerism; celebrity, glamour, and aging,"[80] in other words, the very subjects of much of the Woman's Building art making.

Tanner is, perhaps, most revealing when she discusses the importance of *venue* for "Bad Girls West" and refers to choosing Los Angeles because it is the "very groin of Hollywood's male-dominated entertainment industry."[81] There is not one mention in the catalog, nor in the show, that Los Angeles was also the home of the Woman's Building, the heart of seventies feminist art.

Is it possible, then, that this political erasure is because of the ideological, didactic, polemical, and radical nature of the ideas that emanated from the Woman's Building? That very essentialism that was condemned in the final years of the institution had been a guiding principle for teaching, mobilizing, and organizing. We were definitely not insouciant.

Conclusion

Assessing the influence of the Los Angeles Woman's Building on American life is like trying to assess the influence of feminism on contemporary ideas: too vast and profound and too elusive and embedded. However, we can isolate a few of the saliencies of the Woman's Building legacy.

As a space occupied and controlled by women, the Woman's Building's influence permeates contemporary social ideas and contemporary feminisms. By appropriating, designing, and contesting space the Woman's Building, through its spirit of place, has exerted a significant influence on urban life.

The expanded notions of sexuality and the body are major contributions to the modern and postmodern. If female sexuality is *the* defining component of seventies feminist art, as it reflects women's identities and experiences of living in a patriarchal culture, then what does that say for and about the art of the Woman's Building? To paraphrase Amelia Jones, in the artists' attempts to define sexualities and subjectivities, to analyze political agency, to explore female desire and eroticism, and to reveal the complexities and problematics of female identities, the range of art ideologies and practices was vast.[82]

For all of the advantages of being housed under one roof, as a "family of women," so to speak, or a "community of feminists" or "room of muses," there were drawbacks. The charge of essentialism plagued the Woman's Building for much of its later history. That very essentialism, used programmatically, strategically, and effectively to raise the consciousness of women about their value, their valorized difference(s) from men, and the potential power of their numbers and abilities, was to continue to influence gender identity politics. But it was, dialectically, also to lay bare the racism of seventies feminism in its inadvertent erasure of differences among women.

Ironically, although music, for example, was never seen as a major element in the programming of the Woman's Building, the workshops and concerts that were held were highly influential in disseminating ideas about process and music as a tool for organizing. Women physically using their formerly muted, atrophied voices in solidarity was not a neutral process. This conversion of metaphor ("giving voice") into materiality and actuality is only one example of the didactic power of some of the programs. Many of these same ideas were taken over by women's studies programs throughout the country, i.e., disseminated to thousands of students. Perhaps there is no pair of ideas promulgated by the art workers and activists of the Woman's Building that has more power than the notion of the citizen artist and the idea that art should be in the public interest (and in the public).[83] Although Woman's Building artists were often accused of individualism and self-indulgence because of the highly personal art production, the opposite was true. Art in the public interest was a very important part of Woman's Building philosophy and praxis, e.g., the spirit of guerrilla theater that flourished in the performance and organizing work of Woman's Building activists such as the Feminist Art Workers, and that influenced Women against Pornography and WAC (Women's Action Coalition). Although guerrilla theater did not originate at the Woman's Building, some of the ideas that infuse contemporary guerrilla theater may be traced to cultural feminist ideas. For example, the ecological/spiritual theme of Leslie Labowitz's *It's Sproutime* and the work of Ana Mendieta can be seen in the Greenpeace guerrilla theater. The idea that private fantasies shape public events is a force in contemporary performance art in the public interest and the notion of collaborative art permeates much of contemporary socially conscious art.

In heralding a new era of public art, *Citizen Artist: 20 Years of Art in the Public Arena*, edited by Linda Frye Burnham, a critic who was often associated with the Woman's Building milieu, and Steven Durland, is as much about the art of the Woman's Building as not (e.g., with articles by and about Lacy, Gaulke, and other Southern California artists associated at one time or another with the Woman's Building). The editors feature art as a life experiment and the artist as citizen, and I sometimes felt I was reading a history of the Woman's Building.[84]

Certainly, the three founders of the Woman's Building advocated art in the public interest and the artist as citizen.

Perhaps if the influence of all three of the founders had been stressed by more art historians, and for the right reasons, giving full range to their ideas, the influence of the Woman's Building environment might have been felt more keenly. De Bretteville's influence on American design cannot be overestimated. Her austere design, not to mention her stress on site and the spirit of place, and her insistence on examining the issues of public and private communication, have all been important. As for Raven, she exerted strong influence on art historical ideas, for example, radical feminism/cultural feminism, essentialism as programmatic, the critic as inseparable from the artist, highly personalized art, and her methods of writing art criticism, to name only a few. Chicago's influence has been her insistence on collaboration, on reclaiming art practices that had been dismissed and trivialized as "female," and on the particular visualizations of the body—the central cavity and the roundedness of femaleness. Her spirit of entrepreneurial art, provocation, and female valorizing should not be overlooked as imbuing feminist art and artists with more power.

When one considers these founders and art thinkers/workers as a trilogy, we open up the possibilities for an intervention into art history and lead the way for a stronger interpretation of the influence of the Woman's Building.

In assessing that contribution, we will have to evaluate the Woman's Building's role in Modernism and Postmodernism. Can we see any bridge between the primarily Modernist art of the Woman's Building and what we are witnessing now among some Postmodern feminist artists as Mary Kelly (and including Kruger, Sue Coe, Jenny Holzer, and others) who refuse to use images of women in their work in order to subvert the use of the female image as object and spectacle?

In Kelly's *Post Partum Document* (begun in 1973, but first exhibited in 1979), she presages the eighties.[85] Her work has been an attempt to expose the processes of representation, language, and sexual position and their significance "to show what lies behind the sexual division of labour in child care, what is ideological in the notion of natural maternal instinct, what is repressed and almost unrepresentable in patriarchal language, female subjectivity...."[86]

The autobiographical nature of Kelly's work reminds one that art makers at the Los Angeles Woman's Building were instrumental in valorizing autobiography as a valid premise for art making. This cardinal premise (linked to idea that the personal is political) guided much of the art of the Woman's Building and contributed to our cultural reserve of personal narratives, fantasies, and visual stories. Giving testimony is now one of the most powerful human endeavors, giving voice and agency to "ordinary" people.

Although much of the Woman's Building's legacy has been unheralded until very recent years, there have been patches of acknowledgment. Some well-known male artists, especially performance, installation, and conceptual artists, have recognized the Woman's Building's influence on their work. Tim Miller, for example, cited the Woman's Building as an influence on his work, acknowledging that the work at the feminist institution gave him permission to explore autobiographical material in his performance art.[87]

Yet other male artists have been publicly silent on the issue of feminist influences on their work. Among those who have received a great deal of critical attention and who have utilized feminist strategies of art making (without acknowledging this) is Jim Isermann, who was in Los Angeles during the heyday of the Woman's Building. Isermann knits or crochets large quilts that are his "canvases." Mike Kelley, who was a student at CalArts in the seventies, uses stuffed animals and other materials first utilized by feminist artists. Nayland Blake, influenced by Kelley, is the next generation to pick up the mantle of this genre.[88]

Nonetheless, new generations of feminists and feminist artists are alerted to the significance of their legacy. I have already mentioned the new generation of CalArts feminists who resurrected their feminist legacy. Their pink poster for the F Word conference proclaimed:

[F]eminist art programs of the early seventies are at the center of the dynamic history of feminist art education.

Suzanne Lacy...is an artist who was part of the original Women's Design Program and developed a performance program at the Woman's Building.

Faith Wilding [Woman's Building affiliate]...is an artist and professor who was a member of the Feminist Art Program and *Womanhouse*.

Sue Maberry...is the Director of the Library at Otis College of Art and Design, where the Women's [*sic*] Building slide archives are housed. She has been involved with the Woman's Building for years.

Nancy Buchanan...began using video as a natural extension to performance and installation. Her artworks have been exhibited and screened worldwide....She has participated in various artist-run organizations such as Los Angeles Contemporary Exhibitions, Los Angeles Center for Photographic Studies, and the Woman's Building.

It is certainly to the credit of the CalArts Feminist Art Workshop that they noted their feminist art program's direct descent from the Feminist Studio Workshop, *Womanhouse*, and the Woman's Building. The stated goal of the F Word conference was "to better establish their legacy and to foster understanding of contemporary feminisms... [creating] a dialogue between the different generations associated with feminist practice."[89] That these newer generation feminist artists had to engage in "detective work" to trace their lineage is one of the points of this essay and the collection.

It is clear that some of the artists, critics, and academics of the newer generation are looking at unfinished business. They are not only trying to understand their legacy, but also to acknowledge it publicly.

One piece of unfinished business at the Woman's Building, and in feminism in general, however, is the extant racism in our approaches. Most who were in the arts community associated with the old Woman's Building readily admit that the relationship of women of color to the Woman's Building was never resolved and that we mostly failed in our various quests for a liberated race politics. As I have implied, this element of the Woman's Building past is a legacy of second-wave feminism, in general, and carries over into contemporary gender studies and queer studies. Just as we now have to look at the ways in which women's and men's experiences of the world have been socially constructed, so it is with race and class. Our next task is to do a better job in producing a critical theory that gives examples of how class, race, and gender are constructed and reinforced through representation.

The irony of our failure to wage a partially successful struggle with racism is that we had the tools to do it. A number of the strategies that Woman's Building artists and others used might have been instrumental in addressing racism. Women artists have been trying to negotiate new relationships to the body and to decolonize it in every way. This was a central task of Woman's Building activist artists. We demanded a body that was not negated, was not the "other," was not colonized—a body that was truly liberated—just as we were searching for a truly liberated art practice and theory. That we did not apply this praxis to race politics and that we did not see that body as racialized is a negative aspect of the history.

Our Woman's Building environment was an imagined, a built, and a *living* environment. Some say that women's material culture (as in quilts) has a symbolic language, and therefore, is a vital repository of a group's collective worldview. Another view is that direct actions, such as performance art and squatting, politicize and re-create environments. Or, that we can reveal the oppression of women through art by making public their private lives. The transformation of women's art from use value to commodity in a colonial context is alienation and can have implications for a "culture of resistance." The home, house (and museum and salon) can be seen as subversive "fronts," catalysts for women's creations and a space in which underlying feminist agendas unfold.

This is our vital history and our dynamic present. Denizens of the Woman's Building transformed physical site to conceptual space and invented a vision that was to sustain the community for longer than any women's cultural institution in the country.

The "boundaries" of the Woman's Building were both liberating and limiting— the former realized through our march into the future; the latter through the removal of our site and a politics of memory that was a conscious and unconscious attempt to erase our presence as a force in the twenty-first century of cultural and social ideas. *From Site to Vision: The Woman's Building in Contemporary Culture* is an attempt to address the latter and underscore the former.[90]

Notes

1. Paula Findlen, "The Museum: Its Classical Etymology and Renaissance Genealogy," *The Journal of Museum Collections* 1.1 (1989): 60.

2. Ibid., 73.

3. Ibid., 59.

4. Ibid., 60.

5. Many scholars have pointed to or alluded to feminism's ambiguous and ambivalent relationship to Modernism and Postmodernism. See, for example, Henry Sayre, *The Object of Performance: The American Avant-Garde Since 1970* (Chicago: University of Chicago, 1989); Craig Owens, "The Discourse of Others: Feminists and Post-modernism," in *The Anti-Aesthetic: Essays on Postmodernist Culture*, ed. Hal Foster (Port Townsend, WA: Bay Press, 1983), 57–83; and Lucy R. Lippard, "Both Sides Now: A Reprise," in *The Pink Glass Swan: Selected Feminist Essays on Art* (New York: The New Press, 1995), 266–77.

6. Virginia Woolf, *A Room of One's Own* (Harmondsworth, Middlesex: Penguin, 1945 [1928]).

7. The symposium, which I organized, was held at California State University, Long Beach, in 1983, and was co-sponsored by the CSULB Women's Studies Program and the Center for the Continuing Education of Women.
8. See Arlene Raven's catalog essay for the show in *At Home* (Long Beach, California: Long Beach Museum of Art, 1983).

9. Ibid., and *Womanhouse* (Valencia, California: California Institute of the Arts, 1972).

10. It would be an oversight not to acknowledge the very early feminist work by Louise Bourgeois on the themes of women and house in her series of the 1940s: Femme/Maison. A piece from the series, *Femme/Maison—To Carletto* (1947), is reproduced on the cover of Lucy Lippard, *From the Center: Feminist Essays on Women's Art* (New York: E.P. Dutton, 1976).

11. Some geographers have claimed that women were the first to build shelters, e.g., Carl Sauer, "Sedentary and Mobile Bents in Early Societies," in *Social Life of Early Man* [*sic*], ed. Sherwood Washburn (Chicago: Aldine, 1961), 256–66, especially 260–66. For this reference I am indebted to Arlene Rengert and Janice Monk, *Women and Spatial Change: Learning Resources for Social Science Courses* (Dubuque, Iowa: Kendall/Hunt, 1982).

12. In critiquing early uses of the expression and concept, Ellen DuBois pointed out that perhaps the first use of the term "women's culture" is in Nancy Cott's book, *Root of Bitterness*, in 1972. Most North American students of the "women's culture" concept acknowledge Carroll Smith-Rosenberg's seminal article, "The Female World of Love and Ritual." Ellen DuBois, et al., "Politics and Culture in Women's History: A Symposium," *Feminist Studies* 6.1 (1980): 25–64; Nancy Cott, ed., *Root of Bitterness* (New York: E.P. Dutton, 1972); Carroll Smith-Rosenberg, "The Female World of Love and Ritual: Relations between Women in Nineteenth-Century America," *Signs* 1.1 (1975): 1–28. These are, of course, academic uses; practitioners at the Woman's Building were using the term all along, at least by implication.

13. DuBois, et al., 29. Within the broad framework of "women's culture," others of the same era, in their attempts to define or question a "feminine aesthetic," "the female imagination," and "women and creativity," or to illuminate the "female world," used different terms. See, for example, respectively, Patricia Spacks, *The Female Imagination* (New York: Avon, 1972); Joelynn Snyder-Ott, *Women and Creativity* (Millbrae, California: Les Femmes, 1978); and Jessie Bernard, *The Female World* (New York: Free Press, 1981). An example of the use of the term "women's culture" is Gayle Kimball, ed., *Women's Culture: The Women's Renaissance of the Seventies* (Metuchen, New Jersey: Scarecrow, 1981).

14. Among some of the works reflecting the ideas of the time within art history and art criticism is Lucy R. Lippard's pioneering *From the Center*, 1976. Many of her essays on feminist art are brought together in the *Pink Swan*. Some of Lippard's later works, although not exclusively about feminist art, contain some of the most provocative and stimulating ideas in the field of public/activist feminist art, for example, *Overlay: Contemporary Art and the Art of Prehistory* (New York: Pantheon, 1983); *Get the Message? A Decade of Art for Social Change* (New York: E.P. Dutton, 1984); and *Mixed Blessings: New Art in a Multicultural America* (New York: Pantheon, 1990). *Chrysalis, a Magazine of Women's Culture*, a journal integrally connected to the Woman's Building, presented incomparable contemporary pieces on women's culture, but rarely used the women's culture concept and seldom supplied overarching theories. *Heresies*, the most political of the women-and-the-arts journals, continued for over twenty years to challenge traditional/conventional views of art, most often offering a socialist feminist version of the feminist avant-garde. Nonetheless, in its attempt to politicize and to stimulate activist art, *Heresies* editors neglected an analysis of culture as it relates to feminist precepts.

15. The Woman's Building partisans were no exception to the distrust of "High Theory" and academic theory.

16. Beatriz Colomina, ed. *Sexuality and Space* (Princeton, New Jersey: Princeton Architectural Press), 1992.

17. The standard at the time for studies of nonverbal communication was Nancy Henley, *Body Politics: Power, Sex, and Non-Verbal Communication* (Englewood Cliffs, New Jersey: Prentice-Hall, 1977). For gender spatial relationships, one of the best was Shirley Ardener, ed., *Women and Space: Ground Rules and Social Maps* (London: Croom Helm, 1981). Ardener's book does not explicitly deal with "women's culture" as a totalized culture, but with aspects of that culture or the way women behave as a result of gender bifurcated human culture. I never saw it cited in any feminist art/culture works in the eighties. As for landscapes of the home, neighborhood, and city, few feminists cited Rengert and Monk's modest-appearing work, *Women and Spatial Change*, which gave me a number of ideas for The House of Women symposium. Major studies on the subject include Catharine Stimpson,

et al., eds. *Women and the American City* (Chicago: University of Chicago Press, 1980) and Gerda Wekerle et al., eds., *New Space for Women* (Boulder, Colorado: Westview, 1980). On gender roles and domesticity, a literature that could have shed light on the culture concept, see, for example, Mary Ryan, "The Empire of the Mother: American Writings about Domesticity, 1830–1860," *Women and History* 2/3 (1982); Kathryn Kish Sklar, *Catharine Beecher: A Study in American Domesticity* (New York: W.W. Norton, 1973). In terms of material culture and environment, there was available Dolores Hayden, *The Grand Domestic Revolution* (Cambridge, MA: MIT Press, 1981), as well as Rengert and Monk. Although problematic for many feminists, useful for ideas on psychosexual dynamics of interior and exterior is Erik Erikson, "Inner and Outer Space: Reflections on Womanhood," *Daedalus* (1964): 582–606. Folklore, especially women's folklore, was a trove of unused (by feminists) ideas about women's culture. See, for example, Rosan Jordan and Susan Kalcik, eds., *Women's Folklore, Women's Culture* (Philadelphia: University of Pennsylvania Press, 1985).

18. Gwendolyn Wright, *Moralism and the Model Home: Domestic Architecture and Cultural Conflict, 1873–1913* (Chicago: University of Chicago Press, 1980) and *Building the Dream: A Social History of Housing in America* (Cambridge, MA: MIT Press, 1981); Ann Markusen, "City Spatial Structure, Women's Household Work, and National Urban Policy," in Stimpson et al., *Women and the American City*; Wekerle et al.; and Dolores Hayden, *Redesigning the American Dream: The Future of Housing, Work, and Family Life* (New York: W.W. Norton, 1984).

19. Hayden, *The Grand Domestic Revolution and Redesigning the American Dream*.

20. Hayden, *Redesigning*, 222–23.

21. Hayden, *Redesigning*, 223. By 1983, Hayden, de Bretteville, and others were focusing on "The Power of Place," a feminist restoration project in Los Angeles.

22. For a 1990s study of gendered space, see Daphne Spain, *Gendered Spaces* (Chapel Hill: University of North Carolina, 1992). More recent works by feminist geographers and others have dealt with gender and space, but I am citing the works that were available at the time that the Woman's Building was open and active.

23. Gaston Bachelard, *The Poetics of Space* (Boston: Beacon Press, 1969), 68.

24. Bonnie Engdahl, "Violette Leduc: Autobiography as Self-Exploration," in Sondra Hale, ed., *The House of Women: Art and Culture in the Eighties* (Long Beach, California: California State University, Women's Studies, Occasional Publication 1, 1985) 111–29. This essay is in a section entitled, "The Apron, the Blanket, and the Blank Page: Class, Gender, Sexuality and Self in the House of Women."

25. See Spain, *Gendered Spaces*.

26. Leila Ahmed, "Western Ethnocentrism and Perception of the Harem," *Feminist Studies* 8 (1981): 524. Mary Ellen Mazey and David R. Lee, *Her Space, Her Place* (Washington, D.C.: Association of American Geographers, 1983), 66. Woman's Building feminists restricted access to their house, if not *de jure*, at least *de facto*. When Lucy Lippard posed the question of why so many feminists on the West Coast restrict themselves and their art to a female audience, she responded: "The L.A. Woman's Building's separatism has been necessary to the contributions those groups have made. Women have come together as a community, and only in communities or groups does anything decisive get accomplished." (Lippard, *Get the Message?* 34)

27. Mazey and Lee, 55.

28. Ibid., 64.

29. This comment is in reference to the total remodeling of the inside of the Woman's Building to reflect feminist values and aesthetics. Thus, although the outside frame was built by the male-dominated Standard Oil Company in the 1920s, the inside was built by women.

30. Engdahl.

31. I am making reference to the much-quoted Heidi Hartmann article, "The Unhappy Marriage of Marxism and Feminism: Towards a More Progressive Union," in *Women and Revolution: A Discussion of the Unhappy Marriage of Marxism and Feminism*, ed. Lydia Sargent (London: South End Press, 1981), 29. This essay still stands as a classic in our thinking about materiality and feminism.

32. That feminist analyses of culture are also ethnocentric is, by now, a truism, but I am not going to delve into a cross-cultural analysis in this essay. See the essay by Sondra Hale and Michelle Moravec in this volume.

33. Mary Beth Welch analyzed women taking space in "Space as a Political Commodity: Establishing a Feminist Presence in a Man-Made Environment," in Hale, 69–77. A striking novel about feminists, squatting, the transformation of space, and the empowerment of women is Zoë Fairbairns, *Benefits* (London: Virago, 1979).

34. Margrit Kennedy, "Seven Hypotheses on Female and Male Principles in Architecture," *Heresies* 3.3 (1981):12.

35. Adrienne Rich, "After Twenty Years," *Diving into the Wreck: Poems, 1971–1972* (New York: W.W. Norton, 1973), 13.

36. Wekerle et al., 26. The authors are, in turn, borrowing from Elise Boulding, *The Underside of History: A View of Women through Time* (Boulder, CO: Westview, 1980).

37. Ibid., 27.

38. For example, the early period of Women's Studies in some of the California State University campuses: San Diego, Long Beach, and Sacramento.

39. Some of the other "alternative" spaces into which feminists have poured their culture are: self-help health clinics and counseling centers; feminist credit unions; women's resource centers; feminist bookstores and presses; women's coffee houses/saloons/restaurants; child care centers; food cooperatives/housekeeping cooperatives; legal rights centers; spiritual centers; inter-arts centers; the shelter movement (battering, rape, child abuse, drugs, alcohol); and the special spaces created by and for lesbians, women of color, the elderly, the disabled, and others who have been even more marginalized than those in the general female population.

40. For the distinctions between female and feminist consciousness, see Julie Peteet, *Gender in Crisis: Women and the Palestinian Resistance Movement* (New York: Columbia University Press, 1991); and my elaboration of the distinction in *Gender Politics in Sudan: Islamism, Socialism, and the State* (Boulder, CO: Westview, 1996).

41. Some have proposed that the attempt to manage affairs in a feminist mode, as I have described it here, in the midst of corporate America and in an era of diminished funding for the arts, cooptation and devaluing of feminist ideals, and the erosion of egalitarian principles in general, caused the demise of the Woman's Building.

42. John Berger, *Art and Revolution* (New York: Pantheon, 1969), 27.

43. Here I have borrowed from Zygmunt Bauman, *Culture as Praxis* (London: Routledge and Kegan Paul, 1973), 178.

44. One of the best source books for performance art of this period is *The Amazing Decade: Women and Performance Art in America, 1970–1980*, Moira Roth, ed. (Los Angeles: Astro Artz, 1983). Woman's Building-affiliated artists are well represented.

45. It should be clear at this point that throughout this essay I have been using the "seventies" as a model, not as the chronological truth.

46. Lillian S. Robinson, *Sex, Class, and Culture* (Bloomington: Indiana University Press, 1978), 3; Lucy Lippard has made the point in several publications that art and criticism are political and engaged. See, for example, *Get the Message?* and various issues of *Heresies*.

47. Simone de Beauvoir, *The Second Sex* (New York: Vintage, 1974 [1952]); and Betty Friedan, *The Feminine Mystique* (New York: Dell, 1974 [1963]).

48. Mary Daly, *Gyn/ecology: The Metaethics of Radical Feminism* (Boston: Beacon, 1978); Susan Griffin, *Woman and Nature: The Roaring Inside Her* (New York: Harper, 1978); and Adrienne Rich, *The Dream of a Common Language: Poems 1974–1977* (New York: Norton, 1978). Rich is not usually referred to as a "cultural feminist" or a "radical feminist" because of her socialist tendencies. But certain of her poems are women's cultural tropes, e.g., "Transcendental Etudes," from the above collection.

49. Los Angeles itself was said to consist of the cultural feminists on the west side of town and the more political (e.g. socialist feminists) on the east side (e.g., Silver Lake and Echo Park).

50. Audre Lorde, "The Master's Tools Will Never Dismantle the Master's House," in *Sister Outsider* (Freedom, CA: The Crossing Press, 1984), 110–13.

51. Griselda Pollock, *Vision and Difference: Femininity, Feminism and the Histories of Art* (London: Routledge, 1988), 17.

52. Alexandra Comini, "Vampires, Virgins and Voyeurs in Imperial Vienna," in Thomas Hess and Linda Nochlin, eds., *Woman as Sex Object: Studies in Erotic Art, 1730–1970* (New York: Newsweek, 1972); Carol Duncan,

"Esthetics of Power," *Heresies* 1 (1977), 46–50, and her classic "Virility and Domination in Early Twentieth-Century Vanguard Painting," *Artforum* 12.4 (1973).

53. Duncan, "Virility and Domination."

54. Sylvia Plath, *Ariel* (London: Faber and Faber, 1965); Anne Sexton, *The Death Notebooks* (Boston: Houghton Mifflin, 1974).

55. Ntozake Shange, *For Colored Girls Who Have Considered Suicide When the Rainbow Is Enuf: A Choreopoem* (New York: Macmillan, 1975). See, for example, "sorry" (52–54) and "somebody almost walked off wid alla my stuff" (49–51).

56. See, for example, Shange's "a laying on of hands" in *For Colored Girls* (60–64). See below for further discussion of the themes by people of color. At Woman's Building poetry readings and workshops, both Wanda Coleman and Michelle Clinton spanned all of these three themes. Mitsuye Yamada talked of Japanese Americans in concentration camps, but rarely presented women of color as victims.

57. Rich, 1978.

58. A number of dilemmas were extant. For example, lesbians often asserted that the essentialized and totalized category "woman" generally meant heterosexual women and yet, lesbians were vocal in the "unity of women" stance.

59. This is a play on a comment attributed to Charlotte Bunch—"add a woman and stir"—which was a critique of tokenism.

60. Lippard, *Mixed Blessings*.

61. Mary Beth Edelson represents an exception in her performance piece *Mourning Our Lost Herstory*, from "Your 5,000 Years Are Up" (1977). This performance evoked the kind of nostalgia for lost land, history, and culture that characterized some art by women artists of color.

62. The designation "survivor," as contrasted to "victim," used to refer to women who had experienced rape, incest, or domestic violence, was an innovation of the Woman's Building. According to Terry Wolverton, it was first used in such art events as "The Incest Awareness Project." Terry Wolverton in personal conversation with the author, September 15, 1999.

63. See Guerrilla Girls, *The Guerrilla Girls' Bedside Companion to the History of Western Art* (New York: Penguin, 1998); and the Guerrilla Girls' poster, *Do women have to be naked to get into the Met. Museum?* http://www.guerrillagirls.com/.

64. Shirley Geok-Lin Lim, "Dazzling Quilt," in *The Forbidden Stitch: An Asian-American Women's Anthology*, Shirley Geok-Lin Lim, Mayumi Tsutakwa, and Margarita Donnelly, eds. (Corvallis, Oregon: Calyx Books, 1989); Bettina Aptheker, *Tapestries of Life: Women's Work, Women's Consciousness, and the Meaning of Daily Experience* (Amherst: University of Massachusetts, 1989). Also, see Pam McAllister, *Reweaving the Web of Life: Feminism and Nonviolence* (Philadelphia: New Society, 1982).

65. This piece by Kruger is reproduced in her book *Love for Sale* (New York: Harry N. Abrams, 1990), 58.

66. See the special issue on "The Body as Discourse" in *Women and Performance: A Journal of Feminist Theory*, 3.2 (1987), especially the diagram on 5.

67. Jane Gallop, *Feminism and Psychoanalysis: The Daughter's Seduction* (London: Macmillan, 1982).

68. After the first exhibitions of *The Dinner Party*, a special issue of the feminist quarterly *Fireweed* (Canada) was published and it encapsulated a number of these criticisms. See *Fireweed* 15 (1982), especially Lisa Steele's "The Limitations of 'The Dinner Party,'" 27–31. Chicago's "monumentalism," her "mystification of the role of women as biological creatures enmeshed in private emotion, domestic labour, and the decorative arts" are also criticized in Carol Cone's "Washing the Dishes," 42. In my own work, I have raised these criticisms and others (the whiteness of the subjects, the class bias, and the imperfect nature of the collaborative project), e.g., "Women's Cultural Movement: Atavistic or Revolutionary?," unpublished paper for the Conference on Women's Culture in American Society, 1880–1980, Los Angeles, National Endowment for the Humanities and the Los Angeles Woman's Building, March 21–23, 1981; and "Introduction ...," *The House of Women*.

69. Note that these criticisms are not commonly leveled at the work of women artists of color who use their bodies in similar ways. For example, the early inscribing on the body of Frida Kahlo, the earth sculptures of Mendieta, and the later, Postmodernist photographic series by Lorna Simpson, such as *Guarded Conditions* (1989). I doubt that the lack of nudity in some of these pieces can explain the different responses.

70. Or, "Movies, Monstrosities, and Masks," to quote Amada Cruz in an essay by that name in *Cindy Sherman: Retrospective* (Chicago: Museum of Contemporary Art, 1997), 1–17.

71. See Mira Schor, *Wet: On Painting, Feminism, and Art Culture* (Durham: Duke University, 1997).

72. Lippard, *From the Center*, 1976, 127. I am indebted to Rebecca Schneider for calling my attention to the Lippard quote, in *The Explicit Body in Performance* (London: Routledge, 1997), 35.

73. Schneider, 35.

74. "Bad Girls" was curated by Marcia Tucker at the New Museum of Contemporary Art, New York, and its counterpart, "Bad Girls West," was curated by Marcia Tanner at UCLA's Wight Gallery, Los Angeles, both in 1994; "Sexual Politics" was curated by Amelia Jones at the UCLA Armand Hammer Gallery, Los Angeles, in 1996.

75. Linda Goode Bryant, "'All That She Wants': Transgressions, Appropriations, and Art," *Bad Girls* (Cambridge, MA: MIT Press, 1994), 97.

76. Both Amelia Jones and Rebecca Schneider have updated these seventies and Woman's Building themes in their studies of the body in performance art. Rebecca Schneider, *The Explicit Body in Performance*, 1997; Amelia Jones, *Body Art/Performing the Subject* (Minneapolis: University of Minnesota, 1998).

77. Amelia Jones, "Sexual Politics: Feminist Strategies, Feminist Conflicts, Feminist Histories," in *Sexual Politics: Judy Chicago's Dinner Party in Feminist Art History* (Los Angeles: UCLA Hammer Museum and Berkeley: University of California, 1996), 20–38. As of March 23, 2007, *The Dinner Party* has a permanent home at the Elizabeth Sackler Center for Feminist Art, Brooklyn Museum. Chicago will be *less* written out of history.

78. Marcia Tucker, Introduction, *Bad Girls*, 5.

79. Marcia Tanner, *Bad Girls*, 10.

80. Ibid., 11.

81. Ibid., 11.

82. Jones, *Sexual Politics*, 22.

83. Arlene Raven, *Art in the Public Interest* (New York: Da Capo Press, 1993).

84. Linda Frye Burnham and Steven Durland, eds., *The Citizen Artist: 20 Years of Art in the Public Arena: An Anthology from High Performance Magazine*, 1978–1998 (Gardiner, NY: Critical Press, 1998).

85. Mary Kelly, *Post-Partum Document* (Cambridge, MA: MIT Press, 1996).

86. Griselda Pollock and Rozsika Parker, *Old Mistresses: Women, Art, and Ideology* (New York: Pantheon, 1981), 167.

87. This particular information on male artists who were influenced by the Woman's Building is from Terry Wolverton. Personal e-mail communication, September 17, 1999.

88. Ibid.

89. All of these quotes are from the Feminist Art Workshop's poster for their conference, "The F Word: Contemporary Feminisms and the Legacy of the Los Angeles Feminist Art Movement," 1998.

90. Feminist art is flourishing in 2010, much of it connected to the West Coast in some way. "Nationwide USA The Feminist Art Project," a brainchild of Judy Chicago, has served as an umbrella for a number of projects. The California Caucus for Art Conference (2007) featured feminist art. In Los Angeles, the Museum of Contemporary Art launched "WACK! Art and the Feminist Revolution" on March 4, 2007. The Woman's Building and feminist art will be featured in the massive West Coast collaboration Pacific Standard Time, with exhibitions, a companion volume to this one, and many references. And *The Dinner Party* has a home.

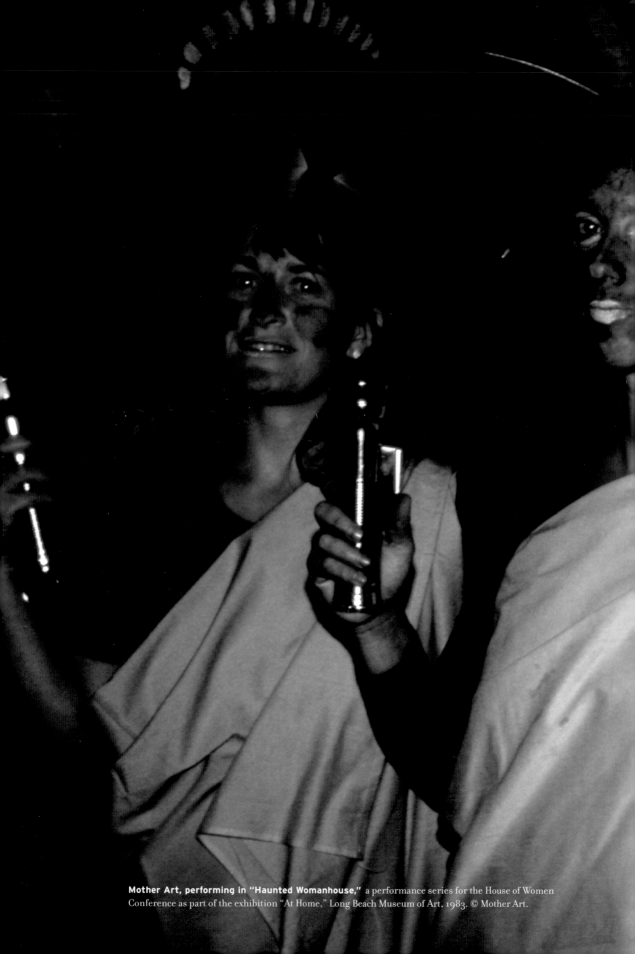

Mother Art, performing in "Haunted Womanhouse," a performance series for the House of Women Conference as part of the exhibition "At Home," Long Beach Museum of Art, 1983. © Mother Art.

THE WOMAN'S BUILDING AND LOS ANGELES' LEADING ROLE IN THE FEMINIST ART MOVEMENT

Laura Meyer

Acknowledgment: An earlier version of this essay was published under the title "The Los Angeles Woman's Building and the Feminist Art Community, 1973–1991," in The Sons and Daughters of Los: Culture and Community in L.A., *edited by David James (Philadelphia: Temple University, 2003).*

Throughout this volume, contributors give credence to the importance of space (e.g. room, house) and its defining role in the development of feminist communities and feminist art. Another significant dimension of space is the city in which feminist activism, culture and art practice take place. Los Angeles, more than any other city, played a defining role in the evolution of the feminist art movement in the seventies. Flowering out of the liberation and protest movements of the sixties—anti-war protests, civil rights, Black power, and women's liberation—the women artists' movement comprised a diverse coalition of artists, educators, and critics who sought to redefine the relationship between art and society. Feminist artists viewed art as both a social process and a symbolic framework that could be used to confront broadly political and deeply personal issues. Many pursued an activist agenda, intervening in public spaces and institutions to address issues of social justice and democracy. Feminist artists also analyzed the relationship between public representations of gender and self-image, critiquing the dominant culture's representations of women and reimagining the possibilities of female identity through art.

The implied and explicit East Coast/West Coast competition in the art world often saw New York as the nexus of the art world and Los Angeles as a frail newcomer, at best. Although New York has remained the largest center of mainstream art commerce and exhibition since the end of the Second World War, however, Los Angeles—in part because of its lack of an entrenched art-world infrastructure—offered women artists in the seventies greater freedom to invent new models for artistic production and reception. Los Angeles witnessed the growth of a thriving cluster of galleries and museums in the late fifties and sixties, and attracted the attention of the international art establishment with the emergence of so-called "Finish Fetish" art, or "the L.A. Look"—polished, shimmering objects fashioned from new industrial plastics and paint finishes developed for the defense and aerospace industries during World War II and the Korean War. By the late sixties, then, a vibrant, if young, art scene had joined Hollywood's film studios, the television industry, and the popular music industry in making Los Angeles the capital of what the Situationists called "the Spectacle."[1] The popular media and the developing art establishment in Los Angeles both became important targets of feminist intervention. Southern California feminists also worked to develop independent, female-governed organizations for educating women artists and for producing, displaying, and critiquing women's art.

One of the principle philosophical underpinnings of the feminist art movement was the goal of creating a mutually supportive community of women artists. In opposition to the popular mythology of the lone (usually male) creative genius, the leaders of the feminist art movement contended that broad-based community support was a necessary condition of creative productivity, and set out to build the kind of support systems—both material and psychological—that women artists historically had lacked.[2] Most of the goals and strategies of feminist artists in the seventies—including political activism, a collaborative approach to art making, and an emphasis on autobiographical and sexual subject matter, as well as the validation of traditionally feminine "craft" materials and techniques—revolved around the central goal of affirming women's personal experiences, desires, and oppression as part of a shared history and culture, as well as a valid subject and source of art. Nationally and internationally, women artists established cooperative exhibition spaces, activist organizations, and other networks to provide support and a sense of community to previously isolated women artists. The Los Angeles Woman's Building (1973–91) was by far the longest-lived and most influential of these feminist art communities.

Given the range and scope of the activities carried out during the Woman's Building's eighteen years of operation, it would be impossible to provide a comprehensive account of its history and impact in the space of this essay.[3] Rather, I will offer an abbreviated analysis of the genesis of the Building, and then examine in some detail several projects sponsored there. These include, among others, the televised protest performance, *In Mourning and In Rage* (1977); a national exhibition network generated under the aegis of the Great American Lesbian Art Show (GALAS, 1980); and a special issue of the Woman's Building newsletter dedicated to the problem of racism in the women's movement (*Spinning Off*, May 1980). The diverse goals and needs of the artists working at the Woman's Building, as well as shifting political and economic conditions, continually challenged the organization to redefine the meaning and role of a "feminist artists' community."

Communities traditionally have been defined by social scientists as geographically bounded spaces in which groups of people live and interact over the course of a lifetime. The shifting group of feminist artists that orbited around the Woman's Building, however, might better be defined as an "imagined community," based on a shared sense of identity and purpose, and mediated by shared artistic and textual reference points.[4] Los Angeles is a notoriously diffuse metropolis, its far-flung neighborhoods crisscrossed by freeways and divided by miles of physical distance, as well as ethnic and socioeconomic barriers. From its two locations within the ill-defined "downtown" region of the city (initially on Grandview Boulevard near MacArthur Park, and subsequently on North Spring Street at the far end of Chinatown), the Los Angeles Woman's Building represented an effort to construct a community within a perceived void. But the most effective means of accomplishing that goal, as well as the target audience, was often a matter of controversy. Building cofounder Sheila Levrant de Bretteville visualized the Woman's Building as a beacon for the general public, personified as a "woman on the street" who would reach out and embrace people from around the city.[5] Performance artists Suzanne Lacy and Leslie Labowitz, among others, used the Building as a base from which to launch feminist interventions into the city's physical and institutional structures, including the media. Other Woman's Building members maintained a more separatist vision, wishing to preserve the Building as a safe haven from mainstream society. Theorists of lesbian social community have emphasized that for lesbians and gay men, in particular, a community of peers often takes the place of family as the primary support network and source of self-definition.[6] The projects discussed in this essay, viewed as case studies, help illuminate the varied goals of the Woman's Building's constituents, and the ways in which art making, as a social process and as a symbolic framework, both betrayed fractures amongst the Building's membership and mediated bonds between Building members, as well as other women in the wider community.

The Feminist Art Programs at Fresno State and CalArts

The earliest prototype for the feminist art community that developed at the Woman's Building was an educational program for young women artists founded at Fresno State College in 1970. The Fresno Feminist Art Program was the brainchild of Judy Chicago, whose 1976 autobiography, *Through the Flower*, describes the profound alienation she felt as a young woman artist in Los Angeles in the sixties, when nearly all critically and

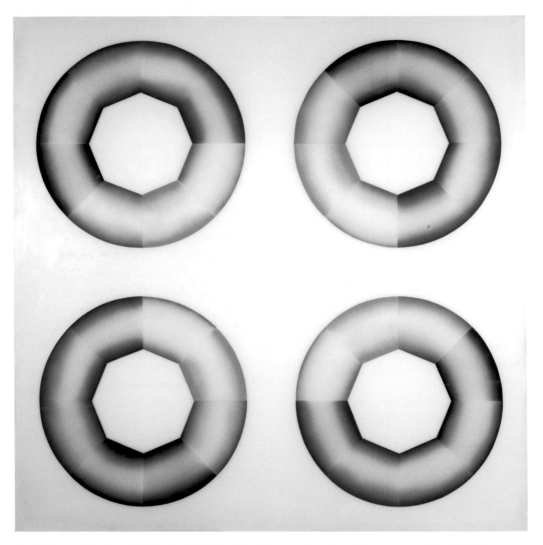

Judy Chicago, *Pasadena Lifesavers: Red Series #3*, 1969–1970. Sprayed acrylic lacquer on acrylic, 60" x 60".
Photograph by Donald Woodman. © Judy Chicago.

commercially successful artists were men, and the cool, industrial look of Finish Fetish art dominated the Los Angeles gallery scene.[7] After graduating from art school at the University of California in Los Angeles (UCLA), Chicago achieved national recognition exhibiting minimalist, geometrical sculpture made with industrial materials. In retrospect, however, Chicago felt that her modest success had been won only at the cost of abandoning her real artistic interests and suppressing her sense of gender identity. She subsequently analyzed her defensive response to the male-dominated art world:

> In an attempt to compensate for the often uncomprehending responses [of men], the woman artist tries to prove that she's as good as a man. She gains attention by creating work that is extreme in scale, ambition, or scope.... She resists being identified with woman because to be female is to be an object of contempt. And the brutal fact is that in the process of fighting for her life, she loses herself.[8]

Chicago conceived of the Feminist Art Program (FAP) as an "antidote" to her education at UCLA and the recurring bias she confronted as an emerging artist in the sixties. The program's first project, accordingly, was to remodel an off-campus studio space where Chicago and her fifteen female students could "evaluate themselves and their experiences without defensiveness and male interference."[9] In direct opposition to the formalist orientation that prevailed at most art schools, Chicago structured her classes around consciousness-raising sessions. She and her students tackled emotionally-charged issues including ambition, money, relationships with parents and lovers, body-image, and sexuality, "going around the room" so that each woman had the opportunity to share her experiences and feelings. Consciousness-raising was a way of brainstorming ideas for artwork; it also encouraged the young women students to confront their personal situations as part of a larger cultural pattern that could be analyzed and changed. Program participant Faith Wilding later recalled the process:

> As each woman spoke it became apparent that what had seemed to be purely "personal" experiences were actually shared by all the other women: we were discovering a common oppression based on our gender, which was defining our roles and identities as women. In subsequent group discussions, we analyzed the social and political mechanisms of this oppression, thus placing our personal histories into a larger cultural perspective. This was a direct application of the slogan of 1970s feminism: The personal is political.[10]

One theme that emerged with disturbing frequency in group discussions was the prevalence of violence and sexual exploitation in women's lives. The young artists confronted and responded to sexual violence in their artwork. In an early student performance described in Chicago's autobiography, for example, a male character violently extracts "service" from a female figure with a milking machine, and then drenches her body with the bloody contents of his bucket. Faith Wilding confronted social attitudes about menstruation in a tableau entitled *Sacrifice* (1971), in which a wax effigy of the artist, heaped with decaying animal intestines, lay before an altar of bloody feminine hygiene products. One of the first public performances to address the topic of rape, *Ablutions*, was created by Chicago, Suzanne Lacy, Sandra Orgel, and Aviva Rahmani in Los Angeles in 1972, in response to discussions that began at Fresno.

Chicago and her students used art to foster an empowered sense of sexual identity. Confronting a cultural tradition in which female sexuality is frequently figured as passive (in "virtuous" women) or else dangerous and shameful (in sexually assertive women), program participants invented myriad so-called "cunt" artworks, "vying with each other to come up with images of the female sexual organs by making paintings, drawings, and constructions of bleeding slits, holes and gashes, boxes, caves, or exquisite jewel pillows," and thus reclaiming a derogatory sexual epithet as a symbol of pride.[11] Cay Lang, Vanalyne Green, Dori Atlantis, and Susan Boud formed a performance group, the "Cunt Cheerleaders." They donned satin cheerleader costumes and chanted lighthearted and transgressive cheers such as the following, which they performed for program guest Ti-Grace Atkinson upon her arrival at the Fresno airport:

> Split beaver, split beaver, lovely gooey cunts.
> Split beaver, split beaver...
> We come more than once.
> Your cunt is a beauty.
> We know you always knew it,
> So if you feel like pissing,
> Just squat right down and do it!
> I hold no pretenses when I pee,
> I kiss the earth and the earth kisses me.[12]

The young artists in FAP also experimented with nontraditional media, including glitter and lace, sewing and crochet-work, costume, performance, and film, thus asserting the validity of so-called feminine "craft" materials and techniques as art. When the program relocated from Fresno to the California Institute of the Arts (CalArts), thirty miles north of Los Angeles, in the fall of 1971, the expanded group's first project involved remodeling a dilapidated house near downtown and transforming it into a series of fantasy environments, entitled *Womanhouse*. *Womanhouse* explored women's traditional roles in the home with a mixture of love, humor, irony, and rage. Installations such as the Faith Wilding's fanciful, crocheted, igloo-shaped shelter, nicknamed the *Womb Room*, as well as the lavish sculpted feast laid out in the collaborative *Dining Room*, embodied an idealized dream of comfort and intimacy in the home. A more ambivalent vision of domesticity and family relationships surfaced in the *Nurturant Kitchen*, created by Susan Fraser, Vicki Hodgetts, Robin Weltsch, and Wanda Westcoast, in which molded foam-rubber fried eggs covered the ceiling and marched down the walls, gradually transmuting into sagging, exhausted breasts. Kathy Huberland's *Bridal Staircase* stood as a stark warning, with a starry-eyed bridal mannequin descending blithely toward a drab gray dead end.[13]

Womanhouse was the first large-scale feminist art exhibition in the United States, and it inaugurated a new phase in the feminist art movement. The installation was open to the public for a month, from January 30 through February 28, 1972, and attracted some ten thousand visitors. To kick off the exhibition, the newly formed bicoastal women artists' network, West-East Bag (W.E.B.), held its inaugural conference there. The national art press and the popular media also gave *Womanhouse* extensive coverage, ranging from a film documentary broadcast on public television to stories in *ARTnews* and *Time* magazine.[14]

As the Feminist Art Program emerged from its isolation, the concept of feminist art and the notion of a community based on a shared female identity drew passionate responses. Since the seventies, debate over the significance of so-called "female imagery" and the true meaning of feminist art has divided feminist critics. One strand of criticism, which reached a peak in the eighties, holds that the emphasis some early feminist artists placed on autobiographical subject matter and so-called feminine media simply reinforces "essentialist" stereotypes; or in the words of art historian Griselda Pollock: "So long as we discuss women, the family, crafts or whatever else we have done as feminists we endorse the social given-ness of woman, the family, the separate sphere."[15] Critics also increasingly voiced skepticism that women with different socioeconomic backgrounds, racial and ethnic identifications, and sexual orientations could be reasonably lumped together into an identity-based community, and whether it was productive to try do so. Yet it is not accurate to dismiss the feminist artwork of the seventies as simplistically "essentialist." The use of alternative media, autobiography, and performance allowed women artists in the seventies to broach previously un-speakable topics, and their pioneering activism laid important groundwork for the critical strategies (and debates) of subsequent feminist theorists and artists, as well as other political art and identity-based art movements.

A Woman in Public: The Feminist Studio Workshop
and the Grandview Building

The success of *Womanhouse* and a rising groundswell of feminist art activism in Los Angeles in the early seventies contributed to a perceived need for a more permanent institutional presence for women artists in Los Angeles. Chicago soon grew disillusioned with the situation at CalArts after the feminist art program resumed its activities on campus and was forced to submit to the administrative supervision of its host institution. She and two other CalArts faculty members, art historian Arlene Raven and designer Sheila Levrant de Bretteville, began laying plans for an independent women's art school, the Feminist Studio Workshop (FSW). Initially, they held informal classes in de Bretteville's living room. By late 1973, however, they had a large enough student base to lease a two-story building in downtown Los Angeles, which was the former Chouinard Art Institute. They shared rent and managerial responsibilities with Womanspace, a new, cooperative gallery for women artists, and several other feminist organizations and businesses, including the Los Angeles chapter of the National Organization of Women, the Associated Feminist Press, a branch of Sisterhood Bookstore, and women-operated galleries and performance venues. In addition to Chicago, de Bretteville, and Raven, several additional instructors joined the Feminist Art Program staff, including performance artist Suzanne Lacy (who had trained with Chicago and de Bretteville at Fresno and CalArts), graphic designer Helen Alm Roth, art historian Ruth Iskin, and writer Deena Metzger.

The Woman's Building opened on November 28, 1973, at 743 South Grandview Boulevard, two blocks from MacArthur Park, a heavily used downtown recreation area. Restaurants and small stores, many of them operated by Guatemalans and other Central American immigrants, encircled the park, while the surrounding streets combined apartment buildings and houses with other local businesses. The mostly Spanish-speaking locals were not especially likely to visit the Woman's Building, but the park and surrounding restaurants attracted a mixed group of Angelenos from other parts of the city. The neighborhood was also familiar to artists and art students, with the Otis Art Institute situated on the far side of the park, in addition to the historical link with Chouinard. Inaugural festivities at the Woman's Building were attended by an estimated five thousand people, many of them artists and former Chouinard staff and students.[16]

A poster advertising the opening of the Woman's Building, picturing a throng of spirited young women flocking to the Building's entrance, embodied the founders' hope that the organization would function as the hub of a vital women's community.[17] When the FSW inaugurated its full-time degree program at the Woman's Building, professors intentionally avoided the hierarchical structure of traditional educational institutions, instead modeling classes on the consciousness-raising format. Former student Cheri Gaulke remembers that everyone, including the teacher, sat in a circle, which struck her as "the ultimate symbol of the Woman's Building, of feminist process, that kind of equality."[18] Students were encouraged to pool their skills and resources with women from other classes, so that writers, painters and printers might work together on the same project. Some of the initial class assignments involved repairing and remodeling the building itself, a tradition that Chicago had begun in the feminist art program at Fresno State and continued at *Womanhouse*. The group effort of

Clockwise from top: **First meeting of the Feminist Studio Workshop at Sheila de Bretteville's living room in Silver Lake**, 1973. Photograph by Lilla Weinberger. © Lilla Weinberger.

Construction of the new space on Spring Street, 1975. Woman's Building Image Archive, Otis College of Art and Design.

Kathy Huberland, *Bridal Staircase*, 1972. Installation, *Womanhouse*, Los Angeles. © California Institute of the Arts Archives.

Sheila de Bretteville hanging up her *Pink* poster in the streets, 1975. Woman's Building Image Archive, Otis College of Art and Design.

constructing their own studio spaces, the collaborative art-making process, and the pleasures and anxieties of learning about one another in consciousness-raising sessions all helped foster a cohesive and intimate sense of community. As Gaulke explains, "your personal life was the subject [of your art], or was a part of [it]...You weren't just there to develop your creativity, your intellect, but also your emotional self."[19]

Building cofounder de Bretteville played an especially important role in defining the Woman's Building's public role during this period, promoting the ideal that feminist art should intervene in the physical and social spaces of the community to create a more egalitarian and inclusive society. De Bretteville explained that she "saw the Building as Woman in public. It's almost as if the Building was a living creature in my mind as a woman on the street. And she was going to be...honored...and she would [bring] the feminine with her into the public realm."[20] Seeking to promote social equality through her artwork, de Bretteville developed design formats that, in her words, would invite the "participation of the broadest possible audience without the privileging of power."[21] Her mixed-media design, *Pink* (1974), for example, produced for an exhibition at the Whitney Museum in which participants were asked to "say something about color," incorporates handwritten comments, photographs and mementos offered by two dozen women of various ages and backgrounds. Invited by de Bretteville to consider "what pink meant to them and their vision of women," contributors offered poignant responses: "Scratch pink and it bleeds." "Pink is childish. I'm not pink now." "The color of pink is used mostly in saying: I Luv You!!!!" "Bazooka bubble gum that makes your throat sore when you first chew it because it's so sickeningly sweet." "The soft inside pink flesh vulnerable." "I hated pink."[22] Utilizing a grid format with thirty-six squares, de Bretteville allotted an equal amount of space to each respondent, purposely leaving several squares empty to encourage museum-goers to add their own thoughts. She also hung a poster version of the project in various neighborhoods around Los Angeles, inviting passersby to contribute their responses. De Bretteville implemented a similar non-hierarchical format for her design of the literary review published by the Woman's Building, *Chrysalis, A Journal of Women's Culture*. Each contributor to the journal had a two-page spread, with open spaces for readers to contribute their responses or additions to the material published.

In the Feminist Studio Workshop, de Bretteville encouraged her students to address the connections between the physical and emotional spaces of the city. For one assignment, students made maps of Los Angeles and indicated the locations where they felt good or bad, where they felt threatened or supported. Next, they made posters showing how they would make a place in the city different. One student persuaded the Los Angeles Rapid Transit District bus line to display her posters on buses traversing the city.

In her administrative capacity at the Woman's Building, de Bretteville facilitated various forms of exchange between FSW students, other Building users, and a broad community of women in Los Angeles and nationwide. Among her first priorities was the acquisition of a printing press for the FSW, so that students and other Building participants could self-publish. She also helped initiate a program of continuing education classes, thus allowing area women to take classes or to teach them without being full-time students or faculty. In the spring of 1974, she conceived a series of conferences that brought together participants from across the nation. The first of these conferences, Women in Design (March 20–21), featured nationally known architects, designers, teachers and editors whom de Bretteville invited to open a national dialogue on feminist strategies among women who "work in public, visual and physical forms." Writers Deena Metzger, Holly Prado, and Deborah Rosenfeld organized a conference for women writers, Women and Words (March 22–23), which brought together luminaries including Kate Millett, Jill Johnston, Meridel Le Sueur, and Carolyn See, and resulted in an ongoing national writers series funded by a grant from the National Endowment for the Arts. The Performance Conference (March 24–27; organized by Suzanne Lacy, Ellen Ledley, Candace Compton, Roxanne Hanna, Signe Dowse, and Nancy Buchanan) featured workshops and performances by emerging and nationally known artists, including Joan Jonas, Pauline Oliveros, Barbara Smith, and Bonnie Sherk, among many others, and established the Woman's Building as an international center of women's performance art. Attended by hundreds of people, these events raised the Woman's Building's public profile and helped establish professional and personal networks that persisted long after the conferences ended.[23]

Suzanne Lacy, a conceptual performance artist and FSW instructor, expanded de Bretteville's model of audience collaboration to create large-scale "performance structures" designed to intervene in the physical and institutional spaces of the city. Lacy has also cited Allan Kaprow, who taught at CalArts in the seventies, as a significant intellectual forebear for his idea that "everyday" actions and "happenings" could be art.[24] While she was at the Woman's Building, Lacy collaborated with Leslie Labowitz to found Ariadne: A Social Art Network, bringing together a broad affiliation of women in the arts, media, government, and the feminist community to create major collaborative artworks addressing specific social issues. For example, in *Three Weeks in May*, denoting the three-week period in 1977 during which the event unfolded, Lacy persuaded the Los Angeles Police Department to release statistics on the occurrence of reported rapes, a subject that was generally kept secret from the public. The visual centerpiece of the project was a pair of twenty-five-foot maps of Los Angeles mounted in the busy City Hall shopping mall. The first map recorded daily rape reports. For each rape designated in red, Lacy added nine fainter pink "echoes" representing the estimated nine in ten rapes that go unreported. The second map listed resources, including telephone hotlines, hospital emergency rooms and counseling centers, that offered services for women who had been raped. Lacy enlisted the participation of the city police, the news media, local politicians, and other artists, staging more than thirty events over the course of the project, including a press conference, self-defense workshops, a rape "speak-out," and a series of art exhibitions and performances.[25]

Lacy next collaborated with Labowitz and writer Bia Lowe to create *In Mourning and In Rage*, in December of 1977. Troubled by the sensationalized news coverage of a series of brutal rape-murders by the so-called "Hillside Strangler," Labowitz and Lacy staged a performance protesting the murders and the media's sensationalist practices, while simultaneously exploiting the public information system to broadcast the event on television and in the newspaper. The performance began at the steps of City Hall with the arrival of a hearse and accompanying motorcade. Nine monumental mourning figures, one for each murdered woman, emerged to confront the audience, draped in black from head to toe. By obscuring the performers' faces, paradoxically, the artists symbolically restored a sense of dignity to the murdered women. While the press had published photographs and titillating details about the personal lives of the victims, several of whom were prostitutes, their draped surrogates, in their very sameness and iconic generality, highlighted the women's shared humanity. Staged as a media event for politicians and reporters, the performance was designed, as Lacy has recounted, "as a series of thirty-second shots that, when strung together in a two-to-four minute news clip, would tell the story we wanted told."[26] The performance led to several public policy changes, including city sponsorship of free self-defense training for women and the publication of rape hotline numbers by the telephone company.

Workshop in Motion and Improvisation at the Performance Conference, March 25-28, 1978, at the Woman's Building, Woman's Building Image Archive, Otis College of Art and Design.

Performance art, as it was developed by Lacy and many others at the Woman's Building, became a powerful tool for activism, for confronting stereotypes and effecting symbolic self-transformations, and, perhaps most importantly, for establishing a sense of community among women. Performance groups based at the Building took their work into a variety of public venues around the city. Calling themselves The Waitresses, for example, Jerri Allyn, Leslie Belt, Anne Gauldin, Patti Nicklaus, Jamie Wildman-Webber, and Denise Yarfitz staged guerrilla events in restaurants and other public spaces, employing satire to dramatize and critique women's traditional service roles. One of their featured characters was the Waitress Goddess Diana, who wore a soft-sculpture costume with a dozen cascading breasts. Another character, Wonder Waitress, came to the aid of harried restaurant workers, confronting impatient customers and intervening with nasty employers. Feminist Studio Workshop graduates Nancy Angelo, Candace Compton (later replaced by Vanalyne Green), Cheri Gaulke, and Laurel Klick founded the Feminist Art Workers performance group in 1976, and embarked on a cross-country road-trip the following year as self-styled missionaries of feminist education. Their performances in community centers, universities, and coffee houses, usually conducted in exchange for food or on the basis of "sliding-scale" audience contributions, highlighted the group's infectious sense of camaraderie.[27] These and other activist performance groups founded in the seventies were the precursors of contemporary activist groups such as the Guerrilla Girls and the Women's Action Coalition (WAC).

The reinvention of performance art as a political statement and as a tool for community building was one of the most important legacies of the Los Angeles Woman's Building. Steven Durland, former editor of *High Performance* magazine, considers the performance work done by Chicago, Lacy, Labowitz, and others at the Woman's Building the best artwork produced during the seventies, and credits it with giving new life to the performance idiom:

> Not only did they take the form and politicize it, but they [oriented it toward] autobiography. Now that's used by artists from cultures outside the mainstream for self- and group-affirmation. It's a way of letting people know that they aren't alone.... In performance art, most of what had come before was formal experimentation. Had feminist art not come along, the form would probably have died a natural death.[28]

The feminist performance art of the seventies gave rise to many of the strategies developed more broadly by artists in the eighties, including autobiography, political activism, the transformation of self through multiple personae, and the appropriation and critique of mainstream culture.[29]

A Building of One's Own: Separatism and the Spring Street Building

De Bretteville's vision of the Woman's Building as a "woman in the street," as compelling as it was, did not meet the needs of some of the women who came to the Building in search of community. Many young women who enrolled in the FSW or attended other events at the Building yearned to create a safe, supportive "family." They preferred to distance themselves from the larger community, having experienced their families of origin, their schools, workplaces, or neighborhoods as hostile environments. De Bretteville recalls making the startling realization that her vision was completely at odds with what many of her students wanted: "I had all these notions about what the Woman's Building was, which in many ways was about women in public. And then when I got there and created it and was with these women, I saw that what they wanted was a private place ... the women came for a home."[30]

The split between those who envisioned the Woman's Building as a beacon for the public and those who saw it as a safe haven came to a head in 1975, when Chouinard decided to sell the Grandview Building, and the Woman's Building was forced to relocate. De Bretteville hoped to find another downtown location that would be spacious enough to accommodate a broad range of activities. Other women lobbied for a smaller space in a more remote location near the beach or in the country. Chicago located a second story space in Pasadena, a small city at the northeast edge of Los Angeles, that

Val's Café, 3rd floor of the Woman's Building at Spring Street location, neon sign by Lili Lakich, 1977. Woman's Building Image Archive, Otis College of Art and Design.

the group gave serious consideration. Ultimately, however, de Bretteville held out for a large building in downtown Los Angeles, and in the summer of 1975 the FSW and other Woman's Building tenants moved to 1727 North Spring Street.[31]

        Paradoxically, the ambitious decision to lease the largest and most centrally located building possible for the Woman's Building probably contributed over the long run to the organization's increasing isolation. The only large downtown building the organization could afford was located in an industrial district that lacked the lively neighborhood atmosphere of the original Grandview location, even though it was just a few miles away. Next to the railroad tracks and the nearly dry Los Angeles River, the Woman's Building now shared quarters with windowless warehouses and a few scattered manufacturing plants. Many of the non-art tenants were forced to leave for want of foot traffic. The FSW and its extension program persisted as the key residents of the Woman's Building. Members also ran a gallery program, an Annual Women Writers Series, the Women's Graphic Center, and the Los Angeles Women's Video Center. At various times during its years on Spring Street, the Building housed a bookstore, a thrift store, a café, and the offices of *Chrysalis* and Women Against Violence Against Women.[32] Nevertheless, the Building held a less visible position in the non-feminist, non-art Los Angeles community than it had at the Grandview Building.

99

The wish to create a safe, supportive haven at the Woman's Building also sometimes outweighed the desire to take an activist role in public during this period. For lesbian women at the Building, in particular, the notion of community often meant something different than it did for heterosexual women. Straight women more often tended to move in and out of the Woman's Building community, devoting time to their families, boyfriends, and other community involvements during their time away from school or work at the Building. For many lesbian members, on the other hand, the Building provided an all-encompassing social network. Cheri Gaulke, who entered the FSW as a self-identified heterosexual and came out as a lesbian three years later, remembers that "the community of women around the Woman's Building...became my spiritual community, my emotional community, my political community. It became everything to me."[33] Terry Wolverton, another graduate of the FSW, who later served as an administrator at the Building, concurs that "the need for reflection and support was a hugely motivating factor [and] often involved leaving behind old bonds....Heterosexual women had more expectation of crossing back and forth over those borders. For lesbians there was less desire or possibility of slipping back and forth."[34] To identify with the lesbian community at the Woman's Building often meant risking the disapproval or outright rejection of one's family and previous social circle.

The feminist art programs at Fresno State, CalArts, and the FSW had always included many lesbian participants, but lesbian issues did not develop into a central focus of discussion at the Woman's Building until the late seventies. In 1977, cofounder Arlene Raven, who also codirected the Center for Art Historical Studies with Ruth Iskin, invited artists who thought their artwork might contain lesbian content to a series of discussions that resulted in the formation of the Natalie Barney Collective.[35] The collective then undertook the Lesbian Art Project in order to "discover, explore [and] create lesbian culture, art, and sensibility; make visible the contributions of lesbians to feminist human culture; [and] create a context for that work to be understood."[36] Events sponsored by the Lesbian Art Project included consciousness-raising groups, a "gay-straight dialogue" at the Woman's Building, gallery exhibitions of artwork by lesbians, a videotaped dialogue among lesbian artists, open houses, salons, performances, and a series of social events including a lesbian fashion show and several all-women dances.[37] After the Natalie Barney Collective disbanded, several new projects focused on lesbian identity and issues emerged. The Lesbian Creators Series, initiated by Raven, brought lesbian artists to speak at the Woman's Building. Terry Wolverton organized a long-term performance project titled *An Oral Herstory of Lesbianism*. The *Oral Herstory* project began as a series of discussion sessions structured around consciousness-raising and journal writing. It culminated in a performance featuring more than a dozen vignettes addressing the tremendous diversity of lesbian experience, as well as the shared struggles faced by lesbian women.

Another performance that grew out of the Lesbian Art Project, *FEMINA: An*

IntraSpace Voyage (1978), sheds light on the sense of vertigo many women felt upon claiming a place in the lesbian community at the Woman's Building, a decision that often meant leaving behind old ties, perhaps forever. Based on a science fiction story by Terry Wolverton, the performance incorporated dance, song, and personal stories shared by each performer to dramatize the departure and journey of a group of women who determine to leave earth for a distant, unexplored destination: *FEMINA*. For the characters, life as they know it has become physically and emotionally untenable; the voyagers are haunted by visions of apocalyptic wars and earthquakes, manifesting "the voice of destruction [that] shrieks like some terrible monster at the way we choose to love…our art…our voices, our bodies."[38] Despite the suffering they have endured on earth, however, it is painful and frightening to turn away from the past. Mustering their courage for the journey, the women ritualistically "bid goodbye to everything and everyone they have ever known," even "the selves they have been on earth."[39] Lingering over the things they will miss most, one performer poignantly laments the loss of "the touch of [her] mother's hand…the sound of rain…the laughter of children."[40]

Wolverton explained in a press release that *FEMINA* was "not about build[ing] an enormous piece of hardware and blast[ing] off," in contrast to the popular, futuristic Hollywood films of the day, such as *2001*, *Star Wars*, and *Close Encounters of the Third Kind*. Instead, by "[w]orking on *FEMINA*, [the performers] learned that the Universe is not separate from our selves, our own bodies."[41] The symbolic journey to *FEMINA* functioned as a metaphor for the performers' collective undertaking to construct a new community and a new sense of identity. During the development of the performance, Wolverton encouraged the participants to suspend disbelief and to embrace their imminent departure, as far as possible, as a physical and psychological reality. The force of their collective fantasy shook some *FEMINA* participants so profoundly that they actually decided to leave the project, too frightened to continue. One woman wrote an apology to Wolverton, "I know no other way to explain it except that I am scared. I am on such shaky ground here in L.A. and I cannot disrupt the existence I've created for myself so far."[42] Another tearfully informed Wolverton that she had to finish school and therefore couldn't leave earth for *FEMINA*.

Although these emotionally extreme responses may seem irrational from our present perspective, they provide insight into the life-altering impact the Woman's Building community had for many women. Gaulke remembers feeling a similar sense of instability, even fear, during her earliest months there. For her performance in *An Oral Herstory of Lesbianism* (1979), Gaulke recounted the story of her first visit to the Building in the summer of 1977. At that time, she still identified herself as a heterosexual. She had cut her hair very short, she explained, as

> part of my sort of radical identity. And I remember I walked into the
> Woman's Building and there were all these women with…very, very

Bia Lowe, poster for *FEMINA: An Intraspace Voyage*, 1978. Silkscreen. © Bia Lowe.

short hair, like shaved heads like me.... And I freaked out because...
I recognized something that was very scary, that I'd sort of been flirting with but hadn't realized in a conscious way. So I immediately
went back to Minneapolis, grew my hair, died it red...[and] took back
the feminine persona again." [43]

Despite her apprehension, Gaulke enrolled in the FSW in the fall. Her fears resurfaced
on the first day of classes:

I remember the very first...thing we did when we got in this big
room of about 50 women in a circle, you were supposed to turn to
the woman next to you and share some story, or something that
happened to you before you came. And I remember thinking that
the woman next to me was insane. I was absolutely terrified and I
thought she was, like, an ax murderer....I still know her and she—
I think she's a nice person now. But there was something about this
new environment...[t]here was an unleashing of self that was just
absolutely terrifying. [44]

By fostering a sense of community among women artists, feminists and lesbians, the
Woman's Building lent women the strength to develop aspects of their identity that
were condemned or denied by mainstream society.

Seeking to assert a positive image of lesbian identity and to increase the public
visibility of lesbian artists, in 1980 the Woman's Building sponsored a series of exhibitions in collaboration with the Gay and Lesbian Community Services Center under the
umbrella title, "The Great American Lesbian Art Show" (GALAS). [45] The series had a
tripartite structure, including an invitational exhibition in Los Angeles honoring ten
acclaimed lesbian artists, a national network that facilitated local lesbian art shows in
cities across the nation, and a slide registry to document the artwork exhibited in the
national GALAS network. [46] In addition to the invitational exhibition, events in Los
Angeles included eight regional shows and a number of performances, film screenings,
poetry readings, and a lesbian graphics show. The whole project was oriented toward
helping lesbians, especially lesbian artists, forge a sense of connection within a large,
creative community.

Although a few writers had assayed a theoretical approach to the issue, there
was no clear consensus about what "lesbian art" might look like. [47] The work included
in the invitational exhibition ranged from minimalist abstraction to explicit photographs of women's genitals and women making love. (The representations of female
genitalia drew the most criticism from the mainstream press.) [48] Yet the artists
concurred that the art-making process played a crucial role in establishing a sense of

personal and sexual identity. As Harmony Hammond described the connection between her artwork and her inner life in a catalog statement about her wrapped ovoid sculptures: "To make art that has meaning, it is essential to make art that is honest.... [I]t is essential that I do not cut off any part of myself.... I came out through my art and the feminist movement. That is, the work gave form to my lesbian feelings as it gives form to all my feelings and ideas."[49]

"The Great American Lesbian Art Show" offered one of the first visible demonstrations of widespread support and solidarity amongst lesbians, and especially lesbian artists, in an otherwise largely hostile society. There were many risks involved in staging the exhibition, for artist-participants and viewers alike.[50] A poignant statement in the *GALAS Guidebook*, "We Are Everywhere," reminds readers:

> It is vital to remember that for each one of us present, there are hundreds of lesbians who have not identified themselves, or who have chosen not to live publicly as lesbians. Their reasons may be rooted in fear of personal or social consequences, or perhaps even ignorance of the options that exist for a lesbian lifestyle. It is our hope that the word of the GALAS project will reach these women, that their lives will be touched by the proud affirmations expressed in lesbian creative work.[51]

At the Horizon of Identity Politics:
Feminist Identities, Feminist Communities

The Woman's Building faced many new challenges during its second decade. Feminist theory and activism in the eighties increasingly emphasized the differences among women, especially in regard to issues of race, class, and sexual orientation. Although administrators at the Woman's Building worked to implement programming aimed at a diverse group of women, the organization faced criticism for failing to address the concerns of some women in the community, especially women of color. Indeed, the very notion of a community based on a supposedly common female identity came into question during this period.[52] Additionally, the destabilizing effects of criticism from the political left was compounded by blows from the political right. Under the administration of President Reagan, who took office in 1980, federal funding for the arts was cut drastically, and as a result the Woman's Building lost an important source of financial revenue. Shifting political and economic trends also had a devastating effect on the FSW, which ceased full-time operations in 1981 due to falling enrollments. As Wolverton assessed the mood in the eighties, "Suddenly, if women were going back to school, they were going into MBA programs, not into experimental feminist art programs. In the seventies, there was a certain ease in choosing a marginalized stance. In the eighties, there was the feeling that you wouldn't survive."[53]

By 1981, the three co-founders of the Woman's Building had ceased full-time involvement with the Building, and a second generation of leaders, including Wolverton, Gaulke, and Sue Maberry, all of whom had studied with the original core faculty in the FSW, took over the task of professionalizing the Woman's Building to meet the challenge of survival in the eighties. Maberry devised a strategy to develop a profitable typesetting and design business at the Women's Graphic Center, making use of the last part of a substantial government grant to purchase type and a letterpress. After completing a professional fundraising training program, Wolverton took on the task of extending the Building's base of support to include corporations and professional women, some of whom might previously have felt alienated by the Building's radical image.

Many of the most dedicated members who worked to keep the Woman's Building afloat during the inhospitable backlash years of the eighties were lesbian women. As lesbians played an increasingly important role at the Building, gay women and straight women jockeyed for control of informal social policy as well as event programming. Both lesbians and straight women felt alienated at times. In the early years of the FSW, before lesbian-oriented groups began to organize, gay women in particular often felt outnumbered and unacknowledged. As the lesbian presence at the Woman's Building became increasingly politicized, conversely, heterosexual women sometimes felt unwelcome. Lesbian members feared that straight members weren't as committed to the survival of the Building as they were. There were also disputes over guidelines for social behavior at the Building. For example, could heterosexual women bring their husbands and boyfriends to Building events, or would that impinge on others' wishes to maintain a female-oriented environment? Was it acceptable for lesbian lovers to kiss in public, or would that discourage walk-in visitors to the Building?[54] Throughout the history of the Woman's Building, nevertheless, there were sizable constituencies of both straight and lesbian women, and a sufficient balance of power that problems could be addressed from within the community.

Women of color, on the other hand, always occupied a minority position at the Woman's Building. Feminists from outside the Building staged an organized challenge to white women's dominance there, in 1980, when the activist group Lesbians of Color confronted the planning committee of "The Great American Lesbian Art Show." Representatives of the group voiced concern that all six members of the GALAS planning committee were European-American, and that their publicity network did not extend beyond the white community. In response to these criticisms, the GALAS collective expanded its existing outreach to minority women's groups and also reserved two exhibition spaces in East Los Angeles and South-Central Los Angeles, in order "to provide Black lesbians and Latina lesbians an opportunity to exhibit their art work in their own communities, as part of the GALAS regional network."[55] The GALAS invitational exhibition at the Woman's Building, which showcased the art of ten lesbian artist "role models," ultimately included work by one African-American artist, Lula Mae Blocton, and one Latina, Gloria Longval.

Diane Gamboa, *Vida*, 1986. From the "Cross Pollination" poster project. © Diane Gamboa.

After GALAS closed, members of the Woman's Building adopted a number of strategies aimed at improving race relations and making the organization a more multicultural institution.[56] Wolverton, who had co-coordinated the GALAS committee's efforts to develop better networks with women of color, initiated a "white women's anti-racism" consciousness-raising group, partly in response to complaints by women of color that they were tired of trying to help white women overcome their racism. The Building increased its sponsorship of exhibitions, writing workshops, and other events featuring work by women of color, as well as emphasizing cultural exchange. The 1986 "Cross-Pollination" exhibition, for example, included the work of local artists Carol Chen, Michelle Clinton, Sylvia Delgado, Nelvatha Dunbar, Diane Gamboa, Cyndi Kahn, Linda Lopez, Linda Nishio, May Sun, Mari Umekubo, Patssi Valdez, and Linda Vallejo, as well as artists from other parts of the nation and the world, and was particularly successful in attracting a broad audience and boosting the careers of several emerging artists.[57] Despite successful efforts to showcase work by artists and writers of diverse ethnic backgrounds, however, there is no evidence that Woman's Building membership among women of color increased substantially during this period. Another strategy for increasing ethnic diversity at the Building involved hiring women of color for various staff positions. This approach often backfired, as the new employees found themselves in the demeaning position of carrying out the vision of longtime members (most of whom were white), without holding much autonomous power.

The history of race relations at the Woman's Building is complex and sometimes difficult to assess. Women of color constituted a small but significant portion of the Woman's Building's membership from the beginning, and many more participated in events at the Building but did not become members. Many white feminists, additionally, considered the fight against racism an important aspect of the feminist cause. Yet women of color often reported deep ambivalence about their experiences at the Woman's Building (and in relation to the women's movement more generally). For example, as the only Asian-American participant in the *Oral Herstory of Lesbianism*, Christine Wong used her performance, *Yellow Queer*, to address the discomfort she felt with white feminists, who viewed her as a novelty and an icon: "I was the first Yellow Queer most of these girls had ever seen / So they had to like me / because I was the only one they had." Nevertheless, the experience of participating in the performance was "one of the most incredible processes," according to Wong, who credited the project with giving her "the support [she] needed to acknowledge [her] ancestry."[58]

The May 1980 issue of the Woman's Building newsletter, *Spinning Off*, addressed "Racism in the (White) Women's Movement." The special issue gives voice to the experience of women of color at the Woman's Building, who sometimes faced patronizing assumptions on the part of white feminists about what others should do or believe "for their own good." In an essay calling for women of color to "Confront white feminists," for example, Arlene Inouye-Matsuo argues that European-American feminists' ignorance of cultural differences often fosters a false sense of superiority: Asian women [working with white feminists]," she writes, "have expressed feelings about being perceived as young, naïve little sisters who lack maturity and sophistication and therefore do not have to be taken seriously. Although Asian women are generally less verbal and tend to avoid conflict, these racist attitudes are not justified.[59]

The Comision Feminil Mexicana, a Mexican-American feminist group that was invited to submit a statement to the newsletter, likewise stressed the barriers imposed by insensitivity to differences in class, race, and religious background:

> One of the problems about the term feminism is that it's been so associated with the Anglo community that anyone that doesn't meet their criteria, whatever that is, gets left out. If you look at the early woman's movement, Anglo women were demanding...to get out of the house...or equal pay and access to executive positions. Most of our women are heads of household demanding jobs, period....When we talk about abortion or sterilization, our perspective is again different this time because of our religious upbringing. Because people don't look at that we get told we are not feminist. We get neglected.[60]

Summing up the position of many, Betty Gilmore expressed the need "to see Third World women at the Building...in important roles...treated with the respect they do not often receive."[61]

The precarious financial situation of the Woman's Building throughout the eighties presented an additional source of instability. In the late seventies, a downtown artists' district had appeared to be on the rise, but the scene fizzled out in the eighties, some say because of a lack of sustained commitment on the part of the city's Community Redevelopment Agency. The defunct Los Angeles Theatre Center, for example, had been intended as the centerpiece of a gentrified Spring Street, a vision that never materialized. Many small theaters and arts spaces, including *High Performance* magazine, the Factory Place, Boyd Street Theaters, and Wallenboyd, either relocated or ceased operations during the eighties. Los Angeles Contemporary Exhibitions, which opened in 1978, remained one of the few alternative performance venues in Los Angeles, although it moved to Hollywood in the early nineties.[62]

Faced with a political backlash against alternative cultural institutions and drastically reduced government funding, the staff of the Woman's Building struggled to develop a business model that could generate corporate and individual revenues without compromising the organization's integrity. The Building leadership proved remarkably resourceful in this regard. The Women's Graphic Center, with Maberry serving as business manager and Susan King as artistic director, provided an especially important financial foundation for the Woman's Building during its second decade,

I felt joy
when she entered the room.
It was another cool summer night
in South Central L.A. 1965.
Mother always came in to say good night.
Her comfortin' words seemed to warm the room.
Some nights she would carry off one niece
to sleep with her. As she pulled the small brown string
the light, my brother began to snore.
dream land.

© 1986 Nelvatha Dunbar

Nelvatha Dunbar, 1986. Poster from the "Cross Pollination" project exhibited at Bridge Gallery, Los Angeles City Hall, 1986. Woman's Building Image Archive, Otis College of Art and Design.

generating revenue from typesetting and design services commissioned by various women's groups, museums, galleries, and local businesses. The Graphic Center also served a vital community-building function in the Building, the neighborhood, and the city, proving a popular resource for local artists and amateur designers. Groups of local schoolchildren, for example, were invited to develop their design skills there, and many of these children returned year after year, developing ongoing relationships with project leader Gaulke and others. Among the most successful community activities generated by the Women's Graphic Center was Gaulke's "Postcard Project," funded for three consecutive years (1985–88) by the California Arts Council, which enabled non-artist participants to learn the skills to design and print a postcard featuring a personal heroine or role model. During the final year of the project, several participants also designed posters that were displayed on city buses. The festive and elegant Vesta Awards, produced by Wolverton and members of the Woman's Building Board of Directors to honor women for their achievements in the arts, also became a popular community event that attracted generous donations from individuals and corporate sponsors. By the mid-eighties, the Woman's Building had recovered substantially from the loss of the FSW in 1981 and a membership low of two hundred, gradually adding classes, exhibitions and other programming, and rebuilding membership to more than six hundred in 1985.

The recovery proved temporary, however. The computer revolution and the advent of computer-generated design dealt the Woman's Building a major financial blow, forcing the Women's Graphic Center out of business in 1987. A growing divide between the few dedicated member/administrators struggling to keep the institution afloat, and the board of directors, who were removed from day-to-day operations, also took a toll. Finally, the Building was partly a victim of its own substantial success in generating institutional support for women artists in the art establishment. With increasing opportunities in the wider art world, young women artists in the eighties became increasingly hesitant to associate with an institution they feared might appear to confer upon them a marginalized status. Unable to come clear of its financial difficulties, and with no clear consensus about its operating philosophy, the Woman's Building closed its doors in July of 1991. As Gaulke reviewed the status of the feminist art movement in 1991, shortly after the Building closed, she stated, "There [was] a real crisis in determining what the feminist art strategy [was].... In deciding to close the public space, the board acknowledged that we don't know...."[63]

The Woman's Building made an indelible mark on the city, as well as the global art scene, during its eighteen years in downtown Los Angeles. The Building largely achieved its institutional goals, "to raise consciousness, to create dialogue, and to transform culture," as Arlene Raven legendarily formulated them. The Woman's Building provided a physical and social framework where artists and other women found the intellectual and emotional support to redefine their sense of identity, analyzing and challenging the dominant culture's often derogatory and exploitive images of women. From this supportive base, women at the Woman's Building intervened in the city's institutional machinery, including the popular media, as well as the art-world infrastructure, to help create a more democratic and more humane urban community. Los Angeles is poorer for its loss.

From the fields of
Colorado came
Two Hispanic
Girls who
Became mature
And loving
Women.

Above: **Dolores Guerrero-Cruz**, 1985. Postcard. Created in the three-year long "Postcard Project: Celebrating Our Heroines" taught by artist-in-residence, Cheri Gaulke. Woman's Building Image Archive, Otis College of Art and Design.

Left: **"D" and "E" pages from *Astounding Alphabet Stories*, 1986.** Artist book created by children from Plaza de La Raza in a workshop taught by Cheri Gaulke. Woman's Building Image Archive, Otis College of Art and Design.

Notes

1. David James, "Popular Cinemas in Los Angeles: The Case of Visual Communications," in *The Sons and Daughters of Los: Culture and Community in L.A.*, David James, ed. (Philadelphia: Temple University Press, 2003), 2.

2. Linda Nochlin documented the historical lack of institutional support for women artists in her provocatively titled essay, "Why Have There Been No Great Women Artists?" *ARTnews* 69.9 (January 1971).

3. More than 1,500 images of people, activities, and events at the Woman's Building between 1973 and 1991 are available on the Web. See the Woman's Building Digital Image Archive, http://www.womansbuilding.org/wb/. Another valuable resource is the Woman's Building Oral History Project, which comprises interviews with more than thirty former Building members conducted by Michelle Moravec, available upon request from the Woman's Building Board of Directors. A comprehensive written account of the Woman's Building is Michelle Moravec's, "Building Women's Culture" (PhD diss., University of California at Los Angeles, 1998). A memoir of her years at the Woman's Building by former executive director Terry Wolverton, *Insurgent Muse: Life and Art at the Woman's Building*, was published by City Lights in 2002.

4. Benedict Anderson, *Imagined Communities: Reflections on the Origin and Spread of Nationalism* (London: Verso, 1983). Anderson suggests that nations are imagined because in even the smallest, members will never know most of their "fellow-members." This differs from the situation at the Woman's Building, where the membership of five hundred or so women probably recognized one another by sight and in many cases had close relationships. But insofar as the community around the Woman's Building was constructed out of a desire to create identity, a sense of togetherness, and a shared vision for the future, it can be viewed as a symbolic community. Verta Taylor and Nancy Whittier's concept of a "social movement community," defined as "a network of individuals and groups loosely linked through an institutional base, multiple goals and actions and a collective identity that affirms members' common interests in opposition to dominant groups" is also a useful model for the community that developed around the Woman's Building. Taylor and Whittier, "Collective Identity in Social Movement Communities: Lesbian Feminist Mobilization," in *Frontiers in Social Movement Theory*, Aldon D. Morris and Carol McClurg Mueller, eds. (New Haven: Yale University Press, 1992), 107.

5. Sheila Levrant de Bretteville, interviewed by Michelle Moravec, Woman's Building Oral History Project, August 12, 1992, Los Angeles, CA.

6. See Kristin G. Esterberg, *Lesbian and Bisexual Identities: Constructing Communities, Constructing Selves* (Philadelphia: Temple University Press, 1997). Also see Deborah G. Wolf, *The Lesbian Community* (Berkeley: University of California Press, 1979); and Taylor and Whittier, "Collective Identity in Social Movement Communities," 104–29.

7. Judy Chicago, *Through the Flower: My Struggle as a Woman Artist* (Garden City, New York: Doubleday, 1975).

8. Judy Chicago, *Everywoman* 2, (May 7, 1971), 25.

9. Faith Wilding, *By Our Own Hands: The Women Artists' Movement, Southern California, 1970–1976* (Santa Monica, CA: Double X, 1977), 11.

10. Ibid., 35.

11. Faith Wilding, "The Feminist Art Programs at Fresno and CalArts, 1970–1975," in *The Power of Feminist Art: The American Movement of the 1970s History and Impact*, Norma Broude and Mary D. Garrard, eds. (New York: Harry N. Abrams, 1994), 35.

12. *Everywoman* 2 (May 7, 1971).

13. Photographic documentation of *Womanhouse* is available in a catalog, *Womanhouse*, designed by Sheila Levrant de Bretteville. Photographs of the installation can also be seen in Faith Wilding's book about the early years of the feminist art movement, *By Our Own Hands*, 24–29; and Arlene Raven's essay, "Womanhouse," in *The Power of Feminist Art*, 48–65.

14. In addition to the catalog, documentation of *Womanhouse* included a forty-minute documentary film by Johanna Demetrakas; reviews in *Time* (March 20, 1972), *New Woman* (April/May 1972), and the *Los Angeles Times* (January 17, 1972), among other publications; and a one-hour television special on KNET-TV, Los Angeles (Channel 28), produced by Lynn Litman in 1972.

15. Griselda Pollock, *Vision and Difference: Femininity, Feminism, and Histories of Art* (London: Routledge, 1988), 9.

16. Lucy R. Lippard described the opening of the Woman's Building in *Art in America* 62.3 (May–June 1974). Reprinted in Lucy Lippard, "The L.A. Woman's Building," *From the Center: Feminist Essays on Women's Art* (New York: E.P. Dutton, 1976), 96–100.

17. See Wilding, *By Our Own Hands*, 62.

18. Cheri Gaulke, interviewed by Michelle Moravec, Woman's Building Oral History Project, August 6, 1992, Los Angeles, CA.

19. Ibid.

20. De Bretteville, interviewed by Moravec.

21. Ibid.

22. De Bretteville, quoted in Liz McQuiston, *Women in Design: A Contemporary View* (New York: Rizzoli, 1988), 22.

23. Wilding, *By Our Own Hands*, 79–80.

24. Suzanne Lacy, interviewed by Laura Meyer, December 19, 2001, Los Angeles, CA.

25. See Moria Roth, *The Amazing Decade: Women and Performance Art in America, 1970–1980* (Los Angeles: Astro Artz, 1983), 114–15. Also see Suzanne Lacy, *Three Weeks in May*, unpublished documentation commissioned by Studio Watts Workshop, 1980.

26. Suzanne Lacy, "Affinities: Thoughts on an Incomplete History," in Broude and Garrard, 267.

27. Gaulke, interviewed by Moravec.

28. Steven Durland, quoted in Jan Breslauer, "Woman's Building Lost to a Hitch in 'Herstory,'" *Los Angeles Times*, January 7, 1992.

29. Terry Wolverton makes this point, compellingly, by way of response to some critics' position that seventies feminist art was unsophisticated in comparison to the poststructuralist critiques of gender favored in the eighties. Terry Wolverton, "The Women's Art Movement Today," *Artweek* 21.5 (February 8, 1990).

30. De Bretteville, interviewed by Moravec.

31. Ibid.

32. *The First Decade: Celebrating the Tenth Anniversary of the Woman's Building* (Los Angeles: Woman's Building, 1983), 4, quoted in Moravec, "Building Women's Culture," 173.

33. Gaulke, interviewed by Moravec. Gaulke explains that although "that's going to sound like a cult or something it was really just a bunch of individuals struggling to figure out who they were with each other."

34. Terry Wolverton, interviewed by Laura Meyer, 1998, Los Angeles, CA.

35. Natalie Barney was an American lesbian expatriate who hosted a famous artistic and literary salon in Paris in the twenties.

36. Lesbian Art Project manuscript, May 24, 1978, cited in Moravec, "Building Women's Culture," 132.

37. See Terry Wolverton, "The Lesbian Art Project," *Heresies* 7 (Spring 1979).

38. Terry Wolverton, *FEMINA: An IntraSpace Voyage*, unpublished script (voice of Dyana Siberstein/ "SeaNee"), 1978.

39. Ibid.

40. Ibid.

41. Lawrence Christon, "Feminism Lifts Off at Woman's Building," *Los Angeles Times*, May 28, 1978, calendar section.

42. Wolverton kept this letter with her archival materials from *FEMINA*, where I later found it. [Editors' Note: Wolverton's archives have since been donated to Department of Special Collections, Charles E. Young Research Library, University of California Los Angeles (Terry Wolverton Papers, Collection 445.)]

43. Gaulke, interviewed by Moravec.

44. Ibid., 6.

45. Tyaga was the principal organizer of the event. The GALAS collective also included Bia Lowe, Louise Moore, Jody Palmer, Barbara Stopha, and Terry Wolverton. Lowe curated the invitational exhibition and Tyaga organized the national GALAS network.

46. The artists featured in the invitational exhibition were Lula Mae Blocton, Tee Corinne, Betsy Damon, Louise Fishman, Nancy Fried, Harmony Hammond, Debbie Jones, Lili Lakich, Gloria Longval, and Kate Millet.

47. One of the first efforts to theorize lesbian art was Arlene Raven and Ruth Iskin's essay, "Through the Peephole: Toward a Lesbian Sensibility in Art," *Chrysalis* 2 (1977), 19–28.

48. In an otherwise enthusiastic review of GALAS in *Artweek*, Neal Menzies dismisses Kate Millet's photographs and Debbie Jones's mixed media sculptures as unclear, poorly crafted, and vulgar. *Artweek* 11.20 (May 24, 1980), 4.

49. Harmony Hammond, *GALAS Guidebook* (Los Angeles: Woman's Building, 1980).

50. The Boston GALAS exhibition was carried out entirely "underground" and only advertised by word of mouth, after the coordinators "spent impossible months finding spaces for the show and then being turned down due to sudden fits of homophobia." They also worried that work in the show might be damaged or destroyed. Nevertheless, the group deemed the event a great success, with sixty artists and twenty-five performers participating, successful fundraising activities, and positive coverage in the gay and lesbian press. Boston GALAS exhibition coordinator in letter to Terry Wolverton, 1980. Terry Wolverton Papers, University of California, Los Angeles.

51. Terry Wolverton, "We Are Everywhere," *GALAS Guidebook*.

52. Cherríe Moraga and Gloria Anzaldúa, eds., *This Bridge Called My Back: Writings by Radical Women of Color* (Watertown: Persephone Press, 1981), xxiii. "In April, 1979, we wrote: We want to express to all women—especially to white middle class women—the experiences which divide us as feminists; we want to examine incidents of intolerance, prejudice and denial of differences within the feminist movement. We intend to explore the causes and sources of, and solutions to these divisions. We want to create a definition that expands what 'feminist' means to us."

53. Terry Wolverton, cited in Breslauer.

54. Cheri Gaulke remembers that straight women sometimes felt persecuted at the Woman's Building, in an ironic reversal of their experience outside. When she decided to participate in workshops for the *Oral Herstory of Lesbianism*, at least one woman threatened to boycott the play if Gaulke was in it. Midway through the project, however, Gaulke decided that she was a lesbian, so the crisis was averted. Gaulke, interviewed by Moravec.

55. GALAS Press Release, February 7, 1980.

56. See Michelle Moravec and Sondra Hale, "'At Home' at the Woman's Building (But Who Gets a Room of Her Own?): Women of Color and Community" in this volume.

57. "Cross Pollination," April 16, 1986, Woman's Building Collection, Archives of American Art, Smithsonian Institute, quoted in Moravec, "Building Women's Culture," 202. The first "Cross Pollination" exhibition was curated by Josine Ianco-Starrels, Samella Lewis, and Candace Lee at the Woman's Building in June 1979.

58. Christine Wong, quoted in "An Oral Herstory of Lesbianism," *Frontiers* 4.3 (1979), 52–53.

59. Arlene Inouye-Matsuo, "Confront White Feminists," *Spinning Off* (May 1980), 1.

60. "Creating a Vehicle for Change: Comision Feminil Mexicana," *Spinning Off* (May 1980).

61. Betty Gilmore, "Racial Prejudice Is a Serious Social Disease," *Spinning Off* (May 1980).

62. Betty Gilmore, cited in Breslauer.

63. Cheri Gaulke, cited in Breslauer.

Lucy Lippard visits the
Feminist Studio Workshop
(Judy Chicago in background),
1974. Photograph by Lilla
Weinberger. © Lilla Weinberger.

Miriam Schapiro, *Mother Russia. 1994. Acrylic, silkscreen and collage on canvas. 72″ x 144″ (fan shaped). Collection of Santa Barbara Museum of Art, museum purchase with funds provided by the 20th Century Art Acquisition Fund and the SBMA Visionaries. Photograph courtesy of Flomenhaft Gallery. © Miriam Schapiro.

Artemisia Gentileschi (1597–c.1651), *Judith and Holofernes*, ca. 1620. Oil on canvas, 78 ⅜″ x 64″. Photograph by Scala/Art Resource, NY, Uffizi, Florence, Italy.

LOOKING THROUGH A NEW LENS: AN INTERVIEW WITH ARLENE RAVEN

Terry Wolverton

Editor's note: Arlene Raven, PhD, was one of the founders of the Woman's Building. She was also a pioneering feminist art historian. Terry Wolverton interviewed her on October 2, 2004, in her Brooklyn studio, on the subject of how feminist art history has changed art. Raven had intended to use the interview as a basis for her own essay about the origins of feminist art criticism, but she became ill with the cancer that eventually took her life— on August 1, 2006—before she could undertake this writing. This interview was edited by M. Gwin Wheatley.

Terry Wolverton: I want to start talking about how you grew up. And especially, when you were growing up, what kind of art, if any, were you exposed to?

Arlene Raven: I was exposed to no art at all. I had no idea who Rembrandt was. I grew up in Baltimore in a working class, Jewish community. You know, Jewish people traditionally don't make images. So there wasn't even, as some of my Christian friends experienced, visual imagery in worship. I did take piano lessons, but never art lessons. I vividly remember the seventh grade where I couldn't color in the lines and was given a "D" on my painting project. So I basically knew nothing about art until I went to college.

TW: This might be hard to reconstruct, but as you think back, do you have a sense of yourself as a visual person, of how you perceived or how you looked at things?

AR: I have a sense of myself as a thinking and philosophical person. I always liked to look, but I wasn't conscious of my perceptions or how they were constructed.

TW: When you went to college, what was your first exposure to art?

AR: I went to college at the age of sixteen. I was made [by my parents] to go to college within the state boundaries of Maryland, so I chose the college that I thought might be the farthest away from where my family lived. This was Hood College, which turned out to be a fantastic place. For about three weeks, I majored in home economics, which included a design course. It was a course in two- and three-dimensional design, sort of an introduction to techniques in art. I found this course really fascinating, so I quickly changed my major.

TW: What fascinated you about design?

AR: It tapped a part of me, a part of my mind and my being, which had never before been tapped. There was a physicality that was at once foreign and delightful. Design was also strangely intuitive for me. As I said before, this was nothing I'd previously experienced, and it certainly was not part of the predetermined pathway to a suburban lifestyle. I found myself equally fascinated with the history of art while in this class, so this first course in design really provided another path for me.

TW: What do you remember about your first studies in the history of art?

AR: I was a real novice. I had no background in art, and here I was presented with a lot of information that I had never considered before. Unlike most of my classmates, who had been to prep schools, I had a huge learning curve. I didn't know any artists, and I didn't understand what the role of art was in history.

TW: Who would you say was the first artist who caught your attention, in that early stage?

AR: It was the Abstract Expressionists.[1] They were my first love and still are—Jackson Pollock, Willem de Kooning, and some of the images of Ad Reinhardt, people like that.

TW: So you were attracted to work that was fairly contemporary?

AR: Yes, in fact I think it was in the early fifties that *Life* magazine had a picture of Jackson Pollock painting in his studio, and I had seen that picture. I went to college in 1961, and Pollock and his cohort were just becoming known outside the art world.

TW: What did you think about it?

AR: The Abstract Expressionists created these spaces in which you could walk with your eyes in an endless kind of a landscape. They created another world—a world to which I was quite drawn. The world as I knew it seemed untenable, so I was quite attracted to this other world. In those paintings, I could wander anywhere. To this day, I wander in my mind, and I'm very entertained and stimulated by reading and by pictures.

TW: Among the Abstract Expressionists, was there a particular artist who emblemized this possibility for you?

AR: Jackson Pollock and Hans Hoffman were my favorites in that group, and I also liked Franz Kline quite a bit. At that time, it didn't occur to me that they were men and that I wasn't studying a single woman artist.

TW: Not one?

AR: There were no women artists to study, according to every textbook. But I honestly didn't even think about it. I didn't have a feminist consciousness then.

TW: Nobody did at that time.

AR: No, but I knew that I was a girl and that I was going into places where I was not supposed to go.

TW: How did you experience that?

AR: Clearly, I felt transgressive. Still, I didn't know how I was going to become a scholar and a thinking person.

TW: What were the signals that let you know that you didn't belong?

AR: For example, the fact that my teacher told me that I thought like a man. That was even as late as in graduate school, in a PhD program.

TW: Was that meant as a compliment?

AR: Yes, his comments were meant as a compliment, but the conformity in my community was so prescribed that there was no deviation. Going to college was okay, but after the second year women were expected to drop out, teach elementary school with a certificate, and be engaged at least. That was just *pro forma*.

TW: But you didn't do that?

AR: No, I didn't. From that first design course and through college and graduate school, I was completely drawn to the material and what was in that body of knowledge. It was also myself in that body of knowledge that was going to determine my life and not a pre-scribed life of marriage and family.

TW: So you knew you were a girl, but you were a girl who thought like a man and you wanted to enter this profession that girls weren't supposed to go into. So how did you? At the time, did that seem like a conflict or an obstacle or that you were the exception?

AR: It seemed like a big conflict, and I didn't know how it was going to play out, because I was still underage when I graduated from college. I still didn't really know all of what I was about, but I did go to graduate school right away. I went into an MFA program at

George Washington University, and thereafter I went into a PhD program at Johns Hopkins. I was in school for a very long time.

TW: On what did you concentrate in the MFA program?

AR: Painting. But by the conclusion of that program, I'd written the longest thesis they had ever received from a fine arts student. It was at that moment I decided that my thinking and my ability to express myself were really rooted in writing—not in making visual statements, but in interpreting them.

TW: Can you describe the way that your visual sense, your perception, changed when it began to be fed with visual imagery and art?

AR: Yes, I remember a painting class, in which, in the manner of Cezanne, we were to paint little patches of color all over the canvas, not simply do the apple and then the orange and such. When I finished that painting I could see all the colors of the universe—not just in the painting, but *everywhere*. That exercise shaped how I see everything. Today, I'll be on the street and I will look at every single thing. I look at people's clothes and their bodies, and I look in shop windows, though I'm not a shopper at all. I like to look at everything. It's a complete feast, the world, and that, I think, is what I can say about how my perception started to change and to develop critically. Also, I was associating with a completely different group of people.

TW: People who were also thinking and perceiving?

AR: People who were not interested in money, who were interested in old things as well as new things—their values were more in line with my own. It was a great relief for me. I didn't want to go shopping every minute and be concerned with the kinds of things my family wanted me to pursue.

TW: After graduate school you went into the PhD program as a writer?

AR: My PhD is in art history. My field was contemporary art, and my particular interest in my thesis was the Washington Color School,[2] which was a slightly later movement than the Abstract Expressionists. I also had an amazing revelation about the Baroque period in Italy in Caravaggio's work, in particular, and I studied that quite a bit, as well as medieval manuscripts and early Christian books. Those were all interests of mine.

TW: What in particular interested you about the Washington Color School?

AR: I was there. I taught at the Corcoran School, which was part of the Corcoran Gallery; that was where the artists of the Washington Color School were gathering. I knew the artists, and I saw them making history. It was a very, very exciting time. I interviewed so many of the artists, and I participated in their art world and recorded my own environment.

TW: What were they doing?

AR: They were painting primarily. They were doing wash painting onto unsized canvas, which meant the paint soaked into the fabric. The paintings were hard-edged geometric paintings, mostly, sometimes on a very big scale. In addition to the interviews, the primary artist I was interested in was Morris Louis,[3] who had already died. I made a timeline that put together all of the artists' work, what was happening in Washington, and what was it about the city of Washington that contributed to the work. I was particularly interested in their approaches to art education. Many of these artists formed an independent art academy, and many of my own ideas about independent feminist education came from this.

TW: Was there a particular visual quality about the work that arrested you or was it really more about the fact that you were in this community?

AR: The visual quality of the work was number one. It has a meditative quality, a stillness and a spirituality that I enjoyed. You could sit and stare at the work.

TW: Where did you go after you got your PhD?

AR: I immediately went to California to work at CalArts in the Feminist Art Program[4] as an art historian.

TW: Did exposure to feminist ideas predate your move to California?

AR: During my graduate studies, I was very much accepted into male circles. At any party I would be talking with men, but the other women would be in the kitchen having a completely different kind of conversation—or so I thought. It wasn't that I didn't like women. I just believed I had more in common with the men, most of whom were fellow students. I also had a lot of male attention at that time because I wasn't ugly. Looking back, I think I was both threatening and alluring to the men I was around. I ended up marrying one of my teachers, not at Johns Hopkins, but at George Washington University. At the time, I was completely unconscious of how I was aligning myself.

TW: So when did it start to occur to you that there were no women in the picture?

AR: I began to see that there were no women when I started teaching modern art history at the Maryland Institute. At the same time, I was going to consciousness-raising groups for the first time, and I was working on a magazine called *Women: A Journal of Liberation* that came out of Baltimore. I was working also at a free clinic. So it wasn't in my profession that I first noticed there were no women; it was through consciousness-raising that I noticed there were no women in my profession. It also raised my consciousness about my marriage and my participation in it, such as making all the meals, doing all the cleaning and the laundry and so on, being a full-time student, and having a full-time job, and my husband doing nothing. That didn't seem unfair to me until I was in consciousness-raising. That was the beginning of the end of my marriage.

TW: When did you start to become interested in women artists?

AR: In Baltimore, before I went to California. Then in California in 1972, I began a study of women artists not at all covered in my PhD program. While my education had given me a wide knowledge of art from the beginning of time to the present, I knew nothing about these women. I didn't even know how to find them. But the books were coming out, and I found them in bookstores.

TW: Who was the first woman artist who caught your attention?

AR: Mary Cassatt, because if there would be a woman artist mentioned at all, prior to the feminist movement, it would be Mary Cassatt. She was a nineteenth century figurative artist, and she painted women and children. Most would look at her work and consider her "a typical girl artist," but, in truth, the relationships between the women and children in Cassatt's work were often erotic, conflicted, and merged. She also did Biblical interpretations. For the Woman's Building of 1893,[5] she did a panel on the tympanum, which was about the tree of knowledge in Genesis, and she depicted all women and children picking the fruit of knowledge. This was radical! Here's a painter who was grudgingly acknowledged as being of historical note and, still, she would be called the student of Degas, if she was included at all. During this time, I was able to begin to see her work as radical. Her work was technically conventional, but she made images of things that were very subversive and that became for me a way to identify a good painting—if it depicted something you hadn't seen before and it was expressing a way of life for a group of people who hadn't had a voice before. That's what Mary Cassatt was doing.

TW: The fifties and sixties, and even early seventies, were so much about formalism in art, forms and surfaces. Content was almost an embarrassment or taboo. It seems to me that as feminists began to consider art from that perspective, there was a shift back to focusing on content in work.

AR: I think the feminist movement in art actually fostered additional awareness of content. Feminists were talking about feelings and personal experiences, and women's experiences were considered to be the proper subject of our art and our art history. Also, consciousness-raising was a part of our program at CalArts. At the time, I engaged in a study of women's visual expressions and writing. I interviewed a number of women and viewed their work, and I tried to find what it was about this work that says "I'm a woman." I tried to consider why we didn't notice or note the gendered aspects of art prior to this time, and I contrasted the women's work with that of living male artists. And it was a huge revelation for me. I had just completed my formal training, and I was using my education not to train students but to explore new, uncharted territories.

TW: We've talked about how when you were a child there was really nothing to look at and so you didn't have an awareness of looking. Then, your visual sensibility opened up in a profound way. When you began to look for women and to read for women's

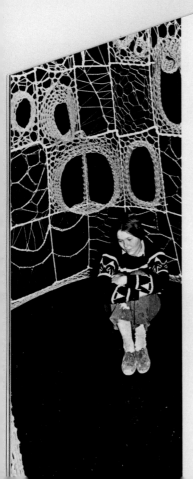

Crocheted Environment
Faith Wilding

Our female ancestors first build
themselves and their families round-
shaped shelters. These were protective
environments, often woven out of
grasses, branches or weeds. I think of my
environment as linked in form and
feeling with those primitive womb-
shelters, but with the added freedom of
not being functional.

Menstruation Bathroom
Judy Chicago

Menstruation is something women either
hide, are very matter-of-fact about, or
are ashamed of. Until I was 32 years old,
I never had a serious discussion with my
female friends about menstruation. The
bathroom is an image of women's hidden
secret, covered over with a veil of gauze,
very, very white and clean and deodorized -
deodorized , except for the blood, the
only thing that cannot be covered up.
However we feel about our own
menstruation is how we feel about
seeing its image in front of us.

experience in the images you were seeing, was this another shift for you in your own perception?

AR: It definitely changed the way I was looking at things. It was reciprocal. I was looking at things in my life and in the lives of other women, and in the lives of men, too, and I was beginning to see it all differently—art and life. To return to our conversation about content—I believe that feminist art really encouraged other people, men and women, to be concerned with what was motivating their art and its contents.

TW: In that movie I was telling you about, *What the Bleep Do We Know!?* [directed by William Arntz, Betsy Chasse, and Mark Vicente, 2004], one of the principles they talk about is that if you have no knowledge of something, you can't see it even if it is there. There's this story about the Native American Indians when Columbus' ships came and how they literally couldn't see them because they didn't know what a boat was. So as feminist perception was dawning, were there things that you had to learn to see?

AR: Yes, I had to learn about being a woman and what it meant. Here I was, putting on all the meals, cooking from scratch with organic everything and never having one thought that this wasn't what I was supposed to do until I had the thought that it wasn't. I went to a consciousness-raising meeting where the topic was doing the dishes, and I realized I did all the dishes as well as all the other household chores. This realization prompted me to ask why couldn't my husband and my stepdaughter do the dishes? This sounds like a simple question, but it had huge ramifications for my work; this question changed how I perceived certain artistic images of women's work. For example, my personal understanding of women's household labor came to influence my understandings of depictions of women's household labor. I began to question the artist's intent in a different way. And I think my own realization was writ large in the community. In *Womanhouse*,[6] the artwork was all about domesticity. It was about dishes and putting food on the table and the bride in the linen closet, but from a feminist perspective. And in fact, the young women who were in that program were not housewives; they were young women who were talking about their mothers' lives, not their own lives. These young women were forging different kinds of lives than those lived by their mothers; the young women were making studios, doing carpentry, learning to have a work ethic—the kinds of things that had been taught to male artists and not to female artists. On the one hand, the young artists were honoring the lives of the women who came before them, and, on the other hand, they were acknowledging the oppressiveness of their predecessors' lives.

TW: As you continued your research project about women artists, eventually you were able to go further back than Mary Cassatt?

AR: Oh, yes, right back to goddess worship and female basket weaving, fishnets, all kinds of useful arts women participated in that weren't even considered in the realm of art. Then I looked at artists who were unknown in the early Christian period, the medieval period, the Renaissance, all the way through the mid-twentieth century. I found particular artists such as Artemisia Gentileschi,[7] an early Baroque artist, whose images were infused with her anger at her own station in life. Over and over again, she would depict a woman cutting a man's head off—John the Baptist. Of course, we in California were not the only people investigating women's art; there were other people, feminists, other women investigating women's art as well. Mary Garrard[8] became an expert on Gentileschi. Previously, it would have been absolutely unheard of for anyone to specialize in a woman artist.

TW: How were images like Gentileschi's read before feminists started looking at them?

AR: They likely would not have even been considered, or they would have been considered as minor, because they were done by women. The art world paralleled the patriarchal society in which it existed.

TW: Nobody was looking at the content?

AR: It's not that no one was considering the content. It's that the work of women artists was simply not considered. Again, in the case of Gentileschi, the content was derivative; it's a Bible story. What is interesting about her work is that she was repeating these images over and over again, and no one was noticing it.

TW: So they just hadn't been studied by anybody?

AR: No, they had not been studied. And to study them with a feminist perspective would be entirely different than studying them without. To employ a feminist perspective means finding meaning in a woman's life, and in Gentileschi's case it would be considering her rape and the lack of support around that rape.

TW: This gets into the area of woman as subject?

AR: Well, I'm talking about women as artists right now. But yes.

TW: Right, but we're also talking about the images that are in the paintings themselves. Because we're not only talking about Gentileschi's rape, but we're also talking about the rape that is depicted in the painting. So how were the women depicted in art perceived prior to the articulation of a feminist consciousness?

AR: Scholars at that time were beginning to notice both woman as artist and as subject. Linda Nochlin[9] has noted that many times women are depicted lying down, frequently nude, eyes averted, as an object to be looked at, but not one who could look back. There were many instances of this throughout art history.

TW: But in a painting like the ones that Gentileschi painted, women were not depicted this way, correct?

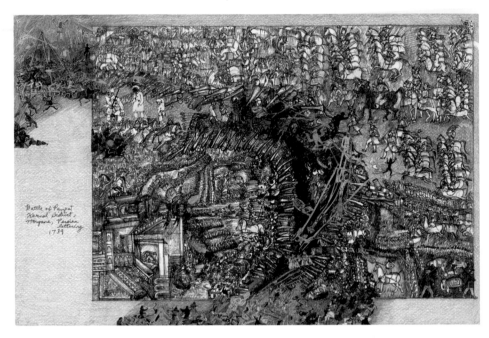

Joyce Kozloff, *Boys Art #8: Battle of Panipat, 1739*, 2001–02. Mixed media on paper, 11 3/8" x 16¾".
Photograph courtesy of DC Moore Gallery, New York. © Joyce Kozloff.

AR: Correct, but historically there are many more supine women than not. Gentileschi's Judith was always twisting around and wielding the knife, and Gentileschi painted from very close range, so it was in your face. She compares to Caravaggio, who was called the painter of dirty feet because he would use peasants as models and you could see that they had dirt on their feet. Caravaggio also had this very close up view, so that you felt as though you were standing right next to them. It wasn't the voyeur from afar looking at beauty, which is symbolized by nude women. These were people doing things.

TW: Once women began to do the looking at this art with a consciousness of being a woman, how did the meanings of those images change?

AR: First of all, you could see that a castration image was about castration. And that if a woman was doing it, it was making a certain statement about her hostility and anger against male privilege and the penis as an organ. Now I don't know what kind of change that is. I think I can talk more about how the perception of the depiction of rape changed. Before the feminist movement, the perception of rape in society-at-large was: "It's the woman's fault. She wore a short skirt. It's not a big deal." From the woman's point of view, however, it was always violation, violence, humiliation, and disintegration. As women artists began to paint rape, the view changed. Not only would the viewer encounter a woman who was more conscious of the things that could happen to one as a woman, but also the painter may have, in fact, had some kind of life experience that infused the work. Another thing that changed was how we began to see earlier work, for example, Harriet Hosmer's work.[10] She was a nineteenth-century sculptor whose work was very large. It was conventional public sculpture, but it was gigantic. In her case, the sheer size of the work is significant. She clearly was bucking convention. And there were others, often lesbians in the nineteenth century, who were artists and writers who defied social conventions in their work and in their art. We rediscovered these foremothers in the seventies. Because our education had not included these women, we felt compelled to study and record their lives for posterity, to enter them in the canon, but also to consider them separately. It was critical that women's art should enter the canon and be compared to men's art and other factors as well, and that we should look at women's art as a body and see what women's art has to say separately.

TW: So there was scholarship in the nineteenth century that included women artists?

AR: There was writing about women artists. I wouldn't really say scholarship, because the art historical writing was done by male art historians and this writing about women artists was not by art historians. They were biographies or memoirs or factual journalistic accounts of women artists. For instance, I found an anthology about girls in art and "ladies who painted." It was sort of a Christmas coffee table book of the nineteenth century. So it was not in the scholarly canon. In order to bring those women into the canon, you really had to be a professional art historian who understood what made up the canon and how to incorporate women's contributions, and that would be in terms of nineteenth century women as well as twentieth century women, even though texts did exist. I saw this as my joyful task, as did many other feminist art historians.

TW: What are the kinds of things that you saw when you took on this task?

AR: I saw things that I would have avoided previously or thought unimportant, such as watercolor painting and china painting. I went into little, rural museums in Italy, for example, and I saw work by women that mostly went unnoticed. I also looked at what women artists were depicting; many employed domestic imagery—childcare, gardening, housekeeping—in secular works to let you know what women did at home while the men were outside the home. Then, I would also see men's depictions of women, how women looked and what they did, first in ecclesiastical art and then in secular art. There were differences, and I looked for these differences as well as similarities. I would try to combine that with my previous knowledge. For example, prostitutes, and many women of the Bible, were depicted in ways that dishonored them. Mary Magdalene was never depicted as someone who had a value even though she did so to Jesus Christ. And the Virgin Mary is an interesting case; men and women artists would give the Madonna and child various interpretations. Some depictions were quite erotic, suggesting incest. I also looked for what wasn't depicted; for example, there were no representations of women as heads of state.

TW: So as we re-enter the seventies and work is starting to be made with a feminist consciousness, how does the work begin to change?

AR: For one thing, in the Feminist Art Program, women who had little art training were encouraged to use materials right at hand. You didn't need to learn painting or sculpture or architecture, but you could put pieces together with what was at hand. This resulted in a lot of performance art, photographs, videotapes, and making art with everyday feminine materials—lipsticks, shoe polish, nail polish. Performance art was like playing dress up in a lot of ways, because we did it not only for an audience but also in terms of role-playing inside of the educational experience. It wasn't only for exhibition. In general, in the United States, a lot of soft materials began to be used, soft sculpture, by both men and women. There was a total rethinking of what is an appropriate art material. Some used eggs, and others drew pictures with their menstrual blood. All of this experimentation gave rise to the pattern and decoration movement, which included men and women artists, but which was inspired by the feminist art movement, in particular by Joyce Kozloff's[11] and Miriam Schapiro's[12] art.

TW: Do you believe the women artists were well served or ill served by instructors not insisting that they gain some particular skills with art-making materials?

AR: Women did develop skills with art-making materials, for example video and construction, but I don't think skills were taught in general at CalArts. Nobody learned to paint at CalArts. People who came after the David Salle[13] and Eric Fischl[14] period learned to paint after they left school. If you wanted to learn those skills you could go to a conservative academy. In general, I don't think that the students in the Feminist Art Program were any less skilled than those students outside of the program. But I think that because of the content of their work, it was perceived as incompetent. I, in particular, remember when Faith Wilding[15] came up for her master's degree and found her imagery ridiculed by the committee. In effect, CalArts had appeared to accept and nurture this feminist program, but many of the traditionally trained academics rejected the work fulfilled by the program.

TW: What was Wilding's imagery?

AR: Her imagery was semi-abstract nature imagery—leaves, spirals, and designs emanating from the center. It was very sensuous, and it wasn't the Conceptual art that some of the other students at CalArts were producing. Her work was not criticized for its craft, but for its content, for the sentiments she expressed in it. Obviously, once you teach women to find their content and to give it a form, the next step is how to make that form the best form, and that's where the skill comes in.

TW: Aside from materials, how else did the art begin to change?

AR: How the work was exhibited changed; it was exhibited in different places—on the streets, in grocery stores, in parades. A lot of the principles of public art that are now not called feminist were developed by those early feminist artists. Make a parade, silk screen the grocery bags at a supermarket, get your message out. That was very unusual. I think that feminists made a tremendous contribution to performance art, especially Barbara Smith[16] and Linda Burnham.[17] While there was a growing performance art movement in Los Angeles at the same time, it was largely male and driven by different ideals. For example, the male performance artist Chris Burden[18] was having himself shot, crawling through glass, and being nailed to his Volkswagen on a crucifix at the same time that *Womanhouse* was expressing what it was that women did. On the one hand, we have the male artist as "hero," and on the other hand we have the woman as invisible domestic. These are clearly two different realms.

TW: Can we talk about the Woman's Building?

AR: Concurrent with the CalArts' Feminist Art Program, we were developing Woman-space, which was a gallery where we also held events that would foster community among the women artists. We had to create a community so that we could *see* the community, making it visible. We had days honoring women's achievements with speeches and other such gatherings. As time went by, it became clear that having a program in someone else's institution is just not the same as having your own independent institution.

TW: What were some of those differences?

AR: In the former, you can control your classroom or your program in terms of teaching whatever you want, as long as it doesn't violate the standards of the whole. At the time, CalArts was one of the most radical schools ever. It was a completely avant-garde school, and they had an amazing faculty. Yet the Feminist Art Program was seen as beyond radical. Many thought it trivial to consider women's experience, and many were simply angered or irritated by our presence. Over time, it became clear that we were operating too far outside the value system of the school, and we were really not considered part of the academic community. Even within such a so-called progressive institution, feminism was threatening the dominant paradigm.

TW: And once the women artists had mutated, if you will, they could no longer coexist at CalArts?

AR: I could foresee that we couldn't go where we wanted to go with our students in the environment of CalArts. So when I had an opportunity with Judy Chicago[19] to start something new, and then Sheila de Bretteville joined us during the planning process, I was very eager to do that. We knew we had to do something that was really different. The bottom-line difference was our value system, not our technique or artistic standards.

TW: Were there other times in art history when a community of artists or a group of artists or a movement of artists was driven largely by nonnormative values?

AR: The Abstract Expressionists in America in the fifties were driven by values different from the norm. The dominant paradigm was the businessman in the gray flannel suit coming home to the woman in the shirtwaist dress and high heels and the two children, and what they appeared to consider important was financial security, fidelity, and domesticity. The Abstract Expressionists didn't look anything like these people, and they didn't share the same values. They were bohemians and nonconformists.

TW: As you look at the contemporary art world now, do you see vestiges of feminist art there?

AR: Many of the same people are still working—Miriam Schapiro, Joyce Kozloff, Suzanne Lacy, Judy Chicago, and many, many others. I think that the challenge today is about what it means to have feminist content, what is the content of feminist content, what is being a woman, and how do we talk about it. That has been under discussion for three decades now, and many different approaches have come to the fore. Some issues not emphasized in the first flowering of feminist interpretation became more urgent and filled out in some way the various points that one could make about art, the things that you noticed about art and artists. Queer art has become a category of investigation. You could even see art made by mothers as a category that would be very interesting to investigate. And I don't know that there are "vestiges"; I think people who were originally in those feminist programs that I knew and were in other feminist groups across this country and whom I'm still in touch with are still working. They may not be in the same organizations, but they are still working.

TW: And have you seen their work shift?

AR: Yes, I've seen their work shift, but neither towards nor away from feminism. Work shifts because the artist finds new materials and grows and changes directions. And yes, we can see a lot of different changes, but I don't think those changes have been necessarily in point of view.

TW: Do you think that the art historical record will retain this work and this movement?

AR: I don't know. Of course, we hope so, but if history repeats itself, we're in big trouble. It's possible that, because of the current level of destructiveness in the world, we might have no historical record of anything. We could have absolutely no legacy. If things stay as they are now, yes, more women will enter the canon, but I don't think things will stay the same. History doesn't move forward in a progression. It's a very complex question, and it depends on things other than the work of women artists.

TW: So often when I encounter people who have been born in the last two or three decades, inevitably they accept how things are right now and they don't understand the enormous shift that occurred to enable them to be how they are now. So I'm wondering if there is anything else that you would want to say to explain to such a person that shift of perception.

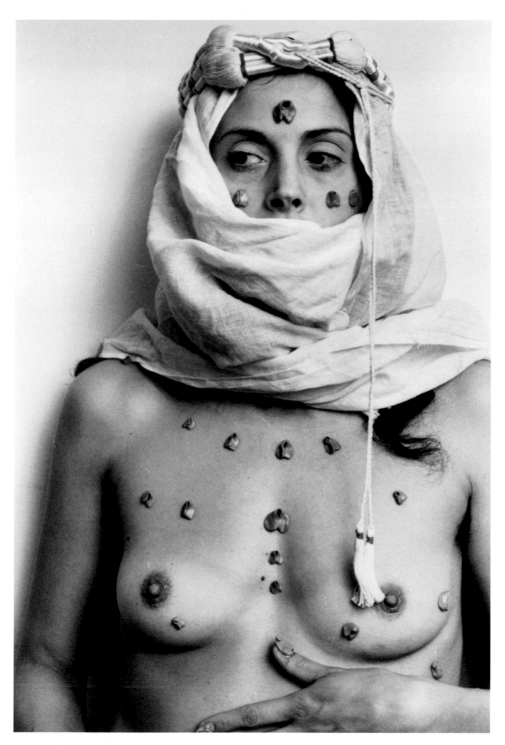

Hannah Wilke, *S.O.S. Starification Objects Series (Veil)*, 1974–75. Gelatin silver print, 40" x 28".
Hannah Wilke Collection & Archive, Los Angeles. ©Marsie, Emanuelle, Damon, and Andrew Scharlatt,
licensed by VAGA, New York.

AR: It's a revolution, and perhaps younger people experience their own revolutions. I don't know what they would be, because I'm in this older generation. We are currently in an exciting period of paradigmatic shift. This shift is not tied to the seventies. What I would say to younger women is this: you will see as you go along in your career where gender will play a role in your accomplishments and then you will understand. There is no other way to really know but through experience. If young women see, for example, abortion become illegal, I expect that they will better understand the role of gender in society. Young women will have their own experiences of gender. Their experiences will be different from ours because the bar is higher now.

TW: I do get concerned by their lack of knowledge of history.

AR: It's not only young feminists who lack history. Art history is not being taught in art schools now, so you have young artists who don't know who the important people in the history of art are, even in their own lifetimes. I work with young artists who don't know who de Kooning is, who might not know who Pollock is. I had been working with a young woman who is doing work about skin, herself, and her body, and she didn't know who Hannah Wilke was.[20] That's a problem of education. And it's bigger than feminism.

TW: Who undertakes that education, if not art schools?

AR: I personally undertake it, but now I'm working in an institution where I have a certain job during a certain period of time. I'm not going to make a new school again; I'm just going to be who I am and educate from where I am and from what I know. I think there are many people like me who are transmitting that consciousness, but it's not programmatic. One of the things I've learned is the limits of one's influence, and I learned this from feminism.

TW: Will you say more about that?

AR: I can be effective as a teacher and as a mentor to students because I know where my effectiveness and their effectiveness in art begins and ends. We truly thought we were changing the world in 1970, and I think that I have learned a great deal about what it takes to change the world and what kind of power you have to have, at what level you have to be. It's a fantasy to think that you are going to paint a picture or write an essay and change the world; you are not. But let's look at what you can do. I think very much that the legacy of the feminist movement resides largely in people who have gone through that experience, through that evolution of self and who are sharing it with others in whatever way they are sharing it. I think change is a pebble dropped into the water and spreading in rings. I think that's the way change happens—from small, discrete acts repeated over time.

TW: People are transmitting the processes, values, and philosophies. Let me go back a little bit. As there was this enormous revolution from the sixties into the seventies, a revolution of seeing and perception of women, it seemed to me that there was another revolution that occurred as we moved from the seventies up to the eighties and into more of a postmodern idea.

AR: The eighties brought a lot of critical perceptions to bear on art. Much of the Post-modern critical apparatus was lifted from literary criticism, but still derived from the feminist approach. Unlike feminist approaches, however, Postmodernism was highly intellectualized and increasingly academicized so that, to me, it got away from its orig-inal intent, which was to be direct. However, I think one learns a lot from Postmod-ernism. For example, invention is not necessary; there might not even be such an action as invention on parts and pieces that make up an apparent whole. Furthermore, Postmodernist thought suggests that one can rewrite history by using parts and pieces. To me this is completely feminist. It's making a collage—taking the fragments of your life and other lives and putting them together. In this same period, there was a lot of conflict between what was called essentialism, which was a belief that there is a true nature of women that can be expressed by female artists, and anti-essentialists, who believe that gender is a construct. The latter is a Postmodern notion. In reality, I think that work has to have both heart and ideas, and in its simplest form that's what that debate was about—heart versus ideas. When one makes a cultural comment, one is also making a statement about oneself—what we would call "identity politics." The statement is both individual and universal. For example, I make distinctions about the quality of art, and these distinctions are based largely on my intuitive reaction to that art, not something that I learned, or so I think. But I cannot separate myself from my learning.

Notes

1. Abstract Expressionism is a type of art in which the artist expresses himself purely through the use of form and color. It is non-representational, or non-objective, art, which means that there are no actual objects represented. The Abstract Expressionism movement was centered in New York City between 1946 and 1960.

2. A visual art movement of the 1960s, the Washington Color School was originally a group of painters who showed works in the "Washington Color Painters" exhibit at the Washington Gallery of Modern Art in Washington, D.C., from June 25–September 5, 1965. The Washington Color School artists painted largely abstract works and were central to the larger Color Field movement.

3. Morris Louis (Morris Louis Bernstein) (November 28, 1912–September 7, 1962) was one of the many talented Abstract Expressionist painters in the United States to emerge in the fifties. He was among a group of artists that were central to the development of Color Field painting. These artists were concerned with the classic problems of pictorial space and the statement of the picture plane.

4. The Feminist Art Program was founded by Judy Chicago in 1970 and housed at California State University, Fresno. In 1971, the program moved to the new California Institute of Arts (CalArts), and was codirected by Chicago and Miriam Schapiro.

5. Designed by architect Sophia B. Hayden for the 1893 World's Columbian Exhibition in Chicago, the Woman's Building housed art and crafts made by women from around the world. It was from this structure that the Woman's Building in Los Angeles took its name.

6. *Womanhouse* (January 30–February 18, 1972) was a women-only art installation and performance organized by Judy Chicago and Miriam Schapiro. Chicago, Schapiro, their students, and artists from the local community participated. Chicago and Schapiro encouraged their students to use consciousness-raising techniques to generate the content of the exhibition. Each woman was given a room or space of her own in a seventeen-room mansion in Hollywood, California.

7. Artemisia Gentileschi (1593–1654) was an Italian Early Baroque painter, today considered one of the most accomplished painters in the generation influenced by Caravaggio (Caravaggisti). In an era when women painters were not easily accepted by the artistic community, she was the first female painter to become a member of the Accademia delle Arti del Disegno in Florence. She was also one of the first female artists to paint historical and religious paintings, at a time when such heroic themes were considered beyond a woman's reach.

8. Art historian Mary D. Garrard is the author of *Artemisia Gentileschi: Image of the Female Hero in Italian Baroque Art* (Princeton, N.J.: Princeton University Press, 1991), and coeditor, with Norma Broude, of *The Power of Feminist Art* (New York: Harry N. Abrams, 1996).

9. Professor and art historian Linda Nochlin is a leader in feminist art history studies. In 1971, the magazine *ARTnews* published an essay whose title posed a question that would spearhead an entirely new branch of art history. The essay was called "Why Have There Been No Great Women Artists?" As the title suggests, the essay explores possible reasons as to why women artists had not achieved the same historical notoriety as their male counterparts.

10. Harriet Goodhue Hosmer (1830–1908), an American sculptor, was born at Watertown, Massachusetts. She studied anatomy with her father, a physician, and afterwards at the St. Louis Medical College. She went to Rome in 1852, where she was the pupil of the English sculptor John Gibson. Her *Zenobia, Queen of Palmyra, in Chains* (1859) is in the Metropolitan Museum of Art, New York City.

11. Joyce Kozloff (b. 1942) was, in the seventies, one of the leaders of the Pattern and Decoration movement, which questioned the positioning of the decorative arts as an inferior, wholly feminine genre.

12. Miriam Schapiro, (b. 1923), originally painted in the Abstract Expressionist style. As her commitment to feminism grew during the sixties, she developed her own personal style, which she called "femmage." Combining such commonplace elements as lace, fabric scraps, buttons, rickrack, sequins, and tea towels, she transformed them into sophisticated compositions that often imply multiple layers of both space and meaning.

13. David Salle (b. 1952) is an American painter. He earned a BFA and an MFA from CalArts, where he studied under John Baldessari.

14. Eric Fischl (b. 1948) is an American painter who also studied at CalArts.

15. Faith Wilding came to the U.S. from Paraguay in 1961. She received her MFA at CalArts, where she was a founding member of the Feminist Art Program. Wilding is a multi-disciplinary artist. She has exhibited and lectured widely in the United States and Europe.

16. Barbara T. Smith (b. 1931) is a pioneer performance artist and art educator. Among the innovators in the field, she did her first performances in Los Angeles in the sixties and subsequently has performed throughout the United States and abroad. She has been among the founders of several early alternative arts spaces, including the Woman's Building in Los Angeles, and part of the women's movement from its inception.

17. Linda Frye Burnham was the founding editor of *High Performance*, a magazine that chronicled and reviewed performance art in the seventies and eighties.

18. Chris Burden (b. 1946) is an American artist. His reputation as a performance artist started to grow in the early seventies after he made a series of controversial performances in which the idea of personal danger as artistic expression was central. His most well-known act from that time is perhaps the performance piece *Shoot* that was made in F Space in Santa Ana, California, in 1971, in which Burden was shot in his left arm by an assistant from a distance of about five meters.

19. Judy Chicago (b. Judy Cohen, 1939) is a feminist artist, author, and educator. In 1971, Chicago and Miriam Schapiro jointly founded the Feminist Art Program at CalArts, where they organized *Womanhouse*. In 1973, Chicago founded, with Arlene Raven and Sheila de Bretteville, the Woman's Building and the Feminist Studio Workshop. Chicago is most famous for her 1974–79 work *The Dinner Party*, an homage to women's history in which hundreds of volunteers participated. It is now permanently housed at the Brooklyn Museum.

20. Hannah Wilke (1940–93; born Arlene Hannah Butter) was an American painter, sculptor, and photographer associated with Conceptual art and Post-Minimalism. Her work explores issues of gender and the body.

Cheryl Swannack spray painting ceiling, construction of the new space on Spring Street, 1975. Woman's Building Image Archive, Otis College of Art and Design.

FEMINIST ART EDUCATION AT THE LOS ANGELES WOMAN'S BUILDING

Betty Ann Brown

"The women's art movement of Southern California undertook the creation of feminist education as a high priority.... The emphasis on education distinguishes the West Coast women's art movement from that in New York, for example, which focuses more on the needs of professional women artists to advance their careers...."
—Faith Wilding [1]

Feminism is one of the great movements for human liberation. The "second wave" of feminism in the United States began in the sixties alongside the Civil Rights Movement and other broad-based initiatives that challenged the authority of the dominant culture. Much of the political action of the decade was sited on university campuses, and the decade changed the face of the academy. (I remember participating in a 1968 sit-in at my college president's office to compel him to institute a Black Studies Program.) In line with the call for egalitarianism (including race, class, and gender), adult education and community re-education were also carried out in community institutions throughout the country. Feminist educators were among the leaders of liberatory education, and feminist artists and historians were prominent among them. The Los Angeles Woman's Building and the Feminist Studio Workshop were among the vanguard in feminist art education.

The first Women's Studies course was offered in the United States in 1966.[2] Within seven years, there were more than two thousand Women's Studies classes taught at various U.S. institutions.[3] By 1970, art historian Linda Nochlin was offering courses on women in the arts in New York.[4] That same year, artist Judy Chicago organized the Feminist Art Program (FAP) at California State University, Fresno.[5] It was the first program of its kind.[6]

In her autobiography, *Through the Flower: My Struggle as a Woman Artist*, Chicago recalled that she and the (male) department chair at Fresno discussed that while many young women took art classes, few became professional artists.[7] Chicago decided to offer an all-woman class. Using her own experience as a model, she focused on "the struggle out of role conditioning that a woman would have to make if she were to realize herself."[8] Chicago had the class meet off campus because she had "ample demonstrations" of how intimidated many young women are in the presence of men...[the male] presence reminded the women of society's tacit and all-pervasive instruction that they should not be too aggressive, so that the men's egos would not be threatened."[9] She told the women that the first step was to locate and prepare a studio for the class meetings. As the students were compelled to develop practical skills in construction and the use of power tools, their physical self-confidence grew.

During the first class meetings, Chicago and the students began what the artist referred to as "a kind of modified consciousness-raising, which combined the expressing of common experiences with...trying to help the women understand the implications of those experiences in order to change their behavior patterns."[10] Chicago believed that consciousness-raising could "revolutionize teaching...because [as] one goes 'around the circle,' one discovers that the strangest people know the 'right' answer."[11]

In the second semester of the Fresno Program, Chicago added a research component to the class. The students began to investigate women artists of the past, in order to rediscover their "hidden heritage," and they started an archive. The archive grew into the first West Coast file on women artists' work.[12]

Chicago encouraged the students to make art out of their personal experiences, rather than solely out of formal issues—form, line, texture and color—that had little to do with their daily lives. They began to create art about shared female experiences—for example, the sensation of having their personal space violated by a man. Chicago recalled that the students began "showing images of feelings and experiences that none of us had ever seen portrayed before; paintings and drawings, poems, performances, and ideas for films, all revealing the way women saw men...The images that day came out with an incredible force, as if they had been bottled up and suddenly released. They were so powerful that they frightened me."[13] (Early feminist art images remain powerful; they continue to frighten. Perhaps that is why they elicit such heated responses from so much of the public. In January 2001, I toured the "Made in

California" exhibition at the Los Angeles County Museum of Art. People crowded around the videotapes of Chicago's early work, and some of the viewers' comments were truly vitriolic. It was the only site in the immense and varied exhibition that brought forth such viewer hostility.)

According to Chicago, the "most powerful work" of the year in Fresno was the performance art work.[14] This led her to conclude that one reason so few women excelled in traditional art educational contexts is that the curricula focused on historically valued media—primarily painting and sculpture—which were precisely the media that men dominated. It is important to note that in 1974, almost two-thirds of students trained in art and art history in the United States were women, but only 21% of the faculty members were female.[15] When I joined the faculty of the art department of California State University, Northridge, in 1975, there was only one full-time art studio professor who was female. Even in 1999, when we hired two women as studio faculty members, several of the men questioned the women's technical competence. One man went so far as to suggest that we needed to bring in a male mentor for one of the new female faculty members because she probably could not handle the classes on her own. Such a suggestion was never made for new male hires. However, with the rise of artistic pluralism in the late seventies and the emergence of new media like performance, video and installation, women artists began to find their creative voices in visual languages previously unheard by the art establishment. Today, women continue to be the majority in art classes and the minority on studio faculties, but the ratios are changing. Chicago summarized the success of her early efforts in Fresno:

> Once I had organized the class, taken it away from the school, given myself and the students a space of our own and a support group, provided them with a positive role model and an environment in which we could be ourselves, growth for all of us was inevitable.... This suggests that what I stumbled on in Fresno has implications for all areas of female education.[16]

Indeed it does.

> It was like being at the moment of birth, the birth of a new kind of community of women, a new kind of art made by women.[17]

Chicago invited Miriam Schapiro, a well-known New York painter, to speak at Fresno. Excited by the program Chicago had established, Schapiro convinced her husband, Paul Brach, who was then dean at California Institute of the Arts (CalArts), to institute a similar structure there, where Chicago and Schapiro could teach together. In fall 1971, Chicago and her new collaborator moved the Fresno Program to CalArts, which is located in Valencia just north of Los Angeles.[18] Several of the Fresno students decided to continue their art education at CalArts. Together with their teachers, they founded the Feminist Art Program (FAP), endeavoring "to establish an alternative context in which one did not have to choose between 'being a woman and being an artist.'"[19] Chicago, Schapiro, and the CalArts students also organized the First West Coast Conference of Women Artists, which took place from January 21 to 23, 1972.[20]

In order to learn about the history of feminist art education, I augmented my library research with telephone interviews of several of the women involved. I spoke with Los Angeles artists Cheri Gaulke, Robin Mitchell, and Linda Vallejo in November and December 2000. Information from the interviews appears below and throughout this essay.

In early 1971, while she was an art student in Southern California, Robin Mitchell heard a radio interview with Judy Chicago. Robin's art education experience up to that point had been overwhelming dominated by male teachers. She remembers one professor commenting, "I don't really like teaching girls; they just grow up and get married. So I'm going to teach the guys. I hope you don't mind." Another blithely said, "Art schools are the hunting grounds for mistresses and second wives." And Robin still has a photograph that one of her fellow students took of the all-male faculty. An image of eight bearded men similarly attired in denim shirts, jeans, and cowboy boots, the photo is titled, "How to become an artist by imitating your teacher."

When Robin heard Judy Chicago talking about the Fresno Program, she was impressed. She wrote Chicago a letter and received an invitation to Fresno in response. Robin drove her Volkswagen van to Fresno in 1971. She recalls meeting Chicago and Schapiro, seeing a slide show of the work of women artists, and being "blown away" by Schapiro's abstract paintings. Robin entered CalArts that fall and enrolled in the Feminist Art Program. She considers her first semester there "very valuable...a haven." She learned about feminist theory, practiced consciousness-raising, and explored new artistic genres.

The second semester was largely consumed by *Womanhouse* [in which artists created installations about women's experience throughout a seventeen-room mansion in Hollywood].[21] Robin learned about and began to produce performance and installation in *Womanhouse*, where both genres evolved out of Chicago's innovative teaching techniques. Robin worked in one of the upstairs bedrooms. Her first plan

Judy Chicago: *A Survey of Four Decades of Art Making*, National Museum of Women in the Arts, Washington, D.C., 2002. Installation view. Photograph by Donald Woodman. © Donald Woodman.

was to line every surface in the room with quilted fabric, but she soon realized that hers was an overly ambitious plan: she simply didn't have the time. So instead, she covered every surface with abstract painting. One viewer later commented that Robin had created "the artist's room," which was a gratifying response for the young painter.

As with many of the other students, Robin was flabbergasted by the huge public response and disconcerted by the glare of the public spotlight on *Womanhouse*. The experience had been so raw and experimental; there had been so many difficult hours of crying and fighting that it was unnerving to see strangers in "her" space. She also remains conflicted about Chicago and Schapiro as teachers and role models. Although she gratefully acknowledges that they changed her life and greatly contributed to making her the artist and teacher she is today, she found both women difficult and overly demanding at times. Neither the CalArts FAP nor *Womanhouse* was an easy experience for the young student.[22]

Womanhouse opened January 30, 1972. Conceived of as a large-scale art project in which women took their societally imbedded but culturally demeaned homemaking activities and "carried them to fantasy propositions,"[23] *Womanhouse* was located in a condemned mansion near downtown Los Angeles. Chicago, Schapiro, and twenty-one students spent three months cleaning and repairing the long-vacant house. As they worked, many of the students began to resent their teachers. The students became angry about the power wielded by Chicago and Schapiro, irritated by their belief that the two professional artists had more authority than they. Although deeply concerned at first, Chicago came to understand that the only female authority figures many of the students had seen were their mothers, and they had many unresolved feelings about their mothers. Chicago realized that the rhetoric of the feminist movement suggested that all women should be equal, but that she and Schapiro, as accomplished professional artists, were not precisely equal to the young art students. Instead, they were "authorities in that situation."[24] Chicago further realized that "[t]he acceptance of women as authority figures or as role models is an important step in female education. If one sees a woman who has achieved, one can say: I'm like her. If she can do it, so can I. It is this process of identification, respect and then self-respect that promotes growth."[25]

(I have often found it difficult to deal with female students who resent my authority position in the classroom because they, however unconsciously, project their mothers onto me. For example, I was a visiting professor at Claremont Graduate School in the early 1990s. At the end of my two years there, I gave a seminar on feminist theory. Most of the women who enrolled in the seminar had already taken at least one class with me, but few had concentrated on feminist theory. We began each class meeting with consciousness-raising, then discussed feminist texts and their relationship to art making. We ended the semester by creating a collaborative art exhibition that we installed in the gallery of my home university, California State University, Northridge. Most of us bonded so deeply that we remain friends; I share an office with a woman who was one of the students in that seminar and am godmother to another former student's daughter. However, some of the students resented me deeply and continually sought to undermine the process. One young woman went so far as to telephone me at home early one weekend morning and yell at me about what she perceived as my preferential treatment of some of her classmates. The intensity of her voice and her heightened emotionality reminded me of the wounded voice of sibling rivalry. I realized she could only see me as a mother figure, never as a professional whose job was to guide her in deepening her awareness of the art process through examination of critical theory. Chicago's accounts of her similar difficulties at CalArts helped me understand that the female authority figure is often a target, even for students of feminist art education).

In 1973, Chicago, art historian Arlene Raven, and graphic designer Sheila

Levrant de Bretteville founded the Feminist Studio Workshop (FSW) in Los Angeles. The FSW was later incorporated into the Los Angeles Woman's Building, which opened in November 1973 on South Grandview Street, at the site of the old Chouinard Art Institute. In 1975, the Woman's Building moved to a new location, on Spring Street, in downtown Los Angeles. The FSW continued to thrive in the new location.

> Cheri Gaulke came to the Feminist Studio Workshop (FSW) of the Los Angeles Woman's Building in fall of 1975. Cheri's original intention was to spend a year in Los Angeles, acquire the skills necessary to develop a Woman's Building program, then return to Minneapolis and recreate the institution there. Her class was the first at the Spring Street location; they spent the entire fall semester (September–December 1975) renovating the facility. Although Cheri understood that one of the tenets of alternative feminist education was that students had to build their own space, that such construction was in itself a significant learning experience, other women in the FSW program were resentful. After all, they had traveled to Los Angeles and invested considerable moneys . . . to do what? Clean floors and windows? Build walls? Learn electrical and plumbing skills?

> In addition to renovating the site, the FSW students also had to create art for the exhibition planned for the Woman's Building's December opening. Cheri and four others created a performance piece that parodied a three-ring circus. Their "The Other Side Show" explored the collisions of public self and private self. Cheri, for example, closed herself into a circus box and appeared to be sawed in half as a metaphor for her internal conflicts.

> During her two years at the FSW, Cheri's primary mentors were performance artist Suzanne Lacy, graphic designer Sheila de Bretteville, and art historian Ruth Iskin, whom Cheri credits with "up-leveling" Cheri's level of professionalism. Iskin's advice was particularly cogent while Cheri worked on curating an exhibition of Grandma Prisbrey's *Bottle Village* in 1976. (Grandma Prisbrey was an extraordinary, self-trained artist who created an entire village out of bottles, cement, and other refuse in Simi Valley, to the northwest of downtown Los Angeles.) Iskin also helped Cheri give herself "permission" to do individually generated art works, rather than solely pieces developed with groups of performers.

Grandma Prisbrey at the opening of *Bottle Village* at the Woman's Building, March 1976. Photograph by Sheila Ruth. Woman's Building Image Archive, Otis College of Art and Design.

When Cheri began classes at the Woman's Building, she was enrolled in Goddard College, an alternative academic program that gave credit for off-site education. In 1977, she completed her master's degree in Feminist Art and Education through her two years of work at the FSW.

For Cheri, the three primary tenets of FSW that distinguished it from her previous educational experiences were the use of consciousness-raising, the emphasis on collaboration, and the focus on creating art out of each woman's personal experiences. She remembers that although there were as many as fifty women enrolled in the program in the mid-seventies, they still took the time to sit in a circle and go around the group, allowing each person to speak to a chosen theme. They often went around the circle a second time before they began to theorize, to extrapolate from the personal to the political. Cheri also remembers that de Bretteville was the first person to raise the FSW students' awareness of the power of the media. De Bretteville exposed the aggressive nature of most mainstream advertising and asserted that there could be a gentler tenor to public communication. De Bretteville also helped Cheri see that she could use public venues, like the mail system and bus stops, to create art, like postcards and billboards, that integrated the personal and political.

Cheri was soon to become an FSW teacher herself, as a member of the Feminist Art Workers. Like many of the women educated at the Woman's Building, she began as student then moved into roles of increasing responsibility. She offered various classes at the Woman's Building, eventually became building manager, and continues to serve on the board of directors.[26]

In 1976, the Woman's Building Extension Program began offering art education classes for students who attended part-time, rather than full-time in the FSW. By the late seventies, feminist art education had become a significant academic concern. Georgia Collins wrote "the first article in art education grounded in feminist theory" in 1977; a year later Renée Sandell finished her dissertation on the topic.[27] At that time, the Woman's Building's classes were attracting a wide and diverse population.

In 1978, the FSW faculty turned teaching and administrative responsibilities over to the Feminist Art Workers (FAW), a group of former FSW students including Gaulke, as well as Nancy Angelo, Vanalyne Green, and Laurel Klick. Chicago was consumed by her work on *The Dinner Party*. De Bretteville and Raven continued offering classes, although Raven was most absorbed by her work with the Lesbian Art Project.

The FSW closed in 1981, but the extension program classes continued. At that time, the extension program was renamed the Woman's Building Educational Program (EP). The EP began by offering classes in the fields of visual arts, performance art, graphics, book arts, video and writing. In the eighties, there was a shift toward professional development, i.e., how to succeed as an artist; commissioned artworks, such as the Gilding the Building project, which invited local artists to create sculptures for the facade of the Spring Street edifice; and funded projects for specific populations.

Linda Vallejo came to the Woman's Building to oversee the funded project known as Madre Tierra Press in 1979. Through Madre Tierra, Linda brought together thirteen Chicanas and taught them how to design and create handmade books. The goal was a series of image and text volumes employing depictions of the Chicano community and women's relation to it. Linda facilitated the collaborative genesis of images and texts. Then she oversaw the plate design, transfer of photographic images to the metal plates, use of letterpress, scheduling and printing of the final plates. Among the participants was Yreina Cervantes, who went on to expand her career through the use of the kind of art developed in the program.

Linda remembers that it was during her time with the Madre Tierra Press project that she was invited by the Woman's Building to give lectures on Chicana art in general and her own art in particular. It was the first time she had done such public lectures. She recalls with gratitude that the Woman's Building staff and participants were remarkably supportive as she planned and delivered the talks.

Linda, whose own artwork was featured in several exhibitions at the Woman's Building and who served on the board of directors for several years, went on to become a prominent artist and community activist, as well as a notable spokesperson for Chicana arts.[28]

In spite of its notable successes and considerable contributions to feminist art education, the Los Angeles Woman's Building closed in 1991. The last EP classes were offered in spring of that year. The Woman's Building Board of Directors remains active; the Woman's Building papers are collected at the Archives of American Art at the Smithsonian Institute, in Washington, D.C.; the collection of Woman's Building slides, which were digitized by Otis College of Art and Design with assistance from the Getty Foundation, are housed at Otis; and these essays have been compiled into a book. In the nineties, the Woman's Building Board initiated an oral history project to document the history of the institution. As of the publication of this book, the oral history project is still underway.

Principles of Feminist Art Education

Urging all of us to open our minds and hearts so that we can know beyond the boundaries of what is acceptable, so that we can think and rethink, so that we can create new visions, I celebrate teaching that enables transgressions—movements against and beyond boundaries. It is that movement that makes education the practice of freedom.
—bell hooks[29]

Linda Vallejo presenting an opening prayer for
the Madre Tierra Press Opening Reception,
1982. © Linda Vallejo 2011.

The principles of feminist art education were drawn from the revolutionary practices of "second-wave" feminism and served to broaden the impact of feminism in traditional and non-traditional educational contexts. Ultimately such principles functioned as vehicles for expanding the influence of feminism on the culture at large.

> In 1977, Faith Wilding listed four principles of feminist art education:
> 1. Consciousness-raising
> 2. Building a female context and environment
> 3. Female role models
> 4. Permission to be themselves and encouragement to make art out of their own experience as women[30]
>
> Later Wilding added:
> 5. Collaborative and collective work
> 6. Exploding the hierarchies of materials and high/low art practices, as well as recovering the positive values of denigrated or margin-alized practices[31]

Peg Speirs introduced her 1998 study of feminist art education (FAE) with the following paragraph:

> FAE collapses the distinctions between research, art and pedagogy, offering multiple paths of approach and application of feminist the-ory in some form of action. In the academy, FAE dissolves discipli-nary borders that serve to perpetuate separation, competition, and isolation to protect disciplinarity. Not to be understood as a new discipline replacing existing disciplines, FAE is an interdisciplinary location that remains in continual motion so that it cannot be fixed to one particular place, methodology, or feminist. FAE exists inside and outside the academy simultaneously as feminists working for social change in different venues. FAE's shifting location multiplies its dimensions and expands its field of knowledge and practice to reach diverse audiences for the purpose of social change.[32]

For the principles of feminist art education to be incorporated into widespread edu-cational practices requires a radical shift in the traditional educational paradigm. Challenges to that paradigm are by no means new, nor are they limited to feminist practitioners. Brazilian liberationist Paulo Freire sought to expose and disrupt the master/servant hierarchy he witnessed in the traditional classroom in his widely in-fluential *Pedagogy of the Oppressed*. Freire critiques the banking model of education in which teachers deposit data into student "accounts," then seek to withdraw it through testing. "Instead of communicating, the teacher issues communiqués and makes deposits which the students patiently receive, memorize, and repeat."[33] Perhaps because I am less economically oriented than Freire, I have always used the preacher/ congregation analogy to describe traditional education. The teacher/preacher—often an older white male, who often wears a suit—stands at the front of the classroom, often separated from the students/congregation by a podium. He delivers what he presents as "Objective Truth" as if he were channeling God's Word. The students/congregation are to receive the Word without question and repeat it back in the call/response of examinations.

Jane Tompkins asserts that the banking model is obsolete for most educators today, "but what we do have is something no less coercive, no less destructive of creativity and self-motivated learning."[34] That is what Tompkins calls the performance model, wherein teachers endeavor to demonstrate how smart, knowledgeable, and well prepared they are. Many teachers, she argues, put on performances whose true goal is not to help the students learn, but to show them "how to perform within an institutional academic setting in such a way that they will be thought highly of by their colleagues and instructors."[35] Like the banking and preacher/congregation models, Tompkins's performance model can be described as a kind of separated learning. But separated learning is not the feminist ideal.

> Imagine knowing as an act of love ... a giving of the self to the subject
> matter, rather than an "objective" standing at a distance.
> —Hilde Heine[36]

Jill Tarule describes the differences between separated and connected learning.[37] Separated learning is based on what Tarule calls the "doubting game." It separates the learner from the delivered information, at the same time insisting that argument is essential to learning. In other words, separated learning is fundamentally competitive and contentious. In contrast, connected learning is based on the "believing game." Connected learning asks questions like, "How is this experienced?" "What does it make you think?" "How does it make you feel?" Connected learning attempts to include the knower in that which is known. It seeks to establish relationship, to value understanding and acceptance. Tarule and her coauthors build on the work of Carol Gilligan and her colleague Nona Lyons, who "use the terms separate and connected to describe two different conceptions or experiences of the self, as essentially autonomous (separate from others) or as essentially in relationship (connected to others)."[38]

Tarule notes that many scholars assert that female identity is defined in a woman's capacity for relationship; by extension, the very act of learning itself can be embedded into relationship. She adds that connected learning may be gender related, but not gender specific. Like Judy Chicago's Fresno Program and CalArts' FAP, the feminist education at the Los Angeles Woman's Building was based on connected learning.

bell hooks argues that when we reject the separate learning paradigm, education can become the practice of freedom. Like Tompkins, hooks notes that teaching is "a performative act." But hooks argues that teachers "are not performers in the traditional sense of the word in that our work is not meant to be a spectacle." She sees the performative aspect of teaching as precisely that which "offers the space for change, invention, spontaneous shifts, that can serve as a catalyst drawing out the unique elements of each classroom...it is meant to serve as a catalyst that calls everyone to become more and more engaged, to become active participants in learning."[39] Particularly the performance art aspect of early feminist art education provided such a space for change and engagement. Feminist scholars such as hooks and Tarule build on the principles of feminist art education developed at the Los Angeles Woman's Building in order to develop connected teaching/learning praxes and develop student understanding. As Belenky et al. write, "Understanding involves intimacy and equality between self and object, while knowledge...implies separation from the object and mastery over it."[40] Expanded for a more inclusive and broad-reaching student population than the all female, all artist environment of the FSW, Wilding's six principles of feminist education might be restated as follows:

1. Teachers can learn to listen—really listen—to the diverse voices of their students. As hooks writes, "It has been my experience that one way to build community in the classroom is to recognize the value of each individual voice.... To hear each other (the sound of different voices), to listen to one another, is an exercise in recognition. It also ensures that no student remains invisible in the classroom."[41] Supporting students in finding their voices can lead to the emergence of what Belenky et al. term subjective knowing: "The move away from silence and an externally oriented perspective on knowledge and truth [to] a new conception of truth as personal, private, and subjectively known or intuited."[42] This move facilitates connected learning.

2. The curriculum can be shifted from Euro-centered, male canons to acknowledgment of the validity of many traditions, from authoritarian paradigms of objective "truths" to recognition that many so-called truths are in fact relative. hooks explains:

Identity politics emerges out of the struggles of oppressed or exploited groups to have a standpoint on which to critique dominant structures, a position that gives purpose and meaning to struggle. Critical pedagogies of liberation respond to those concerns and necessarily embrace experience, confessions and testimony as relevant ways of knowing, as important, vital dimensions of any learning process.[43]

3. Teachers can incorporate many and varied role models.[44] Again, according to hooks:

> Multiculturalism compels educators to recognize the narrow boundaries that have shaped the way knowledge is shared in the classroom.... When we, as educators, allow our pedagogy to be radically changed by our recognition of a multicultural world, we can give students the education they desire and deserve. We can teach in ways that transform the consciousness, creating a climate of free expression that is the essence of a truly liberatory liberal arts education.[45]

4. The teacher must acknowledge that she, too, is involved in the learning process; she must recognize that education is a cycle that moves from life to the classroom and back to life again. As hooks asserts, "The engaged voice [of the teacher] must never be fixed and absolute but always changing, always evolving in dialogue with a world beyond itself."[46]

5. Learning can involve collaboration and teamwork. According to hooks, "Excitement [in the classroom] is generated through collective effort. Seeing the classroom always as a communal place enhances the likelihood of collective effort in creating and sustaining a learning community."[47]

6. Education can focus on dissolving the polarities of male/female, good/evil, culture/nature, master/servant, etc. These are precisely the polarities that Hélène Cixous dissects in her compelling "Sorties."[48]

> The challenging of this solidarity of logocentrism and phallocentrism has today become insistent enough—the bringing to light of the fate which has been imposed upon woman, of her burial—to threaten the stability of the masculine edifice which passed itself off as eternal-natural; by bringing forth from the world of femininity reflections, hypotheses which

are necessarily ruinous for the bastion which still holds the authority.... What would become of logocentrism, of the great philosophical systems, of world order in general if the rock upon which they founded their church were to crumble?... Then all the stories would have to be told differently, the future would be incalculable, the historical forces would, will, change hands, bodies; another thinking as yet not thinkable will transform the functioning of all society.[49]

Today, Robin Mitchell is a feminist art educator. She teaches painting and drawing at the University of Southern California, Pasadena City College, and Santa Monica College. She acknowledges that her time at the CalArts Feminist Art Program shaped her teaching. Because of her experience with consciousness-raising, she is always careful to let each student have a voice. She designs her classes for students to discover what art is, rather than dictating to them her preconceptions. She is aware that the student population has changed since the seventies, that it is much more diverse, and she employs many of the insights she learned as a woman to develop her awareness of multicultural issues. She credits the FAP with strategies for encouraging students to have a voice, to express their opinions with confidence, and to value their personal experiences. While she realizes that most of her students will not become professional artists, she encourages them to remain creative and to appreciate the value of art in everyone's lives.

Robin is troubled that many of her young female students have had little or no exposure to feminism. She is concerned about all the negative stereotypes about feminism she encounters. She is also concerned about the way in which many [male] artists have usurped feminist art images and processes without giving credit to their origins.

Robin finds the contemporary art world as sexist, ageist, and racist—and as narrow as it has ever been. She admits that it took a long time for her to realize that she was editing her work in a male way in order to be taken seriously. Once she realized that, she discovered a new freedom in her art making. She now paints and draws and sculpts passionate, energetic, "hot" abstractions that are widely exhibited and the subject of substantial critical acclaim.[50]

Like Robin, Cheri Gaulke is a professional feminist educator. She teaches art at Harvard-Westlake School, a private institution in Los Angeles that has approximately 750 students at their grades 10–12 campus. Cheri specializes in video classes; teaching video is a skill she learned at the FSW. She believes that Sheila de Bretteville's commitment to giving a different voice to public communication still has a significant impact on her work as a teacher. De Bretteville's influence is seen in Cheri's policy that students must respect and listen to each other, her projects have students create art from their personal experiences, and her emphasis on media literacy/critical thinking.

Cheri asserts that her own art production has been "totally influenced" by the FSW, from her video installations focused on environmental concerns to those exploring teen identity, from public art works like her 1994 Los Angeles Metro Rail commission to her first digital book and website.[51]

Linda Vallejo still offers classes in alternative contexts, at alternative institutions. For fifteen years now, she has facilitated Native American-inspired "sweats" at California prisons. She became involved with sweats while working with a Chicana women's dance troupe that used Mesoamerican imagery as part of the Mobile Art Studios of the Los Angeles Barrio (Chicano neighborhood). The troupe was often included in intertribal ceremonies. At one of these, Linda was asked by an Arizona elder to assist in "pouring water" (i.e., facilitating the ritual) in local prisons. Soon, she began offering rituals for the women incarcerated at the California Rehabilitation Center in the city of Norco. Linda's rituals are multicultural and inclusive. They employ talk circles not unlike the FSW consciousness-raising process, as well as guided meditations for relaxation, several hours in the sweat lodge, and banquets honoring the elders and teachers of the groups. Linda knows that such rituals have become and will remain an integral part of her being. She is committed to teaching native wisdom, to imaging women at the center of all things, and to aiding others in finding their spiritual core, the deep meaning in their lives.

Linda continues to appreciate the generous support she received from the Los Angeles Woman's Building. "You don't really know the mountain until you've started to climb," she says. "You don't know how high and how steep it really is. You imagine that there will be several organizations to support you along the way, but the truth is, there aren't." As she continues to "pour water" in prisons, she remembers the collaborative community context of her classes at the Woman's Building. On the eve of several one-person shows, Linda acknowledges that it was the Los Angeles Woman's Building that gave her some of her first exhibition opportunities and provided the nurturing community necessary for the germination of her successful career.[52]

Although neither the Los Angeles Woman's Building nor the Feminist Studio Workshop is still functioning, the innovative education they produced continues to influence and inspire. That influence can be seen in both the innovative teaching of former Woman's Building/FSW students and in the thousands they have instructed. As the influence continues throughout many generations of students, the practice of feminist education expands its transformative impact on the culture.

Notes

1. Faith Wilding, *By Our Own Hands: The Women's Artist's Movement, Southern California 1970–1976* (Santa Monica, CA: Double X, 1977).

2. Barbara Ehrlich White, "A 1974 Perspective: Why Women's Studies in Art and Art History?" in *Art Journal* 35.4 (1976): 340. From a paper delivered to the College Art Association meetings, January 1974.

3. Ibid., 340.

4. Ibid., 340.

5. At the time, the institution was known as Fresno State University.

6. See Renée Sandell, "Feminist Art Education: An Analysis of the Women's Art Movement as an Educational Force," in *Studies in Art Education* 20 (2) (1979): 18–28. Cited in Peg Speirs, "Collapsing Distinctions: Feminist Art Education as Research, Art and Pedagogy" (PhD diss., Pennsylvania State University, 1998), 5.

7. Judy Chicago, *Through the Flower: My Struggle as a Woman Artist* (Garden City, New York: Doubleday, 1975), 70.

8. Ibid., 71.

9. Ibid., 72.

10. Ibid., 75.

11. Ibid., 77.

12. Ibid., 86.

13. Ibid., 79-80.

14. Ibid., 87.

15. White, 340.

16. Chicago, 78.

17. Ibid., 90.

18. The feminist art curriculum at CalArts ended in 1975, when artist-professors Sherry Brody and Miriam Schapiro left the institution.

19. Chicago, 100.

20. See Wilding, *By Our Own Hands*, 31.

21. *Womanhouse* was an installation created by Judy Chicago, Miriam Schapiro and their students in the Feminist Art Program at CalArts, in 1972.

22. Author's telephone interview with Robin Mitchell, 2000.

23. Chicago, 104.

24. Ibid., 108.

25. Ibid.

26. Author's telephone interview with Cheri Gaulke, 2000.

27. See Speirs, 3–5.

28. Author's telephone interview with Linda Vallejo, 2000.

29. bell hooks, *Teaching to Transgress, Education as the Practice of Freedom* (New York and London: Routledge, 1994), 12.

30. Wilding, *By Our Own Hands*, 10–11.

31. Faith Wilding, "The Feminist Art Programs at Fresno and CalArts, 1970–75," in Norma Broude and Mary D. Garrard, eds., *The Power of Feminist Art: The American Movement of the 1970s, History and Impact* (New York: Harry N. Abrams, 1994), 34.

32. Speirs, iii.

33. Paulo Freire, *Pedagogy of the Oppressed* (New York: Continuum, 1982) quoted in Jane Tompkins, "Teaching Like It Matters: A Modest Proposal for Revolutionizing the Classroom," *Lingua Franca* (August 1991): 24.

34. Tompkins, 24.

35. Ibid., 24–25. Tompkins suggests that in place of the performance, teachers make the students responsible for presenting the material to the class for most of the semester. I have found this a particularly effective strategy in graduate level classes. In my experience, however, making students in introductory classes responsible for material they have had little or no previous contact with is inappropriate. I find I must spend some time helping them assemble the "raw materials" of information and a "tool box" of theories/strategies before they are equipped to present material on their own.

36. Hilde Heine, quoted in Estella Lauter, *Women as Mythmakers: Poetry and Visual Art by Twentieth-Century Women* (Bloomington: Indiana University Press, 1984), 221.

37. Jill Mattuck Tarule, from "Women's Ways of Knowing," paper delivered at Women and Education: Learning, Knowing and Teaching for the 21st Century, a conference held at the Huntington Library, San Marino, California, in January 1990. Tarule's theories are amplified in Mary Field Belenky, Blythe McVicker Clinchy, Nancy Rule Goldberger, and Jill Mattuck Tarule, *Women's Ways of Knowing: The Development of Self, Voice, and Mind* (New York: Basic Books, 1986/1997), especially 100–30.

38. Belenky, Clichy, Goldberger and Tarule, 102.

39. hooks, 11.

40. Belenky, Clichy, Goldberger and Tarule, 101.

41. hooks, 40–41.

42. Belenky, Clichy, Goldberger and Tarule, 54.

43. hooks, 88–89.

44. Teachers must take care not to reproduce stereotypes about oppressed peoples as they work with different cultures. I point to the work of Leilani Clark, Sheridan DeWolf, and Carl Clark (Euro-American scholars at Grossmont College in El Cajon, California) whose article "Teaching Teachers to Avoid Having Culturally Assaultive Classrooms," in *Young Children* (July 1992): 4–6, made me particularly aware of this danger. I also refer readers to Maria Lugones's "Playfulness, 'World'-Traveling, and Loving Perception," in Ann Garry and Marilyn Pearsall, *Women, Knowledge and Reality: Explorations in Feminist Philosophy* (London: Unwin Hyman, 1989), for discussion of how the disenfranchised "learn" negative self-image.

45. hooks, 44.

46. Ibid.,11.

47. Ibid., 8.

48. Hélène Cixous, "Sorties," in *New French Feminisms*, Elaine Marks and Isabelle de Courtivron, eds. (New York: Schocken Books, 1980), 90–98.

49. Ibid., 92–93.

50. Author's telephone interview with Robin Mitchell, 2000.

51. Author's telephone interview with Cheri Gaulke, 2000.

52. Author's telephone interview with Linda Vallejo, 2000.

Estilita Gramaldo (far left) of WomanTours talking to Suzanne Shelton (center) in courtyard of the Woman's Building at the Feminist Eye Film and Video Conference, March 29-30, 1975. Woman's Building Image Archive, Otis College of Art and Design.

An installation by Su-Chen Hung in the exhibition "Viva la Vida: An Homage to Frida Kahlo," at the Woman's Building, 1978. Woman's Building Image Archive, Otis College of Art and Design.

"AT HOME" AT THE WOMAN'S BUILDING (BUT WHO GETS A ROOM OF HER OWN?): WOMEN OF COLOR AND COMMUNITY[1]

Michelle Moravec and Sondra Hale[2]

Join us in the creation of the community of learned women Virginia Woolf believed was possible. Not the daughters of educated men, but the education women themselves controlling their private and professional lives according to their values, sensibility and womanity.[3]

Introduction—Feminism and Community[4]

The Woman's Building of Los Angeles emerged in an era characterized by many homogeneous and somewhat essentializing themes about a need to build and maintain *community*—a women's or woman's community, a feminist community. However, the manifestos, mission statements, and reiterated slogans that characterized the identity politics of the era of "second-wave feminism" were both vague and specific about the nature and type of community envisioned. Some statements expounded on a need for women to invent and build spaces and institutions that were uniquely tailored to women's needs, spirit, and creativity. Whether or not these were actual edifices, they were to be "safe houses," places where *all* women felt "at home."

The concept of "community" remained an elusive one in most of the early feminist literature. Other terms implied community (e.g., "collective"), and essentialist terms abounded (e.g., "woman's world" and "women's culture"), but few ventured into an actual definition of "community." So much was "understood." Even most of the Woman's Building's official statements skirted the terminology while occasionally citing members who used the term.

For example, the publication issued to celebrate the tenth anniversary reproduced a mission statement that uses such terms as "collective identity" and "environment" but not "community." At the same time, one of the founders, Arlene Raven, is quoted as saying, "We are the Woman's Community; we live and grow in the Woman's Building." Active member Deena Metzger asserts, "the Woman's Building is the room of our own, the private space where community begins."[5]

Some early feminist institutions clearly aimed to create community or considered themselves to be one. Sagaris, referred to as "an independent feminist institute," emerged in 1975 as one of the first organizations to deal with feminist education, in the broadest sense.[6] Although not defined as a "community," the question of "what builds women's sense of self and sense of community" was considered in discussing cultural goals.[7] Susan Sherman, however, frames the group that broke away from the larger gathering of Sagaris as an "alternative community," a term that was very common in the 1970s and 1980s. Sherman argues, "With the birth of the August 7th Survival Community, the crucial step had been made from an educational institution run by a collective of eight women to the formation of an alternative educational community run collectively by all the members of the community."[8]

Following in the footsteps of Sagaris was a West Coast institution that chose to use the word "community" in its title. Marilyn Murphy remarked about Califia:

> We call our organization Community to express our commitment to the development of an informed community spirit among Califia women which recognizes and affirms our differences as we celebrate our sisterhood. Califia Community is committed to the development of a multicultural community of the spirit of women through feminist education.[9]

A legacy of this "spirit of community" undergirds a recent book on feminist artists. *Expanding Circles: Women, Art & Community*, edited by Betty Ann Brown, explores community in its diversity:

> People must be given images of different kinds of communities, of communities that are neither patriarchal nor hierarchical, neither authoritarian nor demeaning. Communities that honor the authority of lived experience. Communities that give voice to those often silenced...We write about alternative definitions and identifications of community, about using art and art processes to build community.... We write about community as any group of two or more people who live and/or work together.[10]

Most feminist concepts of community stressed the inclusiveness while trying to pay at least lip service to diversity. However, the question of just how all-inclusive the various feminist movements and institutions of the twentieth century were dominated much of late-twentieth-century feminist writings. Although subject positions have changed as situations change, it is safe to say that any number of self-defined groups have claimed to have been marginalized by "the women's movements": lesbians, bisexuals, transgendered peoples, working-class women, mothers, older women, and the disabled. One such segment of women that has been highly vocal on this matter is the congeries of the various groups that constitute the totalized category "women of color."

One of the problems of feminism and race was the raised expectation based on feminists' *claims* of inclusivity, egalitarianism and the openness and tolerance of "difference" within the moral community.[11] These claims were made despite that fact that schisms of race, class, ethnicity, religion, culture, sexuality, abilities and age permeated the larger society out of which the women's movements had emerged. The ideals of inclusivity were more like wishful thinking, without a clear analysis of what actions might be required to make the vision a reality, or a full understanding of the conditions that created those divisions. With hindsight one is struck by the impossibility of that goal of all-inclusiveness.

Like many feminist institutions of its day, the pioneer members of the Woman's Building of Los Angeles stressed a spirit of community: social relations among members based on ethics and values related to perceived feminist principles. The Woman's Building cofounder Arlene Raven expressed it this way:

> The purpose of feminist education is to create and participate in cultural revolution. Towards that end, feminist creative activity takes place in the context of a community in which women can support one another, validate individual and common experience, create from that experience, and share their work with the public...When women are primarily in a feminist support community, their work reflects female/female support and the different sense of identity which one has in that situation. This is a new and different kind of art, reflecting a new social structure—feminist community structure.[12]

Is Anyone at Home?

In 1983, Arlene Raven curated a show at the Long Beach Museum of Art that celebrated the tenth anniversary of *Womanhouse*, the first of the large 1970s feminist art exhibitions/installations/performances.[13] Raven titled the exhibition "At Home," an ironic reference to the ambivalent embracing of the "home/house" icon and theme by many seventies feminists.[14] An ironic reading of both the "At Home" show and *Womanhouse,* of a decade earlier, questions the safety of the home. Was it a refuge for everyone who dwelled there?

For the purposes of this essay, the ironic reading of "home/house" begs the question of who experienced the Woman's Building and any number of feminist safe spaces as hospitable. Did all feminists and women feel "at home?"

∞∞∞∞

The Woman's Building in Los Angeles took its name from the Woman's Building of the 1893 Columbian Exposition in Chicago.[15] Both projects explored women as "artists," a role that had been historically male in Western society. The Los Angeles institution, founded by Judy Chicago, Sheila de Bretteville, and Arlene Raven to "expand women's ability to express themselves individually and collectively and to communicate their experience through art," served for eighteen years as one of the nation's primary centers for feminist art movements and the main one in southern California.[16]

While always struggling for funding and hardly a prosperous arts institution, the Woman's Building was, nonetheless, better endowed than a number of even more fledgling institutions, especially those organized by women artists of color. It was especially difficult, then, for feminist artists of color to ignore or avoid the Woman's Building. Yet, the claims of "community" expounded by Woman's Building founders, staff and denizens set forth a tension that was to plague the house.

The concept of "community" permeated the doctrine and many of the practices of the Woman's Building. Co-founder Chicago envisioned the Woman's Building as a supportive community that would nurture women's development as artists and provide an appreciative audience for an art that explores women's experiences.[17] Some feminist artists even moved from other cities to take part in the enterprise.[18]

Therefore, establishing a site and supporting women artists were not the only goals. The founders and early participants held a loftier and more elusive ideal: the establishment of a very special "community."[19] Perhaps no one concept was as important to the Woman's Building founders and initial denizens as "community." In this sense, the Woman's Building reflected one of the cluster of goals of "second-wave" feminism: e.g., to build a moral community of women; to maintain the connection between academy and community; to build and expand community through coalitions; to develop a nonhierarchical community; and to mobilize the community toward change.

The problem was (and still is, to a large extent) the totalizing of the concept of "community," as if it were monolithic (or should be), and the cultural hegemony that held sway. Who had the authority to decide what a community was, to *name* the community, to categorize it, and to decide how it should be structured and who was part of it?

Within the context of Los Angeles feminists, the Woman's Building itself was often referred to as a "community." Yet "community" as a concept was only partially defined, and beyond the idealistic expressions in the early years, was under-theorized.

Actually the Woman's Building consisted of several "communities," some of which overlapped. These included founders, faculty, administrators and staff, Feminist Studio Workshop (FSW) students, Extension Program students, specific program/projects/collaborative groups (e.g., Lesbian Art Project, Women's Graphic Center, Women's Video Center, and Feminist Art Workers/Sisters Of Survival), the Board of Directors, and regular audience members. These "communities" defined a series of concentric circles, with those who spent the most time on the premises or took responsibility for its operations serving as "insiders," and those who attended more occasionally often feeling more like "outsiders."

Crosscutting and overlapping with the above were also communities based on ideologies, fragments of which affected community-building at the Woman's Building. After all, this was 1970s feminism—with its splits between and among liberal, radical and socialist feminists (and divisions within these); the "lesbian-straight" split; class divisions; and Jewish/non-Jewish. Within Los Angeles there was even a historical regional division between east-siders (e.g., those who lived in Echo Park and Silver Lake areas) and west-siders (e.g., from Santa Monica and Venice). The former were considered more political and leftist; the latter, more cultural. The Woman's Building was on the eastside and drew from an array of eastside feminists. Yet, its constituency, contrary to the conventional local wisdom at the time, was considered more "cultural feminist" than leftist feminist. Such were the contradictions of the feminisms of the times.

It goes without saying that the essentialized and totalized category of "women of color" had its own divisions, not only ethnic/race, but also class, sexuality, and generation. Furthermore, there existed strong differences about the degree of cooperation and participation with white/Anglo women that would be deemed appropriate or strategically sound. Therefore, while some women of color insisted on inclusion in an institution like the Woman's Building, others favored forming their own communities and institutions. One of the problems, as indicated above, was that the separatist institutions had an even more difficult time with funding and often ended up as "poor sisters" to the ostensibly better endowed institutions dominated by white women.

If the extent of compensatory or corrective programming was any measure of the disaffection or dislocation that many women of color felt about their association with the Woman's Building, then the problem was great. Through the years the Woman's Building staff, board of directors, program committee, and participating artists worked on issues of racism in their programming.[20] It was highly unlikely, however, that an organization like the Woman's Building could resolve a series of problems that the movement(s) as a whole were unable to resolve, or even to address adequately. In the end, only those women of color who shared a similar perspective on feminism as the predominantly white Woman's Building members became heavily involved in the organization.

Were Women of Color at Home?

Although feelings about racism were an undercurrent at the Woman's Building in the late 1970s, as in a number of feminist organizations throughout the country, it was not until the Woman's Building began receiving funds under the Comprehensive Education and Training Act (CETA), that racism surfaced as an issue.[21] Many of the women eligible for employment under this program in Los Angeles were women of color. Although CETA funds provided the Woman's Building with the ability to hire support staff, many of the women of color who were hired were not in positions of authority. This situation ultimately led to charges of racism against one white staff member in particular. Ironically, members of the Woman's Building had sought CETA funding not only to increase their budget, but also because they wanted to draw more women of color to the Woman's Building. They further hoped that the new staff members' friends and families would become involved in the Building. Even when women of color were hired in "executive" positions, the integration of newcomers was difficult and conflicts ensued.

Unexpectedly, the CETA program transformed the issue of racism at the Woman's Building from an abstract discussion to a concrete and more visible situation. Member Annette Hunt points out that prior to the CETA programs, the Woman's Building dealt with the issue of racism as a "rhetorical question—we could all sit around [and] wonder why don't we have more black women here? How are we going to reach more black women, Hispanic women, Asian women?"[22]

The introduction of women of color to the organization grew increasingly tense. Under the auspices of the CETA program, Meg Henson-Flores, an African-American woman, joined the Woman's Building as the managing editor of *Spinning Off*, the monthly publication of the Woman's Building.

Henson-Flores ultimately filed a grievance against Sue Maberry, a longtime member of the Woman's Building who had attended the FSW and served in various administrative capacities over the years. The grievance stemmed from an incident in which Henson-Flores was complaining to a colleague about "the usurping of [her] authority as managing editor." She claimed that Maberry, overhearing the conversation, "wheeled around in her chair and loudly, abusively and disrespectfully demanded that [Henson-Flores] leave 'her' office and 'shut up!'"[23] Henson-Flores accused Maberry of repeatedly "being wholly offensive, accusative, and disrespectful" to the increasing number of black women in the organization.[24] In a written grievance to the Woman's Building Board of Directors, Henson-Flores described the racial climate of the Woman's Building as "abhorrent."[25] In the same document she suggested the establishment of guidelines and disciplinary procedures "to control the mad actions on the part of those abusive women."[26]

Maurine Renville, then executive director of the Woman's Building, responded to Henson-Flores's grievance by conducting an evaluation of Maberry in which it was concluded that Maberry "needs to work on developing tolerance and other ways of communicating with people new to the Woman's Building who do not maintain the same level of commitment and working styles."[27] While acknowledging the need for improvement, this "criticism," nonetheless was an implicit validation of Maberry's unswerving commitment to the Woman's Building. The board "resolved" the problem by lessening Maberry's involvement with *Spinning Off*—and hence Henson-Flores—and relocating Maberry's office to a more remote location. The administrators "communicated to Meg that these actions were taken to remove responsibility from Sue, easing pressure and stress that resulted in her response to the overheard conversation."[28] Nothing was mentioned about racism, despite Henson-Flores's accusations.

Henson-Flores continued to press the members of the Woman's Building to address racism. In a letter to the executive director, she requested that a forum be held about racism at the Woman's Building. She requested also that minutes from that forum become part of the permanent archive of the Building.[29]

Despite Henson-Flores's insistence on a greater problem of racism at the Woman's Building, the people in authority recast the problem as a difficulty between a newcomer and a longtime member of the Woman's Building. This was a fairly common rationale in feminist organizations of the 1970s and 1980s.

According to personnel records, Henson-Flores continued to arrive late for work and ultimately was fired in 1980.[30] She reported the Woman's Building to the California Department of Fair Employment for substandard working conditions. Ironically, by that time Suzanne Shelton, a woman of color, had become executive director and she had to respond to Henson-Flores's accusations.[31]

Because of conflicting stories, it is difficult to ascertain what actually happened in the conflict between Henson-Flores and Maberry and what the motivations were behind it. There is no way to know for sure whether Henson-Flores's firing resulted from racism, poor performance, or retaliation for her complaints.

Clearly, perceptions of racism were a problem at the Woman's Building. However, conflicts between newcomers to the Woman's Building and long-time members occurred frequently, even among white women. It is likely that the issues of racism exacerbated an already existing tension at the building between "insiders" and "outsiders." A case in point was the situation that developed after Valerie Angers, a white woman, became part of the Woman's Building "community" in 1977 as building manager. Angers joined the Woman's Building as part of a group of women who founded the magazine *Chrysalis*.[32]

As an "outsider," Angers faced considerable challenges as building manager, and eventually her tenure at the Woman's Building came to a close. In her letter of resignation, Angers argued that the existence of a closed community within the Woman's Building impeded effective management and that the "coziness" often translated into hostility toward those who did not have a long history with the Woman's Building.

Because of her relatively short history with the Woman's Building, longtime members attributed her criticisms to her inability to understand the organization.[33]

Renville, too, although an "insider," had conflicts with longtime members of the Woman's Building when she constituted a new board of directors. Longtime members of the Woman's Building saw the new board members as "corporate women."[34] Sharon Sidell-Selick quotes one of the Woman's Building founders: "What we got [with the appointment of a new board] was a Board who … did not understand the Building, did not like the Building, [and] had a vision of trying to push the Building more into the mainstream scene in order to be acceptable."[35]

In 1980 the Woman's Building hired Shelton, an African-American woman, as executive director.[36] The board of directors hired Shelton because they hoped she would bring more women of color into the organization. Such high expectations only compounded the difficulties Shelton experienced as an "outsider" at the Woman's Building. Even Sheila de Bretteville, the most outspoken advocate of making the Building accessible to outsiders, "always believed it would never work to have somebody be the executive director who wasn't someone who had been through the Building experience, because they couldn't understand what it was they were directing."[37]

From the beginning Shelton, like all the other administrators, had little autonomy, despite her title of executive director. For example, she hired Terry Wolverton as her administrative assistant, but under pressure from other Woman's Building staff.[38] These conflicts over the autonomy of the executive director prevailed throughout Shelton's tenure at the Woman's Building. Shelton also experienced difficulties meeting the high expectations many of the staff members had that were partially based on her being paid more than anyone else; she earned $18,000 a year as compared to their $6 an hour salaries.[39] Longtime members of the staff behaved as though Shelton worked for them, which in a sense she did. Despite her official position of authority, many of those who had participated in the decision to hire her had more influence than she did.

Shelton saw her mission as clearly defined. In an article written five weeks after she assumed the position of executive director, Shelton outlined her three major goals: to create a secure financial base, to increase the visibility of the Woman's Building, and to involve a more diverse group of women.[40] Five months later, at a board retreat, Shelton had lost much of her enthusiasm. She outlined twelve major problems, many of which had been voiced by previous administrators; these included the lack of leadership by the board, an inability of the board and staff to work together, and a distrust of the executive director by the staff.[41] Further exacerbating the situation, financial difficulties persisted, which perpetuated a crisis mentality.

Some of the issues Shelton raised demonstrated her ideological differences with the founding vision of the Woman's Building. For example, she saw the original description of the Woman's Building—"a public center for women's culture," which served as the unofficial motto for the organization—as "vague and passive." She suggested re-casting the statement of purpose in more active terms, to say what they hoped to "change, alter, affect." She also suggested a shift in programming from an emphasis on process to product, which contravened the very notion of feminist art that the Woman's Building pioneered.[42]

While Shelton may have been correct that the message was not selling any more, her suggestions were anathema to longtime supporters of the Woman's Building. In her literal inability to speak the language of the Woman's Building, she interpreted the emphasis on consensus as a euphemism for the stifling of disagreement, individuality, and initiative, and she heard "accountability" as a mistrust of outsiders.[43] The Woman's Building was predicated on a shared experience and similar values, which Shelton had not had and did not hold.

No matter how hard she worked, Shelton could not integrate into the organization. As her assistant, Terry Wolverton saw a tension between Shelton setting new goals and the board members and other staff—women with long-standing connections to the building—trying to preserve the status quo. In retrospect, Wolverton, a longtime Woman's Building member and administrator, realized that "what they really wanted was a woman of color to come in and really just be a part of the spirit and the vision of the Building as it existed. But the trouble was that this particular woman of color—and probably any woman of color—would have had a slightly different version and a different agenda of what the Building would, could or should be."[44] Sidell-Selick quotes an unnamed Feminist Studio Workshop staff member who was commenting on the Woman's Building's attempt to integrate a black director into a white institution:

> A very disastrous dynamic got started. The staff, not operating out of malicious or deliberate but a very unconscious racism, was unable to see that she [the executive director] was working in the best interests of the Building…We couldn't figure out how to bring in women from different backgrounds and welcome them to the Building. We didn't know how to listen from a different perspective. There has been a lot of lip service about being open to all women but that really isn't true. The Building has a definite cultural personality that defines who can be in it.[45]

Although on the surface it would appear that efforts to remedy racism at the Woman's Building by simply hiring more women of color failed, that is, no doubt, too facile. The conflicts that ensued must have served to raise the consciousness of the Woman's Building staffers and board, perhaps imperceptibly altering the goals and practices of denizens. Nonetheless, armed with the best of intentions, most of the members of the Building did not understand or refused to acknowledge that bringing women of color into the organization would necessitate a change in the mission of the Woman's Building.

Tensions over racism continually exacerbated the already-existing difficulties anyone new to the Woman's Building experienced in trying to gain acceptance. As Cherríe Moraga points out in *This Bridge Called My Back*, "there is seldom any analysis of how the very nature and structure of the group itself may be founded on racist or classist assumptions."[46] Without such an analysis, the women of color recruited into the organization could only function as token figureheads. Failing to consider the racism implicit in the mission and structure of the Woman's Building contributed to its inability to serve as a home for all women.

Anti-Racism Work at the Woman's Building

It was not the recruitment of women of color into the staff of the Woman's Building that was to draw attention to the issue of racism at the Woman's Building. Ironically, it was through criticism of a show dedicated to lesbian art that the issue of racism finally received concerted attention.

In December 1979, members of the Woman's Building began organizing "The Great American Lesbian Art Show" (GALAS). From its inception GALAS made a particular effort to recruit lesbians of color. In the initial letter about GALAS, the organizers explained, "We recognize that for women of color, the difficulties of identifying both as 'artist' and 'lesbian' are significantly greater."[47] In February 1980, the GALAS Collective sent a press release announcing that two spots in the GALAS Invitational would be reserved for Black and Latina lesbians. The organizers of GALAS also worked with a local Los Angeles group, Lesbians of Color, to recruit art by women of color. Despite these efforts, the organizers of GALAS still received considerable criticism of their show as racist.[48]

In 1980, spurred by the criticisms of GALAS and by her own recognition that "it was impossible to live in this culture and not be racist," Terry Wolverton began focusing on white women's anti-racism work.

Wolverton approached the issue of racism as she had the topic of homophobia: she turned to her feminist background for techniques to address these issues. She had discovered an article that provoked "a classic women's movement experience: reading just the right articulation of theory at just the time I needed to move to a new level of consciousness and action."[49] Wolverton had decided to create a white women's consciousness-raising group devoted to anti-racism. She chose to form a group for white women only so that she could "do [her] homework" rather than relying on women of color to raise consciousness for her. Seven women responded to the initial announcement that she placed in *Spinning Off*.[50]

The White Women's Anti-Racism Consciousness-Raising Group formed in the fall of 1980.[51] During the consciousness-raising sessions the women examined their emotions when addressing racism and discussed how feelings of guilt or embarrassment hampered their efforts to combat it. Exploring the ways that children learn

Gloria Longval, *Amor*, 1980. Charcoal and colored pencils, 41 " x 33". Collection of Michelle Smith. Photograph by Slobodan Dimitrov. © 1980 Gloria Longval.

Artist demonstrating
needlework as part of
the exhibition *Textiles
as Text: Arts of Hmong
Women from Laos*, 1986.
Woman's Building Image
Archive, Otis College of
Art and Design.

racism, they analyzed their own early experiences with racism. They also discussed the ways language reflects hierarchical relationships between different races. Several sessions were devoted to evaluating their personal relationships with people of color.

Gradually the group moved beyond consciousness-raising to problem-solving and action. Some concentrated on incorporating more women of color into the Woman's Building, developing an affirmative action program for staff, board, and artists represented in the institution. The members of the action group also attempted to increase staff members' consciousness about racism. They asked the staff to work collectively to compile lists of (1) the ways racism limited them, (2) the benefits that would result in having more women of color working at the Women's Graphic Center, (3) the ways they might achieve greater representation by women of color, (4) the difficulties in reaching their goal of including more women of color, and (5) the ways they each might contribute to this effort.

Efforts to raise consciousness about racism at the Woman's Building had a positive impact. Maberry recalled that prior to the work on anti-racism at the Woman's Building, "There wasn't any way you could talk about your own racist feelings or what it meant to be racist or what was racism and what wasn't."[52]

Other Strategies

Although consciousness-raising may be a necessary condition for altering race dynamics within an organization, it is not a sufficient condition for transformation. While it is true that white women within the organization had come to a greater understanding of their own racism, the Woman's Building, as an organization, retained the same structure, and only broadened its goals to include more women of color. Ultimately, this limited change meant that the Woman's Building would never successfully attract large numbers of women of color.

As early as 1977, there had been a recognition that lack of financial resources might impede the participation of women of color; organizers sought grant funding for scholarships. The Woman's Building received funding from the National Endowment for the Arts to increase the participation of women over fifty, disabled women, and women of color. The New Moves Program offered scholarships to women wishing to participate in various Woman's Building programs. A woman of color who participated in the 1980 Summer Art Program reported:

> [A]fter seven weeks, I had come to view my own and other women's feelings and thoughts as sources of power—a power that could transform the way we looked at ourselves and related to our environments. As a result of the photography and video experience I gained, I made an important career transition and I'm now studying cinema at [Los Angeles] City College.[53]

Advertising for the New Moves Program stressed that the women's movement was for all women. In an effort to recruit a more diverse constituency, the Woman's Building offered programming and activities that reflected the needs and interests of women of color. During the 1980–81 academic year, the education programs primarily sought to reach populations not previously served by the Woman's Building, while also creating relationships with organizations that served communities of color.

In addressing the Asian American community, Woman's Building planners, working with the Asian American Studies Program at the University of California, Los Angeles (UCLA), developed contacts with the Asian American press, and received good coverage of Woman's Building events. The Woman's Building offered an Asian women's history course, poetry readings and writing workshops for Asian-American women. A performance by Unbound Feet, an Asian American performance group, drew two hundred people to the Woman's Building.[54]

Coincident with a greater emphasis within the Woman's Building of the need to answer the charge of racism and exclusion, the political times had changed. During the 1980s members of the Woman's Building struggled to adapt the concept of women's culture and women's community to an increasingly conservative political context. The leaders of the Woman's Building began to emphasize its function as an arts organization for women rather than as a feminist organization. Tragically, in the early 1980s, the Reagan Administration gutted funding for the National Endowment for the Arts, along with the CETA IV employment program, and made it next to impossible to provide the kind of financial support or employment opportunities to encourage participation by women of color. Increasingly, in the 1980s programs at the Woman's Building focused on generating income. This focus on financial survival of the Woman's Building above all else severely hampered efforts to address the issue of racism and to create a climate that was more hospitable to groups of women. Instead of concentrating on building a community, the Woman's Building began to create a more mainstream image in order to pursue more traditional funding sources.

This shift in the mission of the Woman's Building was deeply troubling to some members. Aleida Rodríguez, a Cuban émigré who served on the board of directors from 1981 to 1983, denounced this trend in her acceptance speech upon receiving a Vesta Award in 1984. Rodríguez ultimately left the Woman's Building over the change in emphasis and perceived mainstreaming.[55]

In the mid- to late 1980s, the Woman's Building became more financially stable and renewed its charge to expand the diversity of the organization. In 1986, the Woman's Building hosted "Textiles as Text," an exhibit of art by Hmong refugees, accompanied by a cultural festival; in 1987, it presented exhibits by African-American artist Faith Ringgold and "Viva La Vida," works in homage to artist Frida Kahlo.

In 1990, the Woman's Building conducted a survey of ten Latino cultural organizations to explore the needs of Latina artists. This included conducting informa-

Diane Gamboa and Daniel J. Martinez standing with Gamboa's poster, *Vida,* **at the "Cross Pollination" exhibition**, Bridge Gallery, Los Angeles City Hall, 1986. © Diane Gamboa.

tional interviews at each of the ten organizations to obtain programming information and to offer the Woman's Building as a resource for Latina artists. In October of 1990, the Woman's Building produced "El Dia de Los Muertos," an exhibition of the works of four Latina artists—Laura Aguilar, Barbara Carrasco, Diane Gamboa, and Rose Portillo—along with a videotape of the same title, produced by two Latinas. In addition, the Woman's Building hosted a fiesta complete with three-piece *Norteño* band, a Mexican banquet, and altars where the audience could participated by offering a memorial to their loved ones. Approximately three hundred people attended the opening, and some one thousand viewed the exhibition during its six-week run. Although the group had hoped to produce bilingual brochures and a videotape, instead, in March of 1991, the Woman's Building sponsored Espejo Voz, a bilingual reading of the works of fifteen Latina writers. Ninety-five people attended this event.

Despite these outreach and programming efforts, the Woman's Building was still never able to recruit large numbers of women of color. While the notion of "outreach" to women of color represented an impulse to integrate organizations, some women of color found the concept and practice patronizing. As Cherríe Moraga points out: "We have had it with the word 'outreach' referring to our joining racist white women's organizations. The question keeps coming up—where exactly then, is in?"[56] How included could women of color be in the mission of groups if such "outreach"

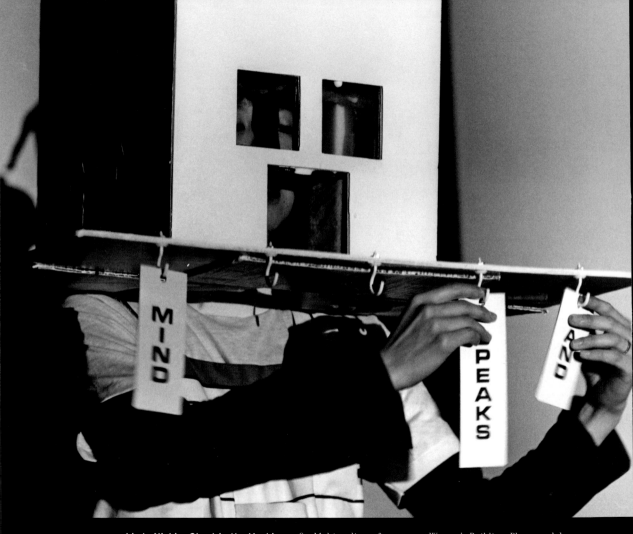

**Linda Nishio, *Ghost in the Machine*, 1983. Multimedia performance at Woman's Building. Photograph by Sheila Ruth. Woman's Building Image Archive, Otis College of Art and Design.

proved necessary? Furthermore, the idea of outreach focused on bringing women of color into the organization as currently constituted, seemingly without consideration for a need for transformation partially brought about by the new needs, goals, and ideologies of women of color.

During its last years, Woman's Building programmers took a number of opportunities to develop programming that would speak to the needs, tastes, or politics of women of color. These endeavors became increasingly sophisticated. Sometimes the program committee capitalized on a controversy, trying to turn a negative event into a positive exploration of racism, diversity, and multiculturalism. Such a controversy surrounded Kate Braverman's Woman's Building reading from her novel *Palm Latitudes*. Braverman, a white woman, spoke from the vantage point of her protagonist, a Chicana. Women of color connected with the Woman's Building challenged the appropriation of a Chicana's voice, and the matter generated heated and healthy discussion about whether or not artists and writers must speak only from their own voices and positionality in terms of ethnicity, race, gender, age, region, class, and sexuality. The discussions, formal and informal, led to a three-part symposium (May 11, 18, and 25, 1989) on "In Whose Voice, In Whose Vision: Culture and Representation." The symposium participants were highly diverse, as was the audience.

Some Women of Color at Home

As discussed above, while many new members of the Woman's Building struggled to find a place within the existing organization, because the Woman's Building was founded by white women, it seemed inevitable that the mission of the institution would more closely fulfill the needs of white women. However, like all such generalizations, things were not so simple. In matters related to social movements and organizational activities, there is often a contrast between what transpires in public forums and organizational disputes and people's individual experiences. Therefore, despite controversy about racism and exclusion, some women of color found the Woman's Building a hospitable place for their art and a supportive environment for them personally.

However, in analyzing the Woman's Building Oral History Project material to explain why some women of color found a community at the Woman's Building, one can see a pattern. I would argue that the women of color who felt most at home and a part of the Woman's Building community all shared the predominant vision of feminist art held by members of the Woman's Building. An exploration of the ideas of some of the women of color who became involved in the Woman's Building supports this argument.

Linda Nishio, a Japanese American artist, began participating in the Woman's Building in the late 1970s after working as an artist for a number of years. She had had formal art education and held a Master of Fine Arts degree. After attending a performance at the Woman's Building, Nishio recalled that she initiated contact with Vanalyne Green, whose performance she had admired. The women became friends, and Green, a white woman, championed Nishio's work. The support led to the inclusion of Nishio's art in several shows. Nishio also found the design work produced by the Women's Graphic Center (WGC) intriguing and, even though the WGC had no job openings, convinced the staff to hire her. She worked there for the next seven years.

Several factors contributed to the ease with which Nishio entered the Woman's Building. Because the friendship network was the most powerful structure within the Woman's Building, Nishio gained access to influential members when she made friends with Green. Nishio felt comfortable enough with her identity as an artist to contact a white member of the Woman's Building about her art. She also possessed the self-confidence to aggressively pursue employment at the Woman's Building, the fastest track to the "in" group in this organization. It is interesting to note that Nishio did not arrive at the Woman's Building as a result of any outreach program, but came because she found the Woman's Building attractive to her interests.

Nishio's work also resonated well with the other art produced by members of the Woman's Building. Nishio recalled identifying with the work performed at the Woman's Building because much of her work dealt with personal exploration, so that she felt "some camaraderie of support among the people there."[57] However, an analysis of Nishio's art during this period illustrates her struggle to address issues of inclusiveness of the woman's movement. Through her art Nishio seemed to search for her "place in the world." In *Ghost in the Machine*, a short film, Nishio appeared with a cardboard house on top of her head. The house kept trying to locate itself in different neighborhoods, but it never quite fit in, an experience paralleled by many women of color in the women's movement.

However, the metaphor of the house or room was also an apt symbol for many of the white women at the Woman's Building. When Nishio entered the Woman's Building milieu, she was well educated, already had a strong art background, and was experimenting with avant-garde art herself. Despite being a woman of color, she was "like" the women at the Woman's Building in her approach to art. Although her work addressed the "exclusiveness" of the women's movement, she made art that spoke intelligibly to members of the Woman's Building. When asked about her attraction to the Woman's Building, Nishio repeatedly expressed a sense of identification with the subject matter dealt with by artists at the Woman's Building. For example, when asked what appealed to her about the Woman's Building, she responded: "It was the performance that on a personal level I felt very much akin to, because a lot of my work was about personal exploration, text and projected film.... I think it was just the identification with the kind of work being done that really drew me to the group."[58]

Even though she was one of the few women of color involved in the Woman's Building at that point, Nishio was accustomed to that situation. She explained, "For me that was the way the world has been." When asked how her involvement in the Woman's Building influenced her work, she commented, "I think what I gained more than contextually ... was a sense of pride about the work, more internal stuff, confidence, self-confidence, the camaraderie among people and I think the self-confidence ... to continue to make art."

As for a sense of community, although Nishio did not use that term, she did describe the Woman's Building as a supportive environment for more than her art: "Actually, I should also say to you that back in '82 my first husband died, and when I was at the Woman's Building it was really an incredible place for me to be at the time, a lot of support and a lot of growth [happened] for me during that time."

While Nishio came to the Woman's Building an accomplished artist, Rosalie Ortega was involved with Woman's Building first as support staff and only many years later as an artist. She came from a Mexican American family who raised her with little acknowledgement of Mexican or Mexican American cultural traditions. Her mother pushed her children to assimilate by speaking English only, moving them to a white suburb of Los Angeles, and teaching them nothing of their cultural heritage. Ortega recalled that her childhood experiences were most similar to those of a suburban housewife. After her parents divorced (when she was twelve), her mother began working outside the home and Ortega assumed responsibility for running the household. She remembered reading *The Feminine Mystique* and relating to the complaints of middle-aged, white, suburban housewives, despite the fact that she was sixteen years old.

Although Ortega did not become involved in any political movements during high school, she read Eldridge Cleaver and Malcolm X and was intrigued by their ideas; she had no knowledge of the Chicano movement. In fact, until Ortega attended an interview for a merit-based scholarship at UCLA, and the interviewer suggested she apply for funds available to Chicanos, Ortega had "[never] really heard that word in relationship to myself."[59]

While attending UCLA, Ortega worked in the childcare center where she met a member of the Woman's Building who introduced Ortega to the organization. Ortega attended a women's music concert at the Woman's Building and then started providing childcare for Woman's Building events. Although Ortega remembers finding the programs offered at the Woman's Building intriguing, she only felt comfortable participating as a childcare provider.

Ortega also became involved in Califia, initially through her childcare work, but eventually as a collective member. She believes, in retrospect, that Califia offered her membership in the collective as part of their effort to increase representation of women of color.

Ironically, it was within the women's movement that Ortega first felt the disparities between her upbringing and the expectations feminists had for a "woman of color," an identity Ortega did not feel described herself. Ortega felt she had "no place to belong" because she did not share the cultural experiences of the other Latinas. She recalled a Califia retreat for women of color in San Diego where she felt quite uncomfortable: "I had no idea about [the women of color's] anger and their experience and was just so confused, and knew deep in my heart that I wasn't a part of them and they wanted me to be, but I wasn't comfortable there. I was more comfortable with the white women, yet I wasn't supposed to be a part of that group."

When a member of Califia accused Ortega of "not knowing who [she] was" in terms of her cultural heritage, Ortega felt so attacked she ceased involvement with the women's movement for several years. During this time, she completed her education and became an artist. Ortega then entered into a second phase of involvement with the Woman's Building, this time as an artist rather than as support staff. She continued to receive information from the Woman's Building and felt drawn to events, but felt "there was something really holding [her] back." Her fear of rejection within the women's movement remained strong, but was overcome by her curiosity about a seminar on women's spirituality.

The curiosity resulted in Ortega attending a presentation by Circle of Aradia, a feminist Wicca coven. She enjoyed the presentation so much that she enrolled in a series of workshops that the Circle of Aradia offered. Within the Circle of Aradia, Ortega finally found the acceptance she had sought. She felt that the Circle of Aradia provided her with a place to heal from her negative experiences with feminism. She joined a coven where she was, "as usual in these groups," the only person of color, but in this situation dealt with it in a different way. As she described the transformative experience: "I think that what I gained from that was a sense of myself as an artist, as a woman with my own spirituality, as a leader." She felt she belonged: "What I loved about their group was that you could be a lot of different things. You could be lesbian, you could be straight. You could be a person of color. You could be whatever it was and it really was okay … it was really a great place for me … It really helped me grow a lot."

Ortega began working as an artist and was invited to serve on the board of directors of the Woman's Building in the late 1980s. She recalls that initially some of the other board members were uncomfortable with her "touchy feely women's spirituality." Unlike her experience with Califia, this time Ortega felt strong enough to resist opposition to her viewpoint and continued to voice her feelings.

For someone like Ortega, the Woman's Building existed first as a symbol, as a place where women could explore feminism. As she grew as an artist, the Woman's Building gradually came to provide a second function in her life, this time as an arena where she could make her own unique contribution to feminism, without having to apologize for her perspective as a woman of color or as a witch. She commented on the spiritual meaning of the Woman's Building for her:

> I've had very indirect involvement with the …physical Building [itself], yet it has …done some incredible things for me in my life. And I think that, maybe that is how some institutions should be. That they are not

just about the physicalness and going in there and doing things, but some things…can have impact that goes beyond that. And I suspect it impacted a lot of other women's lives….Just knowing that it is there may have helped.

Unlike Rosalie Ortega, who learned about the Woman's Building while in college, Gloria Alvarez remembers being "really amazed to find the Woman's Building."[60] Although unversed in feminist art, Alvarez did come from a political family. She had helped organize a Movimiento Estudiantil Chicano de Aztlán chapter at her high school and was involved in student and community groups in college. She considered herself a participant in the Chicano movement and wanted "to take an active role in doing something for my community." While in college she participated in Comision Femenil Mexica, a Chicana feminist organization, and after college went to work in social work, focusing on domestic and child abuse.

Alvarez heard about the Woman's Building from a friend. When she first visited the Woman's Building, she encountered Yolanda Alanis, a Chicana who worked as a receptionist. Alvarez learned about the scholarships available at the Woman's Building, and applied for and received several. She attended Mitsuye Yamada's poetry workshop and became involved with a video project headed by Jerri Allyn that produced public service announcements to raise awareness about forced sterilization, a topic with which Alvarez was already involved.

While Alvarez enjoyed the Woman's Building, as a full-time student and single mother, it was difficult for her to become very involved. Also, she felt real class differences existed at the Woman's Building. While she recognized some women at the Woman's Building really wanted to reach out to Latinas and working class women, she felt this was a somewhat limited group. She remembered having discussions with members of the Woman's Building about the different experiences women of color had with feminism. Alvarez was involved with a group, Lesbians of Color, who worked with the Woman's Building on racism. In part, Alvarez wanted to become involved with the Woman's Building in order to bring a Latina presence to the Woman's Building.

Alvarez, although not actively involved with the Woman's Building, maintained a membership so she would continue to receive information about activities. She searched for Latina names in the materials and when she read that Aleida Rodríguez was offering a writing workshop, she signed up for that group. She also occasionally received calls from members of the Woman's Building about participating in specific projects, usually centering on the video center. Alvarez remained friendly with several women from the Woman's Building, and in 1989 she approached Terry Wolverton, then executive director, about the possibility of conducting a series of workshops on Central American and Mexican immigrant women at the Woman's Building. Alvarez had conducted a few workshops in the community, but thought the Woman's Building was the perfect location for them.

She felt unsure about the reaction of members of the Woman's Building to hosting her workshop, but found, to her surprise, that the women not only wanted the group to use the Woman's Building, but that Wolverton would help her apply for grant funding. Alvarez became an artist-in-residence at the Woman's Building from 1989 to 1991. In addition to her workshops, Alvarez organized a Latina poetry festival and participated in a project to make the Woman's Building more responsive to the needs of Latinas. Although she found a warm reception at the Woman's Building, problems arose when her students telephoned the Woman's Building and no one could provide information in Spanish. Publicity materials were also printed in English only. Alvarez recalled that her students who did attend the Woman's Building "felt good that this was a place specifically for women." Alvarez believed that had the Woman's Building survived it would have become a more multicultural organization. However, she felt conflicted about the separatist aspects of the Woman's Building. While Alvarez recognized the value of women working with women only, she felt that, ultimately, women should also be working with men.

Although Alvarez was critical of some aspects of the Woman's Building and ambivalent about others, she, like so many women of color, was saddened by the closing. When asked about how she felt about the closing of the Woman's Building, she responded:

> Shocked. In a way I kind of took it personally...I kind of felt homeless. But I was really shocked because I felt like the Building was a place that was established and despite whatever problems I may have had with people who were there on staff, still...I thought this...can't happen...it was real hard to accept it...this was the only place spe-specifically for women.

Conclusion

While the anti-racism policies at the Woman's Building and the diversity programming made a difference in the organization, women of color remained reluctant to join the organization in large numbers. Despite early remedial efforts and later more profound and creative efforts, the middle and late history of the Woman's Building is similar to many feminist institutions during "second-wave feminism." Many women of color saw themselves as an afterthought, as add-ons, pawns in the process of tokenism.

Part of the problem at the Woman's Building stemmed from its origins in the mostly white, middle-class feminist movement. As Minnie Bruce Pratt points out, when a feminist organization "gets started by a non-diverse group; if the diversity is not in the planning sessions, a shift later, in how and what decisions are made, is exceedingly difficult."[61]

The repercussions of the Woman's Building having emerged from a mainly white movement and having been founded by all white women were compounded by the identity of the Woman's Building as an arts organization, since art is often seen as the domain of the elite in our society. Other feminist organizations that provided more basic services perhaps drew more women of color in need of them. Art, whether mistakenly or not, was seen as a luxury for many people and most of the poor. As a consequence, it was often the last concern of women of color. Barbara Smith has pointed out some of the problems in integrating identity politics into a concept of women's culture. She argues that women's culture explores and celebrates women's identity, and in that regard, tends to privilege gender over other aspects of identity. This approach privileges a universal oppression, either as lesbians or as women, that does not allow for the differing loci of oppression experienced by women of color and poor women. The authors disagree with Smith's assertion that "social-cultural" issues are somehow less important than "the more stringent realities of class and race."[62] This assessment merely reverses the hierarchy she accuses "cultural feminists" of creating.

Women of color, looking for a new "home" or community, could fit into the Woman's Building in limited ways. Some women, like Rosalie Ortega, felt they did not belong in the community of women of color, despite their matching skin tones. Ortega ultimately felt more comfortable among a mixed group of women. Other women, like Linda Nishio, found a niche in the Woman's Building as an artist already familiar with the spirit of feminist art created at the Woman's Building. Women like Gloria Alvarez may have been more typical, however. She went to the Woman's Building to enjoy the women-only space, but felt that the Woman's Building really was meant for white women. She found it hard to accept what she saw as the separatist aspects of the Woman's Building that potentially divided women of color from men of color.

Ultimately, it is difficult to separate the issue of racism at the Woman's Building from the insider/outsider conflicts discussed above. All new women experienced some degree of difficulty gaining acceptance at the Woman's Building. Over the years, the Woman's Building developed into a tight-knit group of women who assumed responsibility for the organization, making it difficult for any new members to acquire power, regardless of their skin color. Perhaps this division of insider/outsider is inherent in the very notion of community, feminist or not.

Whether or not the Woman's Building experience points to another example of a failure of community building in U.S. feminist movements, institutions, or organizations, in general, is a matter to be explored in another essay. The inability of the Woman's Building to create space for all women had the ironic result of creating that splendid isolation that Woolf craved, the room of one's own. Poet Eloise Klein Healy, a longtime Woman's Building member and leader, observed this final irony: "I feel like I've been sent to my room," she said about life after the Woman's Building, but the thought might just have easily been an ironic statement on isolation.[63]

As I have stressed throughout this essay, the travails of the Woman's Building in building community were not unique. One needs only to look at the recent histories of any number of feminist and progressive organizations to see the parallel with the Woman's Building. However, the spirit of community building and the efforts to confront and deal with racism are among the positive legacies of the Woman's Building and its contribution to the troubled and dynamic history of contemporary U.S. feminism and arts movements.

Notes

1. The play on "a room of her own" is an obvious reference to Virginia Woolf, *A Room of One's Own* (New York: Harcourt Brace Jovanovich, 1991 [1929]). If radical feminism finds its origins in the work of Simone de Beauvoir, then certainly Virginia Woolf stands as the mother of the feminist art movement.

2. This chapter is the result of a writing collaboration between Michelle Moravec and Sondra Hale. Michelle Moravec carried out the original research (oral histories and archival). Therefore, any time the personal voice is used it is Moravec's.

3. This is from a letter, dated April 15, 1975, that was sent to prospective students of the Feminist Studio Workshop (FSW). Woman's Building Collection, Archives of American Art, Smithsonian Institute, Washington, D.C. (hereafter referred to as Woman's Building Collection, Smithsonian Institute). The Woman's Building was founded to house the FSW, an educational program, along with galleries and other feminist enterprises.

4. The material for this essay was partially contained in Michelle Moravec's dissertation on the Woman's Building: "Building Women's Culture: Feminism and Art at the Los Angeles Woman's Building," PhD diss., University of California, Los Angeles, 1998. The work is partially based on interviews Moravec conducted as part of the Woman's Building Oral History Project from 1992 to 1999 in Los Angeles, California, except where otherwise noted. The project involved audio recording fifty interviews with selected participants in the Woman's Building over the years. At the time of publication, the tapes are in the collection of the Woman's Building Board of Directors, Los Angeles, CA. Unless otherwise stated, all interviews referred to were part of that project.

5. Terry Wolverton, ed., *The First Decade: Celebrating the Tenth Anniversary of the Woman's Building: A Pictorial History and Current Programs* (Los Angeles: Woman's Building, 1983). The Mission Statement is printed on the back cover; the quotes are from p. 8 and p. 6, respectively.

6. Charlotte Bunch, "A Note on Sagaris," in *Learning Our Way: Essays in Feminist Education*, ed. Bunch and Sandra Pollack (Trumansburg, NY: The Crossing Press, 1983), 114–15.

7. Jackie St. Joan, "The Ideas and the Realities: Sagaris, Session I," in Bunch and Pollack, 118.

8. Susan Sherman, "Women and Process: The Sagaris Split, Session II," in Bunch and Pollack, 133.

9. Marilyn Murphy, "Califia Community," in Bunch and Pollack, 130.

10. Betty Ann Brown, *Expanding Circles: Women, Art & Community* (New York: Midmarch Arts Press, 1996), vii.

11. "Moral community" refers here to an ethical community—that which is value-laden and is built on social and kin relations as contrasted to political or economic relations.

12. This is a quote from an unpublished work by Arlene Raven, "Notes on a Feminist Education." At the time, Raven was a member of the staff of the Feminist Studio Workshop. Quoted in Ruth Iskin, "Feminist Education at the Feminist Studio Workshop," in Bunch and Pollack, 72.

13. *Womanhouse* (Valencia: California Institute of the Arts, 1972).

14. Arlene Raven, ed., *At Home* (Long Beach, CA: Long Beach Museum of Art, 1983).

15. Undated flier in Moravec's possession. According to Faith Wilding, the Woman's Building received its name when "Nancy Youdelman... found an old book which turned out to be the catalog of the Woman's Building of the World's Columbian Exposition in Chicago 1893." The Wilding quote is from Faith Wilding, *By Our Own Hands: The Women Artist's Movement in Southern California, 1970–1976* (Santa Monica, CA: Double X, 1977), 61. See also Jeanne Madeline Weimann, *The Fair Women: The Story of the Woman's Building, World's Columbian Exposition* (Chicago: Academy Chicago, 1981).

16. Undated Woman's Building flier in Moravec's possession.

17. Judy Chicago, *Through the Flower: My Struggle as a Woman Artist* (New York: Doubleday and Company, 1975).

18. Terry Wolverton, interviewed by Moravec, Los Angeles, CA, July 30, 1992.

19. Most of the fifty Woman's Building participants Moravec interviewed as part of the Woman's Building Oral History Project mentioned the importance of community. While not always defining community (and there were many different kinds), it was clear that each respondent had a particular notion in mind.

20. There was, in fact, a great deal of programming that dealt with racism, cross-cultural issues, and the diversity of Los Angeles. One of the earliest efforts, in 1976, was a collaboration by Chicana muralists, led by Judy Baca, *Las Venas del las Mujeres*. In 1983, artist Linda Vallejo offered a printmaking project, *Madre Tierra*, for Latina artists and writers. *Cross-Pollination* (1986) was a project in which the Woman's Building commissioned twenty artists of diverse ethnic and cultural backgrounds to produce posters that reflected those cultures. A cross-cultural writers series was organized in 1987. "In Whose Voice?" (1990) attempted to deal with the issue of whether or not white women or any group should speak for women of another group in their artwork. Women of color also served as Artists-in-Residence, e.g. Gloria Alvarez in 1990. These are just a few of the programs that women of color instigated or the Woman's Building programmers organized in response to complaints or simply as part of their political agenda.

21. Sharon Sidell-Selick, in her study of Woman's Building management, *The Evolution of Organizational Meaning: A Case Study of Myths in Transition* (PhD diss., The Wright Institute, Berkeley, 1985), 77, comments on the irony of being able to hire more women of color, only to have it create more conflicts. See also Meg Henson-Flores, undated grievance petition, c.1979–80, Woman's Building Collection, Smithsonian Institute.

22. Annette Hunt, interviewed by Moravec, San Francisco, CA, August 8, 1992.

23. Henson-Flores.

24. Ibid.

25. Ibid.

26. Ibid.

27. Personnel Evaluation of Sue Maberry, February 1980. From the personal files of Sue Maberry.

28. Ibid.

29. Meg Henson-Flores to Maurine Renville, April 30, 1980. Woman's Building Collection, Smithsonian Institute. A professionally facilitated forum was held for staff in 1979 or 1980 (recollection of Terry Wolverton, e-mail correspondence, January 13, 1997).

30. Maurine Renville to Meg Henson-Flores, March 26, 1980. Woman's Building Collection, Smithsonian Institute.

31. See Notes by Suzanne Shelton, September 3, 1980, Woman's Building Collection, Smithsonian Institute.

32. *Chrysalis* occupied office space in the Woman's Building, and many members of the Woman's Building were involved with the production of the magazine. Previously, Angers had helped to found the Detroit Feminist Credit Union, an organization with a controversial history in the women's movement. For a concise history of the controversy over the feminist credit unions, see Alice Echols, *Daring to Be Bad: Radical Feminism in America, 1967–1975* (Minneapolis: University of Minnesota Press, 1989).

33. Woman's Building Staff Meeting Minutes, April 13, 1978, Woman's Building Collection, Smithsonian Institute.

34. Sue Maberry, interviewed by Moravec, Los Angeles, CA, September 9, 1992.

35. Sidell-Selick, 74.

36. "New Executive Director," *Spinning Off* (November 1, 1980), 1.

37. Sheila de Bretteville, interviewed by Moravec, August 12, 1992, Los Angeles, CA.

38. Terry Wolverton, interviewed by Moravec, July 30, 1992, Los Angeles, CA.

39. Maberry interview.

40. "New Executive Director," *Spinning Off* (November 1, 1980), 1.

41. Suzanne Shelton, "Vision Statement: Problems/Possible Solutions," c. March 1981, Woman's Building Collection, Smithsonian Institute.

42. Ibid.

43. Ibid.

44. Wolverton interview.

45. Sidell-Selick, 1985, 77, Moravec's italics. Sidell-Selick chose to make her respondents anonymous. Thus, we do not know if we are hearing a woman of color, a white woman, an insider, or an outsider. Nor has she dated her interviews so that we can temporally contextualize.

46. Cherríe Moraga, "La Guera," in *This Bridge Called My Back: Writings by Radical Women of Color*, ed. Moraga and Gloria Anzaldúa (New York: Kitchen Table, Women of Color Press, 1983), 33.

47. Bia Lowe, for the GALAS Collective, letter, December 21, 1979, Woman's Building Collection, Smithsonian Institute.

48. From interviews with GALAS participants: Bia Lowe Interview, November 19, 1992, Los Angeles, CA, and Terry Wolverton Interview, July 30, 1992, Los Angeles, CA. Some women of color threatened to boycott the show unless women of color were included.

49. Elly Bulkin, "Hard Ground: Jewish Identity, Racism, and Anti-Semitism," in *Yours in Struggle: Three Feminist Perspectives on Anti-Semitism and Racism*, Bulkin, Minnie Bruce Pratt, and Barbara Smith, eds. (Ithaca, NY: Firebrand Books, 1984), 89–153.

50. *Spinning Off* (October 6, 1980). Members of the group included Terry Wolverton, Bia Lowe, Mary-Linn Hughes, Tracy Moore, Cindy Cleary, and Ginny Kish. Later, Cyndi Kahn, Barbara Margolie, Jane Thurmond, Pat Carey, Jacqueline De Angelis, Judith Lausten, Patt Piese, and Louise Sherley joined. E-mail correspondence with Terry Wolverton, January 14, 1997.

51. Out of fourteen women involved in a white women's anti-racism workshop, eleven identified as lesbian. Of the three heterosexual women, two identified as Jewish. It may be that lesbians, because of their experiences of exclusion within the women's movement, may have heard the charges of racism against the women's movement with a less hostile ear and that Jews may have embraced "liberation by analogy." A similar argument has been made by Minnie Bruce Pratt, "Identity: Skin, Blood, Heart," in Bulkin et al, 20. However, Terry Wolverton, whose anti-racism work at the Woman's Building is discussed later, disagrees with this interpretation: "For me, the critical difference in [the] willingness [of lesbians working on racism at the Woman's Building] to receive feedback about racism did not have so much to do with being lesbians but with a developmental shift in theory about racisms. We'd been previously stunted by a simplistic analysis that 'Racism=bad, feminism=good, therefore feminists cannot be racist.' We felt we'd been oppressed as women, and could not therefore conceive of being powerful enough to oppress anyone else. If we owned up to racism, we lost our innocence (and our 'victimhood'!). But by 1980, there was starting to be some more sophisticated analysis about oppression, and the complex machinations of multiple strands of oppression (race, class, gender, sexual preference, physical ability) and that one could, in fact, occupy many different positions on those multiple spectra. This allowed us to see, as Elly Bulkin articulated, that the choice was not between racism and non-racism, but between racism and anti-racism. If lesbianism had anything to do with it, it was that within the lesbian community there was more opportunity for interaction across lines of race and class than there might be for heterosexual women in the larger community. Also, politicized lesbians had less investment in the status quo, and were more committed to recreating society and culture at a radical level, and might therefore be more embracing in their analysis." Moravec correspondence with Terry Wolverton, January 13, 1997.

52. Maberry interview, September 9, 1992.

53. Marte Jones from a Woman's Building flier, n.d., c. 1980, Woman's Building Collection, Smithsonian Institute.

54. Joan Watanabe taught in the Woman's Building graphic programs, and Helen Ly was a student in FSW.

55. Cheri Gaulke interviewed by Moravec, August 6, 1992. Other feminist organizations were also forced to resort to such mainstreaming and fundraising methods. For example, in late 1979, the Women's Action Collective, facing a financial crisis, transformed its house manager into a "development coordinator." Nancy Whittier, *Feminist Generations: The Persistence of the Radical Women's Movement* (Philadelphia: Temple University Press, 1995), 46.

56. Cherríe Moraga and Gloria Anzaldúa, "And When You Leave, Take Your Pictures With You: Racism in the Women's Movement, Introduction to Jo Carillo's Poem 'And When You Leave, Take Your Pictures with You,'" in Moraga and Anzaldúa, 61.

57. Linda Nishio, interviewed by Moravec, Pasadena, CA, December 13, 1992.

58. Ibid.

59. Rosalie Ortega, interviewed by Moravec, Pasadena, CA, December 12, 1992.

60. Gloria Alvarez, interviewed by Moravec, Los Angeles, CA, November 19, 1992.

61. Pratt, 51.

62. These comments were made as part of a sister-to-sister conversation between Barbara Smith and Beverly Smith, "Across the Kitchen Table: A Sister-to-Sister Dialogue, Barbara Smith and Beverly Smith," in Moraga and Anzaldúa, 113–27.

63. Woman's Building Oral History Project, October 2, 1992. Woman's Building Collection, Smithsonian Institute.

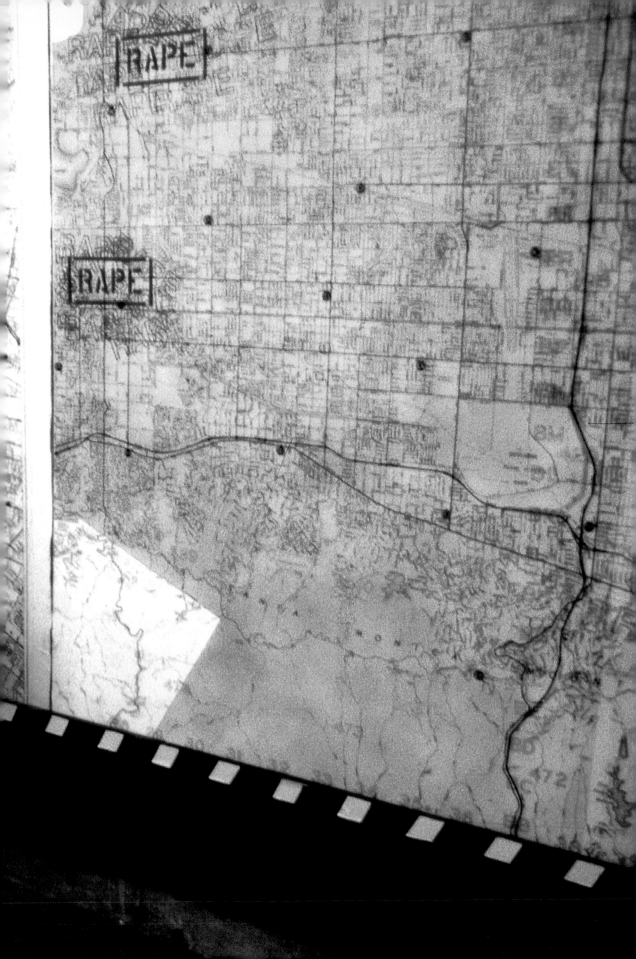

THE RITUAL BODY AS PEDAGOGICAL TOOL: THE PERFORMANCE ART OF THE WOMAN'S BUILDING

Jennie Klein

This essay is dedicated to the memory of Renee Edgington and Matt Francis.

Prologue

I would like to open this paper by recounting an experience that I had on the summer solstice of 1992, when I still lived in San Diego, the southernmost city in California. Because I had developed a local reputation as an art historian concerned with feminist issues, I was invited to a gathering of the Southern California chapter of the Women's Caucus for Art for the occasion of the solstice. Although the invitation did say something to the effect of a ritual dance, I couldn't quite believe (or didn't want to believe) that I was consciously entering into a part of feminism that I thought was best forgotten. Suffice it to say that I arrived at the gathering, which took place at a mountain adjacent to the east county home of one of the caucus members and found myself hiking up a mountain in order to take part in a "healing ritual." After burning sage, invoking the spirits of the four compass points and participating in a "sacred" dance that the teacher had learned from an African dancer "with a really cute butt," I hiked back down the mountain, eager to get away from a group of women who I believed were victims of a deluded consciousness. At the time that I participated in this ritual, I had very little familiarity with the performance art done under the umbrella of the Woman's Building. Had I been more familiar with the work, I would have realized that the ritual in which I participated was typical of the sort of performances produced by the students and

193

faculty of the Woman's Building, and that often this sort of ritual was either a part or a precursor of feminist activism. Suzanne Lacy, who is best known for her public performance events organized to protest violence against women, often did private ritualistic performances in tandem with the larger event. This was the case with *She Who Would Fly*, a totemic performance done at the same time as *Three Weeks in May* (1977), a performance event designed to increase awareness of rape.[1] Cheri Gaulke, who helped found two activist performance collectives (The Feminist Art Workers and the Sisters Of Survival/S.O.S), early in her career performed a private birthday ritual derived from Native American tradition and engaged in an elaborate Goddess-worshipping ceremony on the island of Malta.[2] Anne Gauldin, who along with Jerri Allyn founded The Waitresses, a performance collective of present and past waitresses who did impromptu skits at local restaurants about the plight of real waitresses, created a number of ritualistic performances, including *The Malta Project* (with Gaulke, 1978) and a private healing ritual of her own, which she did with her mother. Many of the women who participated in the 1992 mountaintop ritual had come of age in the mid-seventies. At the very least, they would have been familiar with the performance work done at the Woman's Building, and some of them had probably seen it firsthand. For these women, a ritualistic ceremony honoring a matriarchal tradition was the first step in creating a woman's culture from which they could act politically.

Not being familiar with either the Woman's Building or the performance art done by the faculty and staff of the Feminist Studio Workshop (FSW) at the time, it seemed to me that taking recourse in feminist spirituality was an apolitical gesture that accomplished very little. One of my close friends and mentors was the late artist and AIDS activist Renee Edgington, who founded the Los Angeles-based collective Powers of Desire. Along with Edgington, I believed that the most effective type of activist art was that which challenged hegemonic and oppressive representations and policies with a knowledgeable and calculated re-deployment of oppressive imagery. I was very influenced by the writing of Douglas Crimp and believed that his arguments about the most effective forms of AIDS activist art were equally relevant for other political art forms, including that with a feminist agenda. Following Crimp's lead, I was suspicious of any art that attempted to "transcend" the conditions under which it was made. What I experienced on the mountain that night seemed very far removed from the sort of political intervention in which I was interested. I believed that very little was accomplished that night, other than that the participants felt better because they had done something that cemented their feminist bond and reinforced their feminist principles. Several months later, however, I was invited to protest the Tailhook scandal in front of the Miramar Air Base by the same group of women who had been dancing on top of the mountain. Clearly there was some sort of connection between the political—i.e., public—event that took place at Miramar and the private ritual on the mountain, if for no other reason than many of the same women were involved in both. I do remember being somewhat surprised that there was any connection at all. Nevertheless, I was not convinced that feminist spirituality was necessary or even desirable for feminist political action.

I had plenty of company in my skepticism. By the mid-eighties and early nineties, many feminists had become dissatisfied with the solutions offered by cultural feminism—a separate sphere for women in which everyone participated in a matriarchal society of sharing and understanding. Cultural feminists, with their Wiccan ceremonies and images of the goddess, were perceived by critics from a variety of disciplines as undermining the feminist movement by trading in actions for activism. In her history of radical feminism, for example, Alice Echols suggests that cultural feminism derailed the more politically engaged project of radical feminism.[3] The problem with cultural feminism, according to Echols, was that it "turned its attention away from opposing male supremacy to creating a female counterculture," which often degenerated from the laudable goal of empowering women into a facile valorization of one's personal lifestyle choices, bathed in a hazy glow of Goddess-inflected spirituality.[4] In an extremely influential article, "Textual Strategies: The Politics of Art Making," Judith Barry and Sandy Flitterman-Lewis argue that a truly radical art is not one that glorifies an "essential female art power" through recourse to female spirituality, but rather one that understands the "question of representation as a political question … an understanding of how women are constituted through social practices in culture."[5] Somewhat surprisingly, given their concern with a critique of representation, Barry and Flitterman-Lewis are particularly critical of seventies activist art, writing that "these more militant forms of feminist art such as agitprop, body-art, and ritualized violence, can produce immediate results by allowing the expression of rage, for example, or by focusing on a particular event or aspect of women's oppression. But these results may be short-lived, as in the case of heightened activism resulting from an issue-oriented art work."[6]

In defense of Barry and Flitterman-Lewis, the writings of so-called cultural feminists were often long on poetic metaphor and short on concise political analysis. Much of the language employed by cultural feminist writers such as Mary Daly, Charlene Spretnak, and Susan Griffin, writers who published frequently in *Chrysalis*, the magazine of women's art and culture published at the Woman's Building, was generally a rather uncritical representation of stereotypical qualities associated with (white) women. Nevertheless, they represented an important early attempt to articulate an alternative mode of language and representation that was non-patriarchal in its orientation. Even more to the point, feminist spirituality was an important tool for the Woman's Building artists, who used the imagery and ideas of cultural feminism in order to articulate an alternative representational vocabulary that successfully challenged existing hegemonic representational codes. At the Woman's Building, feminist spirituality worked as a catalyst between the personal experiences shared in

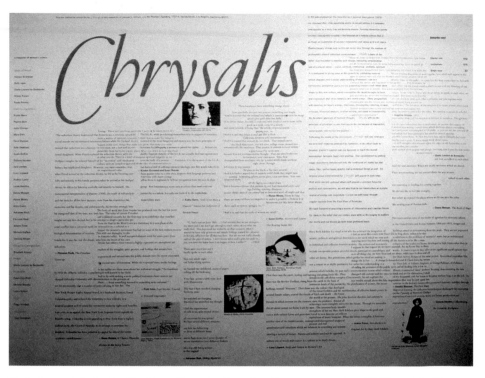

Sheila Levrant de Bretteville, *Chrysalis* poster. Two color offset printing, 23" x 17½". Woman's Building Image Archive, Otis College of Art and Design.

consciousness-raising sessions and the political art that was produced from them, transforming what would have been fruitless sessions of complaining into an enterprise with mythical underpinnings.[7] Such spirituality legitimated the connection between the body and the mind and stressed that the experiences of the sensual, sensate body were as important as those of the sentient mind. It provided a ready-made cache of alternative images of women, images that seemed to fly in the face of patriarchal stereotypes of women. This was particularly important in the case of activist performance art, which was often conceived with the idea that at some point the media would show up and the piece would be on the evening news. Finally, feminist spirituality, with its mythological pantheon of goddesses, fairies and witches, had particular relevance for a group of artists familiar with the history of Western art and mythology. It is little wonder that Suzanne Lacy—student of Judy Chicago and Arlene Raven, faculty member of the FSW, and teacher of Cheri Gaulke, Anne Gauldin, and Jerri Allyn—found Daly's *Beyond God the Father* to be a profoundly influential book.[8] In Southern California at least, feminist spirituality allowed rather than prevented feminist performance artists to articulate a radical reading of the female body as the basis for a feminist consciousness that in turn produced a (feminist) model for an engaged form of art making. Far from derailing activist art, feminist spirituality made it possible.

196

The cultural feminism of the Woman's Building could be characterized (to borrow the words of Teresa de Lauretis) as more a project "than a description of existent reality.... This may be utopian, idealist, perhaps misguided or wishful thinking, it may be a project one does not want to be a part of, but it is not essentialist as is the belief in a God-given or otherwise immutable nature of woman."[9] Writing approximately nine years after the publication of "Textual Strategies," de Lauretis was able to be more charitable about cultural feminism without sacrificing any of her theoretical rigor. Along these same lines, I would propose that the activist performance art of the Woman's Building could be re-read through the lens of postmodern theories of representation and language and not be found to be wanting. In looking back at these activist performances from the seventies, as I propose to do for the remainder of this essay, I am struck by the similarities between this work, which was generally collaborative, colorful, and very public, and the artwork generated from AIDS activism, particularly that of Edgington and the two collectives that she founded along with her partner Matt Francis: Powers of Desire and Clean Needles Now. In comparing AIDS activist work with the activist performance of the Woman's Building, I would like to argue that the visual language employed by these earlier artists worked to re-present oppressive images in the contemporary media, and, what is more, re-presented them in such as way as to implicate the viewer in their critique of the existing social structures. I would also argue that the artists of the Woman's Building did in fact challenge oppressive social structures through the deployment of their own sexualized and particular bodies, and that the presence of these "bodies" was crucial to the success and meaning of these performances. Finally, I want to demonstrate that the so-called essentialism seen in the work of these artists was in fact a late twentieth-century response to the hegemonic representations of women in the media, rather than a refusal to engage critically with the manner in which women were constructed in and by patriarchal society.

I. The Feminist Art Program and *Womanhouse*

Woman's Building members spawned a number of interesting and provocative performances during the late seventies and early eighties. In this paper, due to the limitations of space, I propose to look at three of them: *Ablutions* (1972), performed by Lacy, Chicago, Sandra Orgel, and Aviva Rahmani; *In Mourning and In Rage* (1977), a performance event organized by Lacy and Leslie Labowitz; and *Ready To Order?* (1978) a week-long performance event performed by The Waitresses. I have chosen these three performances because they span a particularly fertile time for feminist performance art in Southern California: from the period immediately before the Woman's Building opened to the period just prior to the Reagan-era eighties, a period that represents the last utopian gasp of this particular form of art activism. Before discussing these three performances, I think it is necessary to give some background on the Feminist Art Program (FAP) and its first performance event, which took place at *Womanhouse*. The

WOMANHOUSE

Top: *Womanhouse*, 1972. Exhibition
catalog cover featuring Miriam Schapiro
(L) and Judy Chicago (R) sitting on the
steps of *Womanhouse*. © California
Institute of the Arts Archives.

Right: *Womanhouse*, 1972. Exhibition
catalog page picturing *Leah's Room from
Colette's Chéri* by Karen LeCoq and
Nancy Youdelman. © California
Institute of the Arts Archives.

Leah's Room from
Collette's Cherie
Karen LeCoq
Nancy Youdelman

Lea's room is a room of lush beauty and
suffocating oppression. The strong,
pungent smell of magnolia, the pinkness
of the wallpaper roses, the hats with
veils to soften an aging face all create
this feeling of oppression and decadence.
Enmeshed in this suffocating
environment was the courtesan Lea, a
woman desperately trying to save her
fading beauty. Her beauty was her
life. Beauty made her pleasing to the
gentlemen, obtained her favors, gave her
wealth and friendship.

The performance piece done in this room,
in which a woman incessantly applies
layer after layer of makeup, portrays the
pain: the pain of aging, of losing beauty,
pain of competition with other women.
We wanted to deal with the way women
are intimidated by the culture to
constantly maintain their beauty and the
feeling of desperation and helplessness
once this beauty is lost.

Feminist Art Program, which Chicago founded, was based on a radically different approach to teaching art, an approach that would carry over to the FSW at the Woman's Building. This approach was premised upon consciousness-raising sessions, a tool used nationally in the women's movement to help women realize that their feelings of worthlessness and depression stemmed from the unequal social conditions in which they lived. "Consciousness raising," according to Faith Wilding, "helped us to discover the commonality of our experiences as women, and to analyze how we had been conditioned and formed on the basis of our gender.... As each woman spoke it became apparent that what had seemed to be purely 'personal' experiences were actually shared by all the other women; we were discovering a common oppression based on our gender, which was defining our roles and identities as women."[10] The consciousness-raising sessions became the basis for much of the art made by the students of the FAP who explored topics that had previously been off-limits, such as women's roles, women's sexuality, and violence against women. When the FAP moved from Fresno State to California Institute of the Arts (CalArts), Chicago and Miriam Schapiro (who was on the faculty at CalArts) decided to begin the FAP with an intense, collaborative project that would involve all of the students and would use the consciousness-raising methodology developed by Chicago. The result was *Womanhouse*, an abandoned mansion in residential Hollywood transformed into a collaborative installation that dealt with the ambivalent relationship that women had with the home. In addition to the installations, *Womanhouse* featured evening performances done by the students of the FAP. These performances, which are documented in Johanna Demetrakas's 1972 film *Womanhouse*, were for the most part fairly straightforward explorations of women's roles in patriarchal society; the two exceptions were *Waiting* and *The Birth Trilogy*.[11]

Although many of the performances done for *Womanhouse* explored the feelings of entrapment and oppression that women felt when forced to confine their activities to the home and child rearing, only one of the performances actually dealt with rape. In the piece *Three Women*, Shawnee Wollenmann's character, Rainbow, describes to her friends a gang rape. A free and easy spirit, Rainbow finds herself at a party where she quickly becomes separated from her "old man." After doing a large amount of drugs, Rainbow fell in with a group of men, who eventually gang-raped her, or, as she put it, "took turns balling me."[12] *Three Women* was developed from the role-playing exercises that Chicago had her students engage in; the events narrated in the piece had some basis in truth but had not actually happened to the participants. Nevertheless, Rainbow's testimony, which Demetrakas included uncut in her documentary film, is absolutely chilling. Speaking in a high, rather vacuous voice, Wollenmann began the narrative by talking about how her old man had given her this marvelous jacket, a jacket that felt so wonderful that she had worn it to the party on the night that she was gang-raped. When she came to after the rape, all of her clothes, including the jacket, were gone. She never saw either the jacket or her old man again. "It was really a bummer man…but, you gotta stay above it, man, you gotta have love, or you can really get brung down…."[13]

The notion that this young woman's body was violated by a group of hippie men who were supposedly more enlightened than their fathers is fairly disturbing. What is even more disturbing is the matter-of-fact manner in which Wollenmann's character accepts the circumstances of the rape. All of her feelings of loss and betrayal are projected onto the jacket, which she seems more upset about losing than she does her "old man." Rainbow's narrative would have been difficult to hear even if Wollenmann had simply stood in the middle of the *Womanhouse* living room and recounted the story in her normal voice. Instead, she was part of a group of three women, all of whom were lounging on brightly patterned pillows and rugs while wearing wildly colorful clothing and wigs and speaking in exaggerated voices. Wollenmann's costume was particularly colorful: a rainbow-colored Afro wig, copious sparkle make-up, flowing robes, and plenty of heavy jewelry. On the one hand, the presence of Wollenmann's corporeal body, or at least the record of the presence of her corporeal body in Demetrakas's film, serves to connect her experience to the Real in a way that no depiction of rape, no matter how graphic, can accomplish. Body art, or the presence of the body in the art, "proposes," as Amelia Jones suggests,

> *proximity*: as a critique exploring rather than repudiating the seductions of late capitalism through specific bodies that force the spectator's own narcissistic self-containment to account (through its reversibility) for the "other" of the artist as the artist accounts for her or his interpreters by performing specific bodies that force the interpreter to acknowledge her or his implication in determining the meanings of the artist/work of art.[14]

Jones's notion of the "proximity" of the performing body is certainly relevant to my own experience viewing the performance. The first time that I saw Rainbow in Demetrakas's film, I found myself wondering whether or not the performing body recorded on film had actually experienced the sexual violation that she was narrating. Identifying with the character of Rainbow through the shared corporeal experience of having a woman's body that is equally vulnerable to masculine attack, I found myself feeling increasingly un-comfortable as Rainbow's tale of a hippie love fest turned into a story of a gang rape. My feeling of discomfort was enhanced by the off-camera sounds of the audience, whose initial laughter upon encountering Wollenmann's over-the-top character had changed to an eerie silence by the time she had finished mourning the loss of the magical jacket.

Three Women, a performance by Shawnee Wollerman (front), Nancy Youdelman (rear) and Jan Oxenberg (not pictured), at ***Womanhouse***, 1972. Silver gelatin print, 10" x 8". Photograph by Dori Atlantis.

Ablutions, performance by Judy Chicago, Suzanne Lacy, Sandra Orgel, and Aviva Rashmani, 1972. Venice, CA. © Judy Chicago, courtesy Through the Flower Archives.

II. Ablutions

On the other hand, the almost clown-like make-up worn by the three women, an effect exacerbated, for me at least, by the overall reddish tone of the film, served to counteract the proximity that the "real" presence that their performing bodies invited. Wollenmann's exaggerated persona and her breathy, little-girl voice reinforced the notion that this was role playing, and that at the end of the performance piece everything would be all right and Wollenmann would revert back to her identity as a feminist artist who was too canny to end up in the same situation as Rainbow. After *Womanhouse* closed, Chicago continued to meet with the students in the FAP's Performance Workshop and explore imagery and ideas through consciousness-raising. The performance that resulted from these meetings was *Ablutions*, which was performed late in the spring of 1972, just before Chicago left CalArts in order to found the Woman's

Building. *Ablutions* was conceived as a means of speaking out against rape and its devastating effects on women. Perhaps it was the desire to present a less mediated representation of the Real rape that caused Chicago and her students—Lacy, Rahmani, Orgel, Jan Lester, and Jan Oxenberg—to seek out women who had actually experienced rape and tape-record their testimonials. According to Lacy, the initial conception of *Ablutions* was to simply seat an audience in a darkened room and play these testimonials.[15] While this idea might not seem terribly radical today, when it is fairly common to turn on the television and catch celebrities and non-celebrities alike testifying to their experience of rape without shame or fear of reprisal, in the seventies nobody even acknowledged that rape existed, let alone talked about it. Lacy recalled that in order to assemble the stories of women who had been raped, she and Chicago had to "literally... go down dark streets and end up in strange places in the middle of the night, tape recording these stories."[16]

In making the decision to include accounts of rape that were connected in some way to the "Real" experience of that rape, Chicago and her students were on to something. One of the themes that appears frequently in the writings of Arlene Raven and other "cultural" feminists is the importance of naming, of having the power to tell one's own story. "The testimony of rape...the telling is exorcism, a ritual of healing through repetition...."[17] Raven's words would later be echoed by Trinh T. Minh-ha, who suggested that "the story of marginality" can only be untold by the storyteller, who speaks to the tale rather than about it.[18] Telling the tale, rather than giving the history, is a crucial strategy for those on the margins who have not traditionally had access to the Lacanian realm of the Symbolic and representation. As drama critic Jeanie Forte has argued,

> Actual women speaking their personal experience create dissonance with their representation, Woman, throwing that fictional category into relief and question. Shock waves are set up from within the signification process itself, resonating to provide an awareness of the phallocentricity of our signifying systems and the culturally determined otherness of women.[19]

Raven rather astutely recognized the way in which the violence of a supposedly neutral rhetoric in fact upholds the gender hierarchy between men and women and is imbricated within actual violence against women. While it is probably too simplistic to argue, as Susan Brownmiller does, that "rape is nothing more or less than a conscious process of intimidation by which *all men* keep *all women* in a state of fear," rape does function, as de Lauretis has suggested, as the sign of a power struggle to maintain, rather than disrupt, a certain kind of social order. Noting that "gender-neutral expressions" such as spousal abuse or marital violence imply that both spouses engage equally in battering each other, de Lauretis argues that even as those terms "purport to remain innocent of the ideology or of the rhetoric of violence, they cannot avoid and indeed purposefully engage in the violence of rhetoric."[20]

III. The Ideology of Rape

One of the stories that ended up on the final version of the tape was that of Raven, who, inspired by her work with Chicago on *Ablutions*, would help to found the Woman's Building the following year.

> Judy Chicago was making the *Ablutions* tape when I visited her in the spring of 1972. I had been raped three days before, and I was experiencing the shock, panic, self-loathing and despair of the raped victim, because I felt so helpless all I could do was lie there and cry. But I rose on the third day anyway to pursue my survival and future, guided by my woman's intuition that they could be divined...by flying three thousand miles to perform a ritual of speaking pain and of initiation with a woman I had met, powerfully, only once.[21]

For Raven, participation in the ritual performance *Ablutions* was an important milestone in overcoming the terror and horror of the violation of her body. It was also the means by which Raven cast off her previous identity and became reborn into the feminist community. Sometime during that first meeting, Chicago suggested that she take the surname Raven as a sign of her new identity, just as Chicago's decision to "divest" herself of the name Gerowitz signified her own new feminist identity.[22] Comparing *Ablutions* to a "Wiccan response to the devil's warlocks," Raven credited the ritual performance with breaking the spell cast by the dark ritual of rape. *Ablutions* gave Raven the means by which to exorcise the rape, to name the violence that was done to her and therefore take control of that discourse:

> As I broke silence, I entered at the same time the healing ritual/performance of *Ablutions*. I see this act, in retrospect, and symbolically, as initiation into the circle of women with whom I would bond over and over to create the feminist institutions, educational methods, criticism, publications, relationships, and the art about which I am now writing.[23]

Telling the tale is clearly therapeutic. Is it enough, however, to simply re-tell the tale, to re-present it from the vantage point of the experiential body? Or does one run the risk of merely opening new opportunities for (self) surveillance, new conditions under which female bodies can and must be disciplined? Rape testimonials, to which the plethora of examples from tabloid television and gossip magazines attests, do not necessarily alter the circumstance by which rape is perceived. Rather, these testimonials serve to reinforce the notion that no woman without the protection of a benevolent male is safe in any situation. Given the ubiquity of the myth/ideology of rape, it was, and is, absolutely imperative to counter that myth, to provide an alternative position from which the story of rape can be retold. The problem that plagued early feminists was how to do that retelling without simply reifying an ideology of the victim or sensationalizing the act of rape. As Hannah Feldman puts it:

> In some ways, it would seem that to name rape, and those who perpetrate it within a culture which condones it, reinforces that same culture's allowance, even prescription, that gender difference be inscribed in women's experience, thereby labeling them already raped or inherently rapable. To some degree, marking the commonness of rape would seem to enhance the culture of fear in which women live.[24]

Feldman's cautionary words against an unproblematic embrace of visibility politics are well taken. However, the alternative—to not speak at all, is equally unfeasible. Arguing that "to name oneself as a rape survivor works to empower the speaker who, by rejecting the silence that usually accompanies rape, reclaims, in part, the subjectivity lost in such a violation," Feldman suggests that the testimonial, the act of enunciation from the "contaminated position of the survivor," provides a real and viable option to the traditional account of rape permitted under the existing legal systems, an account that essentially tells the story of the rapist's desire.[25]

Although Feldman doesn't elaborate on how one can enunciate from "the contaminated position of the survivor," it seems that in order to do so the woman who is raped must somehow "speak" her bodily pain against the rhetoric of violence, the patriarchal ideology of which rape is a violent manifestation. Apparently, the young women who conceived of and performed *Ablutions* came to the same conclusion as Feldman, and realized that, while the testimonial of the experience of rape was important, the method of enunciation was equally so. Gradually, the students in Chicago's performance workshop elaborated upon the initial conception, transforming *Ablutions* into a complex ritual of corporeal actions/representations that took place against the backdrop of the rape testimonials. The final performance, according to Chicago, explored the themes of "binding, like Chinese foot-binding, brutalization, immersion, body anxiety, and entrapment" through a series of images and actions that were indissoluble from the corporeal and gendered bodies of the performers.[26] In choosing to explore ritualistic, mythological images of female bodily pain in tandem with the testimonies of rape, Chicago and her students found a way to enunciate from the position of the victimized body without reinforcing the ideology of rape.

IV. Images of (Not) Rape

Unlike the performance *Three Women*, *Ablutions*, which was performed only once, was never filmed. What remains of the performance for viewers are four photographs, reproduced in Chicago's autobiography *Through the Flower*, which depict first the empty performance space with three metal tubs and broken eggshells scattered around the room, then the performers bathing and binding each other while a fourth woman, Lacy, nails kidneys to a wall. In the last image, three bodies are left bound and wrapped in the space, which has now been connected by a giant spider web of string. As two other photographs of this performance, one published in *The Power of Feminist Art* and the other published in *TDR/The Drama Review* make clear, the spinster was Suzanne Lacy, who is shown holding a very large coil of twine.[27] In addition to these photographs, which by virtue of being taken in black and white have an antique appearance that belies their relatively contemporaneous status, there also exists Chicago's published description of the piece, included in the appendix of *Through the Flower*. This description adds the sequential narrative that the iconicity of the photographs elides. In a space filled with broken eggs and piles of rope, kidneys, and chains, three women took turns immersing themselves in bathtubs that contained viscous substances such as eggs and mud, while a nude woman was bound/spun to a chair. At the conclusion of the performance, Lacy and her accomplice left the bound, wrapped women, while Raven's "I felt so helpless," played again and again. *Ablutions* had a profound impact on everyone who was there. In Lacy's words:

> [T]he audience was stunned.... Apparently, several people just sort of gagged and ran for the door at the end of it. They had never been exposed—not only with that information at that level of detail, but to women's perspective on it. And the rage and the intensity of victimization that was in the piece. In fact, a couple of the women who were in the piece, one of them...had an emotional reaction to allowing herself to participate from the vantage point of the victim.[28]

What is striking about *Ablutions* is the way in which it dealt with the discursive and representational structures that surrounded the ideology of rape. Significantly, *Ablutions* provided an opportunity for the first time for the raped body to speak, both at the level of signification (the taped voices) and the pre-symbolic, or semiotic level (the "bathed" and bound bodies of the two nude women, the kidneys on the wall). What made *Ablutions* so compelling at the time that it was performed was its intertwining of interrelated, but different discourses—the recounting of the rape using the symbolic language of the Father, and the experience of the rape from the perspective of the bodies of the bathed and bound women. By the end of the performance, the audience was brought into an uncomfortable proximity (to borrow Jones's term) with rape, a proximity that forced them to share a corporeal connection with those whose bodily space had been egregiously violated by a patriarchal code of sexual behavior. Certainly the intended message behind *Ablutions* was the oppressiveness of rape; all of the images invoked through the agency of the performing bodies of Chicago and her students were meant to reinforce how dehumanizing and demoralizing the experience of rape was for all women. And yet, the photographs of the event, taken by Lloyd Hamrol, Chicago's then-husband and a well-known Los Angeles sculptor, read differently than Chicago and her students perhaps intended them to. The broken eggshells, meant to symbolize the violation of subjectivity, look like flower petals or cotton balls in both the tiny reproductions in *Through the Flower* and the full-page reproduction in *The Power of Feminist Art*. Meanwhile, the bloody kidneys nailed to the wall, deprived in the black-and-white photographs of the visceral qualities of smell and texture, look like a garland of dark shapes. Finally, the bound women, wrapped head-to-toe in white bandages and suspended in an ethereal web of white twine, seem somehow embryonic and promising, caterpillars waiting to emerge rather than mortally wounded butterflies.

V. An Hysterical Poetics

My reading of *Ablutions*, based on photographs taken after the fact, would seem to contradict the intended meaning of the performance. I would argue, however, that since the meaning of the image often exceeds the stated intentions of its maker, that they compliment that meaning. It seems to me that the strength of *Ablutions* lies in the decision to employ corporeal imagery that simultaneously referenced mythological constructions of femininity and challenged those constructions. Mieke Bal, in her analysis of Rembrandt's *The Suicide of Lucretia* (1666), argues that traditional narratives of rape shape or construct a meaning that often obliterates the violence of the original act. Narratives such as that of Wollenmann, no matter how compelling, ultimately serve to distance the woman hearing the narrative from the actual violence of the act. In the social construction of rape, which Bal rightly characterizes as a public, semiotic act,[29] rape is a type of murder/suicide, in which the victim somehow commits the act herself. Bal is therefore particularly interested in Rembrandt's *The Suicide of Lucretia* because it does not permit "Brutus"—i.e., patriarchal discourse—to discursively structure this rape. In Rembrandt's version, Lucretia is shown at the moment of her suicide, her dress stained with blood, almost as though the corporeal traces of her body's violation had oozed out onto the surface of the painting despite her efforts to contain it. Bal, clearly indebted to the work of Julia Kristeva, characterizes this corporeal ooze as an hysterical poetics, a way that the body can speak both visually (pre-linguistically) and verbally. Speaking from the position of the hysterical semiotic is a means by which the violence of rhetoric (narrative) can be countered. Thus, the testimony of rape must in some way originate, as Feldman suggested above, from the pre-linguistic body that experienced that violence. The excretory and excreting bodies in *Ablutions* gave a corporeal dimension to the taped testimonials. What is more, they created a gap between the violent rhetoric—the testimonials—and the visual images. This disjunction is even more pronounced today, due to the fact that what remains of the performance is little more than black-and-white photographs, through which, I have argued, those bodies speak differently yet again. The performing bodies were not merely acting out the narratives of rape heard over the speakers that night; they were narrating a different experience from a corporeal position and substituting a rebirth of subjectivity for the murder/denial of rape.

It was particularly significant, therefore, that *Ablutions*, which was performed at the studio of Laddie Dill in Venice, California, took place in an art context rather than on the street or in someone's home. The mythology of high art and great masters, firmly in place since the Renaissance, has always worked to deny the way in which art and artists are imbricated by and within patriarchal ideology and narratives. The history of art is full of images of rape told from the point of view of the man, from Rubens's *Rape of the Daughters of Leucippus* (1615–18), Poussin's *Rape of the Sabine Women*, and the plethora of images of rape/conquest in modern painting to the rape/conquest scene in Ayn Rand's *The Fountainhead*, a paean to the generative power of male genius. Bal's reading of Rembrandt, a name which has become so completely equated with high art that it has been used to sell an expensive brand of toothpaste, is an attempt to free his work from the rhetorical straightjacket of narrative, which, although not commensurate with its image, nevertheless supersedes the meaning of that image. Bal makes a compelling case for reading Rembrandt's images differently than the traditional rhetoric of art history might allow; it is doubtful, however, that she could have made an equally compelling case for many other artists.

The decision by Chicago and her students to use rape imagery that originated in an "hysterical poetics" of the body, rather than traditional masculinist codes of representation, was significant for several reasons. First, it revealed, as Bal would say, the rhetoric of violence, the semiotic and corporeal violation that is rape. It demonstrated that rape was in fact a violation on two levels: a crime against a woman's subjective identity and a violation of her corporeal integrity. Second, by virtue of taking place within a high art context, it challenged the very discourse that worked to make rape into rhetoric, to deny the semiotic violence that rape in fact represents. *Ablutions*, in a sense, was one possible answer to Linda Nochlin's famous question "Why have there been no great women artists?" Why indeed, when to be an artist meant participating in an ideological construct that denied female subjectivity, an identity that even the most persistent female artists such as Artemisia Gentileschi and Mary Cassatt were unable to transcend.[30] Art, and art history, have been gendered male. As Griselda Pollock has pointed out: "Women have not been omitted through forgetfulness or mere prejudice. The structural sexism of most academic disciplines contributes actively to the production and perpetuation of a gender hierarchy. What we learn about the world and its peoples is ideologically patterned in conformity with the social order within which it is produced."[31]

The women who conceived of *Ablutions* realized this and attempted to inter-rupt the traditional art historical discourse in which women were turned into the sign Woman and deprived of their own subjectivity. *Ablutions* actually contained many of the elements that make up art's more traditional re-presentation of rape: mythological imagery, female bodies, and rhetorical narrative. What is missing is the ideological sleight of hand that causes these elements to come together to form one (true) meaning. With *Ablutions* these elements remained disjunctive, contradicting rather than com-plimenting one another. It is little wonder that the audience didn't quite know what to say when confronted by the performance.

VI. Suzanne Lacy

Most of the women involved in *Ablutions*, including Chicago, chose not to continue with performance art. The one exception was Lacy, who has not only continued organizing performances up until today, but has done so on a much more public scale. After grad-uating from the FAP with an MFA in art, Lacy was invited to join the faculty of the FSW at the Woman's Building. This association with a fledgling feminist art institution gave Lacy two things that she desperately needed in order to realize her ambitious perform-ances: a group of committed students and colleagues who were able to help and collab-orate with her and friendly institutional support. Along with her main collaborator, Leslie Labowitz, Lacy staged three major performances that dealt with the issue of sex-ual violence against women: *Three Weeks in May* (1977), *In Mourning and In Rage* (1977), and *Take Back the Night* (1978). Together, Lacy and Labowitz also founded Ariadne: A Social Art Network, a collaborative organization that served as an umbrella for facilitat-ing feminist activist performance such as The Incest Awareness Project, performed by their students. Of the three, *In Mourning and In Rage*, conceived and executed on the heels of *Three Weeks in May* and performed quickly as a knee-jerk reaction to the increasingly salacious media coverage of the Hillside Stranglers and their victims, best epitomizes the fusion of the mythological and the media-friendly that Lacy and Labowitz sought in their public performances. The image of the seven-foot female mourners draped in black is one that continues to have currency even today. At the same time, this image is suggestive, as Lacy and Labowitz intended it to be, of pre-his-toric, matristic societies in which female mourners performed a powerful act of socie-tal healing that served to strengthen the community, a community that Lacy and Labowitz began to build with *Three Weeks in May*. *In Mourning and In Rage* can best be understood by reading it through the lens of *Three Weeks in May*, a three-week perform-ance event that began on May 4, 1977. In late 1977, as word of the predatory Hillside Stranglers (so named because they left the often tortured, raped, and strangled bodies of their female victims on the sides of the hills in Los Angeles), Lacy and Labowitz must have realized that counteracting the public rhetoric of rape was not something that could be accomplished with any one action, even one as inclusive and far-reaching as *Three Weeks in May*. *In Mourning and In Rage* was in many ways a condensed version of the earlier performance, designed to hammer home the message about violence against women first articulated in May of 1977.

VII. Three Weeks in May

For *Three Weeks in May*, Lacy installed two large maps in the City Mall, located in downtown Los Angeles not far from City Hall. On one map, she recorded the location of rapes reported to the police by stamping a large red stencil "RAPE" on the site where it occurred. On the other map, she pinpointed the location of rape crisis centers, police precincts, and battered women's shelters. In addition to the maps, she organized a series of events, including three public performances orchestrated by Labowitz, and a self-defense demonstration. The performance was tremendously successful as a piece of activist art, which is the way it has been presented in recent accounts of the piece.[32] What is often overlooked is that *Three Weeks in May* was not simply an activist event in which artists participated, but was instead a carefully orchestrated performance designed to facilitate interaction between various groups and coalitions in order to forge a new dialogue/discourse about rape. *Three Weeks in May* caused elected public officials, activists from the feminist community, media reporters, office workers, and feminist artists—five very different groups of people—to rub shoulders. Lacy could very well have had a disaster on her hands if she had not had an extremely well organized vision of the entire event prior to the opening press conference on May 4. Fortunately, she was organized. She also had an art event that in many ways was difficult for the general public and critics alike to conceive of as art. For Lacy, who has always been extremely concerned with expressing an aesthetic vision in her work, the inability of critics to fully comprehend her performance has been frustrating. According to Lacy:

> *Three Weeks in May* was explained by critics as being about rape (which it was), but never analyzed in terms of its structure—simultaneous juxtaposition of art and non-art activities within an extended time frame, taking place within the context of popular culture. Women's art is a complex integration of content and structure, and neither can be overlooked for a real critical understanding of it.[33]

VIII. Allan Kaprow

The inability of critics and audience alike to recognize the aesthetic elements of this performance can largely be traced to the influence of Allan Kaprow, rather than Judy Chicago and Arlene Raven, on Lacy's work. Lacy completed her MFA under the auspices of the FAP at CalArts where Kaprow was a member of the faculty. Faced with the choice of studying with John Baldessari (the Conceptual artist who trained David Salle and Eric Fischl) or Kaprow, Lacy chose Kaprow, because she believed that his teaching methods and philosophy were much more compatible with feminism. Kaprow's ideas about dissolving the boundary between art and life became for Lacy the means by which she could unite avant-garde art practice with her desire for feminist activism:

> Kaprow's project, to investigate the border between art and life, was a theoretical substratum for feminist artists wishing to unite art, the conditions of women's lives, and social change.... If art could be an articulation of real time and images collapsed into a frame of daily life, as Kaprow argued, then political art need not only be an art of symbolic action, but might include actual action.... At the intersection of the questions Kaprow asked of the artist's role and the challenges Judy Chicago raised to the relevance of female experience, there grew the possibility of feminist activist art.[34]

It was due to Kaprow's influence that Lacy had taken her work outside of the gallery, in the process making art out of non-art events such as self-defense demonstrations and press conferences. Given that Kaprow's aesthetic could be characterized as a non-aesthetic, one could argue that the failure of critics and audience to recognize the art elements of *Three Weeks in May* was symptomatic of its success as a piece of work that effectively bridged the gap between art and life. As I have suggested in my reading of *Ablutions*, however, countering an art/art history discourse was hardly an empty exercise. For *In Mourning and In Rage*, Lacy, along with Labowitz, staged a spectacle whose primary effect was visual and which therefore had a much stronger aesthetic impact than the earlier performance. At the same time, performed as it was in a public forum (rather than the private artist's studio that was the site of *Ablutions*), it was able to obtain the same high visibility as *Three Weeks in May*.

IX. In Mourning and In Rage

On the morning of December 13, 1977, approximately sixty women met to form a motorcade, which followed—funeral style—a black hearse that pulled up before Los Angeles City Hall. Nine women mourners, six-foot-tall actresses wearing heels and headdresses in order to bring their height up to seven feet, alighted from the hearse and moved to the steps of City Hall, where they spoke one at a time in memory of all the violence that had been done to women. One by one, the women, against the backdrop of City Hall and a banner that read "In Memory of Our Sisters, Women Fight Back," stepped up to the microphone. As each woman spoke, the chorus of mourners chanted "In memory of our sisters, we fight back." Finally, a tenth woman, dressed in red, approached the microphone, crying out "I am here for the rage of all women; I am here for women fighting back."[35] *In Mourning and In Rage* concluded with a statement from the artists, a presentation of demands for self-defense and emergency listing of rape hotline numbers, and speeches by local politicians, including Los Angeles City Council-member Pat Russell. In spite of a very loud airplane, folk singer Holly Near sang an a cappella song composed especially for the event, and the Los Angeles City Council Members promised to support the demands of the feminist organizations that collaborated with Lacy and Labowitz on the piece. Six television channels covered the performance, and Lacy and Labowitz were asked to appear on several talk shows.

X. Images of Feminist Anger

In Mourning and In Rage was documented both photographically and in a video made by L.A. Women's Video Center for the Woman's Building. The photographs of the event, which have been reproduced in a number of publications, including *The Power of Feminist Art*, always show the black-clad women with their foot-high headdresses and covered faces lined up in an atavistic row that projects female anger and empowerment. This effect is actually enhanced in the video presentation of the event, shown in conjunction with the photographic documentation in the 1998 exhibition *Out of Actions: Between Performance and the Object 1949–1979*, at Los Angeles Museum of Contemporary Art, which includes a very determined Lacy helping the women to alight from the hearse, and emphasizes the absolute silence of the women, broken only by their short speech at the microphone. According to Lacy and Labowitz, the performance sought to transform the archetypal image of the female mourner in order to create "a public ritual for women to share their rage and grief, to transform the individual struggle to comprehend these assaults into a collective statement."[36] In all likelihood, the powerful images of the female mourners had less of an effect on the immediate conditions under which the brutal rape and murder of young women was being reported than did the presence of Councilmember Russell, the support of the City Council, and the extensive media coverage.[37]

It is these images of black-clad women standing silently in an accusatory line, however, that have continued to resonate in the collective imaginations of feminist activists. Women who are not even familiar with *In Mourning and In Rage* and who would have been too young to have participated in the performance in any case have used the imagery of the performance again and again. In 1989, I participated in a similar performance organized by two pro-choice activists that protested the first Bush administration's attempts to undermine Roe v. Wade. As various feminist activists, including attorney Gloria Allred, spoke about the necessity of keeping abortion safe and legal, I, along with a number of other women clad in black, filed silently on to the platform of the Organ Pavilion in Balboa Park, San Diego, in a silent and symbolic protest against the numbers of women who died due to botched abortions. Although minus the headdresses, we created a powerful image as we stood in the late spring sunlight of Southern California. This mythological "performance" of which I was a part has resonated with me in a way that my other activist actions have not. I somehow felt myself to be a part of something bigger, as though I had tapped into a part of my female essence that was atavistic and ancient. I realize, of course, that my response was predicated not so much on the fact that I had "discovered" a part of myself that was rooted in the chaos of the collective unconscious, but rather that the ideological forces that addressed me in contemporary Western society were powerfully cemented by an originary mythology peopled with archetypal characters. Nevertheless, I think that my response to participating in this type of performance, while certainly not universal, testifies to the effect made possible by the strategic deployment of mythological and ritual imagery. Lacy's and Labowitz's decision to use imagery from feminist mythology was a strategic attempt to provide an image that would resonate in a positive way with those who watched the nightly news. At the same time, I'm not sure that they would have characterized it as merely strategic. Both Lacy and Labowitz had a powerful belief in the sustaining power of a mythology that was feminist in origin.

XI. Feminist Mythology

Lacy's engagement with this spirituality, as mentioned above, began with her association with the Woman's Building. Although Lacy's work in the seventies became increasingly public, she continued to do private, ritualistic performances along the line of *Ablutions*. In *Three Weeks in May*, Lacy had kept the public event—the stamping of the maps—separate from the private ritual—*She Who Would Fly*—out of the belief that a ritualistic performance would not be accessible to a broader audience. Labowitz, on the other hand, had always used ritualistic forms in her work, although it was not until she arrived in Los Angeles that she realized the significance of her imagery: "When I came back to L. A. and met Suzanne Lacy it was like 'Aaaaahhh!' Suddenly all of this stuff started to make sense. I learned a tremendous amount about feminism and the roots of my imagery. We were able to combine ... my direct public approach and her roots in feminist ritual and performance, making it into the form that we are doing now."[38]

The resonant image of black-clad women originated, therefore, not with Lacy and her cool, Kaprowesque aesthetic (at least for her public performances) but with Labowitz, whose career had taken a radically different direction than that of Lacy. Labowitz went the traditional route, getting a BFA and an MFA from Otis Art Institute in 1972. At Otis, Labowitz was exposed to the formalist Conceptual art that was currently in fashion in the art world. Although Judy Chicago had arrived in California and started the FAP, Labowitz herself remained largely uninterested. "I really was one of these typical female art students who had a lot of male friends, who talked about ideas with men, who looked very masculine in the sense of the way everyone dressed kind of ... neutral and not very feminine. Although I had long hair."[39]

Labowitz did do one performance that anticipated her later feminist work while still in graduate school. In *Menstruation Wait*, Labowitz sat at Otis for several days and waited for her menstrual period. The performance was over when her period began. Although *Menstruation Wait* (1972) conceptually and structurally had a lot in common with Happenings and Fluxus-inspired Actions, its external content, as well as its emphasis on the female body, made it very controversial and Labowitz was almost kicked out of school. Ironically, Labowitz, who was married to a German artist, applied for a Fulbright Fellowship in order to execute another *Menstruation Wait* in Düsseldorf, West Germany. Based on that performance, Labowitz became the first woman at Otis to be awarded a Fulbright.[40] In Germany, Labowitz executed another *Menstruation Wait* in the entrance hall of the art academy in Düsseldorf in 1972. The hostile and/or puzzled reaction of the audience taught Labowitz that "the expression of women's experience was not acceptable even in art."[41] Labowitz did find a nascent feminist community with a strong pro-Marxist stance in Germany in 1972. Influenced by the Marxism of her fellow German feminists, Labowitz's subsequent performances were designed to politicize their participants and their audiences. "The performances would work on the level of public ritual, uniting participants and a mass audience in a spiritual bond that creates community by politicizing its members."[42]

XII. Joseph Beuys

Although Labowitz was involved with the German feminists, it was her shaman/teacher, Joseph Beuys, who had the most influence on the fusion of aesthetics and politics that characterized her mature work. In the ruins of postwar Germany, Beuys emerged as an artist of international reputation who became famous for his explorations of German mythology and magic. Prior to his appointment at the Kunstakademie in Düsseldorf in 1961, Beuys had led a rather quixotic life, running away from home as a teenager in order to join the circus and learn performing tricks, and then joining Hitler's Luftwaffe at the age of nineteen. Beuys claimed to have been shot down over the Crimea in 1943 and rescued by nomadic Tartars, who covered him in animal felt and fat in order to raise his body temperature. In 1947, he enrolled in the Düsseldorf Art Academy. In 1955, he disappeared from Düsseldorf in order to work in the fields, reappearing at the end of the fifties with a series of drawings. In 1961, he was appointed professor of monumental sculpture at the Kunstakademie; he was fired from his post at approximately the same time that Labowitz arrived in Germany. In the performance *How to Explain Pictures to a Dead Hare*, done in conjunction with his first one-person exhibition in 1965 at the Galerie Schmela in Düsseldorf, Beuys covered his head with honey and gold pigment, tied a steel sole to his right foot and a felt sole to his left, and spent the next three hours whispering explanations to a dead hare that he held cradled in his arms, a hermeneutic and shamanistic performance designed to suggest the creative mystery of the artistic process.

Beuys's shamanism was particularly appealing to Labowitz because of its political dimensions. After performing an art action on July 20, 1964, (the anniversary of a failed assassination attempt against Hitler) in Aachen, West Germany, that caused right-wing students to attack him, Beuys became increasingly political, founding the German Student Party in 1967, and the Organization for Direct Democracy in 1970. His art actions became increasingly politicized. At the international Documenta 6 exhibition in 1977, he established a Free International University that included discussions on topics such as nuclear energy and equal rights for women. From her mentor, Labowitz learned that political art could be made more powerful through a skillful deployment of imagery. Because she was a woman working in the United States (a nation of media images that seeks to appropriate all histories yet remains curiously devoid of its own) rather than a man working in Germany (a nation that is perhaps overly obsessed with its own mythology), Labowitz took the role of shaman-behind-the-scenes, organizing but not participating in her performance events.[43] Prior to doing *In Mourning and In Rage*, Labowitz had done several performances in which the black-clad women had made an appearance, including a German performance, entitled *Paragraph 218*, against an anti-abortion proposal and her four part-performance *Myths of Rape*, done in conjunction with Lacy's *Three Weeks in May*.[44] *In Mourning and In Rage*, a performance that has been appropriated and re-appropriated for feminist actions, could be considered to be the penultimate expression of Labowitz's use of mytho-political imagery: an imagery that simultaneously appealed to the late-twentieth-century Los Angeles media and yet managed to suggest a time that was far removed from the context in which it had recently appeared.

XIII. The Effectiveness of Political Art

On the day following *In Mourning and In Rage*, the LAPD found the body of yet another woman who had fallen victim to the Hillside Stranglers. *In Mourning and In Rage* might have been successful as a performance event designed to enhance media awareness. It was not successful, however, in preventing yet another brutal torture, rape, and murder of a woman. *In Mourning and In Rage* had sought to change the parameters of our understanding of rape and the patriarchal ideology that shored it up. The seven-foot mourners had thus attempted to place the rape/murders perpetrated by the Hillside Stranglers into a larger context of societal misogyny and violence against women. The fact that a woman was raped/murdered during the evening following the performance is not so much an indication of Lacy's and Labowitz's failure to use performance as a vehicle for change as it was a sign of the profoundly misogynist nature of patriarchal society. In the media coverage surrounding the Hillside Stranglers, the women who fell victim to these predatory men had become little more than sexualized bodies who were (stupidly) in the wrong place at the wrong time: *all* women were potential victims, but sexual women were more likely to fall victim than those women that controlled their sexuality. *In Mourning and In Rage* might have been deemed (and certainly has been

Powers of Desire, *Jillin Jackin' Off Jacket,* **modeled by Renee Edgington,** ca. 1992-1995. Performance group founded by Renee Edgington and Matt Francis. Photograph by Powers of Desire.

canonized) as an unequivocal success in the annals of feminist activist practice. To a large extent it was. Nevertheless, it leaves open the question, posed by Barry and Flitterman-Lewis, as to whether it simply (and facilely) transformed mourning into rage, equivocating on the former in favor of the latter.

The answer to this last question cannot be reduced to a comparison between feminist art that interrogated patriarchal representation versus feminist art that celebrated an innate female power. *In Mourning and In Rage* had an immediate effect because it was able to mobilize fear and turn it into positive action and righteous anger, at least for a while. The problem with any activist performance art, particularly pieces such as *In Mourning and In Rage* that deal with terribly brutal subject matter, is that it is difficult to sustain the initial energy that produced the piece in the first place. A performance designed to be "media-friendly" runs the risk of becoming the flavor of the month. Addressing women's rights was fashionable in the seventies, less fashionable in the eighties and nineties. Drained and exhausted from dealing day in and day out with such brutal subject matter (which was never more than a catchy hook for the local media), Lacy and Labowitz backed off from their earlier agitprop performances. They collaborated several more times after *In Mourning and In Rage*, organizing a performance structured after *Three Weeks in May* for Las Vegas entitled *There Are Voices in the*

Desert (1978) and designing a float under the auspices of Ariadne for the Take Back the Night March in San Francisco in 1978. *Take Back the Night* was the last major perform- ance structure that Lacy and Labowitz collaborated on together, although they contin- ued to work on separate projects under the auspices of Ariadne. Labowitz turned to a more personal, introspective style of performance while Lacy continued organizing large-scale performances that were geared towards exploring the connections that she believed existed between all women.

XIV. Mourning Our Collective Loss

Lacy's and Labowitz's decision to turn away from dealing with the atrocities perpet- rated against women in their later work suggests that they in fact had not permitted themselves time to mourn. As I was preparing to write this paper, I ran across Douglas Crimp's article "Mourning and Militancy." The parallel between his title and that of Lacy's and Labowitz's piece immediately struck me. "Mourning and Militancy," written at the height of the AIDS epidemic, was Crimp's attempt to reconcile the seemingly passive act of mourning (candlelight vigils for the death of people one had loved) with the proactive stance of activist protest. In a powerful argument that interwove Freud's theories on mourning and melancholy with his own personal experience as a Stonewall-era gay man and AIDS activist, Crimp suggested that AIDS activists had "transformed" their sorrow into rage simply because they had to: "Seldom has a society so savaged people during their hour of loss."[45] The process of mourning was constantly interrupted, savaged, as Crimp put it, which in turn resulted in its being transformed into activism. And yet, militancy, which makes all violence external, fails to address the profound sadness engendered by the violence—psychic, linguistic, and physical—that gay men have endured and internalized. Thus militancy functions in some way as a denial of the pain that gay men have internalized, permitting them to continue to deny their own ambivalence. "There is no question," Crimp concluded,

> but that we must fight the unspeakable violence we incur from the
> society in which we find ourselves. But if we understand that violence
> is able to reap its horrible rewards through the very psychic mecha-
> nisms that make us part of this society, then we may also be able to
> recognize—along with our rage—our terror, our guilt, and our pro-
> found sadness. Militancy, of course, then, but mourning too: mourn-
> ing and militancy.[46]

One could make the same argument, of course, for the way in which society had time and again savaged women in their time of need by suggesting that the responsibility for rape rested with the victim rather than the perpetrator of the assault. Although Lacy and Labowitz viewed the seven-foot tall mourners as a transformation of the stereotypical image of the powerless female mourners, they were nevertheless *mourn-ers*, a physical embodiment of psychic pain at the loss of women's lives. Dealing with material such as rape, pornography, and incest was a constant assault on the psyches of all the women involved, a fresh attack that did not allow the psychic wounds from the previous one to heal. It is little wonder that Lacy and Labowitz were unable to continue working on this difficult material. What is amazing is that they were able to do as much as they did.

XV. Powers of Desire

In the end, I think that the success of Lacy's and Labowitz's work can best be gauged by its influence on subsequent activist performance. In 1990, Crimp came to Southern California to teach a class at CalArts. Two of the participants in that class were Edgington and Francis, who subsequently founded Powers of Desire (POD). In many ways, POD was modeled on AIDS activist collectives in New York City and Chicago such as ACT UP and Queer Nation. Like these groups, POD was heavily informed by post-structuralist theories of subject construction and a Foucauldian analysis of the workings of power and repression in every day society. What distinguished POD from these other collec-tives, however, was its location in Southern California, the site of performances such as *In Mourning and In Rage*. Edgington and Francis were familiar with the work that had been done by the feminists in the seventies. What is more, they knew of Cheri Gaulke, a student and then teacher at the Woman's Building. Although they did not subscribe to goddess spirituality in any manner or form, they were extremely sympa-thetic to the notion of doing performance that combined an expression of psychic pain with militant activism. In 1992, they created a performative installation piece for Los Angeles Contemporary Exhibitions (LACE) entitled *AIDS Molotov Mausoleum*, which was a mausoleum wall comprised of memorial plaques dedicated to prominent AIDS activists. Each contained a Molotov cocktail that the viewer was invited to take down and throw at prominent institutions. *AIDS Molotov Mausoleum*, like *In Mourning and In Rage*, permitted the simultaneous expression of mourning and anger. Just as the image of the women standing in front of city hall retrospectively permits the viewer to mourn for women who have been victimized by violence, so too did the *AIDS Molotov Mausoleum*, which created a space for the sort of quietism that had been earlier eschewed by AIDS activists.

The *AIDS Molotov Mausoleum* was in some ways atypical of the overall art pro-duction of POD and its offspring, Clean Needles Now (CNN). In 1987, Crimp had called for a "critical, theoretical and activist" alternative to the "personal, elegiac expressions that appeared to dominate the art-world response to AIDS."[47] For the most part, the art events orchestrated by POD, which took place in the gritty streets of Los Angeles, were a response to this call. It is not surprising, then, that POD became CNN, an activist or-ganization dedicated to preventing the transmission of AIDS from contaminated

needles.[48] As representatives of POD and then CNN, the members wore colorful clothing, drove bizarre vehicles and generally made spectacles of themselves even in Southern California, the home of Disneyland, Hollywood, and Magic Mountain Amusement Park. Although influenced by Crimp's call to activist arms, they were also clearly indebted to an aesthetic that did not originate in New York, but rather in Southern California. The performance collectives organized by Lacy's students exemplified that aesthetic of colorful activism: The Waitresses, the Feminist Art Workers and the Sisters Of Survival. All three collectives dressed in outrageous clothing (the S.O.S. wore nun's habits that were the colors of the rainbow) and performed guerrilla actions (the Feminist Art Workers did a performance where they called women on the phone to verbally affirm rather than assault them), but of the three, it was probably The Waitresses whose work most resembled that of POD.

XVI. The Waitresses

Anne Gauldin and Jerri Allyn founded The Waitresses around 1977; they came up with the idea while driving to Santa Cruz to attend a conference.[49] The original group, which included Denise Yarfitz, Patty Nicklaus, Jamie Wildman (also known as Wild and Wildperson), Leslie Belt, Allyn, and Gauldin, initially met in order to do consciousness-raising and brainstorming about their experiences as waitresses. By 1978, they unleashed their consciousness-raising performances on an unsuspecting restaurant-going audience in Los Angeles. *Ready to Order?* was a weeklong series of guerrilla performances at various restaurants. *Ready to Order?* was loosely modeled after *Three Weeks in May* (for which Gauldin did a performance) in that it included a number of workshops and panel discussions on the history of working women, job discrimination, and assertiveness training. Like the latter performance, it also received a great deal of publicity, as public relations was another skill that Gauldin and Allyn had learned from Lacy and Labowitz. The impromptu performances, which dealt with issues such as sexual harassment and discrimination, were based on incidents that actually happened to the performers when they worked as waitresses.[50] Performances/skits included a pantomime of a waitress looking for a non-existent tip, a snotty Italian "waiter" who intimidated "his" customers into leaving a big tip, and the "Millie" awards—an awards ceremony that included the categories of the longest inconsequential conversation and longest smile.

XVII. Feminist Humor

Probably the best-known image of The Waitresses, however, is that of the waitress-goddess, a late twentieth-century version of the many-breasted Diana of Ephesus. In one typical photograph, she stands left of center, her arms raised, wearing pink grape leaves in her hair, more bunches of (fake) grapes attached to her dress, and a prosthesis with approximately thirteen breasts, some with bright red nipples, some with pink nipples, and some with no nipples at all. Gauldin, whose belief in the power of the goddess as a feminist statement infused much of her work as a Waitress, played the many-breasted goddess. While still a student at the FSW, Gauldin began doing private backyard rituals, which she later translated into performances such as *Coffee Cauldron* (1980), a fusion of Kali (the many-armed female Hindu goddess) and waitress imagery. Gauldin also traveled to the island of Malta, where she did a ritualistic and collaborative performance with Cheri Gaulke, another of Lacy's students.[51] As with Lacy's and Labowitz's performances, the work of The Waitresses combined an interest in contemporary issues that affected women with a mytho-poetic vision of a feminist future. There was, however, one significant difference between the former and the latter: the degree of seriousness with which each collective approached the subject matter at hand. It is much easier to find humor in the plight of a waitress (even though her plight stems from the inequities of patriarchal society) than to find humor in rape,

220

Above: **Powers of Desire,** *AIDS Molotov Mausoleum, Fight AIDS not Arabs*, 1992. Performative installation piece, mausoleum wall with memorial plaques and Molotov cocktails, installed at Los Angeles Contemporary Exhibitions (LACE). Powers of Desire performance group founded by Renee Edgington and Matt Francis. Photograph by Powers of Desire.

Below: ***Ready to Order?***, 1978. The premiere of The Waitresses performance art group in a 7-day, site-oriented, conceptual art structure that took place in various restaurants and cultural sites in Los Angeles. Cofounders Jerri Allyn and Anne Gauldin were joined by Leslie Belt, Patti Nicklaus, Jamie Wildman-Webber, and Denise Yarftiz Pierre. Photograph by Maria Karras at Lafayette's Café, Venice, California. © The Waitresses: Jerri Allyn and Anne Gauldin.

sexual violence and murder, and incest. The element of humor also made it easier to deal publicly with issues that were unpopular in society at large. "The thing I loved about The Waitresses," Gauldin recalls, "is that humor was always a really important part of our work. It was important for us to give feminist information, but it wasn't like cramming it down somebody's throat, it was presenting it in a really fun, upbeat way that people could hear what we had to say.... We were kind of crackpot."[52]

By using humor in their performances, The Waitresses sought to engage what Rita Felski has termed the "feminist counter-public sphere," a term that takes its name from the bourgeois public sphere of the late eighteenth century, "a critical and independent public domain that perceives itself as distinct from state interests" and that related literature and art to an explicitly gendered community.[53] The humorous "counter-public sphere" invoked by The Waitresses in the late seventies was invoked by POD and CNN in the early nineties as they too sought to relate literature and art to the specific experiences and interests of an explicitly gendered community—in this case, those people whose sexuality is considered non-normative. One of the most paradigmatic photographs taken in conjunction with POD was that of Edgington modeling a fancy cowboy hat and coat in which the abundant fringe on the sleeves had been replaced by condoms. Edgington's coat appeared to contain hundreds of small nipples, just as the many-breasted Diana wore at least thirteen larger nipples/breasts on her own garment. In many ways, there is a great deal of similarity between the two photographs, with Edgington standing in a pose that mimics that of Diana. Like Gauldin, Edgington wore the *Jillin' Jackin' Off Jacket* for street performances and activist interventions. Edgington's "fringe," however, is not comprised of nipples. The condom was part of POD's courageous attempt to spread safe-sex information in the face of an aggressive campaign of disinformation and miscommunication on the part of the media. Unlike Diana's nipples, which served as a signifier of a prelapsarian feminist innocence, a sign of the present-day potential for a feminist utopia in which waitresses could be given their due, the condoms were a way of putting a good face on a bad thing, a reminder that safe sex was, by necessity, sex with barriers. Like The Waitresses, POD (and Edgington) used humor, "crackpot" behavior, and an outrageous aesthetic in order to effect social change. Unlike the work of The Waitresses, the performance events of POD never got beyond the desire to ameliorate a less than satisfactory present. POD (and later, CNN) came about precisely because there was no end in sight to the AIDS epidemic, and not because they could envision that end through the agency of their work. Edgington thus wore hundreds of small containers, latex barriers designed to prevent both pregnancy and the spread of disease.

XVIII. Conclusions

"ACT UP," Mary Patten has written, "did not always acknowledge our predecessors— in fact, some of us needed constant reminders that direct action, street theater, and media genius were not 'invented' by us."[54] As I have engaged in my own research on the feminist activist performance associated with the Woman's Building, I have wondered why art done in the name of AIDS activism has not been more open in acknowledging its commonality with the earlier work. Lacy's and Labowitz's use of guerrilla intervention against hegemonic media representations, their perceptive analysis of how the media functioned, and their attempt to put forth an alternate discourse to the ideology of the victim (a tactic that was also adopted by AIDS activist artists) extended and transformed the irruptive moments of Dada street performance into performative actions that could be interpreted as harbingers of the new epistemology of postmodernity because of its gender specificity. Given the commonality between seventies and nineties activist art, I suspect it was the utopian impulses and references to feminist spirituality in the former that has made it difficult for the latter to acknowledge any connections. Certainly this was my problem when I climbed up the side of the mountain over ten years ago. The goddess is deliberately anti-intellectual, or at least anti-theory. She has seemed to exist outside of theory and even history, a fiction that her advocates, with their nostalgic talk of matrifocal societies and female archetypes, have reinforced. And yet, the invocation of the Goddess is profoundly hopeful, a beacon of light in what would otherwise be a dreary landscape. Ten years later, older, wiser, and less radical, I find myself identifying with the words of Erica Rand, another veteran of the AIDS activist and safe sex wars:

> We must create contexts for more broad-based theorizing and strategizing, and recognize that this requires very hard work. It requires, too, professional theorists, like consultants and academics, getting over ourselves—so that we neither presume that we have all the representational expertise nor encourage others to conclude that we do—and vigilant attention about impediments to broad-based theorizing.[55]

The performance art of the Woman's Building encompassed many aspects—autobiography, identity, activism, and feminist spirituality—all in the name of bringing about social change in an active and aggressive manner. As we enter not only a new century but also a new millennium—a time of change, optimism, and hope—it is perhaps finally time to embrace this legacy of the Woman's Building.

Notes

1. For an overview of Lacy's performance work from the early to mid-seventies, see Suzanne Lacy, "She Who Would Fly," interview by Richard Newton, *High Performance* 1.1 (February 1978): 4–7.

2. Cheri Gaulke, interviewed by author, Los Angeles, CA, December 1995.

3. Alice Echols, *Daring to Be Bad: Radical Feminism in America 1967–75*, (Minneapolis: University of Minnesota Press, 1989), 5.

4. Ibid., 50.

5. Judith Barry and Sandy Flitterman-Lewis, "Textual Strategies: The Politics of Art Making," in *Visibly Female*, ed. Hilary Robinson (London: Camden Press, 1987), 106–107.

6. Ibid., 107.

7. This was certainly the case with the formation of the Natalie Barney Collective and the Lesbian Art Project, which were organized under the auspices of the Woman's Building. See Terry Wolverton, "Lesbian Art: A Partial Inventory," *Insurgent Muse: Life and Art at the Woman's Building* (San Francisco: City Lights, 2002.)

8. Suzanne Lacy, interviewed by Moira Roth, Los Angeles, CA, March 16, 1990. Archives of American Art, Smithsonian Institution, Washington, D.C., 28.

9. Teresa de Lauretis, "Upping the Anti [Sic] in Feminist Theory," in *The Cultural Studies Reader*, ed. Simon During (New York: Routledge, 1993), 77. A slightly different version of this essay was also published with the title "The Essence of the Triangle or, Taking the Risk of Essentialism Seriously: Feminist Theory in Italy, the U.S., and Britain" in *Differences: A Journal of Feminist Cultural Studies* 1.2 (Fall 1989).

10. Faith Wilding, "The Feminist Art Programs at Fresno and CalArts, 1970–75," in *The Power of Feminist Art: The American Movement of the 1970s, History and Impact*, ed. Norma Broude and Mary D. Garrard (New York: Harry N. Abrams, 1994), 35.

11. The scripts of these two performances are reprinted in the appendix of Judy Chicago, *Through the Flower: My Struggle as a Woman Artist* (New York: Anchor Books/Doubleday, 1975) 207–19.

12. Ibid., 208.

13. Ibid.

14. Amelia Jones, *Body Art: Performing the Subject* (Minneapolis: University of Minnesota Press, 1998), 50.

15. Lacy, interviewed by Roth, 20.

16. Ibid.

17. Arlene Raven, *Crossing Over: Feminism and Art of Social Concern* (Ann Arbor: UMI Research Press, 1988), 27.

18. Trinh T. Minh-ha, *When the Moon Waxes Red: Representation, Gender, and Cultural Politics* (New York: Routledge, 1991), 12–13.

19. Jeanie Forte, "Women's Performance Art: Feminism and Postmodernism," in *Performing Feminisms*, ed. Sue Ellen Case (Baltimore: The Johns Hopkins University Press, 1990), 251.

20. Susan Brownmiller, *Against Our Will* (New York: Simon and Schuster, 1975), 15; Teresa de Lauretis, *Technologies of Gender* (Bloomington: Indiana University Press, 1987), 32. In order to keep the logic of my argument, I have somewhat abridged that of de Lauretis, which draws upon the work of Wini Breines and Linda Gordon on family violence. De Lauretis is specifically concerned here with looking at case studies on family violence that employ supposedly gender-neutral language. Because of the applicability of de Lauretis's argument to my own, I have extended her comparison to include the way in which rape is discursively structured under the law as a gender-less crime of violence, a position that most feminists are understandably against.

21. Raven, 27.

22. In her second autobiography, *Beyond the Flower: The Autobiography of a Feminist Artist* (New York: Viking, 1996), Chicago writes at length about her decision to change her name legally to Chicago from Gerowitz, her married name. Fighting to maintain her identity in the face of the blatant sexism that plagued the California art world,

Chicago "borrowed" from the Civil Rights movements and publicly and legally divested herself of her surname, an act which required her then husband, Lloyd Hamrol, to sign legal papers. In order to announce her name change, Chicago's dealer, Jack Glenn, had an ad printed in *Artforum* spoofing the macho announcements by male artists that were regularly published in that magazine. The result was the now infamous 1971 photograph by Jerry McMillan of Chicago posing as a boxer with her new name emblazoned across her chest.

23. Raven, 27.

24. Hannah J. L. Feldman, "More Than Confessional: Testimonial and the Subject of Rape," in *The Subject of Rape*, ed. Monica Chau, Hannah J.L. Feldman, Jennifer Kabot, and Hannah Kruse (New York: Whitney Museum of American Art, 1993), 14–15.

25. Ibid., 14, 16.

26. Chicago, *Through the Flower*, 217.

27. The image of *Ablutions* is reproduced on page 169 in *The Power of Feminist Art*. The image in *TDR* shows Lacy nailing the kidneys to the wall, while the twine lies coiled on the floor nearby. For a discussion of Lacy's role in this piece, see Moira Roth, "Suzanne Lacy: Social Reformer and Witch," *TDR/The Drama Review* 32.11 (Spring 1988): 42–60.

28. Lacy, interviewed by Roth, 22.

29. Mieke Bal, *Reading Rembrandt: Beyond the Word-Image Opposition* (Cambridge: Cambridge University Press, 1991).

30. For a more detailed discussion of Gentileschi's work, see Mary Garrard, *Artemisia Gentileschi: The Image of the Female Hero in Italian Baroque* (New York: HarperCollins, 1989). For a more detailed discussion of Mary Cassatt, see Griselda Pollock, *Vision and Difference: Femininity, Feminism, and the Histories of Art* (London and New York: Routledge, 1988).

31. Pollock, 1.

32. See Josephine Withers's account of the performance in her article "Feminist Performance Art: Performing, Discovering, Transforming Ourselves," in *The Power of Feminist Art*, 170–71.

33. Suzanne Lacy and Lucy R. Lippard, "Political Performance Art: A Discussion by Suzanne Lacy and Lucy R. Lippard," *Heresies* 5.1 (1984): 25.

34. Suzanne Lacy and Judith Baca, "Affinities: Thoughts on an Incomplete History," in *The Power of Feminist Art*, 269. While Lacy has stated in several publications the importance of Kaprow's influence, her most sustained discussion of the importance of his teachings occurs on pages 22–24 in the interview with Roth.

35. *In Mourning and In Rage*, which is probably Lacy and Labowitz's best known performance, was documented in Lacy, "*She Who Would Fly*: Interview with Suzanne Lacy."

36. Lacy and Labowitz, "Evolution of a Feminist Art: Public Forms and Social Issues," *Heresies* 2.2 (Summer 1978): 83.

37. Thanks to the performance, Lacy and Labowitz became local talk-show celebrities. Ransom money for the capture of the Hillside Strangler(s) was reallocated for women's self-defense classes. For one night, at least, media coverage shifted from a reification of the mythology of rape to images of women practicing self-defense. Finally, an intrepid reporter went down immediately after the performance to the phone company, who had initially resisted listing the phone numbers for rape hot lines in the emergency listing, and forced them to back down.

38. The Woman's Building, "Moving Out: Leslie Labowitz and Ruth Iskin on Social, Feminist and Performance Art," *Spinning Off* (April 1979): 3.

39. Leslie Labowitz, interviewed by Michele Moravec, transcript, August 25, 1994, Woman's Building Collection, Archives of American Art, Smithsonian Institution, Washington, D.C., 3–4.

40. Labowitz, interviewed by Moravec.

41. Labowitz and Lacy, "Evolution of a Feminist Art," 78.

42. Ibid., 78.

43. Probably the closest thing that American feminism had to Beuys was Rachel Rosenthal, who deliberately used her (constructed) personae in her performances. For an excellent overview of Rosenthal's work, see Moira Roth, ed., *Rachel Rosenthal* (Baltimore: Johns Hopkins University Press, 1997).

44. Whereas Lacy would start first with an image of her performance and then would make her politics work with the initial image, Labowitz was always conscious of coming up with imagery that could work politically. In her best-known performance, *Paragraph 218*, Labowitz deliberately used "clear, direct images in order to avoid mis-interpretation." At the time of the performance, supreme court judges were debating whether to reinstate the law making abortion illegal in West Germany; *Paragraph 218* was performed at the city hall on the eve of the judges' vote. Part of a program put on by a women's organization, *Paragraph 218* was performed before approxi-mately five hundred spectators, most of them women, who held up torches to light the performance area. Three women dressed in black pointed hoods and capes representing the German supreme court judges stood on a stage holding signs with 218 hands printed on them. On either side of the judges stood two women in red hoods. A woman wearing street clothes entered the performance space and screamed at the judges, "Why can't anybody hear me?" The two women in red then wrapped her in white gauze. When they were done, they threw a bucket of red paint over the by-now kneeling and wrapped woman. Finally, another woman wearing a short skirt and high heels entered carrying a six-foot long, gold penis, which she handed to the judges. The judges held it aloft, and then threw it at the audience, where it broke in pieces. In *Paragraph 218*, Labowitz deliberately created a performance that had a somewhat "raw" look, which she saw as indicative of a work that grew out of the *volk* rather than the *gesallshaft* of German society. Produced for about $25, *Paragraph 218* was deliberately crude in a Brechtian sense in order to provide contrast with the slick images of femininity in the media. The reaction to the performance was all that Labowitz could have desired. "It was very emotional," she recalled. "After it was over, there was a period of silence where our spiritual connection could be felt throughout the group." After living in Spain for a year, Labowitz returned to California, where she very quickly became involved in the feminist com-munity. Introduced to Lacy by the performance artist Eleanor Antin, Labowitz found herself participating in *Three Weeks in May* almost before she knew what she was doing. The four performances that Labowitz executed for *Three Weeks in May* recycled much of the imagery from *Paragraph 218*, including the gauze-wrapped woman and the judges in pointed, medieval-looking hats. In *Myths of Rape*, which was performed on May 19, 1977, six blind-folded women in black representing society's blindness carried hand-painted signs with myths and facts about rape. The women alternately assumed positions of defense and defenselessness while Labowitz handed out liter-ature to the office workers on their lunch hours. For the second performance, on May 20, *The Rape*, Labowitz collaborated with the Women Against Rape, Men Against Rape Organization. A woman was circled by per-formers wearing signs identifying themselves as social institutions, while being wrapped (and silenced) from head to toe in gauze. She was then carried out of the mall on a stretcher, a "rape" victim that had been raped a second time by an unfriendly legal system. The third performance on May 21, *All Men Are Potential Rapists*, was performed and created with two men from the Los Angeles Men's Collective. In this performance, the men recreated childhood games that fostered attitudes condoning violence against women. The final performance on May 22, *Women Fight Back*, was performed on the day of the closing rally by members of the Woman's Building. Several women hid in large black cones with statements such as "gouge eyes" and "turn fear into anger" written on them. Another woman on the outside was bound by ominous figures, while the "cone women" struggled to break free. The performance ended with the rescue of the bound woman.

45. Douglas Crimp, "Mourning and Militancy," in *Out There: Marginalization and Contemporary Culture*, Russell Ferguson et al, eds. (New York: The New Museum of Contemporary Art, 1990), 237.

46. Ibid., 243.

47. Crimp, "AIDS: Cultural Analysis/Cultural Activism," in *AIDS: Cultural Analysis/Cultural Activism*, Douglas Crimp, ed. (Cambridge, MA: MIT Press, 1989), 15. First published in October 43 (Winter 1987).

48. Under the auspices of Clean Needles Now, Edgington and Francis were able to open a storefront for needle exchange in West Hollywood, a space that has remained open even after their untimely deaths in an automobile accident in the summer of 1998.

49. Unless otherwise noted, most of my information comes from Anne Gauldin, interviewed by Michelle Moravec, September 20, 1992. Collection of the Woman's Building Board of Directors.

50. My description of the performances comes from Pamela J. King, "They also serve those who waitress," *Los Angeles Herald Examiner*, May 7, 1978. In one performance, a rude customer and a demanding employer drive a harried waitress to distraction—until she turns into "Wonder Waitress," complete with satin jogging shorts. In another performance, a comfortably garbed waitress is urged by her boss and a redneck customer to "spruce up" her appearance. She dons hot pants and high heels, and improves her tips significantly even though she spends more time flirting than working.

51. *The Malta Project* took place in the summer of 1978, as a collaborative performance executed for the partic pants in the Edinburgh Arts Project and the startled inhabitants of Malta. The piece begins in a church, where Gaulke, dressed like a priest with red high-heeled shoes, told the story of her father, the Protestant minister. Moving outside, Gaulke put on red shoes and danced until she collapsed at the feet of the goddess in Tarxien, the above-ground temple. Gaulke was then carried through the streets to an underground temple where Gauldin performed a healing ritual dance over her body.

52. Gauldin, Interview by Moravec, 13.

53. Rita Felski, *Beyond Feminist Aesthetics: Feminist Literature and Social Change* (Cambridge, MA: Harvard University, 1989), 164.

54. Mary Patten, "The Thrill is Gone: An ACT UP Post-Mortem (Confessions of a Former AIDS Activist)," in *The Passionate Camera*, ed. Deborah Bright (New York: Routledge, 1998), 389.

55. Erica Rand, "The Passionate Activist and the Political Camera," in *The Passionate Camera*, 378.

Images and words that reflect the authentic and varied life experiences of women are seldom valued or visible in public, printed communications, undermining our connection to the dominant culture. Lacking the graphic skills valued by that culture limits access to professional work and the skills developed within women's subculture are rendered unavailable to society at large.

Women's Graphic Center's classes, presses, galleries and outreach network provide a uniquely supportive community in which you can discover, explore, and communicate your experience, as a woman. For 6 years women have been designing and printing books, posters, and postcards at the Women's Graphic Center. By encouraging women to maintain ethnic and sexual identity in graphic communications, the personal connection to work is made, creating a bridge between private experience and the public world.

Speak your own language

Writing, artmaking, design and printing are taught by professional women, providing a necessary link to job related information.

WGC Core Faculty

Sheila Levrant de Bretteville
Eloise Klein Healy
Susan King
Sue Maberry
Mary McNally
Cynthia Marsh

1980 Visiting Artists

Frances Butler
April Greiman
Judy Hofberg
Deena Metzger
Jane Rosenzweig
Betye Saar
Deborah Sussman
Kathy Walkup
Teresa Woodwood
Linda Vallejo

I've got things to say

Please send me more information

name
address
city   state   zip code
phone

Women's Graphic Center
at the Woman's Building
1727 N. Spring Street
Los Angeles, CA 90012
213 221-6161

THE COMMUNITY OF DESIGN / THE DESIGN OF COMMUNITY: AN EMAIL DIALOGUE

Sheila Levrant de Bretteville and Bia Lowe

Dear Bia:

It is a bright, crisp, sunny day. I am working on my public art project for 207th Street,[1] working still with some of the same notions regarding participatory democracy and design with which I formed the Women's Design Program in 1971 and the Woman's Building [in 1973].[2] The neighborhood around the A train subway stop as an expression of everyday life over time is the subject there, and the participants are of different classes, genders, and ethnicities.

I'd like to propose a "conversation" with you via e-mail regarding our days at the Woman's Building. I am very interested in those moments when we were both in the same place at the same time and where our memories of an event overlap and diverge, as well as where our interpretations are alike and different. Can we find those nodes? And then coalesce our comments around them?

Part of my interest in doing this with you is that you were there in 1971 in the Women's Design Program at CalArts, and in 1973 in the Feminist Studio Workshop, and then the Women's Graphic Center at the Woman's Building. It seems to me that we have a special opportunity to look at our differences and similarities, and see whether we are able to locate convergence or divergence to traditional categories of age, class, or sexual preference.

Tell me what you think.

Love,

Sheila

Dear Sheila,

You're on!

I met you at CalArts when I was twenty—a young twenty, very passive, inse-
cure, a virgin. I fancied myself as creative but didn't trust my own ability to make
forms. Feminism challenged the prevailing psychological model of being female, and
gave me a radically new insight into my gender, my sexuality, my fear of my own powers.
I was ready for the Women's Movement, and in particular, an intelligent community
of women who would delve into "consciousness-raising" as well as (excuse the jar-
gon) find empowerment through the process of form making. And, there you were.
The Women's Design Program was custom-made for any woman whose feminism
had a cultural bent, whose sense of self-in-the-world could be nurtured through
creative work and a grounding of feminist analysis.

Your first design assignment had us begin with two rudimentary materials:
an Avery dot label and a blank piece of paper—one unit, a singularity, a self against a
ground. Slowly we were to add more dots to the paper, to discover the resonance of
one thing to another, and then, of course, to consider the whole. From there we each
took our composition of dots and reduced it photographically, making sixteen reproductions. From those, we worked within a grid to assemble a quilt of our dot images.
Each in turn could be reduced and reproduced sixteen times, to assemble more and
more intricate compositions, as many times as we wished. Like the Eames's film,
Powers of Ten, some of the results looked like clusters of supernovas, while others
coiled like strands of jewel-like DNA.

In the process, we learned a great deal about photo reproduction, and saw how
design, rather than being a formidable realm controlled by an unseen Oz, is simple
assemblage: a human satisfaction, completely within our grasp. From there it was not
difficult to extrapolate to other designed realms, say fashion, architecture, city planning and beyond to the subtle, and not-so subtle, elements that influence our lives as
women. If we wanted to change the world, indeed, our own lives, what aspect of the
culture, of public life, could we influence through creative work?

A bit of alchemy, something of the empowerment I was hoping to find, happened
with your next assignment. We were to choose a text—something particularly pleasing
or disturbing—and manipulate it using the design and conceptual skills we had
learned in the previous exercise. I chose a passage from *Last Exit to Brooklyn*, the rape
of the character Tralala. I first took my photo reproduction of the text and cut it up so
that all the words related to the victim (Tralala, her clothes and body parts) made up a
sphere, while all the predicates (the rapists, their body parts, their actions, and their
implements) composed a kind of arrow bearing down on the sphere. This solution
seemed simplistic, too literal. I wanted to go deeper. I then arranged all the nouns, be
they related to the victim or to the perpetrators, so they appeared to be falling off right
the right edge of the page, and assembled all the verbs so they appeared to be falling

off the left. This solution was a more discerning portrait of rape, of dissociation, wherein people and actions were in freefall.

I had deconstructed a brutal passage from a controversial novel, and saw I had the power to diffuse something hurtful in the dominant culture. I wanted to do more of that, to become an actor in my world. You gave me the permission to play, to trust I would find a form that could bring deeper levels of meaning to the content. The alchemy of that assignment has served me well, especially as a writer. Like design, writing is a process of arrangement, aggregation, of organizing information. I work until the whole is bigger than the parts. I trust the process until the gestalt glistens.

So, if I haven't already said as much, thank you.

Love,

Bia

Dear Bia,

The way you describe your writing style, as "a process of arrangement, aggregation," would seem to map well onto the way we are talking with each other via e-mail.

It is truly a delight for me to hear that an assignment I gave in 1970 could be helpful to you long after. I barely knew what could come from what I was asking and doing with the students who chose to be in the Women's Design Program. I wonder whether my intentions, if told now, would have meaning for you as a writer, or for others who design, make art, or teach.

Teaching for me was almost entirely about structuring a situation in which I could question what I had been taught and what was being made and taught by others at the time. In design schools, students taught by teachers steeped in modernism, as I had been, were often given a short text to manipulate formally: first only the size of the type was allowed to change, then space, then weight, and finally an image was permitted to augment the specificity and power of the visual communication. At the time I began teaching, graphic designer Dan Friedman gave his students a weather report to manipulate in this way, and the results were published in The Journal of Typographic Research. *The work was beautifully cool and elegant. I thought students could learn the same typographic skills by choosing the short texts themselves and manipulating the typography according to the meaning those texts had for each of them, rather than starting with a text to which they might have no personal or meaningful connection. It seemed to me that the resultant work would not look the same as those where formal exploration was disconnected from a particular person's unique connection to the text. It seemed to me that the invitation to choose your own text would reflect not only the diversity of the texts and the depth of connection. The aesthetic aspects would reflect the individual woman's own visual voice. I was quite surprised to learn that a powerful emotional connection to the subject matter can make slow, controlled, formal manipulation much more difficult to do, and to teach; at the same time it was totally*

233

worth the effort. I saw work that was unpredicted, unique, and particular.

I remember that you chose a section from Hubert Selby's Last Exit to Brooklyn—*the rape of Tralala—a powerful and brutal text about which virtually any woman would have strong feelings. Would it be possible to see yourself as separate from the text, to step back from it, and work with it formally at the same time? I had no idea what visual forms would develop from this investigation, or where teaching in this way would lead.*

I am so very relieved and pleased to learn that a process of moving words or images around until the "gestalt glistens"(!) evolved from this. Excellent!

I worried sometimes that the Women's Design Program participants would not bond to design. I was too new to teaching to know that most college students do not go into the fields they study but use what they learn in whichever way their own paths take them. By teaching you differently, I was concerned that each of you was not being inducted into the field of design in a way that would encourage you to become designers deeply connected to your work, as designers and authors, in the way many of my students now see themselves. I tried to show work that I thought demonstrated how people who loved to make things were also looking at society as a made thing.

Love,
Sheila

Dear Sheila,

The images in the dominant culture were—and continue to be—abusive, targeting the glandular. Images are meant to arrest the viewer, to stimulate reactions of fear, excitement, deprivation or shame. We intended to change the world, but did we want to deliver our content with the same low blows? Or could we combat those images with female values? And if so, what forms would suit our feminism?

You were all about female values, many exemplified by your use of the grid: a quiet field the viewer can step into and encounter. The grid demonstrates respect for that viewer, her own relationship to information, and her own pace of discovery. The grid is both democratic and participatory. I am thinking now about all our talks concerning democracy and anarchy, and our interest (this, in my memory, was particular to you and me) in the Italian design group, Superstudio.[3] We loved their futuristic posters of landscapes superimposed on a grid, within which people migrated according to their needs or interests, carrying few personal possessions, linked by a worldwide grid of information. Information was to replace materialism, to free us from ownership and therefore from all human bondage.

Twenty-eight years later, I'm living in that utopia, plugged into the Web, migratory between Los Angeles, New York City, and Ireland. The Internet has been the vehicle for a more global/anarchic/decentralized existence, but it has also enabled tribalism to flourish and allowed us to become detached. And at the same time, the

234

Superstudio (Adolofo
Natalini, Cristiano Toraldo di
Francia, Roberto Magris, G.
Piero Frassinelli, Alessandro
Magris, Alessandro Poli)
1970–72. *Fundamental Acts*,
from *Life Supersurface. Pulizie
di Primavera (Spring Cleaning)*.
© Superstudio 1972.

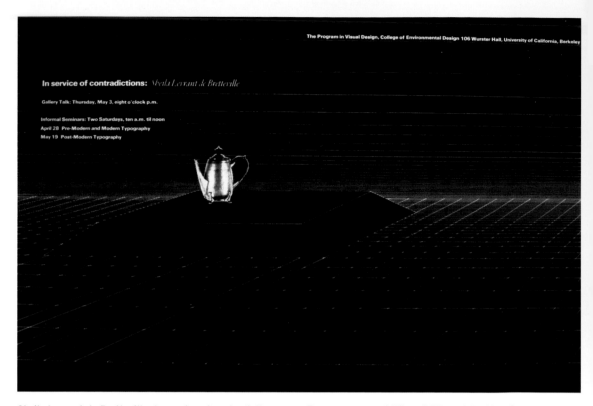

Sheila Levrant de Bretteville, *In service of contradictions*, 1979. Diazo sepia print 16 ¾" x 24". Woman's Building Image Archive, Otis College of Art and Design.

virtual environment conspires as a collective mirage, making it harder to engage with the difficulties and joys under our noses, within our grasp.

And it's forced us to question the veracity and meaning of so much information, and what controls, if any, we have over what goes out or comes in to our thoughts. We are more mistrustful of information and of discourse…and that bodes ill, I fear.

But now to bed…

xx, Bia

Dear Bia,

The slides I showed you in 1971 from Superstudio were also an attempt for me to connect my new life in California with my recent life in Italy. I showed the work that fascinated me: designers who initiated and gave form to subjects that captured their imagination. The Superstudio architects made graphic images and wrote texts that translated what they feared and what they wanted into vivid and powerful metaphors. It seemed to me then, and still does now, that Superstudio's dystopias and Italo Calvino's Invisible Cities *were capable of inspiring graphic designers who could move the profession beyond status quo positions. I wished I had done what Superstudio had—those visual presentations of fictional cities, which gave form to feared outcomes of current social problems! I optimistically hoped to inspire you and myself to imagine desired, as well as feared, outcomes—I wanted especially to see our hoped-for futures.*

I was not nearly as reflective as you might have thought regarding my own interiority, and I had not investigated which of my needs made working with women so compelling. I was aware of pushing myself and my work toward questions without answers much more than acting out of knowing what should be done or what knowledge would be the most meaningful and appropriate to present and transmit to my students. I had read Paulo Freire and wanted to teach in America with this notion of students having as much agency—or more—and as much knowledge—but different—than I had.

In the late sixties, I saw Superstudio's and my own sense of the grid as a metaphor for equal access, a structure for equality. Now the grid is a jumping off place, or some old corset to be thrown off in exchange for more loosely related narrative structures, more loosely connected and sometimes ambiguous and indeterminate relationships of images and texts to one another. Perhaps that is parallel to the indeterminate and loose relationships one has on the Web. Hundreds of people e-mail me and most of them I have not seen! I have a connection with a group of designers in Australia—Tess Dryza and Robyn Stacey at the University of Western Sydney—who are working in their communities with goals much like those that inform my work, and we try to connect online. They saw similarities in what I had written and wanted to explore them in real time on the Net. This kind of communication that brings "virtual" communities of interest together is only partially satisfying. Although I feel "seen" and understood in the way that I understand myself, I still want more. I want to meet them, see them in flesh and blood, so to speak—and they are trying to import me next year! Because I so seldom work at getting published, it is particularly valuable to me to have people halfway around the globe understand the kind of connection and participation I create in the public art work I do now. I look for where in each neighborhood are connections as well as disconnections, and where and how people care for one another. I find this is something I crave and I keep trying to recreate a form to hold it wherever I go to do my public artwork.

Dear Sheila,

I remember you, in 1970, freshly back from Italy, beautiful, pregnant, and ambitious in your ideals. I trusted you instantly. I recognized, though I didn't have the brains to articulate it then, that you had a healthy ego (rare, I think, for leaders, particularly in "minority" movements, where powerlessness and victimization are the road conditions). You created a field for me and the other women in our group to enter and explore. It was real leadership, the power of inspiration and encouragement.

So, of course I followed you from CalArts to the Building, but I was also afraid of it and of what feminism was offering me. I both wanted and feared a sexual relationship with a woman, and I remember when asking you about whether I should go to the Woman's Building, my inquiry was spiked with a kind of prurient anxiety: "Are there really a lot of lesbians there?" You responded with your typical neutrality, probably simply because you've always been secure about your sexuality.

Twenty-eight years after I met you, after I became a grown woman, a feminist, an artist...and a lesbian, I'm still confronted with my capacity for self-denial. How very different from what I imagined I'd be!

And so here we are in reflection, 28 years later. Is this the legendary Saturn Return? The 28-year orbit of Saturn around the sun, and in its wake the life lessons we're bound to reexamine? I know I feel visited by familiar ghosts, by a circularity, but I think it bodes well.

For one thing I believe we'll see a resurgence of feminism. I see its portents percolating in the women around me. I see us stepping into our lives with integrity, intimacy, real power. We are still to do our best works, and I believe we will.

xx, B

Bia, how could you have seen me pregnant; Jason was born in July of 1970, and I created the Women's Design program in 1971?

Sheila

Dear Sheila,

Hmmm. Perhaps my imagination hankers for a mother image of you? We are not that different in age, yet as my mentor, you mothered me...

I do remember you from the first year at CalArts, before you created the Women's Design Program there. Also, I remember you at an outing the Design School took to Esalen. It was traumatic for me because I didn't want to go into the famous nudie baths and be naked with everyone. I felt that I must be quite hung-up to steel myself away from the crowd. Afterward, Richard Farson, the Design School dean, gave me a lecture on being too uptight.

Yours,

B

Dear Bia,

I am about to go into holiday cooking mode in preparation for a relatively smaller crowd here than in Christmases past. But you have jostled my memory and many of the names of people you knew then strike a warm chord. Not that outing at Esalen though. I did not feel comfortable in the Esalen baths either because I felt too much stripped bare and on view. I was nursing at the time and my breasts hurt and were full. Worse still, Richard Farson (then Dean of the School of Design at CalArts) mentioned them several years later as being splendid! So you were right to demur! I was on show in ways I was not attuned to at the time, nor did I know then how much I resist being on view or in the limelight! It was traumatic and ill considered! Those men were seldom aware of how manipulative and controlling their ideas and processes were. I remember a session at CalArts where Farson had Bill Shuts, the director of Esalen, come to do a workshop with faculty and students. At one point everyone was asked to mill about among one another. When Bill Shuts said, "Stop," whomever you were in front of at that moment was the face you were to explore with your hands. I called him "Bull Shits" from that point on, knowing that this amount of intimacy and familiarity between students and faculty was a questionable thing, especially for me, the only woman in the design school faculty and not much older than most of the students. I was trying to figure out in what ways I was at all different than the students, and this kind of exercise hardly helped!

I also didn't go into the pool at CalArts where nude bathing was de rigueur because I did not want to be everyone's first look at a post partum person.

Peter and I had only that September returned to the States from Italy, where I had been working for Olivetti in Milan, and I was working as a freelance designer using a desk in the New York offices of Studio Works. I was doing the office logo for the designer John Saladino, and "tchotchkes" for Creative Playthings in New York City, and camping out in friends' apartments. We moved west in early December of 1969. Jason was born at the end of July and CalArts opened in the CalArts buildings that September 1970, which is when I first began to teach.

I was ready to have a child, and when I did not become pregnant immediately, I went to a doctor in Los Angeles, who said I had to give my body a chance to get over stopping the Pill and traveling on planes and when I had settled down a bit I would get pregnant. Sound advice, except…I was already pregnant! Jason was born seven months later, and he was not premature according to the doctor who delivered him at Good Sam's [Good Samaritan Hospital]—the only place I could find near my neighborhood that practiced Lamaze "natural childbirth" at the time. It was the beginning of my awareness that the medical establishment did not really know as much as one might think they knew about women's bodies!

I was hired to design all the publicity for CalArts while it was being planned in a building facing MacArthur Park, around the corner from the Chouinard Art School. I looked out at MacArthur Park and tried to figure out what being in Los Angeles meant; it was far more foreign to me than Milan. Herb Blau, the provost of CalArts and dean of the Theater School, had arranged for a special issue on the founding of CalArts for Arts in Society magazine. He and the deans were too busy to write the text, and I was asked to put the magazine together, to be both designer and editor. It was the first time I had the opportunity to fully shape the meaning of a publication, to choose which texts and images were in it, and sequence both to create what would now be called a "disjunctive narrative."[4] It was a very exhilarating feeling to be able to fully shape both the content and form of that publication.

To everyone's surprise, Jason came out before the magazine was done. I was speccing type in the hospital. My dear friend Marianne Partridge worked closely with me on that publication; she was then the secretary to the PR director of CalArts and had yet to discover her great talent as an editor. She followed me from school to hospital and into our home to finish the magazine during that first month of Jason's life, and became his self-appointed godmother. That fall, when CalArts opened, I began to teach for the first time.

I had been the only woman on the Design School faculty for two years, and by that time I decided I would create a program for women. Dick Farson was no longer dean; Victor Papanek had been his most vociferous critic. I did not trust Victor, although his book featured innovative, adaptive uses of materials in nonindustrialized countries. Papanek replaced Farson as dean. What I remember more than that irony of that succession were the astonishing and egregious comments Papanek made in response to my request to restrict my teaching to two days a week in a Women's Design Program that would run concurrently with the new Feminist Art Program. Victor had two objections. One was that my choice would mean none of the male students would have access to a woman teacher, to which I responded they should simply hire more women teachers. Then he shocked me by giving me permission to do this new program while saying he thought it foolish that I wished to separate out the women because, like the Jews in ghettos, this made it easier to kill them. I was totally horrified by that analogy and considered him a Nazi from that day on. Victor died this past spring, and I have often thought of him on Yom Kippur, when forgiveness is in the cultural air. Oh, it does seem like such a long time ago!

The earthquake of 1971 occurred when graphic designer Keith Godard and architect Katrin Adam were living with us on Waverly Drive. They were the first of many who lived with us for various periods of time. I have come to understand that I was recreating my childhood home where, all throughout my earliest childhood, in the years from 1940 to 1948, a stream of refugees, related to either one or the other of my parents, lived with us. Katrin and Keith thought the flashes and sounds of that earthquake were those of World War II. During that first earthquake experience, I told Peter there was a dog under the bed. After a second or two, he reminded me we had no dog and our bed was a mattress on the floor. All our dishes broke in the earthquake but otherwise I was unfazed by it, and did not link it to the war.

During the first two years at CalArts, I shared an office in the Granada Building on South Lafayette Street with the West Coast version of Studio Works, until Arlene Raven, Judy Chicago, and I created the first Woman's Building around the corner on Grandview.

Love,

Sheila

Dear Sheila,

The Sylmar Quake forced me to move out of my all-too-private little hole of an apartment and into the dorms at Valencia. There I met my pal, Bernard Cooper, and began to participate, finally, in the curriculum at CalArts, which eventuated in meeting you and finding my way to the Women's Design Program. Finally locating myself in a community of artists and feminists, I realized at long last I had a connection, and an obligation, to make work, to communicate ideas, to make—if it's not too precious to say—art. It was the beginning of a grand and heady time.

I think of the old days at the Woman's Building with both fondness and cynicism. Along with the exhilaration of our actions, thoughts, discussions, works, etc., was the mania of our youth and our inability to examine the darker aspects of our idealization. We were going to change the power structure, yet there was much bullying and victimization, horizontal hostility, and literal braying at the moon.

One of the things I remember about you, and loved you for, was your apparent ability to maintain your Self on the roller coaster. I like to remember (though I know you wouldn't like to be memorialized for this) your participation in one of those marathon "gay/straight" dialogues. Everyone was going around the room in "C-R" [consciousness-raising] fashion and talking about their sexuality in lofty, political terms (the straight women less lofty, less sure of expressing themselves). Anyway, what I remember (or how legend has revisioned the event) is you saying, "I don't know... I like to suck cock, what can I say?" A showstopper. It was the best and proudest expression of a woman's sexuality in the room, explicit and without one mote of apology.

I remember, too, you had a real interest in both the discrepancy and flow between private and public. Twenty years ago, making the personal political was a necessary step in creating change. Now our most banal thoughts and mundane achievements are up for grabs. There is no privacy, no discretion, no life without a public. How our world has changed! Americans have an unfortunate reverence for celebrity and psychology, and a rage for identity that seems nearly nonexistent elsewhere. U.S. feminism seems narcissistic, while elsewhere in the world it is real.

Friends often ask me about women in Ireland...how does such a Catholic country treat women? Well, there have been two women presidents since the founding of the Republic...more than I may ever see in my own country in my lifetime. What does that say about our American hubris, our self-examination, our precious psychological bent, and our ability to make real change?

But back to those days, when the personal was political. I want to talk more about cultural feminism, which was the work at the Woman's Building, and so maligned by political feminists, who felt that art, or cultural work, was...What? Worse than secondary...incidental? Elitist? A diversion from the "real" work of social change?

At the moment, I am thinking about the Incest Awareness video project and what a transformative experience it was for those of us who created that environment or

Equal Time in Equal Space, 1980. Collaborative video installation directed and produced by Nancy Angelo. Photograph by Bia Lowe. Woman's Building Image Archive, Otis College of Art and Design.

who worked on the video, *Equal Time in Equal Space* [ETES].[5] We were working counter to the secrecy and isolation that incest had created in our lives, making community not only out of shared victimhood, but also out of a sharing of labor, skills, and ideas. It was great to be doing something groundbreaking (very little public work had been done on the subject), but also to have taken great care in making it aesthetic. For example, the floor of the screening room was painted pink, to create a warm inner circle, and one could not wear shoes, to establish an environment that one entered with a sense of shared vulnerability.

The aesthetics of participatory democracy, of feminist design, informed the piece. Nancy Angelo conceived and co-produced the project. In it, six women were each videotaped during a series of consciousness-raising sessions concerning their experience of incest—what had happened to them, how it had impacted their lives, how each had shouldered the task of her survival. Nancy had carefully choreographed these discussions so that the broadest range of incest experience would be represented, and that the speakers would reflect a range of class and ethnic backgrounds. During the screenings, the audience was invited to sit inside a large circle of six monitors, each synchronized to play back a woman's testimony and responses, as though interacting in real time. It was a virtual C-R group!

242

One of the many things that was brilliant about ETES, as we called it, was that it demonstrated the respectful, ritualized listening of consciousness-raising, wherein each participant is given the time she needs to speak without interruption, and in which each acts as a leader. I think that community project had many long-lasting and wide-ranging effects in the culture at large, including the introduction of the term "incest survivor."

I'm also fondly reminiscing about the conferences in the old Woman's Building on Grandview. Women came from all over the country to attend the Women in Film Conference, Women's Words Conference, and Women in Design, I was gobsmacked by many of the great writers there, including Tillie Olsen, Audre Lorde, Adrienne Rich, and Meridel Le Sueur. It was a groundbreaking assembly, and an inspiration to young, yet-to-be artists like me. I have a lovely memory of women gathered around the fountain in that beautiful Spanish courtyard, each in lively, intense conversation. With every breath we were making women's culture, and we believed that culture would change lives. Everyone was high on it.

I am also thinking about Val's Cafe and Nan's store[6] and how the Spring Street building kept morphing, kept accommodating exhibitions, enterprises, and tenants. It was glorious. But then, towards the end, it shrank like a sick person in the last stages of a terminal disease. I loved both buildings, loved the spaces like you'd love a lover's body. I felt such protectiveness.

The Woman's Building was emblematic of my own growth and emerging creativity, my own self, and I wanted it to be beautiful…and indestructible!

Grrrrrrrrrr!

Bia

Good morning Bia:

I am in that quiet, tired, peaceful state that comes after an event; we had a party here last night for a friend, the large format photographer, Dawoud Bey, and while I have work I must do this weekend, I have decided that answering e-mail is what I can do for starters. Calling up your e-letter also dredges up my version of the same events.

Hubris, gay/straight dialogues, conflating private and public:

Perhaps our hubris came from exhilaration, optimism. I felt incredibly freed by leaving CalArts and creating the Woman's Building. I was completely enthralled by what we were doing and what it could mean in terms of equitable, luminous change. I enjoyed the freedom of listening to what I was thinking, seeing, reading, and of having the time and support to listen to myself, to be curious about my own responses. I felt completely immersed in my life but did not know where it was going. I remember Suzanne Lacy was very interested in five-year plans and invited someone to lead one of those magic marker/ newsprint discussions. I only knew that in the future I wanted to be doing precisely what I was doing then, and thought that when I did not want to be doing that, it would be time to do something else. For othose first years at the Woman's Building, my imagination was captured by the women involved in it; the physical, emotional, and educational structures that we were building to accommodate us; and by the work we were doing and still had yet to do. That sense of possibility, of invention—which needed no explanation or permission—gave our efforts an aura of invincibility and self importance, and produced quite a bit of that hubris you mention, Bia! We certainly had a great deal of naiveté and hubris about our project. At the same time, I think that, in contrast, we worked hard and with seriousness as well. I know that in my own graphic work I was experimenting with forms and underlying structures that could more easily include and accept that which is messy, unconventional, and inexplicable, as well as provide the needed acceptance and acknowledgment that each woman (including me, but largely unbeknownst to me) craved.

My thoughts about my own sexuality were rather ordinary. I did question whether I could have or would possibly have a sexual relationship with a woman. While I found women attractive, and my response was not about making love to them, I was and still am truly attracted sexually to my husband and deeply committed to my relationship with him and to Jason and to the life we were and are constructing together. What I worried about had more to do with being available for women and concerned about how exhausted I felt at the end of the day—the scrambling necessary, the lack of day care, the juggle of getting Jason to and from where he was to be: school, flute lessons, soccer—and being someone who was more than a shred of myself at the end each day. But that was later, when everything began to pile up. In the beginning, at the Grandview building and earlier at CalArts, I could simply bring Jason with me. We campaigned and succeeded in getting day care provided by CalArts, so I then had someplace near me to leave him when I went there. And at the Woman's Building, there were women who entertained and took care of Jason: Phranc, Nancy Fried, and Maria Karras were all very generous.

I remember the performances that dealt directly with lesbian experience at the Woman's Building in the Feminist Studio Workshop. During the early seventies, there was so much talk around me about how heterosexist society was that I began to see all images from that perspective. It seems odd to say this again, but our shared, public environment was full of images that only presented the prevailing, dominant view. Advertisements on billboards to sell almost anything showed smiling women looking up at men. Although I had not written an essay since college, I wrote an article looking at the visual and physical environment for the way in which the genders were presented, with the essentialist goal of arguing for the attributes associated with women to be liberated for use by all. I began to reexamine all my assumptions and sense of comfort or discomfort. I remember Arlene saying, "Comfort is highly overrated." But because of my heterosexuality, I was slow to speak out or act in an environment so largely lesbian for fear that my responses were stereotypical.

Student-teacher liaisons seemed unfairly imbalanced to me regardless of whether the participants were of the same sex or not. Even more difficult for me was when a woman

Bia Lowe carrying a sign board at the Women's Words Conference at the Woman's Building, March 22–23, 1975. Woman's Building Image Archive, Otis College of Art and Design.

therapist who rented space in the Grandview Woman's Building had an affair with one of the Feminist Studio Workshop students. I put clamps on my outrage to rethink in loco parentis, because my initial reaction was that the therapist and the colleague were taking advantage of their positions of power in relation to younger more vulnerable women.

I, too, remember gay/straight dialogues, and those seemed to pit cultural feminism against radical lesbian feminism in what was, to me, a very rigid, ideological discussion, without respect or interest in different origins, experiences, or ideas. No new ideas ever seemed to come from these encounters. What in particular were you referring to as "bullying and victimization"?

One performance that may relate to the event you recounted involved a student with a banana who did a rather untransformed monologue relating her disgust with the penis. As I watched and listened, I thought, I do not feel that way…I cannot believe I ever said the words "cock sucking," yet "oral sex" sounds like a euphemism. I stayed, I think, in the world of mental image, reluctant to be the heterosexual voice, and perhaps I did a disservice to those students who would have preferred I speak from heterosexual experience and its relation to the dominant culture. I do not remember saying what you heard, but I know the performance and my sense of difference impressed me and made me wonder about whether it was odd that I was there, if anyone else in the group thought as I did. In retrospect, I wish I had spoken and made that part of the discussion. But at the time, I felt that position was abundantly present in the culture outside the Woman's Building, and the women inside did not need it spoken of there.

The flow between PUBLIC and PRIVATE is forever of interest to me and I have, like many other people in the intervening decades, tried to look in a more nuanced way at how these two aspects of myself interweave. Clearly, there is a hunger for exposure and access to the intimate facts with little interest in socially constructed notions we possess, the pathologies at work, or whatever complex needs and desires create these events.

I came to the Women's Movement sans experience with therapy, and while many friends had confided in me, I had not probed my own interiority and had no idea what I felt or thought about much of my early experience. I grew up with a politically left wing father who did not join the Communist party and had quite a bit of anarchist literature in our house, as well as records of Longfellow's poems and Paul Robeson singing "Ballad for Americans." Born in 1940, I grew up during WWII, with my father having repeated heart attacks, my mother having monthly migraines, and our house filled with refugees, many of whom had numbers tattooed on their arms from Nazi concentration camps. I simply lived with that past and barely examined it or the present.

With a big dollop of magic optimism and a disregard for ritual and family of origin, Peter and I thought we were creating our lives, making a family from friends. I thought I saw a mirror of that at the Woman's Building, although some women did this because their families of origin would not accept them as lesbians. I saw the positive, self-affirming aspect of those friendship connections, and saw the pain of rejection as theirs, not mine. I understood that "private" at the Building meant time to look at past and present experience in ways that would allow each woman to transform and condense her content into art. And when each woman felt her work could be seen by others, then an exhibition could be put up in the Building, and the work would become "public." I do not think you participated in that class I taught, "Private Conversation, Public Announcements," in which women made posters about places in Los Angeles. They created enough of a relationship with the people at those places for their posters to be accepted as publicly displayed statements about that place and that woman's feelings about being there. Each put up her posters in public, and then the "PUBLIC" could become people instead, and each could talk with other people who saw the posters about the work. I have sweet memories of each woman doing this, particularly Jerri Allyn, Rita Wright, Helene Ly, and a tall Dutch woman, Tiny Beunk. I was fascinated by how the content of each poster drove its formal language. We printed them all by the exceptionally inexpensive diazo process. It was one of several projects I did using that red "blueprint" paper because red is a color that demands attention and opens up issues of contested propriety. The confluence of women and the color red in the public spaces of the city evokes associations—old notions of woman's spaces being hidden away, of red light districts, of injunctions to not call too much attention to oneself or risk endangerment. All these associations hovered behind those women's red posters about and for public places.

Thems are me thoughts, m'dear, and now I had better get back to making some lunch and doing some work.

Warmly, and in sisterhood, as we used to say, but it seems so sweet but dated now?!

Sheila

Dear Pinkie,

...As "Pinkie" you were to many. Your fans—and you had a loyal following Phranc, Nan Fried, Adrienne Weiss, me, Linda Norlen, Susan King, Michelle Kort, Sue Maberry, Cheri Gaulke, all the graphic girls, and many more, all called you Pinkie. It was a great name for you and your determination to use the color.

Pink is, ironically, a kind of dark color for women, shadowy in the Jungian sense, the banner of softness and vulnerability. Pink is the flag of our oppression, and interiority. We resist what it conjures in our desire to assimilate, to see ourselves as strong, immortal, masculine, in control. You were bold to use pink in the vernacular of the public, of printed matter, of the almighty Oz...again the weave of Private and Public. For a time pink was an element of everything you touched, all the Woman's Building calendars, the stationery, and of course, your *Pink* poster.[7]

Your determination to maintain a fluid membrane between the private and the public sphere was compelling. The personal is political, but some of us did not transform our content with the intent of taking it into the public realm. There was an inward focus at the Building, some of it protective and nurturing, but some

247

America blue to the Rose Parade) and it once was the only main street in Pasadena for shopping, business, transactions, and entertainment not known as downtown Pasadena until the ending of World War II.

So that's where my project lies—in the rivalry of the two main streets of importance to the total picture of Pasadena. I find that the intersection of Colorado Boulevard and South Lake Ave. is a public expression of tension in my personal experience. As people from various cultures move through the crossing of these two main streets, I balance the richness of my imagination with my daily experience as a young urban artist.

self-obsessed. In hindsight, it was not altogether productive. Some of us lost touch with the rest of the world.

In the fever of our youthful idealization, there was a failure to look at the darker side of our natures. I am thinking now of a teacher at the FSW. I don't know if she's the one you referred to. She had a sexualized relationship with a student, a friend. Can I forgive the teacher for her misjudgments, her misuse of power, her probable lack of self-esteem? Can I forgive the student, my friend, for her low self-image? My outrage at that says little for the inward looking and compassion necessary for real change. Here was a situation that conflated power, sex, internalized homophobia—all the struggles we preferred to locate outside the walls of the building. And what did I do? I was angry and saw the teacher as a bad, bad mommy, and I channeled my indignation through gossip.

Making family from friends was wonderful, freeing, and comported well with being young (it is much harder now for me to make new friends.) But it also meant—particularly where acting out was sanctioned by therapies—that many of us were recreating the Woman's Building in the image of an incestuous and abusive household. Many of the difficulties from which we tried to liberate ourselves came home to roost.

Feminists now have the rap of having been sex-moralizers, sex police. And looking back, that's not entirely a misrepresentation. There was much rigidity and moralizing. That was evident to me in my story of the gay/straight dialogue, the inability of many in that room to accept your sexual nature, as it was so—at least in my memory—directly expressed. I remember sitting in that circle of women and being unable to think of sexuality in terms of pleasure and intimacy, only idealization. My life did not honor pleasure as a value in itself, as an indicator of self-love or care for an "other."

There was a moralism that prohibited the hairy parts of life from cohabitating with our ideals. Nature in its various forms—men, boys (and by some weirdly concocted extension) dogs, sex, power struggle, meat eating, pleasure, anger, etc.—were largely unwelcome at the building. I have never witnessed, nor experimented with, so many varieties of fasting!

A few years ago, I saw a documentary on the restaurant Chez Panisse, another cultural institution born of the seventies, and I got to feeling sad and resentful that people my age were having so much pleasure at that time, eating everything, drinking everything, laughing and talking with dogs and children, and all the many sexes doing all the many things the many sexes do. It was Dionysian in the best sense.

The "Westside women,"[8] as we called them, seemed even further detached from pleasure. I thought they cannibalized themselves with their politics. That kind of rage for purity reminded me of the Conceptual artists I had hung out with at CalArts. They had rationalized themselves out of beauty in order to have the ideal…in order to be right. I remember all sorts of threats of boycotts and harsh criticism from the "Westside women" for our cultural bent, for our belief that cultural forms and culture making are transformative. It all seemed so pointless and annoying to have those women as our adversaries, when really we were all trying to do the best we could.

I think communities can be re-envisioned, still keeping with this beautiful image of yours—of the grid. That is, a congregation of adults who are not endowed with equal gifts, interests, or values, but who have equal access, a true democracy with leeway for individual freedoms, privacies, and styles.

I wanted to touch on the performance you mentioned, the one with the woman eating a banana and talking about her distaste for penises. I don't remember it, but it's a great example, if not the perfect parody, of much of that artwork. Performance art of that period seemed either to be agitprop or tribal magic and ritual, and so much of it was bad, embarrassingly so. The desire to be transgressive, to shock the status quo (as if shock value alone made the art good) was in itself embarrassing.

When I look back, I see a kind of collage of eggs yolks, breasts, self-inflicted wounds, and contrived confessionals. I love reminiscing about those performances, and I need to laugh at them. There is much about those works and ourselves that was beautiful and innocent, disturbing and funny. It hopefully makes us wiser today.

Yours in yolks,

Bia

Dear Bia:

Your outrage is powerful and impressive. I feel remiss and dim in contrast. I was gingerly feeling my way in those situations that were unfamiliar and not my experience. I identified and empathized, but because much of what was being said and done was new, perhaps I had a damper on my responses. I did not want to be insensitive and heterosexist. Although I was listening deeply and carefully, I unfortunately missed hearing your rage. Very belatedly I apologize, because, had I known better, I might have found ways to open up the brackets around experience and name the bullying that must have been going on.

For me the pleasure was the freedom to question premises. Perhaps I was too drunk on that freedom to check every assumption for its veracity. But something must have blinded me. I wasn't in the know, so to speak, about the struggles with addictions. Living in my extended family where all women worked, I had not known or understood the problems of women in the suburbs who were bored and abused. Although some people in my family have some substance abuse issues and outcomes, I did not think in terms of addictions. I remember coming into the Building with a bottle of wine or champagne to celebrate something and learning that many of the women were in Alcoholics Anonymous. And Ruthie [Ruth Iskin] and Arlene [Raven] were forever on different diets, and Suzanne [Lacy] was eating her "rabbit food." I still ate everything, as I was slender and healthy without any effort to be so. The only problem for me, since puberty, was an anemia that made me faint sometimes and for which I took iron pills and ate all the foods with iron in them: raisins, spinach, broccoli, anything to help. But nothing did until I started to hemorrhage in my early forties; after five years of Chinese herbs and acupuncture and acupressure, I had a hysterectomy and have not been anemic since!

 Sheila

Dear Sheila,

 I think the fact that I was immersed in righteous indignation and that you were optimistic says something about our natures (for me, I do not think this bodes well). Your enthusiasm and good will for those around you made you a good leader, an inspiration. I can't imagine how you could feel remiss for not being more sensitive when you were doing so much at the Building and with your family, and finding enjoyment in both to boot. I think I was still hungry for the mirroring and modeling that are absent for lesbians in their formative years, and that, added to the passivity and privilege I came with, made for the bad combo platter. Many of us were struggling with basic identity issues, mommy issues, family issues, work issues; thus our expectations and disappointments were, I think, out of proportion. I think we are all surviving magnificently, and, as I said, I believe many of our best works are still to come.

 Thanks for reminding me about all the inebriation. I was only thinking of the temperance. There was a lot of pot smoking and rotgut wine drinking going on, and I'd say, in general, a level of unreality was present. God knows I did my share. Both things were true and coincided: denial of pleasure and soddenness. Maybe it just takes a while to learn how to live a sensual and sensible life, a life of pleasures that is also fully and bravely awake. It was certainly a difficult time, particularly, I think, for those of us who were struggling with our sexualities, not to mention the other challenges that liberation invites.

 Yours in wrinkled, but still menstruating, sisterhood,

 Bia

Dear Bia:

 I wanted to say to you, but not necessarily for publication, that the optimism I brought to the Women's Design Program, the Woman's Building, and to each new public art project and class of students here at Yale, has, of course, its other side. I knew little of the other side in the seventies and agreed with Arlene Raven that we were trying to live in the present on an image of the future. That idea was attractive in part because it let me continue to try to control uncontrollable fears I could not handle then, and do a slightly better job with now. I do not have the words to describe my internal structure to others well and simply do not talk about what I cannot understand or accept. Through living with me, Peter—who is different than I in many ways and is not haunted by the same stuff I am haunted by—can add levity and humor to the inconsequential stuff that I imbue with terror and desperation. I am doing a terrible job of explaining this to you. Suffice to say that this has little or nothing to do with sexuality and a lot to do with my childhood understanding of the Holocaust survivors in our home, the economic problems and illness with which I was surrounded, and a magic optimism and alchemy I concocted that made me think, far past childhood, that I could transform things into what I wanted them to be, to construct a form or place that would make a magical difference in people's lives. I was so into that magic making that I missed a lot at the Woman's Building: where it did not work and where the victimization and bullying you felt were going on. It is that for which I feel remiss because my job, as I saw it, was to make sure that did not happen!?! Oh, the omnipotence of youth!

Perhaps righteous indignation and magic optimism are not so far apart and bode equally well, or not, for our future. Now I think I have less unconditional good will for those around me as I had then. I am much more aware than I was then of feelings that having, owning, or being anything desirable is dangerous; being visible is dangerous and makes others not only admire and appreciate … but covet, envy, want—and take it all away. How's that for a dark fantasy ever-ready to haunt?! This fear is more attached to being homeless than to being a woman. And "doing so much" was as much an unconscious compulsion to try to make everything better everywhere at the Woman's Building, and with my family, that I missed the ways Peter felt left out, and who knows what Jason will complain about when he turns to examine how his imagination was constructed!

When the woman who ran the travel agency at the building invited me over for dinner one night, and I came there with Jason, I realized that she had a fantasy life in which I played a significant role—seen in the journal she had kept and showed me. I had no idea anyone was looking at me with that intensity, and I was not sure I could handle the responsibility of that attraction. Similarly, one of the FSW women became deeply immersed in her fantastic identification with cats and the letters X and Y, and sent me her drawings and journals for years. When she asked me to come to see her, I brought my friend Jane Stewart, a psychologist, because that level of derangement, with me in a role I did not choose, is too far from what I know how to handle. I did not want to go alone and not know how to be there. When I left Los Angeles, in 1990, I made up a big box of all her drawings and raving writing. I called her and asked if she wanted them back. She did, and I gave them all back to her, happy to see she was doing well.

Jane Stewart often said that none of us had the mothers we needed for the lives we were creating. Rather than dwell on that lack, my thoughts ran to Sonia Delaunay and Florine Stettheimer, and I felt sustained by their work and their lives. As I say that, I realize that both of them were women who started out in situations of privilege, but that was not what I noticed then, or usually! I still adore Florine and came home early last night to watch "Saints in Three Acts," to see her scenery as much as to hear Gertrude Stein's words, Virgil Thompson's music, and the beautiful singing. Florine's pink tinsel cellophane world that I love so much, her flowers, and lithesome sisters, and the privacy she was able to keep all her

Florine Stettheimer, *Spring Sale at Bendel's*, 1921. Oil on canvas, 50"x 40". © Courtesy of the Philadelphia Museum of Art.

life. And Sonia's abundance, perseverance, and her overflowing ability to work in any medium she needed or wanted to: paint, fabric, paper, designing cars, a six-foot-long book, clothing, and advertising. The quilt she made when her son Charles was born was one of my inspirations when I designed the poster about pink and the FSW brochure/poster that preceded it. Their agency and choice, which perhaps were the result of privilege or support from family, were what I wanted and needed, and got vicariously through their work. My family could not provide that; they were distracted by economic difficulties, health problems, and people who had experienced the worst horrors of torture and degradation the twentieth century could provide. We lived near Coney Island, and the abundance of fantasy, cotton candy, sparkling lights, and all the tinsel aspects of streets filled with people always loomed larger in my imagination than the dirty and tawdry parts, the danger, the rip-offs, and the funky surrounding poverty of it all.

I thought there were many models for lesbians: Sappho and Radclyffe Hall, Arlene [Raven], Ruth [Iskin], Kirsten [Grimstad], Susan [Rennie], and the numerous artists being discovered and revealed by lesbian scholars in the seventies. I thought the passivity of privilege could be transformed by these women who were willing to be who they were publicly as well as privately, and to me it seemed they all were able to create their own lives. I thought lesbians at the Building were creating a new kind of family based on choices of those who could and would be there in a time of need—the way the biological family so often could not or would not be for the women who had come to the Building, and cannot be, given the extreme expectations of what we think family should do for us. "Basic identity issues, mommy issues, family issues, work issues" are the stuff we seem to be working on all our lives, not just in our twenties and thirties. Expectations of family that cannot be fulfilled might be seen as parallel to expectations of what the Woman's Building should have provided (even as it did provide sometimes—most of the time?—for some of us?). In an alchemical, magical, optimistic way, I thought the Woman's Building could make everyone into creative survivors, able to live in the world fully as feminists and as women, whatever that category of people is. That thought was possibly one of the ways we led ourselves into disappointment at the Woman's Building—as if the Woman's Building was not just us?! I agree that although there always has been and always will be conflict, ambiguity, extremes and moderation, they are difficult and continue to be unpopular. Let's go with your belief that "Many of our best works are still to come!"

I am in Boston all day Monday with Susan Sellers. Did I tell you a bit about that new artwork project for the Massachusetts State House I am doing there? I will, but doing so reminds me to ask you to tell me more about your books and the way your writing has its origins in your visual making, and how the form, content, and existence of it relate to the discussions within our conversation. In the broadsheet we printed in the Women's Design Program, and at the Woman's Building, we looked for a way to bring what we created in the privacy of the studio into public view, to transform and condense it into art, and to "make it public and known." How we came to be women who choose to speak out and be heard in

254

public is helpful to me now, as it is the subject of this project, HEAR US, *in Boston.*

In June, I had decided I could not do another project if I was to have time to dawdle, gape, think, and let whatever happen during my sabbatical this Spring. But then last June I received a request for my slides from Pamela Worden of Boston's Urban Arts and then a letter asking me to do a proposal to honor six women in the Massachusetts State House. This piece could be another expression of my work about people who have been left out, voices seldom if ever heard, and hidden histories of a specific site. But it would not take place on the edges of cities and out in the public realm, subject to the elements, like Biddy Mason: Time & Place *and* Remembering Old Little Tokyo *in Los Angeles;* Search: Literature *in Queens;* Path of Stars *in New Haven; and* At the start... At long last..., *at 207th Street Station in New York City; and* West End Railings *under construction now in Boston. In each I had the freedom to choose where on the site my work would take place and who and what images, texts, people would become public and known. This work [*HEAR US*] would be in the center of town in a public place, protected, indoors. Evidently a legislator saw a TV broadcast and noticed that most of the American suffragists were from Massachusetts, and the next time he walked through the State House to the legislature he noticed that there were no images of women there. A committee was assembled but they could not decide on one woman and instead decided to honor six. I was told who was to be honored, where the artwork would be, but not how to present them—except that what we did should be fitting with the place. Where does being outrageous fit in here?!*

When I read the materials sent to me, I first asked why six women all in one place, why not women throughout the building? It made me angry that we were being put together all in one place, in a ghetto of girls! But then it was at the entrance to the building and would not be missed by thousands of visitors a year! I did not go the obvious protest route. Instead, I tried to think about what people coming to the state house in a hundred years might be concerned with and whether the gender of the people represented would be the vital issue, or race, or something else. Certainly, Boston has had a particularly egregious history of race relations. I thought it would be better to do this project with another woman, in the spirit of sisterhood— past, present, and future. When Carrie Mae Weems responded to my queries regarding collab- oration that she would be in Berlin all summer, I asked Susan Sellers to be my partner. I asked her because I like her, she is talented and intelligent, and she is different than me in ways that we could see play out as we did the project: she is almost half my age and would not be subject to a seventies feminist pull on the project. And she has studied women's history but does not see herself as an activist, nor has she been politically involved in the ways I have been. I had begun to think about using marble because there is much marble in the floor of the build- ing, and to make busts of the women in bronze as there are many bronze statues of men, and it would make all the women of color. I kept drawing the women entwined with the marble, and I did not want to make them entwined. They never knew each other and had very different life histories, although they are all from Massachusetts, all born in the nineteenth century, and all public figures and activists. I did not want this project to be only about them

255

being women, so Susan and I wrote our proposal so that it never used the word woman but rather focused on our desire to make each as different as she was similar and unite them all in their activism. Their public speaking was the subject and therefore this would be less a ghetto of girls.

The Woman's Building, by necessity, was a ghetto of girls. It was appropriate to be that then, but that is not what this new project needs to be about—at least for me and for Susan, but perhaps not as much for the women who worked so hard to choose these six honorees.

Tomorrow Susan and I are going to Boston to meet again with our colleagues who work in stone and bronze and to go the state house with the actual-size model I have made of one of the panels. This will be done for a celebration on October 19, [1998,] in which the scholars who worked on the biographies of each of these six honorees will discuss what they think the women would have thought of the new artwork! I am sending the written part of our proposal as an attachment for your pleasure!

Yours in wrinkled but still coloring my hair sisterhood,
Sheila

Dear Sheila,

I loved your last e-mail, and p.s., I actually think much of it is very appropriate for publication. It was sad and scary to hear those stories. There was a level of un-reality at the Building, and it both protected and encouraged women to act out. I remember when Jere Van Syoc was coming to be the guest artist for the Lesbian Art Project and Maria Bloom[9] was brought to the airport to greet her as her bride-to-be, wearing a black velvet robe and little else. They had never met, but the notion of possibility, and of creating our own lives and living with risk and magic, was in the air…so…why not? Maria was starting to slip down the slippery slope at the time, going a little bats, but I think her condition was thought to be "witchy." It was sad and outrageous, though I suppose a case could be made that it was nice that she had a community of people to be in, and that, for a time, she functioned as an important part of it. I think the reason that this all makes me nuts now, and that still makes me cling to my precious moral indignation, is that I participated in it. This is the shadow part of identity politics.

What do you mean when you say "magic optimism"? Are you referring to a fantasy world? Was it cultural, familial, private?

And since you asked: I am going through a complete change with regard to my writing, which I will tell you about later when I have a bit more time. It's an identity crisis!

In sisterhood, complete with white hair, and odd acne (premenopausal?)
Bia

Happy Valentine's Day, Bia!

This would be a perfect holiday for Florine—pink cellophane and little sparkling, scarlet hearts. Let it be a holiday for us, too; only work if you want to! I participate more often in a kind of "magic optimism," whereby my fear-driven desire to make the world sparkle takes over, turns me on, and motivates me to make my kind of magic: alchemy on stone, granite, and concrete—permanent, hard materials with which the hidden becomes visible and the ordinary becomes extraordinary.

Sheila

Dear Sheila,

My orientation to writing has been largely one of autobiography. From Deena [Metzger]'s writing classes at CalArts and the Woman's Building, and from the works of most women poets and writers, I learned to trust my impulse to plumb personal content for material. Writers, especially "minority" writers, hone in on forbidden content as the tastiest and most significant. The unexpressed areas in life are, as in the life of the psyche, often the most soulful. At any rate, I married my love of nature writing with my love for confessional, autobiographical writing. I was especially lucky to have Eloise Klein Healy as a teacher. Her passion for poetics and her candor were inspiring and contagious.

I was a happy puppy writing my first book, *Wild Ride*. I was able to stitch together personal experiences with creatures and occurrences outside myself in the natural world. My engagement with the world was ecstasy.

Unfortunately, some of the revelations and disclosures of that book backfired. For one thing, I disclosed privacies about many of the people in my life. I wrote about my lover, from whom I've since separated, as "my mate" and "better half," and I wrote about her body in very intimate terms—all of which pains me now, and I can only imagine how it affects her.

Recently I've been working on a new book about love, again with the intention to weave natural history with personal history. But this time I'm daunted. I fear it might be destructive to mine real lives and real relationships for material, to exploit privacy for art. How can I honor and protect the privacy of those I love, to secure intimacy, while making an inquiry into the territory? How do I explore the landscape of love without compromising my beloved's privacy, her control over what's public in her life? I've confused privacy with hiding, and wanted to tear down the walls, but at what cost? It's a conundrum.

At any rate, I've reached a crisis with this book, and in general the confessional bent of my work. This inward focus of my work has kept me insular, introspective, and among the navel picking. I really need to have my work challenge me more, push me into areas of research and observation, get me out of myself. Force me to find out what makes things not-Bia tick. What I enjoyed most about *Wild Ride* was writing about events and creatures, particularly those, like bats, who could use some serious PR and who should be redeemed in our mind's eye, thus making our souls more whole, more rich. What I know from writing poetry is that the natural world provides an extraordinary resource and vehicle for the expression of content.

One of the things I loved about design work is that there is an aspect of it that is entirely selfless, entirely in service of the content and the client. The ego is so tied to language and to telling stories about itself that writing can become a dangerous medium for self indulgence. And sometimes it can trick the writer into thinking she is writing for some higher purpose.

Stitching together the inner and the outer worlds, making a weave, is what I think of as feminine in my work. Making it public has required me to utilize my feminism, to analyze public strategies, and all the interpersonal crap that goes with networking and having a career and dealing with authority. All the people who helped me with *Wild Ride* were feminists: agents, editors, and publicists. Marketing was another bag of worms. My sales suffered from the book being marketed as "lesbian." I wanted it to have a larger exposure, but that was not to be. For better and for worse, this was the market research moment for "Gay & Lesbian Writing," and my little book got squirreled away into the that section. I understand what you meant when you said your new project was not going to be about a ghetto!

Anyway, these are my thoughts lately about my work. I am trying to locate "what" it is I want to write about now…and get back to the ecstasy I felt writing my first book!

Yours in narcissistic career crisis, but unflagging hear-me-roar sisterhood,

Bia

Dear Bia:

Thank you for this rich and full description of your work and what you want it to be. Lest you think I am pleased with where I am now in mine, I find what I do falling a bit apart. In the 207th Street project, I talked with 207 people in the neighborhood, in the street, in bars, in the park, in the senior citizen centers, and on the phone. The result was a huge number of tiles with about thirty to thirty-five words on each that deliver the history of Inwood.[10] There are other parts to that project that try to make sense of this activity. As it is the first and last stop on the longest line of the A train, I have written large in bits of mirror the words "At the start…" and "At long last…," and the quotes are assembled following those three dots, arranged in the themes that developed through talking with people. There are other parts, too, terrazzo pieces in the floor derived from Taino petroglyphs. A renters' rights organizer in Inwood told me that the Tainos were the Indians that populated the area of the Caribbean from which many in that neighborhood now come. I researched those petroglyphs, and was struck by them: figures smoking (inhaling whatever substances, having whatever visions) looked like letter A's blowing horns. Billy Strayhorn wrote [the jazz standard] "Take the 'A' Train," and was of African descent, gay, and very private. I asked most people I interviewed about their enjoyment of music. I have a real suspicion that it won't all hang together and that all this talking with people is neurotic on my part and overdone in the world of public art. All the works I have done have involved lots of hanging out in the community, getting close to people whom afterwards I will never see. This has uncomfortable echoes for me and is not what I want to always do. While the Massachusetts project, too, will have quotes that enable viewers to listen directly to the voices of the people honored, there are only six people. Although there is lots of going back and forth between me, Susan, and Ellen Rothman at the Massachusetts Humanities Council and her colleagues, it will never come even close to the amount of time and physical energy I have expended in all my other projects. I worry whether what I am doing is art or design or simply the inordinate amount of pleasure I get from hanging out in these communities and talking with the people I meet there. And I worry if anyone ever wants me to do this work in their community, as they may begin to see that I am not a part of it in ways I forget when I am wherever I go! And I get tired, Bia, and want more and more to have some down time, alone time, private time— if only to rest and to see what would happen without all this people contact. Strange, but when I finish this e-mail and send it off to you wherever you are, I have to go write seventeen letters and get waivers for the seventeen quotes from people who used to live in the old West End of Boston. Their words are to be cut in the steel handrails that will guide pedestrians through a concrete complex that has ghosted into it an abstracted image of their "tenement" with no respect for the quality of the lives led there. Hopefully, those quotes will show what was lost when the neighborhood was razed. And cut into the concrete are eight-foot-high letters that proclaim what was and what is to be THE GREATEST NEIGHBORHOOD THIS SIDE OF HEAVEN. Will I ever stop working on the same thing over and over and over?

But then there is this conversation with you, which when I read it seems delightfully ordinary and extraordinary, rambling and focused, new and old at the same time. I hope it is as tearfully, happily, and hysterically fun for others as it has been for you and me.

Come visit me, Bia, in my round home studio…

In simple sisterhood,

Pinkie

Pinkie,
So, should we talk about the legacy of the Woman's Building?
Love,
Bia

Dear Bia,

Legacy? I shrink from that notion of us deciding our legacy. It seems self-aggrandizing or institutionally aggrandizing. We who started the Woman's Building and labored within it are perhaps the least likely to know what its legacy might be. That is for those who regard it in the future.

Or do you think this is the future now, and we who were a part of it determine its legacy? It was and is my hope that our conversation limited the fictionalizing and aggrandizing of the past by circling in on how we understood what it was we saw accomplished and did not.

Participatory democracy[10] captured my imagination before feminism did and influenced my work as much. My use of a fragmented visual field of equal parts owes its formal existence equally to ideas of "women's time," formulated in 1970, and the desire for a form that allowed each person to represent themselves through their own speech. That is true of my newspaper for the International Design Conference in Aspen in 1970, the Pink *poster in 1975, and my public art in the 207th Street station of the A train completed last year.*

Feminism is content, making it possible for the public to listen to women and to understand women's experience, and to learn to value what and who has been overlooked. To the extent that any design carries that content, it can be said to be feminist.

Who women are is complex. It is not anywhere as simple a position as our inquiry might have led us to think in 1970.

I find myself aligned with Judith Butler and Pedro Almodóvar, and enjoy the notion that gender is totally up for grabs and constructed. At the same time, women are being murdered and raped in Afghanistan solely because they are female, and in the United States, women still are paid seventy-five cents to the dollar paid to males.

What I think women need now, or what I need, is not to be limited by any prescribed forms. Design and feminism are splintered. We have gone far from needing a grid to hold an equality of parts. In fact, for me the crazy quilt is a better visual symbol than the grid, as every shape can be in it and it is not in any way adjusted to fit into a prescribed order.

In sisterhood,

Sheila

Dear Sheila,

Your point is wise and beautifully articulated.

During my time at the Building, I thought I could see the impact some of our efforts had on the culture at large. The Incest Awareness Project would be a good example. Public discourse was stirred in the local media and that, I presume, had some ripple effects.

On the other hand, it's hard to know to what extent the Incest Awareness Project was a cause of change in the culture, or an expression of an effect already set in motion. In hindsight, I wonder if, for example, the term "incest survivor" was really ours to invent, or if it already existed in the collective consciousness of the time, if it was already beginning to burble and find its usage in conversations both private and public. To what extent were we the pebble, the ripple, or simply part of the pond? Which isn't to negate or minimize the importance of the Building. That it existed at all was probably its greatest achievement and its most significant legacy. The existence of the Building represented a commitment to women and to women artists (including, of course, designers, musicians, etc.) and to the variety of creative forms those women had developed, or would develop. It raised the level of seriousness about women artists, the way Linda Nochlin's essay "Why Have There Been No Great Women Artists?" (1971) did. It upped the ante.

[The Woman's Building] was a focal point or a window through which one might witness the effect that feminism was making on consciousness. As such, it would be still fomenting within each of those women who participated in the Building—into how each wove her experience of the Building into a sense of possibility for herself: her sexuality, her ambition and entitlement, her range of content and expression, her knowledge of her history, and her willingness to change.

That's all I'm gonna say right now…, except I LOVE the crazy quilt!

Mucho love to you on this starry night,

Bia

Dear Bia

I continue to think that we do not determine our legacies. And it is self-aggrandizing to claim we do. Even the notion that the Woman's Building "upped the ante" creates some question in my mind. I feel reluctant to claim what it did for each woman who participated in art making or events there, and I would like to leave it for her to define and express her revisionist history of her experience there. We each weave our own narrative of what influenced us.

I prefer the notion that we were part of the groundswell of our time. The Building was a symbol as well as a place, and for each of us, I think, it symbolized something slightly different. I know I idealized the importance of it being a stand-alone building, a separate building with presence. The solidity and stand-alone-ness mattered to me. Cheryl Swannack was a good partner in the building search, and it was with her that the second Woman's Building was found. We both stood on the roof and were filled with an indescribable glee at how big and solid it was. Nothing Judy Baca could say about the gangs nearby could in any way cloud the pleasure I felt when we found it.

In some ways, I think of the Woman's Building a bit like all of the public artwork I have done and am doing, in that I am reluctant to say these works create change. Rather, they stand for a desire to reflect and sustain the communities in which they exist—in all their contradictions and complexity. I expect that the Woman's Building and anything I make will mean different things to different people at different times. I totally agree with you that its largest meaning resides in the fact of its existence, and its memory continues its existence beyond its physical presence.

Can we two decide to leave this discussion of legacy with the hope that each woman who came to the Woman's Building found support for inventing herself according to her own design?

Best to you, dear Bia,

Sheila

Notes

1. For her public art project for the A line of New York's subway system, *At the start… At long last…*, de Bretteville created wall tiles with texts about neighborhood history, large texts created from a mosaic of mirrors, and floor tiles of contrasting cast stone and text. —Editors

2. "Participatory democracy" is a process of emphasizing the broad involvement of constituents in the direction and operation of political systems. —Eds.

3. Superstudio was founded in Florence, Italy, in 1966, by Adolfo Natalini, Cristiano Toraldo di Francia, Roberto Magris, Gian Piero Frassinelli, and Alessandro Magris. Through their designs, Superstudio produced provocative and subversive visions of the future that were critical to the transformation of architecture and design from the late 1960s through the 1970s. —Eds

4. A disjunctive narrative is marked by breaks or disunity, so that the narrative is out of sequence. —Eds.

5. Conceived by artist Nancy Angelo, and sponsored by Ariadne: A Social Art Network, *Equal Time in Equal Space* was a multi-system video installation created and exhibited between 1980 and 1982. —Eds.

6. The Store was a thrift shop created and managed by artist Nancy Fried between 1977 and 1979; it was intended to generate revenue for the Woman's Building but also served as a resource for women who wished to explore alternative personae through performance and costuming. —Eds.

7. This poster, created by members of a design class in the early days of the Feminist Studio Workshop, grew from an assignment in which class members were asked to respond to the color pink on a square of paper. The responses, which included typed and handwritten text, drawings, and photography, were reduced in size and quilted together to comprise the poster. Responses tended to explore the social ramifications of the color— the way it spoke to a kind of imposed femininity and women's anger over this. As one respondent scrawled, "Scratch pink and it bleeds." —Eds.

8. The community of feminists who lived on the Westside of Los Angeles tended to be more politically than culturally oriented. —Eds.

9. This name has been changed. —Eds.

10. Inwood Hill Park is largely undeveloped land at the northern most tip of Manhattan Island. —Eds.

Sheila Levrant de Bretteville, 1981. Photo by Maria Kellet. Woman's Building Image Archive, Otis College of Art and Design.

Jane Grabhorn at work at her press. Photograph courtesy Arion Press.

BOOKS IN A NEW LANGUAGE

Kathleen Walkup

In 1973, two events occurred that changed the landscape of creativity for many women writers and artists across America. On their separate surfaces these events did not appear to be connected, but their accidental convergence has had a signal impact on the way many women intersect with art and art making, the implications of which are still unfolding. The more profound of these events was the establishment of the first independent feminist art education program in the country. The Feminist Studio Workshop was founded in Los Angeles by an artist, a graphic designer, and an art historian, each of whom was evangelical about the messages of feminism. This program, and the building subsequently chosen to house it, "were created by women to end the isolation and silence experienced by women and encourage a sense of community and caring within our shared culture. Through the exhibition of the accomplishments and contributions of women, the future potential of women individually and collectively can be recognized."[1]

The repetition of the word *women* was not accidental at a time when women were consistently referred to as girls no matter what their age; equally deliberate was the emphasis in this statement on the *exhibition* of women's accomplishments and contributions, as opposed to the undertaking of the work itself. This mission statement implicitly acknowledged that women were already accomplishing work that was eminently worthy of attention; what was needed now was broad cultural recognition for what they were doing.

Across the country in March of the same year, Moore College of Art in Philadelphia opened an exhibition entitled simply "Artists Books." The exhibition itself contained work not by women but by the important, predictable male artists of the day (David Hockney, Robert Motherwell, Dieter Roth, Jim Dine, John Cage, and the Los Angeles Pop artist Ed Ruscha, whose work is often credited with initiating contemporary artists' bookmaking). Moore College's curator, Diane Perry Vanderlip, coined the term for the title that would help to define a "new" art movement, one with deep roots in the avant-garde. Vanderlip's criterion for what was to be included in "Artists Books" was deceptively simple: "… [I]f the artist conceived his work as a book, I …generally accepted his position."[2] The breadth of this definition allowed the exhibition to expand to more than two hundred and fifty works.

For the fledging students at the Feminist Studio Workshop, who were exploring the parameters of both form and content in art as adaptable to fit a new feminist consciousness, the artist's book became a logical extension of that exploration. These women had stories to tell. What better platform than books for these private stories to move into the public arena of exhibition and publishing?

New Beginnings at the Woman's Building: One Story

As one of the first group of women to travel to Los Angeles in the fall of 1973 to become part of the Feminist Studio Workshop at the newly organized Woman's Building, Susan Elizabeth King joined a cohort of thirty women, ages twenty-two to fifty, who left their homes or academic institutions to relocate in an environment of feminist artists, designers, writers, and critics. King and two of her colleagues at New Mexico State University (NMSU), where King was finishing her MA in ceramics, had, in the spirit of art historian Linda Nochlin and many women artists in the early seventies, begun to question the invisibility of women in the art world. Through the auspices of a grant from the National Endowment for the Arts, King and her sister students invited the artist Judy Chicago to visit the university as a guest artist. Chicago, who was in the process of traveling the country to proselytize on behalf of the Feminist Studio Workshop, accepted the invitation.

Chicago's pioneering work with the emergent issues of feminist art began in the Feminist Art Program, which she founded in 1970 at Fresno State College (California) and relocated a year later to the California Institute for the Arts (CalArts). At CalArts, Chicago was joined in her endeavor by the painter and fiber artist Miriam Schapiro, whose husband was teaching at CalArts when Chicago arrived there. Located amongst the strips of Hamburger Hamlets, big-box stores, and amusement parks just outside of Los Angeles, CalArts had been incorporated only ten years earlier. With funding from the Disney brothers, Walt and Roy, CalArts was (and is) dedicated to a nontraditional curriculum in visual and performing arts. Even this setting, however, did not sufficiently support Chicago's feminist vision.

After two years there, Chicago left to begin a brand new program, which she intended to develop from the ground up with her CalArts colleagues Sheila Levrant de Bretteville, who had founded the Women's Design Program at CalArts the same year that Chicago and Schapiro had joined the faculty, and the art historian and critic Arlene Raven. The three women came together to establish a space where their vision for a truly alternative education in feminist art theory and practice could be realized. A chance discovery by a student, described by Chicago in her autobiography, led them to name the space the Woman's Building in honor of the 1893 building of the same name at the World's Columbian Exposition in Chicago, which was demolished after the fair.[3]

Meanwhile, Chicago's fortuitous visit to NMSU resulted in King and several of her colleagues examining not just the backstory, but also the very direction of their art. While working in the glaze room, they hatched plans to attend the new workshop that Chicago had so enthusiastically brought to their attention. In the summer of 1973, three of them packed up their belongings and their newly earned MAs and drove to Los Angeles. They arrived in time to help sheetrock the rented space of the Chouinard building at 743 S. Grandview and re-christen it the Woman's Building for its official opening in November.

(Chicago left the staff in 1974 to work on her monumental installation *The Dinner Party*. When the Chouinard building was sold in 1975, the Woman's Building founders began major fundraising efforts toward finding and renovating another building. Supporters such as Lily Tomlin, Meg Christian, and Holly Near helped to raise money for the renovation of a derelict building on Spring Street near a diverse triangle of the as-yet-unrenovated Union Station, Chinatown, and Olvera Street in downtown Los Angeles.)

The Feminist Studio Workshop

The core of the Woman's Building philosophy was housed in the Feminist Studio Workshop. Here the feminist principles that the three founders had evolved in their various teaching practices were to find fruition in a fully developed program of education in the visual and performing arts, design, and creative writing. The goals of the program were not modest. At its most basic in terms of art making, the three women intended to attract women who would go on to share responsibility in "push[ing] the boundaries of the notion of 'new form for new content'.... Since we planned to work out of a content base, which would allow the fusing of emotion and idea, we intended to ask women to think about all the possible ways they might express their subject matter and then help them learn whatever techniques were necessary for the realization of their ideas."[4]

In an interview with the art historian Lucy Lippard, Chicago describes the programs she founded at Fresno and CalArts as "the first step in building an alternate art community."[5] She goes on the describe the Woman's Building as a locus for "education, exhibition, criticism, documentation of feminist values." Later in the interview, Chicago tells Lippard that it was the Woman's Building structure, as it existed outside the mainstream, that had allowed her to "transform [her] circumstances into subject matter," to use her personal circumstances to "reveal the whole nature of the human condition," the fundamental building block, to Chicago, of great art.[6] Ten years after the Feminist Studio Workshop opened its doors, de Bretteville wrote that the goal of feminist design education, along with design practice itself, should be nothing less than to provoke an "alternative vision of the world" that would strive to "transform the dominant culture" and allow women to be equally participant in every aspect of life.[7]

The Feminist Studio Workshop's initial classes in design met in Sheila de Bretteville's house off the Hollywood Freeway. There the students began to explore with de Bretteville a larger context for art making, one that incorporated de Bretteville's ideas about communication beyond the "loft, gallery and museum-going elite, when we make our communications using mass media technology."[8] In these sessions de Bretteville presented her version of the separated and hierarchical worlds of fine art and graphic design. In her words:

> [A]n artist traditionally speaks to a narrowly defined audience (other artists, collectors....) The result is often an incestuous and elitist atmosphere for the arts. The designer, on the other hand, reaches a broad audience and speaks a common language.... The limitation of design is that the designer represents the voice and image of the firm she works for and very seldom feels any personal connection to what she creates.[9]

For Susan King, de Bretteville was reinforcing a lesson she had learned earlier in an important book for her, *Finding One's Way with Clay*: in art making, taste and style are not enough.[10] King began to understand in these early lessons that her relocation to California was simply one small step in a process whose goal was nothing less than the redesign of her entire life.

The Origins of Bookmaking at the Woman's Building

Chicago and de Bretteville worked from very different approaches to their professional practices, but their joint concerns about helping women find new ways of merging form and content in their art making led many of their students to an interest in the book form. While Chicago's artwork did not directly involve books as a form, her paintings and drawings did sometimes include text, and the direction of works such as *The Dinner Party* was pointing toward the narrative. De Bretteville's interest in books and publishing was much more direct although, again, she did not herself make or publish books (or in fact publish much writing of any sort). Throughout her career as a graphic

designer she has had a pronounced interest in typography; among many other professional commissions, she was for a time a designer at the *Los Angeles Times*.

De Bretteville also positioned her work in feminist design education at the
intersection of the private and public spheres of women's lives. Just as feminist
activists in the nineteenth century recognized the importance of moving "women's
work" into the public arena of speaking and lecturing, writing and publishing, and
employment outside the home, de Bretteville and many of the newly voiced feminists
in the burgeoning second-wave movement recognized the vital need for women to
come out from behind their shells of private invisibility into the public light. For de
Bretteville, this move into the public sphere was a social necessity: "Once a woman is
able to locate and articulate a connection to the public world, she is able to feel more
responsible and caring toward it."[11] De Bretteville chose the Women's Graphic Center
as the appropriate program in which this connection could be made. The stated goal of
the program was clear on this issue: "It is the intention of the Women's Graphic Center
to provide the education, equipment and support necessary for women to make the
bridge from the personal to the public world."[12] At the Women's Graphic Center the
bridge would be built largely through the production and publication of books.

Books and publishing were very much in the foreground of second-wave
feminism. Feminist publishing was seen as a critical antidote to the silencing women
had experienced in the realm of mainstream trade and academic publishing. One
early entry, *Women and Their Bodies* (continuously in print since 1970 as *Our Bodies,
Ourselves*) provided an important model for the newly essential dissemination of
information and narrative about gendered issues. Throughout the early seventies,
feminist presses were popping up all over the country, from Cambridge, Massachusetts
(Alice James Books) to Oakland, California (Diana Press, an offshoot of the Women's
Press Collective). Many published mainly or exclusively poetry, but there were titles as
well in oral history, social and cultural issues, political analysis, and the recovered
works of earlier generations of women, some of whom, like Anaïs Nin, who was still
very much alive but working on her diaries in some obscurity, suddenly found themselves in the enviable position of having become icons to the young women coming of
age in the movement.

Nin was in many ways the perfect embodiment of a revered elder (a description she would probably not have appreciated) to the young women at the Woman's
Building seeking role models for their new found ways of writing. She had come of age
in her native Paris at the latter edge of the avant-garde movement there. Like many
of her female colleagues during that time, Nin was unable to find a publisher for her
poems and surrealist novels; and like them, she turned to self-publishing as a temporary solution to seeing her work in print. Her self-promotion included being
photographed, sitting down with her legs discreetly crossed, hand setting type for a
book of her own poetry. By the early seventies, Nin, now a naturalized American citizen

Ed Ruscha, Every Building on the Sunset Strip, 1966. Photographic book, black offset paper folded and glued, 7.1" x 5.6" x .04" (closed dimensions). © Ed Ruscha. Courtesy Gagosian Gallery.

and revered for the candor in her voluminous diaries (which would eventually run to eleven published volumes), was living in Los Angeles. Through her connection with Judy Chicago, Nin conducted private tutoring sessions in her Hollywood home for some writers associated with the Feminist Studio Workshop, even holding a book signing at the Woman's Building for one of the diaries just before her death in 1977 at the age of seventy-four. Susan King describes the arrival of Nin at the 1973 opening of the Woman's Building this way: "The sea of people parted as she floated up the patio staircase."[13]

Concurrent with this fired-up passion for seeing women's work into print, if not entirely into distribution (many of these presses would come painfully and, finally, terminally face-to-face with the economic difficulties of their missions by the late seventies) another movement centered on books was developing, this one in the arena of Conceptual art. While the origins of contemporary artists' books are as contested as their definitive descriptors, the synchronicity of the Moore College of Art exhibition and the founding of the Woman's Building and particularly the Women's Graphic Center does provide a tantalizing space for dialogue between the form of one and the goals of the other.

Well before the Moore College exhibition, Lippard, whose work would go on to have an important bearing on the reception of artists' books, brought these early book forms forward through her writing on dematerialization as a foundation of Conceptual art practice. Although the idea of a dematerialized art object has been questioned often since its first appearance in print, Lippard coined the term with her colleague John

Chandler to trace not only the development of what they refer to as ultra-Conceptual art, but also to describe work in which, as Lippard puts it, there is a denial of expected identity. In Lippard's view the book work of artists such as Sol LeWitt and in particular Ed Ruscha represented the ideal ultra-dematerialized art as objects that were inexpensive, endlessly reproducible, conceptual in content, and above all were able to be distributed completely outside the mainstream gallery world. Lippard went on to co-found the New York artists' book collective Printed Matter in 1976, which opened a retail shop in New York while also acting as a publisher and distributor of artists' books. Although she would shortly repudiate her early enthusiasm for these books, at least in their potential for revolutionizing the mainstream art system (Lippard initially envisioned these books replacing thrillers and bodice rippers on supermarket checkout lines), the idea was by then taking hold that artists' books provided an alternative pathway for the creative voice as "instruments for extension to a far broader public...."[14]

Early Influences: One Story Continued

For Susan King, the increasingly public profile of the new feminist presses and their products would have certainly been a part of the ongoing conversation at the Women's Graphic Center. Two events in particular became central for King during this early period of the Women's Graphic Center. Both revolved around Helen Alm, the Women's Graphic Center's first director: the acquisition of a small commercial letterpress shop, and an afternoon class that remains vivid in King's memory.

Alm bought the contents of a small letterpress shop that was going out of business for the Chouinard Building site in 1974. Included in the purchase was a ten-by-fifteen-inch Chandler & Price platen press and some metal Melior type. The C&P, a venerable mid-sized press of a style known affectionately as a clamshell because of the way it opens and closes to accept and release the hand-fed paper, became the cornerstone of the letterpress studio. The excited students at Feminist Studio Workshop voted on a second metal typeface to augment the Melior, choosing Bruce Rogers's elegant Centaur from the catalog of the Los Angeles Type Founders.

The second event took place during Alm's design class. On that bright Friday in the courtyard of Chouinard, Alm showed the gathered students several examples of artists' books and other work from her own library and from the collection of de Bretteville. Two groups of books immediately resonated with King: Ed Ruscha's and Jane Grabhorn's.

Ruscha's work with books began in 1966 with what would become the icon of conceptual artists' books, *Every Building on the Sunset Strip*. The book unfolded into a long accordion that mimicked Sunset Boulevard in Hollywood and displayed photographically literally every building that lined the street in a flattened perspective that resembled the maps of the stars' homes sold on the street corner in Beverly Hills. Intentionally unpretentious, the book was produced in an open edition in defiance of

273

the idea of the singular or limited artworks available through the gallery system or the fine press publisher. Ruscha claimed in one of his infrequent interviews that he was not interested in the book form per se, but in the lack of preciousness inherent in the idea of the multiple. This statement seems somewhat disingenuous given the narrative content of several of his books, particularly his graphic novels or the classic *Royal Road Test* (1967), in which Ruscha and some of his friends describe a trip to the Nevada desert where, while moving at a high speed, they tossed a Royal typewriter out the car window, then went back to document the results, photographing the remains as they lay scattered along the roadside.

While Ruscha was already a staple in any discussion of artists' bookmaking by the time Susan King and her sister students began to address this form, Jane Grabhorn was unknown outside of a small and elite group of West Coast aficionados of fine printing. The wife of the well-known printer Robert Grabhorn, whose work with his brother Edwin in San Francisco's Grabhorn Press was legendary, Jane had toiled at the composing bank of the press since its establishment in 1919. Somewhat later she also ran her own publishing house, Colt Press. Exasperated at times with the exacting nature of fine printing, Jane Grabhorn demanded her own means of production away from the Grabhorns' elegant machines; Robert purchased her a tabletop letterpress with the brand name Jumbo. This press became the namesake for Jane's irreverent commentaries on fine printing and its perfectionist demands: "Don't be tied down like dunces and fools / To quads ems picas and man-made rules./In this kind of trif-eling, let the male wallow,/For women the freedom of wind and of swallow."[15] King fell in love on the spot with Jane's brand of idiosyncratic printing. The combination of freeform, highly individual content and tightly controlled and skillful craft provided King with a model for moving her own work into the book form.

Alm had exhibited an interest in artists' books while a printmaker at Cal [University of California, Berkeley] and adopted the "mass production technology"[16] of offset printing during her tenure there. A representative book is *Revealed to Me* (1972). The ten-page book is comb-bound and offset-printed in black ink in a nearly square, oversized (ten-by-eleven-inch) format. *Revealed to Me* offers a compelling look at the way in which some icons of Western art might be reinterpreted through an individual sensibility. In the first image, the central grouping, a Renaissance family at the table, is presented as oblivious to the chaotic figures that surround the table. A gnome, a dwarf in heavy makeup, and a Glen Baxter figure in twenties swim attire appear to be partaking of the meal; a snake sleeps on the table and a small dog pulls at the tablecloth. In the next collage, the scale is interrupted and a pointing finger directs the viewer to events outside the window. From that point the collaged elements become increasingly chaotic and iconographic; religious and political symbology take hold, and the viewer is left to interpret and deconstruct the various meanings imbedded in the pages. Most intriguingly, Alm herself catalogs these images in a three-page index in which the

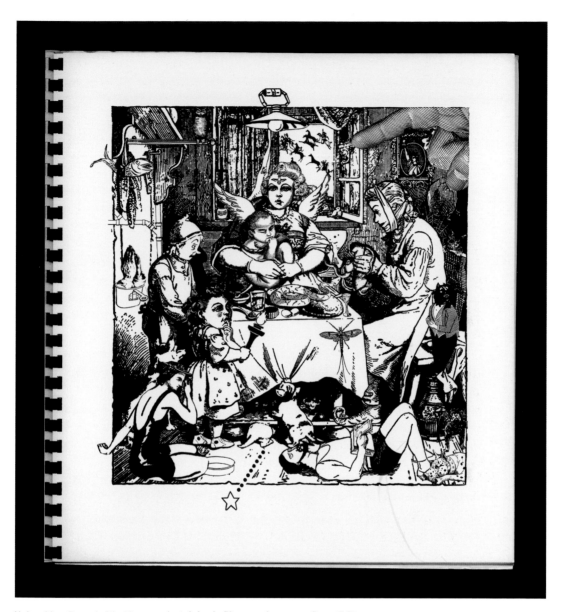

Helen Alm, *Revealed to Me*, 1974. Artist's book. Photograph courtesy Susan E. King.

various bits of imagery are separated and pictured singly inside small, square boxes, suggesting that the viewer might engage in a game of locating the disconnected images (the snake, a telephone, metal tubing, a lamb cinched around its middle and dangling from an armature) in the complex collages. In a subsequent description of the book, Alm gives very little interpretation, writing only, "I allow images that interest me to take on a symbolic interpretation...."[17]

These three models—the dematerialized work of Ruscha, the irreverent doggerel of Grabhorn, and the subverted iconography of Alm—offered diverse influences for King. But she had also begun developing content for her work through the process, new to her, of autobiographical writing. The writing, another strong component of the Feminist Studio Workshop, was taught under the auspices of the Women Writers Program, led initially by the poet Deena Metzger. Metzger, who sometimes also taught classes in her living room, drew on novelists such as Marge Piercy and Doris Lessing, whose *Martha Quest* series had electrified many newly formed women's groups throughout the seventies. By 1978, the poets whose inspiration drove the writing workshops included Adrienne Rich, Susan Griffin, Diane di Prima, Honor Moore, and the work of the four women who were teaching the workshops: Eloise Klein Healy, Martha Lifson, Holly Prado, and Metzger.

King, who came to the Feminist Studio Workshop as a visual artist, remembers that the concept of using one's own stories for artmaking was strongly promoted beginning in 1974, the second year of the program and the year that would come to mark King's own beginning as a writer. Like many women across the country during this period, King and her sister students at the Feminist Studio Workshop were struggling to find their own voices on a range of levels. For King, the autobiographical writing was the most difficult aspect of the workshop.

One of the first book projects that King undertook was a diazo print project, *Dark & Bloody Ground* (1978). The diazo project, proposed by de Bretteville for an eight-session workshop, was to result in a group of printed broadsides meant for "posting, distribution and exhibition."[18] The diazo print was not an arbitrary choice. De Bretteville, whose awareness of this process was likely promoted by her husband, architect Peter de Bretteville, understood diazo to be an economical method for the production of multiples. De Bretteville further prescribed red-print rather than blue-print, both as way of calling attention to itself and because of the red/read homonym that would be implicit in the final work. The projects were meant to reflect both of these spellings, and the assignment sheet listed several meanings for each word in order to help define the project's intention: read, to derive means from; red, any of the various colors resembling blood. (Interestingly, the assignment did not acknowledge another characteristic of diazo printing, its inherently ephemeral nature.)

King's work took the suggestion of blood literally in both its title and its content. She did not, however, adhere to the suggested broadside form. The piece instead became a small book, folded into a concertina. Text completely dominated the work, obviously a major change for a ceramist; the visual aspect was limited to the white type reversed out of the blood-red background. The content was an autobiographical memory of a journey from Los Angeles back to King's hometown in Kentucky. (The dark and bloody ground in the title is the Native American designation for it.) In this work, King established several themes that would continue to resonate in her books: the importance of place, the pull of family, the search for identity as an artist, the importance of materiality to the development of her ideas. King's work as an artist's bookmaker had begun.

King would go on to work with the foundations of this project in many of her subsequent works. In 1977, she produced another diazo print book, this one in blue-print, titled *Pacific Legend*. The band that wraps around the covers refers to this book as, "A mapping of a year's mythology. A personal journey with images." This dual description appears to suggest the dual voices—one public, multiplied, audienced, the second private, reflective, a mirror of the personal—that de Bretteville stressed in her teaching. *Pacific Legend* introduced this duality, and repeated the material experiment of the red/read print assignment, including this time its implicit ephemerality.

Critical evaluation of the work King and her colleagues undertook was not a particular aim of the program, which was intensely engaged in a way to help women "gain confidence in the possibility of expressing personal reality in . . . the public world."[19] This lack of the standard expectation for critique and judgment left women free to explore their own voices in a largely non-judgmental environment. In King's words, the general thrust of instruction was toward, "being kind to people who were making things."[20] Clearly, this operating principle melded well with de Bretteville's concept of the feminist designer as needing to critique "the elements of our culture that demean women" while encouraging "strength, grace and warmth."[21]

Consciousness-Raising and the "Great Art" Construct

With the publication in 1971 of Linda Nochlin's essay, "Why Have There Been No Great Women Artists?," the landscape of art history began to develop the contours of the feminine. Nochlin's essay outlines a feminist analysis for contextualizing the concept of "greatness" within the sociological and institutional frameworks of the culture rather than relying on the traditional idea of a god-granted or inherently gifted personage, a construct that had always privileged the white male in Western culture. At the same time, Nochlin takes exception to two aspects of what she characterizes as contemporary feminist practice with regard to an examination of the history and practice of art. First, she states that feminists were attempting to reconstitute minor women artists as "great" artists using the same (male) criteria that had always been in place. Second and more unsettling is the "mistaken" feminist concept about what constitutes art, attributing to feminism the "naïve idea that art is the direct, personal expression of

277

individual emotional experience, a translation of personal life into visual terms."[22]

There is some ambiguity in the position of the Feminist Studio Workshop with regard to these positions in the many early statements explaining its founding. Certainly one major aim of the Woman's Building was to acknowledge, according to de Bretteville, the fundamental importance of "reviv[ing] names and faces, plans and actions from history," in order to "create a future from expanded resources."[23] Raven called the Woman's Building "an act against the historical erasure of women's art and an acknowledgement of the heritage we were beginning to recover."[24] There is no particular claim to the inherent greatness of the women whose names were being reclaimed in this recovery; in fact Nochlin's essay and her other writing, with its lists and critiques of "lost" women artists, helped to define the territory. Chicago referred to Nochlin's essay in *Through the Flower* not for its theoretical stance but for its historical examples of strong women artists.[25]

The "naïve idea" that art is the movement of personal experience into visual mediums could on the other hand be seen as central to the creative philosophy of the Feminist Studio Workshop. In *Through the Flower*, Chicago discusses the work of the women in her class at Fresno State: "Theirs was content-oriented art. Although I never instructed them to make any particular kind of work, I had encouraged them to use the content of their lives as the basis of their art and that had stimulated the production of a lot of work."[26] De Bretteville's mission statement for the Women's Design Program at CalArts states, "Starting with ourselves, we have used our own experiences as appropriate subject matter."[27] The dynamic that supported the development of content in the art of the "fusing of emotion and idea," as the original goal stated, was the method being repeatedly tested and developed throughout second-wave feminism: consciousness-raising.

Consciousness-raising was a fundamental element of the various feminist art and education programs developed by Chicago and her colleagues at every venue in which they operated. There are numerous references to consciousness-raising in *Through the Flower*, whose index lists ten citations, several spanning ten to twenty pages, with related subjects ranging from "alternative female art community" to performance. Consciousness-raising was at the root of nearly all training at the Feminist Studio Workshop. In one undated schedule of classes for a fall term at Feminist Studio Workshop (possibly 1978), consciousness-raising sessions appear in three separate weekly time slots. Monday afternoons were partially dedicated to "C-R on Political Issues," conducted by the CalArts student turned Feminist Studio Workshop faculty member Suzanne Lacy. On Fridays the entire morning was given over to consciousness-raising groups, in this case leaderless and "democratic." And on Sunday morning the Natalie Barney Collective held three hours of consciousness-raising along with its meeting.[28]

When de Bretteville set up The Women's Graphic Center Program at the

Woman's Building in 1973 to train women in the technical processes of offset printing and publishing, she used "modified" consciousness-raising during the group discussions that anchored the Sunday workshops. Although the specific nature of modified consciousness-raising is not clarified in the course syllabus connected with these workshops, the discussion format is described as one of "support, criticism, suggestions response to problems [*sic*], possibilities, similarities and [di]fferences."[29] For Chicago at Fresno State, modified consciousness-raising had a specific intended outcome: "I didn't know about classical consciousness-raising then. Instead we did a kind of modified consciousness-raising, which combined the expressing of common experiences with my trying to help the women understand the implications of those experiences in order to change their behavior patterns."[30]

This forthright intent toward implementing a "new" paradigm for women's lives as expressed by Chicago in the early seventies—in which her role seems based on the patriarchal therapeutic models of the time—appears to find refinement as the Feminist Studio Workshop developed its ideas about the purposes of feminist education. Descriptions of de Bretteville's Sunday critiques in the Women's Graphic Center Program are filled with nouns and phrases such as discussion, get-together, support, suggestions, response to problems, often avoiding the word "criticism," or putting it last in a string of words, in an implicit acknowledgement of its problematized connotation. A critique becomes a "discussion with an effort to locate contradictions and consistencies in our responses to the materials."[31]

Ruth Iskin, whose practice as a feminist art historian led her to an early leadership role at the Feminist Studio Workshop, declares in an interview, "Feminist education assists women in developing their full potential while developing new form and content in art, form and content which are related to their experiences and lives as women and to feminism."[32]

A 1977 booklet by the British independent art historian Mary Michaels suggests that the initial enthusiasm for an unmediated platform for this new form and content combination might have been mitigated by the quality of some of the products of this exploration. Michaels, in her insightful and well-written pamphlet on her experience with the second annual, ten-day-long, summer Feminist Education Workshop held at the Spring Street Woman's Building, briefly explained Chicago's teaching methodology at this time: "Judy worked with us on visual art: tackling the problem of how to get women making images out of their sense of themselves, rather than a culturally imposed idea of 'Art'; and then, of helping to develop those images into something that would have a wider validity and resonance—art."[33]

Later Michaels paraphrases Chicago in the context of an evening critique at the Feminist Education Workshop: "You mustn't pretend it's art when it isn't, but you have to find ways of combining critical acuity with human support."[34]

For Susan King, the complex overlay of production workshops, consciousness-raising, writing, and her own background in visual, three-dimensional art making, underpinned by the positive support of her teachers, mentors, and peers, led to a commitment to the juxtaposition of form and content in increasingly experimental and individualistic books.

Women and the Printing Arts

King and other emergent artist bookmakers shared an interest in an audience for their work; that audience would presumably be situated outside the mainstream and chauvinistic gallery system. As evidenced in the 1975 catalog *Women and the Printing Arts*,[35] the books being produced through the Feminist Studio Workshop and the Women's Graphic Center focused on serial scheme and a strong connection to the literary. They embodied, by their very nature as feminist documents, or even as documents created and produced by women, the denial of expected identity that underlay Lippard's theory. The catalog also served as an implicit critique of the failure of mainstream publishing to make public enough women's voices.[36]

 Women and the Printing Arts cataloged the exhibition of twenty-five women and one collective whose work was shown in a 1975 exhibition of the same name at the Woman's Building. The exhibition was not limited to women working at the Woman's Building: about half (thirteen women plus the Helaine Victoria Press collective) were from the Los Angeles area, with the rest spread across the country. (The furthest away geographically was Ann Williams in Glover, Vermont.) The catalog was produced as a series of cards, like those of a hard-copy (non-digital) library catalog, held together by a metal ring. Books, posters, and cards were exhibited, but books dominated; in all there are twenty-two books among the twenty-six participants. The catalog offers only written descriptions of the work, not images, and emphasizes three aspects of each piece: production techniques, the fact that they are produced in editions, and the implied presence of an audience.

 The absence of photographs in the catalog is justified in a statement following the introduction which says that the "modesty" of scale, color, and size of the works coupled with their complexity of organization (i.e., books) meant that little would be communicated through photography of the individual pieces. While it is possible that the absence of photographs was primarily due to the technical difficulties of including them in this early attempt at a catalog, the apparent lack of focus on the visual aspects of the work is explained by de Bretteville in her introduction, in which she strongly privileges production, distribution, and the idea of invited response, speaking of "activity" rather than creativity. De Bretteville writes of "mass produced personal statements," and asks each catalog contributor to comment, in the brief participant statements, on both the production and distribution methods she has employed, as opposed to the content of the work itself.[37]

 This emphasis on production is consistent with de Bretteville's role as a graphic designer, in line with the often-pronounced disparity between the "high" art of the visual arts and "low" art of design. In general de Bretteville rejected the "elitist" gallery system in favor of the grittier populist methods of the designer, who by definition must work for an audience of consumers. In her Women's Graphic Center classes, de Bretteville asked her students to consider the "implications" as well as the similarities and differences of working with, for example, handmade objects, handset type, or photographic images in fine art or vernacular traditions, always in the context of these questions: "What do you want to make, what do you want the receiver to experience, what processes do you intend to use and why, how many do you intend to make, what materials do you intend to use and why?"[38] At the root of these questions is a focus on the tangible products of the makers as opposed to the conceptual foundations of the work being undertaken. In the Graphic Center course description there is no question that asks: What do you want to say? Instead, the focus is on the works' reception. On page one of the same syllabus, de Bretteville expresses her goals for the course this way: "What is being communicated, who is the audience, what is of value to you, to society, in the work?"[39]

Of course, the Feminist Studio Workshop, which would have had students in common with the Women's Graphic Center, was focused on supporting women in the pursuit of their own voices. In addition to the several weekly consciousness-raising sessions, the fall term (1978?) schedule of classes includes two to three hour sessions on Our Work and Our Lives, Feeling to Form (co-taught by de Bretteville and Jane Rosenzweig), and two writing workshops directed by Deena Metzger, one of which took place in Metzger's living room. Still, a comprehensive evaluation of the various education programs issued in February 1980 states in a critique of the Feminist Studio Workshop that the program would benefit from "decreased emphasis on process for its own sake and increased emphasis on process related to creating art."[40]

The emphasis on audience and the concomitant repudiation of the traditional workings of mainstream art parallel Lippard's views. In 1977, Lippard wrote an appreciation of women's artists' books for *Chrysalis*, the feminist periodical that was not coincidentally published out of the Woman's Building, with de Bretteville as both editorial board member and designer. The essay, which notes both *Women and the Printing Arts* and its 1977 sequel, about which more will be said later, also includes in the postscript an explicit critique and a somewhat guarded concern about the content of some of the books being produced by women:

> The feminist art movement has evolved from talking to oneself...
> to talking about oneself...and is now becoming increasingly
> concerned with talking to an economically broader-based audience
> without losing the intimacy of the personal/communicative mode
> natural to women.

While the form of artists' books, posters, and postcards is ideally suited to this evolution, their content is too rarely formulated with these ends in mind. Most feminist artists tend to be torn between expressing themselves as strongly as they can and making that expression accessible to others. It is a conflict that will not readily be solved as long as there is an art world and an avant-garde. Yet the notion of feminist art carries within it, by definition, a profound concern for other women.[41]

The Pioneering Presence of Cindy Marsh

One of the exhibitors in *Women and the Printing Arts* was Cynthia Marsh. An early de Bretteville recruit, Cindy Marsh came to the Woman's Building from a bifurcated background of art and technology, making her an ideal candidate for de Bretteville's vision. Marsh was raised in the Boston area, where she took advantage of the ambience of Harvard Square to experience alternative art and music in the sixties. After her schooling at, interestingly, Moore College of Art in Philadelphia, a women's college, and at Rochester Institute of Technology, where her MFA studies emphasized the technical aspects of both fine art and offset lithography, Marsh moved to Los Angeles because, she claims, she wanted to meet one of her art heroes, the ubiquitous Ed Ruscha.[42]

According to Marsh, de Bretteville dropped by Marsh's Hollywood apartment one day and invited her to join a new organization, the Women's Graphic Center, which had received some grant money to pay an offset printer. Marsh wandered down to the Chouinard Building the next day to look at the facility and ended up taking the job, despite some hesitations, because she needed a place to do her own work. Marsh's hesitation partially revolved around the issue of sexual orientation. Marsh, a heterosexual who took her boyfriend with her to inspect the new space, wanted to be certain she would be accepted into the community. Marsh's concerns were echoed by many women approaching the Woman's Building. Heterosexuals were uncertain of their reception in a community that, in supporting gender separation, might also, some surmised, be interested in promoting lesbian separatism. Lesbians (bisexuality and transgendering were hardly considered at this time) who had spent their lives experiencing overt prejudice wanted the assurance of a safe space for both their work and their personal actions. These conflicting tensions continued to require dialogue throughout the life of the Woman's Building.

Marsh stayed to teach at the Women's Graphic Center, where she quickly became a co-director with de Bretteville and Alm, as well as at the Feminist Studio Workshop. Her six-hour class at the Women's Graphic Center focused on offset printing techniques, which she taught on the AB Dick, a duplicator-type offset press that was compact and relatively simple to learn for Marsh's students, many of whom nonetheless did not master its operation, preferring the more direct and accessible

THE SPORTING LIFE
1975

Fat Heart Publications
LOS ANGELES, CALIFORNIA

WOMEN'S COMMUNITY PRESS

Cynthia Marsh, *The Sporting Life* 1975. Offset, silkscreen and letterpress. Fat Heart Publications, printed at the Women's Graphic Center, six pages, edition of 50 copies. © Cynthia Marsh.

technique of letterpress. Marsh often worked on the larger offset press, the RotoPrint, which could feed an eighteen-by-twenty-four-inch sheet of paper. Marsh described this press as an "albatross," a designation that did not prevent her from subsequently buying it from the Woman's Building and "dragging" it home to her studio.

In addition to her innovative use of the commercial technology of offset, Marsh incorporated a variety of media into her own work, including letterpress and silkscreen. Her education and creative sensibility made her the perfect teacher and role model at the Woman's Building. Her highly individualized combination of art and design coupled with her understanding of both the commercial use of and the creative potential for current technologies (offset printing had supplanted letterpress as a commercial technology in the sixties) meant that she embodied the Woman's Building ideal of combining fine art and commercial production methods in the service of an audience. Marsh noted this idiosyncratic combination of interests early on in her work. At Rochester Institute of Technology, critiques of her work, "tended to come down to, 'Well, is this a print or are you selling something?'" Lippard described her work at the Women's Graphic Center as a group of prints that "comment on the joys of printing and the consumer life, like an esthetically satisfying mail order catalogue."[43]

These works, labeled by Marsh in the *Women and the Printing Arts* catalog as books, were in fact large-format suites of prints. *The Sporting Life 1975* is representative. The nine, ten-by-twelve-inch sheets, printed on heavy card stock, combine photography with the reproduction of found objects such as a band-aid, a wood screw, button earrings, and jars of enamel paint that might be used for painting airplane models. All are placed in seemingly random order and juxtaposed with photographs of page spreads from open books. The images are offset printed in both black and white and color, and there are silkscreen additions, including on one print a ring from a coffee mug. There are no explanations for the various images, whose presentation resembles a sparsely designed mail-order catalog whose clientele comes from Tristan Tzara's mailing list.

These suites have the undeniable characteristics of an artists' book in concept and content (strongly thematic in a randomly-built sequence); the obviously multiple prints resemble largish book pages in form and substrate (inexpensive commercial paper rather than photographic or printmaking paper). One in particular, a two-sided, black-and-white piece that has on one side a photograph of a vintage John D. MacDonald paperback opened out to show both covers and on the other captures a random page spread from the same novel, both set at slightly rakish angles, seems to capture the essence of the conceptualized, dematerialized object, a clearly Postmodern form. Marsh saw the objects in *The Sporting Life* as remnants of the "visual noise" of the year in which she printed them.[44]

Marsh lists among these influences the artists Dieter Roth and of course Ruscha (whom she did meet), along with the work of Something Else Press, particularly

Allan Kaprow, and other Fluxus artists. Stephen Bury describes Something Else Press as creating an "ennoblement of the ephemeral." Marsh's captured representations of everyday objects were another form of ennobling the ephemeral, one that she made her own in these idiosyncratic collections.

The Northern California Connection

While King was developing her highly distinctive voice in the burgeoning field of artist bookmakers, she cemented her connection with the Woman's Building by moving from a position of founding student to that of studio director for the Women's Graphic Center. King traveled between her apartment, which fronted the Venice boardwalk, and downtown Los Angeles in her aging Volkswagen bug, often accompanied by one of the many visiting artists and printers that she and the other leaders in the Women's Graphic Center brought in for teaching, lecturing, and curating. King continued to develop the letterpress studio, building on the initial donations of type and equipment and issuing invitations to visiting artists and printers, many from the San Francisco Bay Area. These women were attracted to the energy and focus of the Woman's Building, an entity without parallel in Northern California, which had instead a preponderance of male, literary, fine-press printers working separately in their shops filled with metal type and letterpresses, and a long and illustrious history but little collective energy. These Northern California women welcomed the opportunity to be in a community that teaching at the Woman's Building offered. In turn, they brought newly minted letterpress production experience, often gleaned via casual instruction from veteran printers such as Adrian Wilson, Alfred Kennedy, and Clifford Burke, to their Southern California sisters.

At the Woman's Building these two groups of women, the feminist artist/publishers in Southern California and the feminist writer/printers in the north, met to exchange ideas and, more immediately, production skills. Bonnie Carpenter, of Effie's Press in Berkeley, and Jaime Robles and I, of Five Trees Press, conducted weekend workshops in letterpress production methods, which both presses were using exclusively to produce their small-edition chapbooks. The work at Five Trees and particularly at Effie's was largely poetry by women and was printed in standard chapbook style, either minus illustrations other than title page decoration or accompanied by relief prints. Robles undertook most of the illustrations for those books at Five Trees Press, including H.D.'s *The Poet & The Dancer* (1975), one of the earliest of H.D.'s works to be resuscitated in a legitimate, non-pirated edition, as well as for *Crocus/Sprouting* (1974), the first book issued by Five Trees, with poetry by Jane Rosenthal and design and printing by Cheryl Miller. At Effie's, located in a warehouse in Emeryville, an industrial town tucked between Berkeley, Oakland, and the calm waters of the San Francisco Bay, Carpenter used hand-set Goudy types to print her poetry chapbooks by writers including Adrienne Rich (*Twenty-One Love Poems* [1977]) and Mary Mackey.

TWENTY-ONE
LOVE POEMS

Adrienne Rich

Effie's Press
Emeryville, California

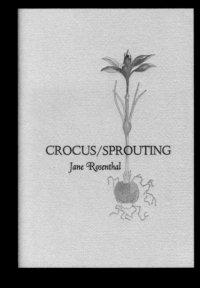

CROCUS/SPROUTING
Jane Rosenthal

One Night Stand

Mary Mackey

Effie's Press
Emeryville, California

Clockwise from top-left **Adrienne Rich, author, Bonnie Carpenter, publisher, artist, book designer and printer,** *Twenty-one Love Poems*. 1976. Letterpress and woodcut graphic. Effie's Press: Emeryville. © Bonnie L. Carpenter.

Mary Mackey, author, Bonnie L. Carpenter, publisher, artist, book designer and printer, *One Night Stand*. 1976. Letterpress and woodcut graphic. Effie's Press: Emeryville. © Bonnie L. Carpenter.

Jane Rosenthal, author, Cheryl Miller, printer, Jaime Robles, illustrator, *Crocus/Sprouting*. 1974. Five Trees Press: San Francisco. Photograph courtesy Kathleen Walkup.

Clockwise from top **Kenneth Davids**, author, Betsy Davids and James Petrillo, cover design, *The Softness on the Other Side of the Hole*. 1976. Oakland: Rebis Press. © Kenneth Davids.

Betsy Davids and Ed Moore, authors, Betsy Davids, title page design, *Double Rising Eyelids Rolling Blue*. 1972. Letterpress book. 10¨ x 8¼¨. Berkeley: Rebis Press. © Betsy Davids and Ed Moore.

Johanna Drucker, illustrator, *As No Storm or the Any Port Party Test*. 1975. Letterpress. Berkeley: Rebis Press. © Johanna Drucker.

Mackey's book, *One Night Stand* (1976), is a rich admixture of traditional typography and cream-colored paper encased in a dazzling, orange, glossy Kromecoat cover; on the title page the words *One Night Stand* are encircled by an IUD. The first poem begins, "You were a four-star fuck." The book, printed by Carpenter in an edition of five hundred copies, sold for $4.

Two other women whose work was often more hybridized (literary and visual, in approximately equal parts) also traveled from Berkeley to Los Angeles to teach at the Women's Graphic Center. Betsy Davids of Rebis Press and Frances Butler of Poltroon Press, along with their respective press partners Jim Petrillo and Alastair Johnston, used the medium of letterpress to generate both text and relief images in their books. Rebis Press often stressed collaboration in its editioned works. Davids, a writer and Renaissance scholar, worked with other writers such as Ed Moore, an ex-student from Davids's English classes at California College of Arts and Crafts (CCAC, now California College of the Arts), on Rebis's first book, *Double Rising Eyelids Rolling Blue*, and with Carole Peel on *Her Her, Her & Her, Her vs. Her, Her-Her*, a large-format portfolio of poems published in an edition of 150 in 1974. Other early publishing efforts included the re-issue of Kenneth Davids's erotic novel, *The Softness on the Other Side of the Hole* (1976), originally published by Grove Press, and *As No Storm or the Any Port Party* (1975), with words and images by Johanna Drucker, a student in Betsy Davids's very first class at CCAC. These last two books—one printed on brown paper-bag stock and bound in thick plywood boards, the other bound in canvas with a spine lashed in thick rope—are indicative of Rebis's experiments with the material form of the book. Although Davids would later say that all of Rebis Press's nontraditional bindings were a product of her reluctance to learn the conventions of hand bookbinding, the books bore implicit references to both earlier *livres d'artistes* and to Conceptual artworks of the sixties.

Poltroon's publications, beginning with its founding in 1975, also challenged materiality, but in this case the work drew more heavily on the tradition of the British artists' book movement and its practitioners, such as the environmental artist Ian Hamilton Finlay and the works of Coracle Press. Butler's contributions to the press were most often visual, beginning with the large-scale chapbook *Confracti Mundi Rudera* (1975), written by both partners and illustrated using black-and-white, often pointillist images. Butler was experimenting throughout this time with very large format photo-engravings, using film prepared in her basement studio and printed on the Vandercook proof press using a free-form inking style. The resultant posters were introduced at the Women's Graphic Center, where Butler traveled at one point as often as twice a month to teach. At the Woman's Building, Butler's contact with Cindy Marsh, whose intelligence as an artist Butler found very impressive, resulted in a sense of shared goals of, in Butler's words, "awaking interest in what were soon to be superannuated industrial techniques as viable creative tools."[45] Like Marsh, Butler taught skills in the various aspects of offset pre-printing, such as the use of the process camera. At the time, these skills were helping to move artists with access to the equipment toward freedom of production.

Women and the Printing Arts Redux

Freedom of production would be meaningful only in the context of freedom of expression. Although production aspects are strongly privileged over content in the second *Women and the Printing Arts* catalog, published in 1977, the titles of some of the pieces hint at the direction toward personal revelation and discovery that many of the women were heading. Among the most important of these works was Suzanne Lacy's *Rape Book*. Lacy created the first iteration of this book in 1972 while working with Chicago and de Bretteville at CalArts. Lacy left Fresno State in 1969, where she was earning a master's degree in psychology, to follow Chicago there. At CalArts, Lacy encountered Allan Kaprow, who along with John Baldessari was helping to define the philosophy and direction of this new institution. The joint influences of Chicago, the feminist artist for whom the personal was political, and Kaprow, the apolitical conceptualist for whom art was life, led Lacy to a politically based commitment to public art that primarily took the form of performance. The subject of rape was an early and compelling one for Lacy, who co-developed *Ablutions* as a performance piece in 1972. Lacy, Chicago, and two colleagues presented the work to an audience of artists in the Venice studio of one of Chicago's friends. Lacy says of this performance: "It was the first piece I know of that was about rape.... For us, going public to the art world was a big step."[46]

Rape Book (1976), a landmark artists' book, effectively combined the personal, political and material into an offset-printed, editioned work of forty-four pages. Lacy initially printed 300 copies, but from the beginning she acknowledged the book's potential for a wider audience by indicating that she would accept orders for subsequent printings.[47] Lacy's artist's statement in *Women and the Printing Arts* was short and straightforward: "Propaganda is more accessable [sic] in mass production." Her description of *Rape Book*, which is considerably more informative, articulates issues about its form—its book-ness—in terms not often discussed in any context during this time period:

> I see the book as an analogy for a woman who is in unity with herself when alone. The glossy white pages are her life—clean, untainted by assumptions and perceptions of women. The intrusions are the black type, the constant recurring experiences which are forcibly placed in the center of each page, in the same way they intrude deeply into a woman's life. I want the reader to enter the book, enter forcibly, enter into a woman's perception, and realize the ways in which women are raped, both psychically and physically.[48]

Lacy created this sense of forcible entry into the book by sealing each copy closed with a large red sticker on which the word RAPE was printed, so that the reader had to tear open the sticker—to violate the book—in order to enter it. Once inside the pages, the reader would encounter definitions of rape that challenged the conventional ideas of the term.

The 1977 version of *Women and the Printing Arts* had a more direct intention than the earlier version. This second iteration was developed as a distribution catalog as opposed to being primarily an exhibition one. In several ways the second catalog reflects an obvious growth and sophistication. First, no fewer than twelve women are listed as members of the collective that produced it, including the two signatories to the first catalog, Helen Alm (now Helen Alm Roth) and Sheila de Bretteville. Cindy Marsh was not part of the collective, but is listed as a "supporter"; Susan King appears for the first time. Second, the catalog bears a copyright notice, in the name of the collective; the first catalog contained no such notice. Third, the catalog indicates the critical support of the Women's Graphic Center and therefore by default of the National Endowment for the Arts (NEA). The NEA at this time was an important contributor to many fledgling small press endeavors across the country, including the many women's presses that emerged during the seventies and early eighties. Finally, and perhaps most importantly for the usefulness of the catalog as a distribution tool, each of the works represented was displayed this time in a black-and-white photo that was printed to bleed off all four sides of the five-by-seven-inch cards; evidently the modesty and complexity of the works were no longer seen as barriers to their visual depiction.

In this second catalog somewhat fewer women and presses were represented (twenty-two as opposed to twenty-six in the first version). Perhaps not surprisingly, the geographic spread is much smaller: only five women were from outside the Los Angeles area (of those none were from the San Francisco Bay Area). Seven women (Alm Roth, de Bretteville, Lacy, Marsh, Carol Bankerd, Vaughan Rachel [Kaprow], and Rachel Youdelman) had work in both catalogs.

If geography was not playing as big a part, books were. Of the twenty-eight works included in the catalog, sixteen were described as books, with another three works arguably able to be included in this category.[49] Nearly all of the work in the catalog is reproduced by offset printing, an indication of the persistence of production emphasis and the public voice of the multiple. Interestingly, the production methods of the women most closely associated with the Woman's Building—King, Marsh, Lacy, Alm Roth—are the most complex. Of these, King is the only one to use letterpress (in this case in combination with offset in the book *Passport*); Lacy is the only artist who uses the designation "limited edition" for her work, the book *Falling Apart*, which is hand-typed and hand-bound in an edition of twenty. Also in this catalog, Lacy's *Rape Book* had acquired the more direct and personal title *Rape Is*; this time her print run was 1,000 copies. (The price, $5, remained unchanged.)

RAPE IS

when your shrink suggests
an affair with him
would be therapeutic.

Top: ***Women and the Printing Arts*, catalog (2nd edition, illus.),** 1977. Printed at Women's Graphic Center, Los Angeles. Woman's Building Image Archive, Otis College

Physical Entity to Spiritual Experience

In 1984 Susan King left as studio director of the Women's Graphic Center. In the interim she had moved from her Venice apartment, with its voyeuristic picture window allowing an uninterrupted view of the skaters, beach bums, and tourists on the beach boardwalk, to the relative seclusion of West Los Angeles, just off Pico Boulevard. Here, behind a modest bungalow, King settled into a two-story, architecturally designed studio with two letterpresses, some metal type, and room for the occasional apprentice. That year she published *I Spent the Summer in Paris* with grants from both the NEA and the New York State Council on the Arts; the book was printed at Visual Studies Workshop in Rochester, New York. This book represents an important conjunction of elements—textual, visual, structural, and material—that would define King's work as an artist's bookmaker. The *Paris* of the title is actually two places: Paris, France, where King traveled for rest and inspiration in the summer of 1983, and Paris, Kentucky, her childhood home, where she returned after her trip to France. King juxtaposes the stories of these two places, with their entirely disparate geographies, into a unified work about her art and her influences. The translucent papers and the intricate, accordion-fold binding create further layers of text and meaning in a mere seven double-folded pages.

When King decided to leave the Woman's Building, eleven years after her arrival there, to pursue her career as a professional artist, she left behind a significant legacy of students who acknowledged the influence she had on their work as artists and as printers. One of these women, Bonnie Thompson Norman, stayed on to take over the studio directorship of the Women's Graphic Center. Thompson discovered her interest in fine printing while working for several years at a Los Angeles bookseller. There she met the highly respected proprietors of the Plantin Press, Saul and Lillian Marks, whose elegant, letterpress, limited edition books were exemplars of the style and craftsmanship of the private presses. To learn this craft, Norman went to the Woman's Building in 1980 to study with King, an experience she later described as "an exciting turning point."[50] In 1991, when the Woman's Building closed, Norman moved the entire letterpress studio to a converted dance studio at the Armory Center for the Arts in Pasadena.

While Norman's interest continued to reside in the area of limited edition publishing, she also recognized the necessity of teaching younger generations the value of books and bookmaking. She designed courses for children in this satisfying medium, as well as finding time to teach women in prison and to create classes in bookmaking for the developmentally disabled. Her classes at the Women's Graphic Center included, in addition to the letterpress printing classes for which she had been trained by King and others, related craft classes such as suminagashi paper marbling and the making of several types of book structures.

Norman's teaching in turn influenced a young designer named Katherine Ng, who in many ways represents the transitional point of the Women's Graphic Center from physical entity to spiritual influence. Ng first made contact with the Woman's Building in the latter eighties through a class taught there by artist and poet Karen Holden, who was supported in her teaching by a year-long California Arts Council grant. The class, *Poetry & Bookmaking*, continued the trajectory of study begun by de Bretteville and her colleagues in its combination of writing and visual art. Although most of Holden's students were interested in the writing, Ng, who was studying advertising design at Los Angeles City College, came for the bookmaking. She stayed on after the formal conclusion of Holden's class to rent studio time at the Women's Graphic Center and, incidentally, to continue her poetry studies with Holden. Even this informal class unintentionally followed a Women's Graphic Center tradition by meeting in Holden's living room in Venice.

In 1991, Ng, by now a printmaking student at California State University, Northridge, was studying book art there under the tutelage of none other than Cindy Marsh. Marsh became an important teacher and mentor to Ng, encouraging her to "write dialogues and write from the heart" and "debuting" her at "Book Fair: Celebrating Women Who Make Books" at Mills College in November 1994.[51] Continuing her interest in bookmaking, Ng took several workshops in artists' bookmaking as well as at least one book structure workshop from Norman while she was still at the Spring Street Woman's Building. Through her work with Marsh and Norman, Ng gained proficiency on the letterpresses at both the Woman's Building and at Cal State Northridge. This skill allowed her access to the Woman's Building studio, which by the late eighties was run as a public access studio; Ng was one of several women and men who paid a monthly fee to work on their own projects there. To complete the circle of influences, Marsh introduced Ng to Susan King, who accepted Ng as an apprentice at her West Los Angeles studio.

Ng received support from both Marsh and King for her autobiographical artist's books, in which she explores her identity from various perspectives as an "Asian woman, a manic-depressive, a lesbian." In *Banana Yellow*, Ng writes brief anecdotal stories with titles like "Identity," "Short," "Stereotype," and "ABC" (American Born Chinese) to describe her encounters as a Chinese-American with mainstream American culture. In the first story, Ng describes one particularly poignant moment on her first day of kindergarten when she wanders around the classroom looking for her name, which she hadn't understood was now Katherine and not, as she was called at home, Mui-Mui.

Banana Yellow's presentation, a trapezoid book suggestive of takeout Chinese food containers, emphasizes Ng's ongoing interest in both writing and origami. The latter originally led her to sculptural book forms such as the diamond fold books of Anna Wolfe, the pop-up structures of Beth Thielsen, and the work of Carol Barton, whose book *Tunnel Map* Ng found particularly compelling. The bookbinder Daniel

Katherine Ng, author/artist, *Banana Yellow*, 1991. Artist book. © Katherine Ng.

Kelm's use of metal and wire as hinges helped inspire *Banana Yellow*'s wire loop binding and handle.

Given the circle of teachers and mentors with whom Ng has worked, her replacement of Bonnie Thompson Norman as studio director at the Armory Center seemed destined. In this position she introduced many students to the field of book art. In particular Ng, who earned a secondary art education credential in 1998 and an MA in Art Education from Northridge in 2001, instructed elementary and high school teachers in ways to incorporate bookmaking into their classrooms. She also oversaw the letterpress studio there, and in that capacity explained to her classes the provenance of the equipment. Ng and the other artists and teachers who used the mirror-lined, former dance studio did their printing beneath the banner that hung at the Woman's Building. This is a copy of the image for the catalog of the first Woman's Building in turn-of-the-twentieth century Chicago; it shows a painting by the nineteenth century artist Madeleine Lemaire. This symbol of the shared mission of the edifices, but more importantly, the ongoing work accomplished by the women at these spaces, was a constant reminder to Ng of the most powerful legacy she carried with her from the Woman's Building: the sense of community that she gained there.

Book Art Moves into the Academy

Ng's work as a teacher took place outside the academic setting, just as did the teaching at the Woman's Building. The Armory is one of a small but growing number of centers that either incorporate book art into their curriculum or are founded as community centers for book art. The latter include the Center for Book Arts in New York (which is well past its twenty-fifth anniversary), the Minnesota Center for Book Arts in Minneapolis (founded in 1983), and the San Francisco Center for the Book (founded in 1996). Centers for book art are appearing all over the country, from Massachusetts to New Mexico to Florida.

Academic institutions, some of which had traditionally housed private publishing presses, began to expand into book art programs in the late seventies. In California, two of the most long-standing programs are housed at women's colleges. In Southern California, the Scripps College Press continues an active program of student-involved publishing that has been under the direction of Kitty Maryatt since 1986. (Susan King preceded Maryatt at Scripps.) Each semester students in Maryatt's publishing class collaborate on a theme-based book that explores a topic chosen by Maryatt. The resulting books, produced in small editions, are distributed primarily to a standing group of collectors.

An early book from this class, published in 1987, included four students—Rosalind Hopkins, Sarah Knetzer, Sherry J. Perrault, and Suzanne Rybak—who interviewed eighteen women in book art for *Los Angeles Women Letterpress Printers*. Of these women, seven claimed connections with the Woman's Building, including the artists Vida Hackman and Susan King, and some women King trained, including Robin Price and Marion Baker, who had been a student with King in the Feminist Studio Workshop. There is even a third-generation connection: Nancy Turner studied with King's student Bonnie Thompson Norman. (The seventh woman with Woman's Building connections is Jaime Robles, who was a teacher there.) Although the range of work represented by these women is broad and their influences multiple, they can claim a common connection through the foregrounding of strong production values, the use of letterpress as a reproductive method, a shared appreciation for the edition or multiple book, and the potential for a layered confluence of texts. As Price says in *Los Angeles Women Letterpress Printers*, "I hate one-line art. I like the layering of information." Price, a 1984 graduate of Pomona College who studied typography under Christie Bertelson at Scripps, also had an apprenticeship with King; she calls it her "most cherished job experience."[52]

Like Scripps, Mills College, in the San Francisco Bay Area, has a contemporary program that has grown from the legacy of an earlier institutional private press. At Mills a librarian and Mills alumna, Rosalind Keep, established the Eucalyptus Press in her campus home, now demolished, in about 1930, primarily to publish manuscripts connected to the college. Following a moribund period after Keep's death in 1961, the Mills program was revitalized through course offerings in letterpress printing and binding. Artists such as Claire Van Vliet, a Vermont printer and MacArthur Fellow with California roots, and Hedi Kyle, a binder and conservator living at that time in New York, taught workshops at Mills that had far-reaching influence. King, always generous to a fault in her teaching, gave several workshops to Mills students on her innovative techniques, some based on Kyle's structures. More important, however, were King's critiques of student work. At these King insisted on depth and complexity in the simplest of projects, declining in particular to support the "one-line" book, as anathema to her as to her apprentice Price.

King's books continue to inspire a new generation of students at Mills and elsewhere across the country. The combination of her own creative content, innovative book structures and use of contemporary materials provide models for students in creating their own artists' books. Many students choose to write their own texts as a basis for their books in an unconscious echo of the FSW's focus on individual writing. Although these texts do not always rely on the direct, personal experiences that anchored the writing at the FSW, much of today's academic book art teaching uses some form of the fundamental pedagogical construct of FSW: Working from a content base that encourages the fusion of emotion and idea, asking students to explore the broadest range of possibilities for their subject matter, and teaching them the specific techniques they need to fulfill their vision.

At Mills College the integration of individual creative writing with the form of the artist's book has led to the first MFA in Book Art & Creative Writing Program in the country. Students are challenged to explore and expand their writing within the framework of the artists' book, the latest iteration of new form for new content.

At Mills and in the rest of the graduate and undergraduate book art programs that are proliferating across the country,[53] the support for individual work, the acknowledgement of the place of editions in art practice, and the use of a variety of mark-making and production methodologies combine to create an environment of exploration and process that is as critical to the making of books today as it was to Chicago, de Bretteville, and Raven when they adopted their revolutionary vision.

Notes

1. "Introduction to the Woman's Building," Woman's Building archive, n.d. [1980], Collection, Archives of Archives of American Art, Smithsonian Institute, Washington, D.C.

2. Diane Perry Vanderlip, "Foreword," *Artists Books* (Philadelphia: Moore College of Art, 1973), 5. As quoted in Stefan Klima, *Artists Books: A Critical Survey of the Literature*, (New York: Granary Books, 1998), 12.

3. Judy Chicago, *Through the Flower: My Struggle as a Feminist Artist* (Garden City, NY: Doubleday, 1975), 150.

4. Ibid., 194–95.

5. Lucy Lippard, *From the Center: Feminist Essays on Women's Art* (New York: Dutton, 1976), 218.

6. Ibid., 220.

7. Sheila Levrant de Bretteville, "Feminist Design," *Space and Society/Spazio e Societa* 33 (1986).

8. Feminist Studio Workshop brochure, spring 1973.

9. Women's Graphic Center program description, n.d. Woman's Building Collection, Smithsonian Institute.

10. Paulus Berensohn, *Finding One's Way with Clay: Pinched Pottery and the Color of Clay* (New York: Simon & Schuster, 1972).

11. Sheila Levrant de Bretteville, Women's Graphic Center program description, n.d. [1978?], 1.

12. Ibid., 2.

13. Susan King, email correspondence with the author, September 15, 2004.

14. Lucy Lippard, "The Artist's Book Goes Public," in Joan Lyons, ed., *Artists' Books: A Critical Anthology and Sourcebook* (Rochester, NY: Visual Studies Workshop Press, 1985).

15. Jane Grabhorn's Typographic Laboratory, *A Typographic Discourse for the Distaff Side of Printing: A Book by Ladies* (San Francisco: Jumbo Press, 1937).

16. Helen Alm, personal statement, *Women and the Printing Arts*, Sheila de Bretteville and Helen Alm, eds. (Los Angeles: Woman's Building, 1975), n.d.

17. Ibid.

18. Feminist Studio Workshop handout, n.d. [1975].

19. Undated draft of a program description by de Bretteville, probably 1978.

20. Susan E. King, phone interview with the author, July 15, 2001.

21. De Bretteville, "A Definition of Feminist Design," February 1982. Published in the Women's Graphic Center newsletter, summer 1982.

22. Linda Nochlin, "Why Are There No Great Women Artists?" in *Woman in Sexist Society: Studies in Power and Powerlessness*, Vivian Gornick and Barbara K. Moran, eds. (New York: Basic Books, 1971), 483.

23. De Bretteville, "A Definition of Feminist Design," 98.

24. Arlene Raven, quoted on Woman's Building website: www.womansbuilding.org.

25. Chicago, *Flower*, 149.

26. Ibid., 90.

27. De Bretteville, *icographic* 6 (1973): 8.

28. The Feminist Studio Workshop held a punishing schedule of classes and meetings six days a week, with only Saturdays off. Each day began at 9:00 or 10:00 a.m. and, except for an early dismissal on Friday afternoons, scheduled its last meeting or class session was at 7:00 p.m., ending around 10:00 p.m.

29. The Women's Graphic Center program schedule, 3. Courtesy Susan E. King.

30. Chicago, *Flower*, 75.

31. The Women's Graphic Center program schedule, 1

32. "Institutions of Women's Culture: Interview with Ruth Iskin," in *Women's Culture: The Women's Renaissance of the Seventies*, Gayle Kimball, ed. (Metuchen, NJ: Scarecrow Press, 1981), 289.

33. Mary Michaels, *Learning to Be There: An Account of a Feminist Education Workshop at the Woman's Building, Los Angeles* Worcester, England: Sea Cow Press, 1977, 13.

34. Ibid., 18.

35. De Bretteville and Alm, *Women and the Printing Arts*.

36. In 1975 the Feminist Studio Workshop and the Woman's Building were, like second-wave feminism itself, just becoming aware of their own lack of sensitivity to the concerns of women of color or even white working-class women. The participants in *Women and the Printing Arts* looked very much like the students in the Feminist Studio Workshop or, in fact, like the participants in nearly any march or demonstration under the leadership of the women's liberation movement: white and middle class.

37. De Bretteville and Alm, *Women and the Printing Arts*. The 1977 catalog of the same name acknowledges a debt to the original catalog while explaining that the second iteration was organized by a collective whose intent was to promote sales through the individual artists. This second catalog, also organized as cards held together with a metal ring, includes a photo of each of the works, which are described on the back of the card.

38. De Bretteville, general schedule for Women's Graphic Center Program class sessions, n.d. [1975–76?], 3.

39. Ibid., 1

40. Feminist Education Graphic Project, February 10, 1980, 9.

41. Lucy Lippard, "Surprises: An Anthological Introduction to Some Women Artists' Books," *Chrysalis* 5 (1977): 84.

42. Cynthia Marsh, interviewed by the author via email, August 6, 2001.

43. Lippard, "Surprises," 80.

44. Marsh, email interview.

45. Frances Butler, email communication with the author, June 30, 2001.

46. Suzanne Lacy in conversation with Betty Ann Brown in *Expanding Circles: Women, Art & Community*, Betty Ann Brown, ed. (New York: Midmarch Arts Press, 1996), 164.

47. Suzanne Lacy, artist's statement in *Women and the Printing Arts*, 1975.

48. Lacy, *Women and the Printing Arts*.

49. Susan E. King's *Letter Portfolio* would by any standard be included in the category of artists' books; Cindy Marsh's portfolio *Lifestyle 1976* is very similar in structure to her other portfolios, identified by her as books. Bea Nettles's *Mountain Dream Tarot*, a suite of 78 boxed cards, would be considered a random-sequence artist's book multiple (the edition ran to 800 decks, a prodigious undertaking).

50. Bonnie Thompson Norman, interviewed by Rosalind Hopkins, in *Los Angeles Women Letterpress Printers*, Hopkins, Sarah Knetzer, Sherry J. Perrault,and Suzanne Rybak, eds. (Claremont, CA: Scripps College Press, 1987), 18.

51. Katherine Ng, interviewed by the author via email, July 13, 2001.

52. Hopkins, Knetzer, Perrault, and Rybak, 6.

53. There are currently six graduate programs in book art in the U.S.: University of Alabama Tuscaloosa, University of the Arts in Philadelphia, Columbia College Chicago, University of Iowa, Corcoran College of Art + Design, and the Mills College program.

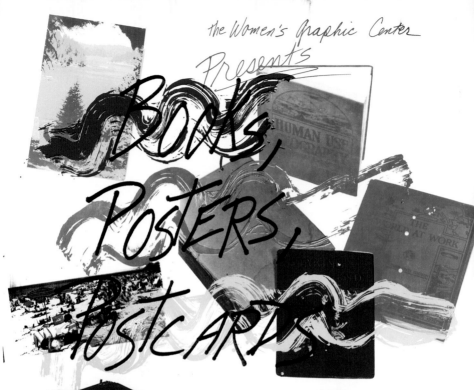

the Women's Graphic Center

Presents

BOOKS,
POSTERS,
POSTCARDS

at the WOMAN's
BUILdinG

1727 NORTH SPRING STREET   LOS ANGELES   (213) 221-6161

OPENING DECEMBER 16 8PM
$2.00 Suggested Donation

Dara Birnbaum, *Technology/Transformation: Wonder Woman*
1978–79. Still from videotape/color, stereo, 5 minutes 50 seconds.
Image courtesy of the artist and Marian Goodman Gallery,
New York/Paris. © Dara Birnbaum.

STORIES FROM A GENERATION: VIDEO ART AT THE WOMAN'S BUILDING

Cecilia Dougherty

Introduction

In 1994, Elayne Zalis, who was at the time the video archivist at the Long Beach Museum of Art, brought a small selection of tapes to the University of California at Irvine (UCI) for a presentation about early video by women. I was teaching video production at UCI at the time and had heard from a colleague that Long Beach housed a large collection of videotapes produced at the Los Angeles Woman's Building. I mistakenly assumed that Zalis's talk was based on this collection, and I wanted to see more. I telephoned her after the presentation. She explained that the tapes she presented were part of a then-current exhibition called "The First Generation: Women and Video, 1970–75," curated by JoAnn Hanley. She said that although the work from "The First Generation" was not from the Woman's Building collection, the Long Beach Museum did in fact have some tapes I might want to see. They had the Woman's Building tapes, and there were more than 350 of them.[1] Moreover, I could visit the Annex at any time to look at them. I felt as if I had struck gold.

Eventually I watched over fifty of the tapes, most of which are from the seventies, and unearthed a rich and phenomenal body of early feminist video work. A considerable amount of the material was based in autobiography, performance, documentation, and political interpretation of popular culture. I was interested in how the work compared to the larger picture of artists' video at the time, and I wanted to know why this work had been all but lost to the history of video. I could cite neither the fact that it was by women, nor that it was feminist in content, as the only reasons for the cultural amnesia surrounding the collection. Artists such as Dara Birnbaum and Valie Export, for example, had made unequivocally feminist tapes in the early and mid-seventies, and Joan Jonas, one of video art's pioneers, created in her best-known work a persona called "Organic Honey" that was assertively female.[2]

The answer is more complicated. The political logic behind the Woman's Building as an art center lies in sharp contrast to some of the standard art practices that interpret new media in traditional terms. A canon of exceptional individual artists in video was established early on by curators, critics and museums, perhaps to prepare the world for the experience of artists' video in traditional art terms and to make space on the landscape for the new medium. An official history of the medium developed based on a narrative of individual pioneering artists who eventually became masters. This story prevails today and manifests in the phenomenon of expensive blockbuster museum exhibitions, which raise the stakes on all media artists, especially those who work collaboratively or with small budgets.

The Woman's Building's founders wanted the space to engender an actual women's art community that could exist not only as a support network, but also as the social foundation of an ideology influencing every aspect of the individual artist's life. This perspective guaranteed that most of the video work at the Building, especially in the early years, would be produced collectively or would be an expression of shared experiences and common lives. It also seems to have guaranteed obscurity for most of the work.

Male artists also used video in the early seventies to investigate personal identity, psychology, and social interaction—themes that seem to have links to feminist theory about individual roles within politicized contexts. They did not have a feminist theoretical framework, however, and the tapes produced are seldom read politically. Interpretations of early work by Chris Burden or Vito Acconci, for example, lean towards discussions of the psychology of power, aggression, trust, and danger. The artist becomes situated in opposition to not only an art world power structure, but also to audiences and participants. These artists expressed or created situations within the work that were considerably outside the social norm, which directed the dialogue about their work.

The strategy was successful. Nonpolitical readings of early video, however socially transgressive the work may have been, preserved a romance about the alienated artist as a prominent part of the narrative. The myth of individual ownership of ideas lingered even through contemporary notions towards the de-commodification of artwork. Interpretations within this narrative preserve the bias towards Modernist models of genius, rebellion, creativity, invention, purpose, and individual initiative. The true story may be obscured by an attractive fantasy of art adventurers and daredevils engaged in Modernist escapades through uncharted mental, aesthetic, cultural, and

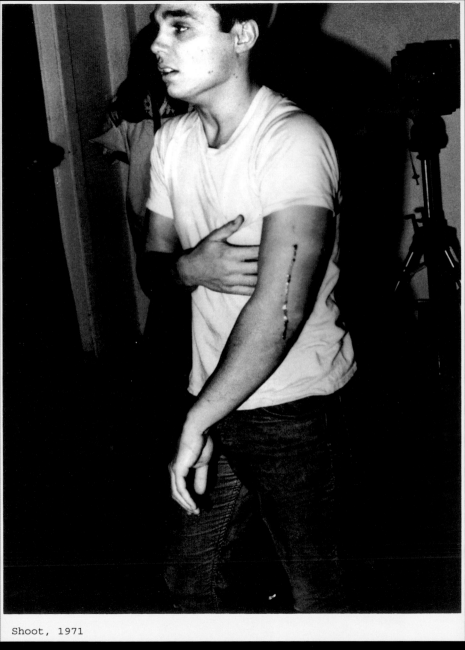

Shoot, 1971

Chris Burden, *Shoot*, F Space, Santa Ana, CA, November 19, 1971. At 7:45 p.m. I was shot in the left arm by a friend. The bullet was a copper jacket .22 long rifle. My friend was standing about fifteen feet from me. Photograph courtesy Gagosian Gallery. © Chris Burden.

Above: **Lynda Benglis, *SELF* (Still from *Female Sensibility*, 1973)**, various dates 1970–76. Portfolio of 9 pigment prints, 23" x 34", edition of 25. Image courtesy of Cheim & Read, New York.

Left: **Kate Horsfield and Candace Compton, L.A. Women's Video Center**, Summer Video Program July–August, 1976. Photograph by Sheila Ruth. Woman's Building Image Archive, Otis College of Art and Design.

economic territories. Myths such as these unravel in the consideration of collectively produced works, especially political or autobiographical works by women. The collective strategy, exemplified in the body of work produced at the Woman's Building, was in fact transgressive. In terms of Modernist art practices, this was a daring and confrontational moment.

Video in the Hands of Artists

There was a great deal of enthusiasm about the power of video in the hands of artists, regardless of the priority of art institutions to establish a hierarchy among practitioners. To artists, the possibilities seemed endless. In the early seventies, the rules had not yet been written, and the field was still wide open for the creation of a new electronic language. Artists such as Peter Campus, Nancy Holt, Richard Serra, Bruce Nauman, and Lynda Benglis were making the most rudimentary discoveries about video.[3] New York and Boston public television stations sponsored and broadcast entire series of video art that, if broadcast within the conservative climate surrounding public television and the arts today, would prove to be a prohibitively expensive risk. Video was an intensely popular medium for women at the Building as well. The tapes from the seventies represent the most interesting part of the collection—both as works and as manifestations of the ideals and goals of feminist art making. The work was in tune with a general fascination with video among artists on an international scale and was developed within an art context that functioned simultaneously as an organized political community.

The video makers at the Woman's Building carried out their experiments in video, placing a wildly optimistic and imaginative set of ideals about Postmodernist art making onto a detailed and unyielding feminist ideological ground. The results set this work apart. Feminist art as a genre includes process and methodology as part of the product and has personal, political and social history at its foundation. Given traditional art historical models for recognizing and validating work, it is easy to make connections between the politicizing of artwork and the erasure of politically based works from art history.

Ideological Background

In 1976, Kate Horsfield and Lyn Blumenthal were in Los Angeles to conduct a summer workshop at the Woman's Building. Together they had founded the Video Data Bank three years earlier and were involved in both feminist issues and in trends in video art. During a subsequent visit to the Building they taped an interview with Arlene Raven, one of the Building's cofounders. The tape, currently distributed by the Video Data Bank as *On Art and Artists: Arlene Raven*, is a document that reads like a manifesto, a pure statement of ideology about feminist art education and the role conceived for the Building as a force within a community of women artists. Raven insists, for example, that within contemporary societies women are a class of people and as such, women's class oppression had led directly to relationships structured by systems of competition. Accordingly, women's oppression occurs chiefly within psychological contexts of crushing isolation and silence. Female artists could turn it around through "supportive criticism and self-criticism," a concept that fuses art criticism and individual responsibility towards a healthy collective progress.[4] Raven's assertion seems to be not only about responsibility and collective struggle but also contains the language of self-diagnosis, correction, redemption, and healing—a powerful mixture of influences within an interpretive feminist logic.

Raven's explanation marks a path into a revolutionary system of self-evaluation and group liberation. Supportive criticism, a key element of the theory, is accomplished through the invention of what Raven terms "Sapphic education," which in her words, "proceeds from a feminist education entering all areas of life." Women must take the opportunity to share information about their everyday lives as part of a "mutual educational process," with the assumption of "peership among women, everyone having something to offer," and "ridding oneself of power dynamics" in personal and professional relationships.[5] Out of this process comes art making.

The women who worked in video seem to have taken the promises of a redemptive and progressive approach to heart. They created one of the most interesting and phenomenal bodies of experientially based works in video that exist today. The tapes show not only the makers' interpretations of formal concerns and issues of content as passed through an energizing filter of "Sapphic education," they also document the development of an entire school of feminist art video.

In the Beginning

Initially, video was used to document absolutely everything at the Woman's Building. It was used constantly and avidly as an experimental art medium as well. Considering that the ideological task at hand incorporated the psychology of the artist as well as the psychology of art making, it is not surprising that there were about 350 videotapes produced at the Building, many within the first decade. The tape collection consists of video art, documentaries, cable television programs, performance documentation, public service announcements, unedited source material, and footage so raw and unprocessed that it is difficult to define. Much of the work is black and white, produced on portable, reel-to-reel equipment and edited with a tape splicer—techniques that are daring by today's practices.

For years many of the videos were stored in boxes in Annette Hunt's garage in Los Angeles.[6] Hunt rightly saw the videos through the lens of her own memories and experiences, having worked on many of them. She was admittedly too close to the material, however, and too familiar with the context of its creation to assess its historical value. One morning she moved the boxes of tapes to the curbside, where they awaited disposal by the Los Angeles Department of Sanitation. That same day, Hunt received a telephone call from her former Woman's Building video colleague Cheri Gaulke. Gaulke was calling to let Hunt know that the Long Beach Museum wanted to archive the tapes. The timing was remarkable, and Hunt rescued the tapes from the curb before they disappeared forever.

Along with the rest of the collection, the tapes were cleaned; transferred from the original half-inch open reels to cassettes (where necessary); and catalogued with generous assistance from the staff at the Long Beach Museum of Art Video Annex. With the cleaning and transferring of many of the tapes, the enormous scope of the video project at the Building is only now coming to light.[7]

According to Hunt, the video makers at the Building did not self-consciously question what it meant to use video. There was a portapak and an abundance of opportunity to shoot. Hunt and other women therefore undertook an extensive project of documentation.[8] They shot everything in and about the Woman's Building that could possibly be documented, and every aspect of what they shot illustrated the ideas that were the Building's political foundation in practice. The architecture and organization of the space, the exhibitions, the 400 to 500 women who renovated the building, the street that it stood on and the approaches one took to reach the front door, the visiting artists at work, and the art and writing workshops in session were all recorded. There are video tours of the site, many interviews, staged scenes, and ordinary conversations among women. The camera was everywhere.

By 1976, women who had already been producing tapes established their own workshop, calling it the Los Angeles Women's Video Center. Hunt, Candace Compton, Nancy Angelo, and Jerri Allyn set up the Women's Video Center as an entity apart from the Feminist Studio Workshop (FSW) in order to become eligible for public funding. Members applied for and received CETA (Comprehensive Employment and Training Act) money to be paid a salary of eighty dollars per week for teaching video and making tapes. According to Hunt, they had it made.

The Tapes

The tape collection is studded with gems of early video. Performance and Conceptual art strategies were put into practice as well as straightforward documentation of events. Most of the makers represented are not currently part of art or academic communities, but some are. One finds tapes by well-known artists such as Suzanne Lacy, Gaulke, Vanalyne Green, and Susan Mogul throughout the collection. Some of their work is among the most intelligent and video-centered. But thinking back to Raven's description of the theoretical environment at the Building, it makes sense that the art process was itself the main point. The process, which was often performance based, led the maker through a transformation. The product was understood as a record of how the transformation took place, and for most of the video artists whose work is untitled and uncredited, the tapes are traces of their struggles in earnest for self-realization.

Kate Millett, *Naked Ladies*, 1977. Sculpture. Woman's Building Image Archive, Otis College of Art and Design.

Mogul's *The Woman's Building: FSW Video Letter* (1974) is a notably unself-conscious, funny, and enthusiastic tour of the Building. It begins as role-play, in which a young woman, carrying a large suitcase and supposedly new in town, asks an older gentleman for directions to the Building. He points out the way and her gaze frames the viewer's introduction to the space. The actor here is Pam MacDonald, a member of the FSW, whose words ring like a testimonial—"I have changed so much [since becoming involved with the Woman's Building] I have to race myself to the mirror every morning." Mogul, who wears a bulky thrift store coat and a broad smile, follows MacDonald to the door, unhindered by portapak, cables, and microphone. Once inside her camera turns to any available subject for an impromptu interview. She finds Judy Chicago. Chicago, resplendent in a Jewish Afro, wide-collared shirt, and large sunglasses, tells the camera: "Old techniques, abstract work, are not meaningful," "[the] traditional art context is unsatisfying," and artists have a need to create "responsible communication" to "make your statement public."

Constructive Feminism (1975), by Sheila Ruth, is a documentary about the Building featuring interviews with cofounders Sheila Levrant de Bretteville and Raven, as well as students from the FSW. This tape is important because it delineates how the

Building became a metaphor for real power through political change; a sense of collectively enjoyed pride and responsibility runs through the piece. The video opens with Ruth at the entrance to the Building with microphone in hand, wearing what appears to be a corduroy pantsuit featuring elbow patches and bell-bottoms. She is the reporter as well as tour guide who gives the viewer her first glimpse at the Building in operation.

The reporter is not objective, of course, and as the camera roams the different spaces, some of which are still under physical construction, Ruth talks about the Building as a "public center for women's culture." The tape includes photographs of women reconstructing the Building's interior, documents that reveal the optimism and confidence the workers experienced. Additionally, the photographs borrow a social realist aesthetic, within which the common person is rendered extraordinary. A connection is made between having the physical space available and realizing ideological goals. From a distance of more than twenty-five years, whether or not these ideals were achieved, or were achieved on a regular basis, is no longer the point.

Ruth interviews the workers, asking how they feel about the process of renovation. Says one, "It takes out the frustration. When I'm through, I can stand back and see something that I have built, see something that is actually visible." This statement is simple and amazing. The worker addresses her work as actually changing the specific relationship of herself, and by feminist logic all women, to the everyday world, the world in which we were kept ignorant of the details of its very construction.

The Artist-in-Residence program is the focus of another series of tapes, including Claudia Queen and Cyd Slayton's 1977 documentation of Kate Millett's visit to the Building, titled *Kate Millett*. Millett, with cigarette in hand and appearing glorious in a white dashiki, is surrounded by fans and followers, many of whom are helping her create sculptural pieces for an installation. These are rather gigantic, *papier-mâché* "ladies" that, in Millett's words, "overwhelm their situation." They do indeed. Eventually, one such sculpture was installed on the roof of the Building to celebrate its fifth anniversary.

An uncredited tape called *Single Mothers: Two Personal Perspectives with Anita Green and Debra Alford* (1979), is one of the most distinctive, if seemingly unfinished or abandoned, pieces I viewed. In this tape, Green and Alford sit at a table, on top of which are a pot of coffee and a microphone that is poorly concealed in a vase of flowers. Behind them is a wall of now-vintage feminist posters. They are having a strained discussion about the problems encountered by single mothers, which appears to be rehearsed, but the tape progresses seemingly without an idea of its own future.

What makes the *Single Mothers* conversation specifically feminist? With statements such as "all mothers feel guilty," and "not a lot has changed," the real themes of isolation, loneliness, and resentment emerge through the language of hopelessness and desire. At the end of the conversation both women face the camera and the image slowly fades out. The moment is honest, awkward, and beautiful.

One of the best-known pieces produced at the Woman's Building is *Nun and Deviant* (1976), by Nancy Angelo and Candace Compton. *Nun and Deviant* is a performance tape that provides an extraordinary, step-by-step description of how to recognize, understand, and identify selves that may lie only slightly beneath the surface. As the tape begins, Angelo and Compton sit facing one another at a card table in an empty parking lot. Angelo puts on a nun's habit as Compton gets into dyke/juvenile delinquent drag; they use each other as a mirror, asking each other if the desired effect has been accomplished. The answer is always "yes."

Each woman takes turns walking to the camera for a close-up shot, with her performance partner in the background smashing crockery on the parking lot ground. In close-up, the "nun" or "deviant" each tells a story about her identity,[9] as the emerging personas become increasingly defiant. They could be talking to themselves, since they used the camera as a mirror. On playback, however, the image reflects the audience rather than the performer, universalizing the narratives and inviting the viewer to find herself in the characters. Angelo and Compton's relationship to the camera creates the intimacy of a confession, while the background performance of dishes being smashed provides the psychological context for each story. At the end of *Nun and Deviant*, the performers rate themselves in a few brief moments of self-criticism, concluding that they did a good job. They also clean up the parking lot!

Angelo uses the "nun" persona in another tape called *Part 1, On Joining the Order: A confession in which Angelica Furiosa explains to her sisters how she came to be among them* (1977). There are two main shots: one an extreme close up of Angelo as Sister Angelica Furiosa, the other of a rose being dipped in honey. Sister Furiosa's confession unfolds in a softly worded story of incest. The language Angelo uses to describe one particular incident of abuse is filled with painful irony and poetic double-speak, as she tells the story of a girl's rape by her father in terms of a mutual betrayal of the mother. It is obvious who has been betrayed. At first the tape appears to be structured as Angelo's attempt to untangle an emotional knot of righteous anger, regret, and guilt. The beauty of the tape, however, is in how it requires the viewer to rearrange logic, to turn lies into truth, and to untangle the knot herself.

In 1979, Angelo constructed a video installation called *Equal Time in Equal Space: Women Speak Out About Incest*. For this piece, Angelo taped six women talking individually about their experiences of incest. To create the installation, she placed six monitors and decks in a circle, each showing a different woman's story, to be played simultaneously. Chairs were set between each of the monitors and the installation itself replicated the form of a consciousness-raising group. The women on the monitors were a part of the circle, as were the audience members seated on chairs. Pillows on the floor made it possible to accommodate extra members of the audience. The decks were synchronized by pausing and playing each deck at the same time because there was no technology available to insure that the six tapes would play simultaneously.

Nancy Angelo and Candace Compton, *Nun and Deviant*, 1976.
Documentary photograph of video production. © E.K. Waller Photography.

Angelo invited children from Los Angeles public schools to view the installation, and it received positive local news coverage. *Equal Time in Equal Space* was groundbreaking. Angelo entered and explored an area that was taboo, invited others in for discussion, and brought the theme to children, who may have benefited from it the most. The installation was part of a two-year project (1979–81) at the Building called "The Incest Awareness Project," which involved visual art, workshops, panel discussions, media events, and an exhibition called *Bedtime Stories*. In 1981, *Equal Time in Equal Space* traveled to the University College Playhouse at the University of Toronto.

Candace Compton's work went in a different direction. In her *Women Communicating Series: #1 My Friends Imitating their Favorite Animals, #2 Some Very Good Jokes and Stories as Told by My Friends, and #3 Some Very Good Jokes and Stories as Told by My Friends* (1979), Compton's "deviant" persona has become less arrogant and more flirtatious. One gets the impression that the flirtation is not only with the camera. In each segment, Compton introduces herself and gives a brief introduction in turn to each of her friends. Individual segments begin in the same empty backyard space. The friend enters the frame and creates what appears to be in impromptu performance.

It was typical in organized women's communities at the time for work, politics, and love relationships to intertwine. *Women Communicating Series* illustrates the interconnection of work, friendship, art making, and love in her circle so effectively that Compton's introductions become humorously predictable. A considerable number of the women "sharing and teaching" or "imitating animals," have also shared apartments, lovers, job skills, have belonged to the same publicly funded carpentry collective (aptly named Handywomen), and have played on the same baseball team (Catch 22). Compton's flirty introductions, which initially seem immature, are an effective device for illuminating the viewer as to what sharing and teaching really meant in the context of a consciously formed lesbian community.

The collection includes other performance-based videos, such as a series of obscure short works produced by Suzanne Lacy in 1974, which are visually and conceptually extraordinary. *Three Works for the Teeth Series* (1974) contains three performances totaling less than eight minutes in which Lacy (1) brushes her teeth using an over-abundance of toothpaste while looking into a mirror, but not into the camera; (2) is spoon fed by an unidentified woman while wearing plastic false teeth that render the feeding almost impossible; and (3) is telling a story about false teeth, most of which the viewer cannot decipher because once again Lacy's mouth is full of plastic teeth. The impact is powerful, rendered by its utter visual simplicity, absurdity, and defiant logic.

In a better-known performance tape, entitled *Learn Where the Meat Comes From* (1976), Suzanne Lacy performs a spoof on television cooking shows directed at housewives. Initially, the camera follows Lacy's hands as she fondles different sections of a lamb's carcass. The camera seems to disregard her face, until the viewer is gradually

Suzanne Lacy, *Learn Where the Meat Comes From,* 1976. Video, Los Angeles. Photograph by Raul Vega. © Suzanne Lacy.

Leslie Labowitz, *Record Companies Drag Their Feet*, 1980. Video production still. © Leslie Labowitz.

made aware that Lacy is "growing" teeth. Lacy devolves from a helpfully hinting house-wife to a raw meat-eating vampire, with the aid of plastic teeth. The real emphasis is on the body of the lamb, however, which looks disturbingly nude and evokes other meanings related to sexualized violence. The parallel between the lamb and the woman preparing it as a meal is strikingly clear. "Where does the meat come from?" she asks. "It comes from you," she answers.

Documentary work from the Video Center includes documentation of two notable public performances, *In Mourning and In Rage* (1977) and *Record Companies Drag Their Feet* (1979). *In Mourning and In Rage* is a well-known performance by Suzanne Lacy and Leslie Labowitz staged solely as a media event. It was created to protest the failure of the police department to apprehend a serial murderer known as the "Hillside Strangler," who had been raping and killing women in the Los Angeles area. The pow-

316

erful documentary footage of the performance evokes the anger and sadness that originally inspired the event. It makes one wonder if we could ever again be so strongly unified and uncompromisingly creative in a collective response to sexual terror.

Record Companies Drag Their Feet, by Labowitz, was another performance-based media event that involved a feminist analysis of pop music album covers. Images of women as victims of sexual and other types of violence that were used to attract customers and promote record sales were specifically targeted. Today, issues of censorship, sexual freedom, and freedom of expression would most certainly be used to complicate this classic feminist analysis of the relationships among sexual imagery, the economy, and the quality of women's lives.

Some of the videotapes are impressive because of their brave and naïve honesty, the de-centering of ego, or the sheer inventiveness of the electronic language. *Effects of Atmospheric Pressure on Sculpture* (1977), by Elizabeth Canelake, is an ironic and subtly powerful six-minute, sculpture-based performance tape. An unidentified woman, presumably the artist, uses an air gun to position blocks of an unidentified sculptural material on the studio floor. She is creating a piece of sculpture, a performance piece, and a videotape simultaneously. There is neither explanation nor voiceover, and the artist's self-consciousness before the camera is matched only by her determination to complete the installation. The camera never focuses in close-up on the performer, which makes her and her activity read as inseparable. Canelake uses video as well as sculptural processes effectively in a doubling of concepts.

A tape by Judith Barry, also from 1977, called *The Revealing Myself Tapes*, is quite the opposite. Barry enacts a long performance in a room full of junk, toys, food, and trash, which have been scattered over a particularly bad, large painting. The accompanying monologue switches from first person to third, but the logic of this tactic is not clear. According to the monologue, the installation and performance are about reorganizing the past, but the final effect is a confusing and unsuccessful word play. Barry herself seems bored by the end of the performance. One wonders if there is a limit to the effectiveness of making artwork from a chiefly internal dialogue. The connection to larger issues seems to have been short-circuited in the unsuccessful attempt to make public an anguished inner voice.

Other short experimental works from the mid-seventies include a particularly timeless monologue called *Snafu* (date unknown), by Leslie Belt.[10] Claiming that she is "fearing the worst" about herself, Belt talks to the camera about depression and self-help strategies from her position on an old sofa. She exudes a disturbed restlessness. The camera is not in focus and its positioning looks uncertain—the shot itself is centered on the sofa, as though the performer merely happened to enter the scene. What results is a tense admission of personal crisis, ostensibly a performance but seemingly more authentic as the piece unfolds.

What is remarkable by today's standards for performance art is that much of the work does not take into account an audience able to identify characters or personas on the basis of head shots or eye contact. An imagined audience is sometimes addressed, as in *Snafu*, but most of what is communicated is done through the process of making the tape rather than through rehearsed monologues or development of a script. The artist's identity is not a key factor. In fact, in some of the tapes we never actually see what the performer looks like. Close-ups simply do not matter. Three other performance-based pieces that exemplify this are *Tuna Salad* (date unknown) by Chris Wong, *Jealousy* (date unknown) by Antoinette de Jong, and *Quandary* (1976), by Linda Henry.[11] *Tuna Salad* is the most enigmatic of the three, involving no language and framing the performer's body in abstracting close-ups. At first, the performer places a speculum and a mirror between her thighs, and then she stuffs her bra with tissue. The camera is not only a mirror; it is a tool of self-examination, without revealing the subject's face.

In *Jealousy*, by de Jong, the performer sits on a chair framed in a medium long shot, which places her awkwardly in the lower half of the frame. For eight minutes she rants against an unfaithful lover. The awkward framing suddenly makes sense: she needs to shout, to "get things off [her] chest," and this requires plenty of headroom.

Henry's *Quandary* is much quieter, as the camera focuses on plates of food set in front of a performer whose face is out of the frame. A monologue ensues about the order in which bread, wine, apples, and cheese should be consumed, and it begins to seem like an illustration of obsessive-compulsive disorder (OCD). Nothing else happens and OCD is not named, but the obsession about the manner in which the food should be eaten is unrelenting. As in *Tuna Salad* and *Jealousy*, there is no need to explain, identify, or provide meaning outside the performance itself. That the artists do not show their faces, or show them only in long shot, completely counters more contemporary performance videos that are primarily invested in close-ups of the performer, and where the artist's identity and reputation provide content. These women are evidently more interested in catharsis achieved in the process than they are in asserting individual identity or inventing personae.

Transformations into the Late Seventies

Performance video moves into experimental narrative in *On the Road to...* (1976), by Vanalyne Green and Nancy Angelo, and in *Eclipse in the Western Palace* (1977) by Cheri Gaulke. While many of the women who made work at the Building did not continue as artists (Angelo, for example, has become an organizational psychologist), both Gaulke and Green currently have careers as video makers. *On the Road to...* is an eight-minute tape of tightly framed imagery. Feet, flowers, petit fours, clocks, and cornucopia are positioned for the camera. What happens is much less a performance than a series of actions, colors, and events, visual metaphors for exploring new territories.

Eclipse in the Western Palace is another performance enacted specifically for the camera that relies on video framing to develop content. A naked female body, with head completely out of the shot, seems to consume women's shoes. High heels of many colors, cork wedgies, and other seventies footwear are guided "into" the performer's vagina by virtue of clever camerawork, creating a somewhat monstrous sight gag.

Gaulke, Angelo, and Green created precursors to what was on the horizon in video art in general. Their visual language seems obvious today, and the feminist message seems direct, but the two tapes discussed above are distinctly in contrast with much of the earlier work. Tapes from the early and mid-seventies were based on a reconsideration of familiar popular representations of women, reclaiming female imagery from arenas of male identification. Faces and bodies moved, talked and gestured in reaction to a newer set of guidelines and took to task popular conceptions of what a woman may be, what women may look like, and what women do. The early works suggest that women start over by creating alternative representations. Work produced a few years later begins to look and sound different. In addition, the equipment and editing facilities had improved enough by the late seventies to include color cameras and a switcher with a special effects generator, all of which guaranteed that a great deal of the work would look and sound different. However, technology does not account entirely for the transformation.

Performance on tape was still popular at the time, but some makers had discovered that framing and placement of objects might communicate visually as much as a performance in front of the camera might communicate narratively. Losing control on camera as a performance strategy was eventually displaced by a gaining tighter control of both image and editing. As the picture begins to contain a visual language based more on the camera's ability to frame objects specifically, what is conveyed exists outside a reference to real time. The ability to establish fictional space, non-space, and illusionistic space evolved from a previous necessity to establish an authentic place. The new video frame reflects the ability to create original meanings based on how the imagery is sequenced using new, and not necessarily linear, narrative logic. Documentation and affirmation of real life and common lives no longer dominated the content of the work. Creating journals and reenacting actual events fell out of practice, and it was no longer necessary to play in front of the camera. What was placed before the mirror had changed, and video space was discovered.

Legacy

One wonders what is the influence of a body of work virtually ignored by art historians, with most of the work still unknown to contemporary curators and audiences. The ideals of feminist art practice as enumerated by Arlene Raven in her 1979 interview seemed to incorporate obscurity into the work they engendered.[12] Videotapes were made under conditions and with goals opposite those that might lead the makers to receive recognition in the mainstream art world. While some of the women who made videos at the Woman's Building are well known today as artists and educators, the legacy is not to be found in individual successes.

Since the mid-seventies, people working with extremely limited funding and very little access to equipment have been part of a community of independent producers, and they have generated major dialogues around issues such as identity politics, appropriation and media, interactive and Internet strategies, and activist media. Students, people of color, and people within queer and activist communities have all picked up camcorders, creating a grassroots movement of independent media. Small organizations such as Pittsburgh Filmmakers; Chicago Filmmakers; 911 Arts Organization, in Seattle; and Artists Television Access, in San Francisco, were founded by film/video makers and performance artists in the seventies and eighties. However, independent video makers today are not especially aware of the work by their predecessors, and indeed do not realize that the history of their own work may be related to the feminist video experiments of the seventies.

The gay film festivals that emerged in the late seventies and function today as launching points for women video makers of all persuasions are clearly related ideologically to the feminist art movement. Media artists such as Jocelyn Taylor, Suzie Silver, Cheryl Dunye, Barbara Hammer, and Sadie Benning all received recognition and audience followings at these festivals. Frameline: The San Francisco International Lesbian and Gay Film Festival, the oldest and largest of the gay festivals, first showed video in 1985, nine years after its first organized film screenings. The video presentations were hosted in a barroom called The Firehouse across the street from the Roxie Cinema, which was the film venue. We sat on barstools or leaned against a wall, pints in hand, staring at a nineteen-inch monitor. It was a beginning. Today there are many venues throughout the world for work by and about sexual minorities, and engaging civil rights and feminist issues. While festivals are always looking for new feature films to showcase, they also provide screening venues for the lesbian, gay, feminist, and alternative video community that continues to encourage new makers. Of course, now our videotapes are shown alongside the films.

Showing a keener interest in video, and perhaps one of the liveliest festivals on the circuit, is the New York Experimental Lesbian and Gay Film Festival, known simply as the Mix Festival. Mix was founded in 1987 by writer Sarah Schulman and filmmaker Jim Hubbard and began showing video in 1991. Programming decisions are based on issues close to the hearts of artists and independent media producers. Mandates for particular thematic strains, industry-compatible production values, or narrative logic do not exist. Curating is done collaboratively, based on work submitted in an open call, and not on what may be perceived as the hottest topics in an already over-canvassed queer community. Mix screenings are frequently packed with audiences who genuinely appreciate experimental work. While the festival in San Francisco has become as mainstream and commercialized as other international non-gay

Barbara Hammer, *Double Strength*, 1978. Film. Production still of Terry Sendgraff on trapeze with Hammer holding a camera. © 1978 Barbara Hammer.

festivals, the intrepid Mix Festival continues to invite work from a variety of quarters—queer, alternative, experimental, progressive—resulting in unceasing originality from many directions.

Other venues such as Artists' Television Access in San Francisco and Dyke-TV in New York were organized within communities of video makers and performance artists rather than in terms of festivals. Artists' Television Access (ATA) is a nonprofit screening and postproduction space founded in 1984 by Marshall Weber and John Martin, local artists hoping to begin a private video art gallery in the South of Market art scene. The private venture failed and an artists-run, nonprofit venture was born. ATA became an alternative space, attracting many feminist-oriented and lesbian video makers such as Leslie Singer, Azian Nurudin, Lise Swenson, Julie Murray, Valerie Soe, and me. ATA provided a supportive space for practicing complete freedom from conventional programming considerations and invited presentations of oppositional or genuinely difficult material. ATA currently describes itself as "a nonprofit breeding ground for road-less-taken thinkers, an artists-managed media arts center."[13]

New York experienced an explosion of video activism and a collectivization of talent in the eighties around the AIDS crisis. In 1987, Testing the Limits was founded as a collective that used video to record history as well as to influence action. In 1989, some of the Testing the Limits collective formed DIVA (Damned Interfering Video Activists) TV, including Jean Carlomusto, Ray Navarro, Catherine Saalfield, Gregg Bordowitz, Ellen Spiro, and Costa Pappas. Video activist James Wentzy became involved in 1990, and from his Tribeca basement apartment, he revived the cable access program DIVA TV.[14]

Dyke-TV, also in New York, hosts a cable access program and holds classes in video production and postproduction specifically for lesbians. It began operating in 1993 as the brainchild of video makers Harriet Hirshhorn and Mary Patierno. The goal of their biweekly, half-hour news program "for lesbians and by lesbians" is "to present lesbian lives—in all our variety—with intelligence and humor."[15] Dyke-TV's tactics are a combination of documentary and guerrilla television. They take cameras into the heart of political organizations and proceed from the interview scene to the scene of a public action, legal demonstration, and sometimes civil disobedience. The line between news gathering and participation in the action being covered is crossed many times in the process.

In the eighties and early nineties, lines were being drawn and re-drawn in attempts to categorize and eventually ghettoize identity-based video. While like-minded video makers formed working collectives, the downside was that many artists became known only in terms of their sexuality, politics, or by whatever cultural affinity their approach to media may have suggested. For example, one frequently encountered work simply labeled as "lesbian," or "African American," or "AIDS activist," as though these terms alone could provide real descriptions of content, strategy, and formal invention.

The identity-based media movement of the past did indeed include post-colonialist, feminist, and lesbian and gay themes, as well as a focus on the perspectives of communities of color. The old liberal issues were turned inside out as artists and academics began a close reexamination of the representation of difference, marginality, and mainstream culture. Formal aspects of artwork underwent a process of reinvention and reorientation through experimental documentary, narrative, and non-narrative film and video work. Communities who had been misrepresented or under-represented in popular culture became allied not only through shared screening venues and a shared desire to displace the norms of culture, race, gender, and sexuality in representation, but also through formal innovation. By way of the identity politics movement, artists engaged in renegotiating the terms of cultural participation, expanding narrative and documentary visual languages, and making new imagery accessible to artists and audiences alike. The next generation may already be rejecting the identity politics movement, but not without inheriting its goals, and not before refining its creative language.

A chief consideration of new generations working in video and film today is distribution. A number of new micro-distributors have sprung up with a priority to make films and tapes available to a young audience of very limited means. In 1995, Portland video maker Miranda July founded Big Miss Moviola, a film and video distributor specifically for work by women. July was interested in distributing work either as part of the interactive Chainletter Tapes series, or in compilations, which she calls the Co-Star series. According to July, "To be included on the Chainletter, you send in a copy of your movie and something for the Chainletter's companion Directory (anything you want) and include $5 (to cover both dubbing and postage). Then you sit on the curb and wait for your Chainletter Tape and Directory to arrive. It will have your movie as well as 9 others."[16] The Co-Star series is a compilation curated by July and screened at venues such as ATA in San Francisco, 911 in Seattle, and at lecture tours on college campuses. In 2000, Big Miss Moviola was renamed Joanie 4 Jackie, and continues to distribute compilations of work by women, producing traveling video shows and in-person lecture tours.

From Durham, North Carolina, Mr. Lady Records and Videos is becoming one of the best known of the small video, music, and CD-ROM distributors. Mr. Lady, founded by Tammy Rae Carland and Kaia Wilson, came into being in 1996 with a minuscule thirty-four dollars in start-up capital. The initial thirty-four dollars was backed up by a sincere passion for women's music and video, and a strong belief that female artists must take control of their own situations. Carland teaches photography and video on the college level, and Wilson is lead singer and guitarist for a dyke band called The Butchies. Wilson also works at Ladyslipper, one of the country's oldest distributors of women's music. Their mission at Mr. Lady is direct and uncomplicated:

Mostly we felt like there *weren't enough Women-&/or Dyke-run record labels* (although we also take this moment to honor those that came before us and are thriving/struggling—and in doing so have made this possible for us). We also wanted to create an *affordable and accessible means of distributing work by independent video artists and film makers*...[and] *cross the borders between music and visual work* in an attempt to break down preconceived notions that one is more accessible and the other more elitist.[17]

Mr. Lady distributes tapes and CDs, mostly by women, a majority of them lesbians, as well as work by gay men. These include video and electronic artist Leah Gilliam, Nguyen Tan Hoang, Elisabeth Subrin, video and installation artist Mary Patten, and Carland herself. They also distribute CDs by female musicians such as Azalia Snail, Le Tigre, and of course The Butchies. Last year I contracted with Mr. Lady to have some of my early video work made available. The key word is *available*. The purchase price for a videotape runs between $15 and $25, as opposed to the usual price of between $125 and $500 set by art and academic distributors, who mainly sell or rent tapes to institutions. Low prices provide the video devotee or young media maker with an affordable way to see and collect artists' work. Most of the business is conducted via mail order. For the artist there is an advantage in selling work at such a low price. A broader audience may emerge outside the more common venues of college film, video, and theory classes; art galleries; and film festivals.

Finally, perhaps a direct line from the Woman's Building's vast videotape collection to a similar contemporary video community cannot be so easily drawn without showing many detours and alternate routes. I cannot find most of the wonderful tapes produced at the Woman's Building listed in video distribution catalogs, nor are my favorite titles and makers described in the pages of video and media theory books. Sometimes this work seems beyond esoteric—one must be a researcher, a detective, or a confirmed videophile to know that it exists at all.

What is evident is that a thriving community of electronic artists continues to organize screenings and festivals of work that can only be described as having grassroots origins. The politics have evolved from liberation movement dogma to critical theory and global awareness. The participants live miles or even continents apart, and collective identity becomes more virtual than actual.

There are nevertheless strong ideological and methodological ties to the Woman's Building's experiment in video. Video continues to be the primary medium for performance artists, for confessional language, for identifying the self and its relationship to ideological and formal contexts, for direct address, and for recording the history of ideas through its participants. Every show of alternative work, every nonprofit postproduction house and small distributorship, and every group of artists that curates itself into a weekend of screenings is evidence of the link from the seventies to the present.

Of course things have changed. The route taken by artists may still reflect how arts communities are defined, but now community identities are presented as more fluid, more comprehensive, and less fixed in singular ideologies. Form and process lead to a currently popular aesthetic of unresolved endings, and new technologies combine with the old to create a desired vision of un-mappable destinies. The personal and the political have merged in the possibilities of the medium, and we cannot yet see the "building" we are constructing.

Notes

1. Since the time this essay was completed, the Woman's Building video collection has been moved to the Department of Contemorary Programs and Research, Getty Research Institute, Los Angeles, CA.

2. Joan Jonas used a persona she called "Organic Honey" in several of her early videotapes and in performances. Organic Honey wore a feminine mask with a costume of Harem pants, jeweled bra, and a large, feathered headdress. This persona appears in Jonas's most celebrated early piece, *Vertical Roll* (1972).

3. Many of the discoveries about video as a new medium may have been first made by Ernie Kovacs in the late fifties and early sixties, in his live, unscripted television shows.

4. Kate Horsfield and Lyn Blumenthal, *On Art and Artists: Arlene Raven*, video recording (Chicago: Video Data Bank, 1979).

5. Ibid.

6. Annette Hunt is a video artist who worked at the Woman's Building and was one of the cofounders of the Los Angeles Women's Video Center in 1976.

7. The Woman's Building video collection is now part of the Long Beach Museum of Art Video archive housed at the Getty Research Institute.

8. Annette Hunt, interviewed by the author, Los Angeles, CA, March 20, 1997.

9. For a detailed description and an interesting analysis of *Nun and Deviant*, see Chris Straayer, "I Say I Am: Feminist Performance Video in the '70s," *Afterimage* (November 1986): 8–12.

10. Many of the tapes have not yet been dated, but I would judge this piece to be from 1976 or 1977, based on the dates of other tapes on which Leslie Belt is credited.

11. Similarly, *Tuna Salad* and *Jealousy* have not yet been dated, but appear to be from 1976 or 1977.

12. Horsfield and Blumenthal.

13. Quote taken from the Artists' Television Access website, http://www.atasite.org.

14. For more details see "A Report on the Archiving of Film and Video Work by Makers with AIDS," by Jim Hubbard on the ACT-UP NY website, http:// www.actupny.org/diva. This site lists all tapes produced by DIVA TV as well.

15. Quote taken from the Dyke-TV website, http://www.dyketv.org.

16. Tara Mateik, "Surveying the Scene: Excerpts from the D.I.Y. Distro Resource Guide," interview with Miranda July, *Felix: A Journal of Media Arts and Communication* 2.2 (1999): 317.

17. Quote taken from Mr. Lady Records and Videos' first catalog. Italics in original. [Mr. Lady Records and Video closed in 2004. —Eds.]

Mary Lou Hughes, printing on the letterpress for the "Postcard Project: Celebrating Our Heroines," 1988. Woman's Building Image Archive, Otis College of Art and Design.

Terry Wolverton at the Vesta Awards, 1986. © Mary Whitlock.

WORDS, WRITERS, WOMEN

Michele Kort

Editors' Introduction:

Although literature is not always characterized as belonging to "the arts," the literary arts were a core part of the Woman's Building's artistic programs. Under the initial tutelage of poet and writer Deena Metzger, the writing classes offered through the Feminist Studio Workshop took as their mission to locate or invent new language and new forms by which to communicate the shifting consciousness and experience of women. These structures and lexicons were not based in the historical myths of Western patriarchal culture, but rather strove to articulate the possibilities of a female-centered society.

This approach emphasized process over product, content over craft, and relied on a process of supportive and constructive criticism to nurture the development of the work. Students were encouraged to delve deeply into the imagination, to explore the mythic and the sacred, and to utilize the content of their own experience as the means to elucidate larger social and cultural concerns.

In addition to its educational focus, the Woman's Building also engaged with the larger local and national community of women writers. The first feminist bookstore in the United States, Sisterhood Bookstore, opened a branch in the Woman's Building when it premiered on Grandview in the MacArthur Park neighborhood of Los Angeles in 1974. This fostered increased awareness of and access to the burgeoning body of feminist literature and theory from across the United States and around the world.

A signature conference, Women's Words, sponsored by the Woman's Building in 1975, propelled the quest for female forms and structures in writing—the journal, the letter, and similar nonlinear forms geared more toward inner exploration than to the neat contrivances of plot. From that time on, prominent feminist writers made pilgrimages to the Woman's Building—Margaret Atwood, Meridel Le Seuer, Kate Millett, Adrienne Rich, and Alice Walker, among many—to share their work and further dialogue with the women of Los Angeles.

Through proximity to the Women's Graphic Center (also housed at the Women's Building), women writers were encouraged and given means to publish themselves and gain experience in actively cultivating an audience for their work. Given control over "the means of production" of their work—often right down to painstakingly setting their own type, character by character—encouraged writers to take risks with their work, knowing that it would not have to fulfill an outside publisher's agenda to find its way to a readership.

To develop this essay, journalist Michele Kort conducted interviews with five women writers—Gloria Alvarez, Wanda Coleman, Eloise Klein Healy, Terry Wolverton, and Mitsuye Yamada. A sixth interview, with Deena Metzger, was conducted by Terry Wolverton. Unless otherwise specified, quotes below were taken from the interviews with these six women who participated at the Woman's Building in various ways—as authors, teachers, and/or students.

When the Woman's Building came into being in 1973, its focus was on making art not words: visual art, graphic design, and art history. Yes, cofounder Arlene Raven's art history and criticism required words, and certainly cofounder Sheila Levrant de Bretteville's approach to graphics was very much concerned with using words—in a "conversational tone," as she put it. Even cofounder Judy Chicago used words in her early-seventies paintings, such as *The Rejection Quintet*, and wrote an autobiography, *Through the Flower: My Struggle as a Woman Artist* (1975).

But Deena Metzger, a poet and novelist who taught at CalArts at the same time de Bretteville was there, remembers,

> We were coming to understand that women were different, certainly different from the predominant society, that they had cultural vision that was completely different, that it contained certain values that were no longer respected by the society, that this was exceedingly precious, brilliant, had its own genius, and that it needed to be nurtured. And we knew we had to have a language for what we were perceiving and understanding and hoping to create. It needed a language to hold it just like it needed a building; that was one structure and language was another structure.

Top: **Deena Metzger and Barbara Meyerhoff, Women's Words Conference**, March 22–23, 1975. Woman's Building Image Archive, Otis College of Art and Design.

Bottom: **Portrait of Deena Metzger** by Maia.

Metzger continues,

> I was teaching a class in women's literature, teaching Virginia
> Woolf's *To the Lighthouse*, and I was literally mesmerized by the light-
> house going around. I gathered that this was an image of women's
> sensibility expressing itself in a literary form, that the lighthouse was
> the form. Certain segments of light or consciousness came and then
> they faded, and there was a kind of egalitarian response to the cir-
> cumstances of life.

But it wasn't until the Women's Words conference in the spring of 1975 that these
explorations blossomed into public expression at Woman's Building.

It was de Bretteville who asked Metzger to organize the conference. "It meant,"
Metzger recalls, "that we had to enter even more deeply into the question, 'What is
women's literature? And what was the history? And were there forms?' We felt there
were forms that had come up, like this lighthouse form of Woolf's. We felt that there was
a legacy, there was a lineage, and we had to find it and then we had to find what was
being done now."

And soon Metzger, along with poets Holly Prado, Martha Ronk Lifson,[1] journalist Marcia Seligson, and others, was contacting some of the most prominent and
powerful women writers of the seventies. "It was like we were weaving the literature
together, the body of literature," says Metzger. She particularly remembers the "extraordinary letter of refusal," she received from novelist Doris Lessing. "At the end of it,
Lessing said, 'You must understand that all a writer has is time,'" Metzger recounts. "So
it was a no, but it was a yes, you know?"

The conference ended up featuring Jill Johnston, Kate Millett, Meridel Le
Seuer, Kathleen Fraser, and Barbara Meyerhoff, and the thread running through all
their writings was an emphasis on the autobiographical and personal—an undertaking
often degraded at the time for being too "confessional."[2] Metzger remembers the
injunction that to be a gifted writer, "you must never talk about your life and [to do so]
is completely degraded. The fact that women were doing this was a 'terrible' thing that
we were willing to honor. It was [as if] personal writing was shameful and women were
terrible, and here we were honoring them."

I attended the conference as a young writer-to-be, and what is most memo-
rable to me were exactly those confessions. The famously confrontational Johnston, for
example, held a public dialogue—right in the middle of her talk—with an ex-lover seated in the audience (the dialogue was about them being ex-lovers). Meyerhoff, the late
anthropologist who brought a loving intimacy to her research, shared aloud with
Metzger the letters they wrote each other each day, despite living only a mile, or a phone
call, apart. Artist Susan King, who was co-administrator (with me) of the Woman's

Building, was so inspired by Meyerhoff's and Metzger's presentations that she insisted we start our own frequent correspondence, although we, too, saw each other nearly every day at work. Things could be written, Meyerhoff had seemed to suggest, that could not be spoken or, at least, never would be spoken. There could be some depth of intimacy attained in that congress of pen and page. Feminists of the time period craved this intimacy, not only with one another, but also with their own minds, and hungered to discover parts of themselves that had never before been allowed expression.

The women writers who attended the conference in the Woman's Building's small, packed auditorium, remember it as the beginning of a new sense of community and possibility. "I was totally isolated from all of that women's art world stuff," says poet Eloise Klein Healy. "I didn't know another woman poet. And suddenly I go to this conference, and there are 300 women writers there. Literally, it was other worldly."

This whetted Healy's appetite for further involvement. She recalls,

It was the first time that I had ever found any kind of community that had to do with art or feminism. I remember one of the hardest decisions of my life was to be able to say that I was a poet, even though I had already published a book at that time. But the reason it was so hard was always that notion that women were somewhat second-class poets; you could do it but you might not ever be really good. There was no room for you in the big ball game. Really. You could be a bench player. But you were never going to start first string.

It was like Edna St. Vincent Millay. You know, I have this picture: Edna St. Vincent Millay is sitting down there holding a bat waiting to go on. But she is not going to be one of the people who runs out onto the field after the Star Spangled Banner.

So [the Woman's Building provided] a really pivotal understanding that I wasn't alone, I wasn't isolated, I wasn't the only person who was trying to figure out how to do this. There were lots of other people who had the same desire and the same interest and, not only that, they were interested in helping each other. What a concept!

Out of *Women's Words* grew an ongoing Women Writers Series at the Woman's Building, featuring famed authors and poets from all over the country (plus the stellar Canadian, Margaret Atwood). Pages from the growing body of women's literature came alive at the Woman's Building on Grandview and, later, Spring Street. You could listen to one of your literary heroines read, then purchase her book at the pioneering Sisterhood Bookstore, which maintained a branch at the Building. "That was the first place I saw Judy Grahn and Adrienne Rich and Audre Lorde," says Healy of the writers' series. "I wouldn't have had the same intersection with those people without the Building being there. It wasn't just *book* learning."

The Women Writers Series also nurtured the talents of local women writers. Poet Mitsuye Yamada recalls, "The Woman's Building asked me to read there, and they were the ones who first recognized my poetry once it was published. I was totally ignored by the Japanese groups and the Asian groups until later."

Poet and fiction writer Wanda Coleman concurs. "I did a lot of readings [there]. I read with Audre Lorde. I read with Kate Braverman. In fact that reading was famous for my earrings flying off." She laughs, "Charles Bukowski wrote it up in one of his novels about my earrings flying off at the Woman's Building."

Metzger joined the faculty of the Feminist Studio Workshop and, shortly after, Healy began offering workshops through the Extension Program, and thus words became even more tightly woven into the arts fabric being created.

The educational programs of the Woman's Building offered a unique approach to learning in the arts. Metzger recalls,

> [We were] speaking to women about their lives and encouraging them to poetic writing and internal writing and their own vision and their own stories and their right to speak, trying to create a fiction with characters who were more independent, substantial, aware of their circumstances but not crushed by them.
>
> We were always inventing new forms and the question in terms of making literature was always: "What do you want to say? What's the form that will hold it? Don't be limited by the forms that exist."

Metzger elaborates,

> In my teaching, when we listen to each other read, we are really invested in each other's excellence and we don't do that kind of cut-throat critique. We ask ourselves, "Is there anything I can say here to help that person get to the next step?" And that's what happened at the Building. So it was a sanctuary where your intelligence was recognized and encouraged, and your work was supported and sent out into the world. The Woman's Building is where those values were practiced. We left CalArts because CalArts could not house the Woman's Building, couldn't house the values of noncompetition.

What made the Building unique as a writing venue wasn't only its feminist outlook, however, but the presence of the Women's Graphics Center. Not only could one write a book, but typeset, print, and bind it—an immediate and concrete realization of one's efforts that was both inspiring and mind-expanding.

"The idea of making your own book was fascinating to me," says Mitsuye

Yamada, who was drawn to the Building for the emotional support it gave her at a time when the higher education system still denigrated women's art. "We made our own paper and sewed our own books," says Yamada. "It was quite exciting. And I learned type-setting for the letterpress. It was so much fun to pick up the tweezers and set type, to get hands-on and feel how a book is made."

"It was definitely the aesthetic of the place that if you were a writer, you better learn about typefaces, because it mattered," says Healy. "I think that came directly from Sheila Levrant de Bretteville... saying, 'You can't depend on publishers to get your work out. If you really feel like you're not going to get yourself published, learn letterpress, learn offset, learn whatever it takes so that you can make it in multiples.' That was what she was always promoting for the writers. *Make it in multiples*."

"I know that when I've had things published in books," Healy continues, "I've really been a stickler for what kinds of typeface my poems get set in. Most poets don't have a clue about that. Nobody ever said anything to them about that, so they don't know." The intersection with de Bretteville's and others' design sensibilities at the Woman's Building taught writers that a work's visual presentation on the page con-veyed another layer of meaning that might support, contrast, or deepen the meaning of the words themselves.

Words integrated with graphics, as well as with the other art forms percolating at the Building (including performance art), so writers became artists and artists became writers. Susan King had come to the Building as a potter, but soon began mak-ing artists' books, using text and images in her work. Similarly, one of the first things Terry Wolverton did when she came to the Building from Michigan was create a book combining her poetry and prose.

"I wanted to self-publish," says Wolverton, who had previously been involved in feminist theater as well as writing, "and by the end of my first year at the Feminist Studio Workshop (FSW) I had done it. All the women from the FSW came to a party and celebrated with me, and it was a huge moment in my life to have that. All these people *cared* that I had made this thing.

"There was always an emphasis on audience," Wolverton continues, "to whom are you speaking, and what are you saying, and how are you reaching them? This wasn't about private little things you keep in a drawer somewhere, although of course you were free to do that. But because we were feminists and wanted to change the world, we saw our work as the vehicle to do that. So of course we had to think about how to get it into the world."

Although artistic product was the overt goal for writers at the Building, it was the process that became paramount, Wolverton says. She learned from Metzger, one of her mentors, that, "one was on a journey, and the journey was more important than the destination.

"You could start on that journey and not know what the destination was,"

Wolverton continues. "The process would be a process of discovery—you would write about what you didn't know, rather than writing about what you already knew."

In those early years at the Building, more emphasis was placed on content and experimentation than on craft. "We weren't taught a lot of rules. Partly that was because we were trying to discover our stories and validate our life experiences," says Wolverton. "That had been forbidden, really, prior to the women's art movement."

Yamada agrees: "I went through the whole American educational system without ever being in touch with who I was, as a Japanese-American or a woman. When I was writing in college, the writings were never personal. They were always about something...but not about myself. At the University of Chicago [where I attended graduate school] we were all trying to write like men. The worst thing that could be said was, 'You write like a woman.' Women writers weren't recognized as real writers."

Coleman had a similar experience. "I was always paid this compliment: 'You're as good a writer as a man.' And I was looking forward to the day when someone would say, 'You're one hell of a writer.'"

For Metzger, the Building provided a space to flesh out women's experience, women's dreams, women's erotic lives, and women's language. She says, "I was very concerned then, and still am, that women would be called into the public room, but they would be called in as *men*, to work with male ideas and in male forms."

There were other reasons why content took precedence over craft in the Building's early days. According to Wolverton:

> There was a great suspicion across the women's movement about notions of quality. Standards of quality had always been used to exclude women, and there was a tendency to reject that altogether. Also, I think there was the idea that form had confined or restricted women, and women writers were trying to throw off that form and discover what would be a female form—a circular form instead of the arc, or the hero's journey, that characterized male formal structures in writing. So there was a kind of deliberate rejection of some of the traditional forms, and an investigation of what else form might mean.

The Woman's Building became a place for women to test their wings as writers. "The Woman's Building was one of the campuses of my University of the Streets, as I call it," says Coleman, who considered herself a "gadfly" around the Building and did a number of readings there. "I was driving this little '73 Pinto, and I used to tear across town from South Central and Hollywood to the Woman's Building on Spring Street, where it was dark and spooky and there was always a problem parking. But I really found it exciting that inside the darkness there was this wonderful welcoming warmth."

The warmth gave permission for Coleman to provoke discussions, which she

Clockwise from top:
**Eloise Klein Healy
introducing writers for
the Women Writers
Series**, 1985. Woman's
Building Image Archive,
Otis College of Art
and Design.

Mitsuye Yamada, 1982.
Woman's Building Image
Archive, Otis College of
Art and Design.

Wanda Coleman.
© Mark Savage.

**Photograph of poet
Gloria Alavrez**. © David
Urmston, NCRR.

found stimulated her work even when they became testy. "I was constantly learning, and I would engage people in argument—it was useful to me," she says.

Although she was one of the few African-American women involved at the Building, Coleman says she didn't feel like a "token" (although she did feel frustrated by the lack of discourse about working-class economics). Yamada did feel tokenized at the Building, which, like other cultural institutions, gained "diversity points" for supporting the work of non-white writers, but she took advantage rather than umbrage. "I knew at the time I was being asked to be the token American-Japanese/Asian woman," she says, "but that was OK. It was better than not being recognized at all! I really do owe a lot to the Woman's Building simply for being there."

Poet Gloria Alvarez, who at the time was a student, Latina activist, and single mom in her early twenties, took the lack of non-white women at the Building as a personal challenge. She had been excited by the existence of the Building, and encouraged in her writing by Yamada, but wanted to bring more Latinas into the programs. "I felt there was a need for the Building to do outreach, but I had to do my part also," she says. So Alvarez established the writing program *Taller Espejo*,[3] which held classes for Mexican and Central American women at both the Building and in the Pico Union district. "It merged the different communities and different languages and brought everybody together," says Alvarez. "There were women with little or no education, and women with doctorates. It was wonderful. We did an artist's book and some radio programs in Spanish; we did readings. Out of that some women started their own groups to perform and publish."

If dedicated women at the Building were successful in overcoming racial barriers, gender barriers could be harder to circumvent. At a time when a more separatist atmosphere was pervasive, men could feel excluded at the Building—as subject matter and even as allies. "I found that my love poems, paeans to black men—to men, period—were usually not welcome," Coleman laughs. "It forced me to really examine these various issues as I was living them. Because ironically when I was most active in the Woman's Building I was involved in an abusive relationship with an alcoholic man." She came to understand that, "If I was to strengthen my work I had to really get some perspective on the issues it raised."

Yamada experienced an even more fraught situation when, because she was suffering serious back pain, she prevailed upon her husband to drive her to a Building-sponsored women's writing workshop she was leading in the Mojave Desert. He remained for the weekend, helping with tasks such as building campfires, and thus drew the unspoken ire of some participants.

"People were so rigid back then," says Yamada.

> I think now they would think it was totally cool that a man would be
> serving the women. But then, I heard that some of the women were

very upset that I was permitting a man to wait on me. In retrospect, the whole trip was to teach us to be independent from male domination, so I understand what the problem was. And it's a thing about all women's groups, not only the Woman's Building, that somehow all of the trauma we collect from the outside world we bring into the group and kind of unload on each other.

The world outside the Woman's Building was not always welcoming of the processes entertained within. Eloise Klein Healy remarks,

> I know in my academic jobs there were sometimes judgments made about me because I did come out of an activist arts background, because I was a feminist activist. I remember one time I was standing at the elevator and a senior faculty member in the English Department, a woman, said, "I hear you're going to go down and teach in women's studies. What is wrong with you? Emily Dickinson didn't need feminism." And I said, "Yeah, and without feminism, we wouldn't know about anybody *but* Emily Dickinson, would we?"

In retrospect, other pillars of Woman's Building philosophy of the time (from the early seventies to the mid-eighties) no longer seem necessary for the structure to hold. "We've evolved beyond the idea that we should only read women writers, or only learn from women writers," says Wolverton.

> At that particular point in time, most of us had been through a traditional education where we encountered almost no women writers. Maybe Charlotte Brontë, but that might be it. So we needed that kind of insularity then, a kind of corrective education; I was right there on the bandwagon. But if that's one's only input, it too is self-limiting. Certainly the people who were teaching us, such as Deena [Metzger], hadn't come from that space of only reading women writers.

While the philosophy and practice might change and evolve, many rue the demise of the Woman's Building in 1991. When Alvarez heard it was going to close, she says, "I was shocked. I felt like, this can't be true, it can't happen. This was the only place specifically for women. I keep dreaming that something like it will happen again, but that this time it will involve everyone, including women of color, at the base."

And Healy talks about the struggle to make known its legacy. Recently, an organizer of a weeklong festival of women in the arts said to her, "What's the Woman's Building?" "And I realized, you know, it's the same old story," Alvarez says. "Whole big chunks of cultural history just go plunk."

Still, Alvarez takes comfort in the fact that women

> keep reinventing it at the cultural level, at the level of some kind of arts. It wasn't the dentists who put that festival on. It was a bunch of wacky women poets. Definitely grass roots, young women, feminists, whatever.
>
> And that made me feel both amazingly happy about it and amazingly troubled that we couldn't keep the Building going, we just couldn't. There was just no way. And I'm wondering why these things happen. But they do. And luckily some other gals get the bug and they decide it has to be done, for there is nothing for them in the regular culture. They look around and they say, "There's nothing here that interests me."

Many of the writers trained and nurtured at the Woman's Building incorporate the processes and philosophy of the Woman's Building into their current teaching. In 1997, Wolverton founded an independent writing center, Writers At Work, where "creativity thrives in the context of community" fostered by several ongoing weekly workshops. These workshops utilize processes of constructive criticism that Wolverton first learned at the Building.

Healy promotes feminist values within an academic context at Antioch University Los Angeles, where she founded an MFA program in creative writing. "The Woman's Building still is alive here in my writing program. We pay very good attention to the ethnic mix and the racial diversity of the faculty. We do a lot to make sure that underserved communities get taken care of. We look to hire people who are going to participate in a more community-based notion of how to teach people, how to be with people, how to get people to learn."

Woman's Building alumnae have also created an impressive body of work since its demise. A smattering of their many publications includes Healy's poem collections *Artemis in Echo Park*[4] and her recent *Passing*[5]; Coleman's poetry book *Mercurochrome*[6] and her novel *Mambo Hips and Make Believe*[7]; Wolverton's novel in poems, *Embers*,[8] and prose novel *Bailey's Beads*,[9] along with numerous gay and lesbian fiction anthologies she has edited; Alvarez's writings for theatrical pieces directed by Peter Sellars; Yamada's poems collected in *Desert Run*[10]; and Metzger's most recent novel, *The Other Hand*.[11] Other Building-involved writers of note include Bia Lowe, author of the essay collections *Wild Ride*[12] and *Splendored Thing: Love, Roses, & Other Thorny Treasures*[13]; poet Aleida Rodríguez, whose recent poetry collection is *Garden of Exile*[14]; Jacqueline de Angelis (who, with Rodríguez, published the literary magazine *rara avis*[15]), and Michelle T. Clinton, author of *Good Sense & the Faithless*.[16] These women remain teachers, activists, and keepers of the flame for women's writing.

Deena Metzger offers an explanation for why Woman's Building writers have gone on to achieve so much. "I think the confidence that we have now in the creative genius of women—of course not entirely, but to a great extent—can be traced back to the Woman's Building. Everything in me that does things in unconventional ways, that feels supported and that feels right to do it, came from the Woman's Building."

Wolverton agrees. "The most important thing the Woman's Building taught me as a writer was to take risks. What's more important than trying to please or impress someone else is to discover something for yourself."

The Woman's Building served as a *Taller Espejo* of its own, providing women with a mirror in which they could see themselves and reflect themselves back to others. It brought women writers face to face with other women writers, who became their mentors or role models. It turned students into teachers and leaders. Most of all, the Woman's Building gave weight and import to the power of women's words.

Selected Works by Writers at the Woman's Building

Excerpt from *Tree*

I am sitting in a hospital room, crosslegged on a hospital bed, typing a new book at 11:30 p.m. No, I will not have a sleeping pill. I can't afford to lose another dream. The moon rose at 9:30 p.m. and appeared in the window like a plump fruit. She did not look like a woman. Now, it glances down at the paper from the roof top. Hidden as by a veil of purdah. Only the eyes showing. She does not look like the man in the moon either. "For years you have wrestled with death," Jane said. Oh yes, I was brave and I came close, but I have decided to reverse the journey, to go back the other way. I am about to wrestle with life and discover what that means. Having faced the lesser demon, I feel ready to take on the greater power. Almost everyone is afraid to live. I am not saying, "I am not afraid," as I am also trying to give up arrogance. But I am going to try to look fear square in the eye.

This is a warm-up. Bare prose. A woman alone in a room. It could be a prison. It could be a cell. It could be the bare room of a nun. It could be the widow's bedroom or the tiny bedroom of some-one's maiden aunt, the one who never married—you know who she is. But I don't want to stop in these rooms, only to point out to you that they exist, that we have always known about them, have always suspected that they are created especially for us, that the rooms where men live alone are noisier, are full of newspapers and brown paper bags and stiff jeans and textures, which rub and crinkle. Women's rooms are quiet. So we do not know what goes on in them. I have written about silence since 1965. Now I want to write about noise. But I am not interested in just any noise. Keening, for example, which always fascinated me, keening and laments and dirges—I am not interested in these. If I am going to come out of silence—and I am determined—then it will be with a big noise. A woman's noise. But not to exclude the man's noise. But of that later. Alida says this time we must go out into the world together. But then every one of us must be ready and everybody must put on party clothes and everyone must change their noses and collars and transform. And there are dancing lessons to be had—oh yes—dancing is required.

∞∞∞∞

This is a book about the kinds of silences that must be broken. Some I know and some I don't know. And it is also a book about the kind of stillness which must be preserved. And the confusion which exists between these. But first I would like to sing a little song, because not knowing how to sing, I have always maintained a silence here. So I think we shall have a little ritual silence-breaking. And I will do what is difficult to do—and you can hum along if you like. Now I assure you I have never been able to sing "Happy Birthday" and knew only two lullabies to sing to my sons and those I sang poorly. When I sing this song now it is with a flat and shaky voice and without knowing what words will come ... the song created as quickly as my fingers can record it and the tune itself also improvised, but that is the best kind.

—Deena Metzger, 1977 [17]

Selected Works by Writers at the Woman's Building

Poem in Support of the Woman's Building

yo & yo & yo girlfriend / the world is like a spinning impulse to do art / from the heart
wrapped by the bindings of the body & culture / so if you're a woman & you got a
vagina & so what? / except if it's now / america what ever year / & maniacs prowl the
streets of dirty cities & leave baskets of fear / & maybe you got a problem with that / or
you got somebody to love in a closet / okay / where you gonna do your art / where you
gonna howl & spit & crawl / out that hammered down spirit / where you gonna dance &
dream the steamy hope that pounds like a heart / that hammers like a pretty smart
muscle / where you gonna find other bitches with a problem / with the problem that
dirties the air or our world?

one time i was on a panel to witness judge to some poems by humans mind you we
wasn't talking about no women's nothing but human poetry & these nice boys, boys i
had fed dinner in a past life, boys claimed to be hip to the feminist cultural movement,
i'm talking the fringe of caring men, and also literate male poets & me was judging the
work of humans who turned out to be women who used words like wishbone & pussy &
blood & these good boys, ones we don't got to worry about weird touchings of small
daughters or fists in the faces of their wives, these boys was strangely & coincidentally
not impressed with our wishbones & our bloody wine, my goodness i thought ain't this
a bitch.

& so yo & yo & yo girlfriend / so once i got to write a poem with a jewish woman's visual
art about the holocaust / & parallels with negroes who drown down into the white bones
 of the sea that didn't love them / i pin racism & cultures of dominance on leadership of
men / & our silly circles of women wanna do art about it / oh yes / okay so it was the
woman's building binded me to the pulse of this jewish woman / ain't we bold / ain't we
talking on the hardest art / ain't we taking on the most dangerous shit / the wounds of
our pussys / our color/ the color of our blood always red / call me radical / call me red &
black / & always counting on the woman's building to count me in / & give me space /
to spread out a wild women's trip /

so i'm grateful

—Michelle T. Clinton, 1988[18]

Selected Works by Writers at the Woman's Building

Excerpt from *Insurgent Muse*

The Woman's Building. A public center for women's culture. In that terse descriptor spins a universe of deas, of history: the way you, as a woman, searched in vain to find yourself reflected in the mirrors of culture. What did you find? Dull-eyed beauties whose gaze evaded yours; mounds of flesh arranged like bowls of voluptuous fruit; evil temptresses, corrupters of men. More often, you found nothing at all, a curious silence. Culture proved to be a funhouse mirror, distorting and diminishing, a surface into which you walked and then disappeared.

Still you kept searching until one day your eyes caught the glimmer of refracted light, a spark in the night sky, and like all such luminosities it drew you, lured you all the way across the continent to its very edge, Los Angeles. That spark lodged in your imagination where it burned for years. Where it smolders still.

The Woman's Building. What other city but Los Angeles could have given birth to such an edifice? City of extremes, pressed against the brink of the Pacific, the endpoint of our restless explorations. City of dreams, where multitudes flock to reinvent themselves, to live out their personal myth. City that has slipped from the yoke of tradition, eluded the burden of history. City that levels and starts anew.

You came here to do that too, left behind the constricted fictions of the Midwest, its constipated possibilities, the cold, the drab, the predictable gaze that would not see you in your full dimensions. You came to put the fragments of your life together, following that spark, to re-knit the woman to the artist, the body to the brain, the spirit.

It was a journey worthy of Ulysses, a mythic voyage: departing wizened expectations, resigning from the family, the clan, abandoning the marble fist of culture that had closed against you, traveling two thousand miles to arrive at the home of women's culture, founded in the city of dreams. What could you have expected? Gleaming columns, a vast expanse of lawn, carved fountains spouting sparkling streams of water that glimmered in the afternoon sun? Anything, perhaps, except this neglected red brick building in a dour industrial district, an iron gate across the door bolted with a padlock.

In one way the site was perfect, no accident at all, a seamless representation of women's place in culture: a once-grand, now run-down structure on a remote street in an obscure part of town where toil goes unrecognized, pushed against the margins of a river choked in concrete; hard-to-find, down-on-its-luck, a derelict part of town. It was anger at this circumstance that had struck the spark, anger that provided the fuel. That, and the ether of imagination.

And imagination is keener than broken glass, tougher than pavement, wider than the smog-filled vistas you can see from the top of the bridge. The truth is, there was not one, but two Woman's Buildings: the one that squatted modestly beside the railroad tracks and the one that blazed, like an idealized lover, inside your brain. Entering the first, you inhabited the second, the parallel home of women's culture, the one with wide hallways and open courtyards on a sunny, tree-lined street, a city landmark wherein every woman's act gained its deserved significance.

Women all over the world knew this second Woman's Building, women in Tokyo, in Mexico City, in Amsterdam, women who'd never set foot on North Spring Street still walked the vast rooms of this other Woman's Building, seized it as their Mecca, their "room of one's own."

You could never understand when others failed to see this second Woman's Building, so brightly did it shine for you. Walking newcomers through the edifice on North Spring Street, you'd puzzle at their dismayed glances, their diffident enthusiasm, and wonder at their failure of imagination. For you it was never a question—you dwelt in both buildings, each as real to you as the scent of your own skin. Huddling in winter in the unheated corridors of the first, you warmed yourself by the glorious fire in the second. And sometimes, when the art was brilliant and the rooms were full of women who were happy to be there together and the words were spoken from the deepest place in the heart, those twin images would blur, begin to swim together, two architectures becoming one.

...No one could ever describe the Woman's Building. It would require a language of multiple dimensions, of texture, a language that could encompass the passage of time as well as contradictory points of view. Perhaps no language could accomplish it. Perhaps only music would be capable of sounding those myriad notes—the harmonies, the dissonance, syncopation, counterpoint—to arrive at a composition of the whole.

Like the blind men in the parable, groping sightless at the surface of their elephant, each woman's grasp of the institution was fragmentary, partial and particular. The Woman's Building was a place. An institution. A gathering of women. It was an eighteen-year experiment. It was a collision of history and politics and art. It was poetry, painting, performance. It was the one night you went there for a dance and it was the thirteen years you spent trying to keep it ablaze.

It was the day you showed up with hennaed hair only to find that five other women had hennaed their hair the night before too. It was the rope straining in your hands as you hoisted the ten-foot-tall sculpture of a naked female figure onto the roof of the building, from which vantage point the entire city was her domain. It was a field of crosses planted on the lawn of City Hall by women dressed in nuns' habits the colors of the rainbow, in protest of nuclear arms. It was a wall made of bottles, a tree of dolls' heads. A circle of women who stared unflinching into the video lens and told the stories of their sexual abuse.

It was the dope you smoked on the fire escape, the Friday nights you stayed late trying to figure out how to pay the bills. It was the first book you self-published on the antique printing press; it was the consciousness-raising group you hated.

Language splinters under the complexity, the immensity, the tens, perhaps hundreds of thousands of women whose imaginations and emotions and lives touched and were touched by the Woman's Building. All their stories, their dreams. And it was the art that was made within its walls, yes, but also the art that was made by some woman in some little town, work that came into being because she'd heard that the Woman's Building dared to exist.

The Woman's Building offered up a spark, and this was the message in its glow: that you, a woman, could be an artist too, and that your woman's life—whatever its particulars—could kindle your art, and that in turn, the act of making art would ignite that life, and finally, that a community of women, engaged in the twin acts of making art and making a new life, would transform the mirrors of culture into windows through which you all would fly, like sparks, into the night sky.

—Terry Wolverton, 1995[19]

Selected Works by Writers at the Woman's Building

On Lesbian Writing

In the interests of examining the connection

to the lives we are living we must ask does the bond run in the blood or is it as some
believe directed by the power of the moon or as others say by the power of a woman
effects on your angle of vision but of course some don't bother to say or didn't say but
even in casual photos the distinctive tilt of the chin speaks volumes and the incredible
glance that lives on in the one standing next to you who has as well included as a
personal style just the most impossible shading of arrogance which indicates and
welcomes an understanding that goes beyond cultural boundaries as when the lights
go off and one fingertip after another gauges the dimensions of sensation on the
surface of the naked skin or under cloth or leather or beaded and gathered stuff
arranged ever so wonderfully you can't believe in looking at the photographs and the
paintings that nobody thought anything of the display and took no opportunity to
comment on the most distinctive manner of ornamentation and posture which acts
almost but not quite as an affront to the received and applied rules of behavior while
making a territory alongside of or just out of reach of the norm in which she and
whomever she wanted to be with simply blossomed

      —Eloise Klein Healy, 2002[20]

Selected Works by Writers at the Woman's Building

Drowning in My Own Language

My world is a brain
shaped island encrusted
from decades of crevices
rumblings seethe
without cracking

the open half
of me is
sinking on a small
land mass into the sea

as I watch rows
of animated people in
white suits
converse on dry
land inches away with
out seeing
me single-handed
clawing
my way up grasping
exposed root ends
crying
out
slow
ly
still
sinking

tas-keh-tehhh

wrong language
the line of white heels
in half
moons over my head
fade away
waves scoop
more land
I look round-eyed
fish in the mouth

helllllllllllp

still
wrong language

I will come up for air
in another language
all my own.

—Mitsuye Yamada, 1976[21]

Selected Works by Writers at the Woman's Building

Excerpt from Ostinato Vamps

i am the daughter of earthquakes
dissonant and disruptive in my reign over Deathland
            i stole
from god-slinging hypocrites in chaps, chinos, & spurs
from the sacred tribe of water-headed satyrs
on an abstinence from abstinence binge, shysters given
judgeships, panderers governing media, sanctioned gamblers
sapping the strength of negrodocious communities—there's
the necessity of music cut with blood weepings

i stole it because it was mine
doowopshewopdewop ohsocherry

as committed as murder, i am inspired by heavily
cologned and powdered harridans plum narcissistic and brain-strained under Kelly
green neon in the
            throes of supremacy, making
white noise proclamations of inappropriate behavior
syndrome synonymous with and analogous to congenital
            boneheartedness

i stole it back cuz twas mine from da get-go
brown thighs meeting white west of The Pacos

in our bed my absence   whispers beneath   his weight

need to fornicate/blindly penetrate
(a bad season spent chained to a filing cabinet
bosses like dogs barking for important files
the rain of empty talking riving the intellect—no place
to run. work—a necessity in these hind quarters)
            all shook up
a rumble mama burped and there i was. take these rhythms as evidence, my splendid
rock-and-roll

            —Wanda Coleman, 2003[22]

Notes

1. Currently publishes under the name Martha Ronk. —Eds.

2. "Confessional poetry" was a term coined to describe the work of poets such as Robert Lowell, Sylvia Plath, Theodore Roethke, and Anne Sexton. These poets reveal intimate details of their lives using the pronoun "I." —Eds.

3. Translated: "Mirror Workshop." —Eds.

4. Eloise Klein Healy, *Artemis in Echo Park* (Ann Arbor, MI: Firebrand Books, 1991).

5. Eloise Klein Healy, *Passing* (Granada Hills, CA: Red Hen Press, 2002).

6. Wanda Coleman, *Mercurochrome: New Poems* (Santa Rosa, CA: Black Sparrow, 2001).

7. Wanda Coleman, *Mambo Hips and Make Believe: A Novel* (Santa Rosa, CA: Black Sparrow, 1999).

8. Terry Wolverton, *Embers: A Novel in Poems* (Granada Hills, CA: Red Hen Press, 2003).

9. Terry Wolverton, *Bailey's Beads: A Novel* (Boston: Faber and Faber, 1996).

10. Mitsuye Yamada, *Desert Run: Poems and Stories* (New York: Kitchen Table/Women of Color, 1988).

11. Deena Metzger, *The Other Hand* (Granada Hills, CA: Red Hen Press, 2000).

12. Bia Lowe, *Wild Ride: Earthquakes, Sneezes, and Other Thrills* (New York: HarperCollins, 1995).

13. Bia Lowe, *Splendored Thing: Love, Roses, & Other Thorny Treasures* (Emeryville, CA: Seal Press, 2002).

14. Aleida Rodríguez, *Garden of Exile: Poems* (Louisville, KY: Sarabande Books, 1999).

15. *rara avis* was edited by Jacqueline de Angelis and Aleida Rodríguez. Seven issues were published from 1978 to 1984 by Books of a Feather, in Los Angeles.

16. Michelle T. Clinton, *Good Sense & the Faithless* (Albuquerque, NM: West End Press, 1994).

17. Deena Metzger, *Tree: Essays and Pieces* (Berkeley, CA: North Atlantic Books, 1997).

18. Michelle T. Clinton, "Poem in Support of the Woman's Building," in *Fifteen Years and Growing*, Terry Wolverton, ed. (Los Angeles: Woman's Building, 1988). Clinton's poem was created for this commemorative booklet for the Woman's Building's fifteenth anniversary.

19. Terry Wolverton, *Insurgent Muse: Art and Life at the Woman's Building* (San Francisco, CA: City Lights, 2002), 6.

20. Healy, *Passing*.

21. Mitsuye Yamada, *Camp Notes and Other Poems* (San Lorenzo, CA: Shameless Hussy Press, 1976).

22. Wanda Coleman, *Ostinato Vamps* (Pittsburgh, PA: University of Pittsburgh Press, 2003), Pitt Poetry Series, www.pitt.edu/~press.

HER SHE. K

SSES HER

**Terry Wolverton dances with
Katja Beizanz at the publication
party for *Blue Moon*.** 1977.
© E. K. Waller Photography.

LESBIAN ART: A PARTIAL INVENTORY

Terry Wolverton

Summer 1977

Two black-and-white photographs, eight-by-ten-inch glossies shot by a professional, portray a group of five women posing in a garden. We are the Natalie Barney Collective,[1] five women from the Feminist Studio Workshop[2] (FSW) who have come together to conduct the Lesbian Art Project (LAP), an endeavor consisting of equal parts art historical research, community building, activism, group therapy, heavy partying, and the kind of life-as-art performance sensibility inherited from the Fluxus[3] artists and so prevalent in Southern California art of the seventies. This labor of love will define the next two years of my life.

The companion photos are a study in contrast, the subjects' attire, stances, and attitudes wildly variant from one image to the next. In the first shot, we scowl into the lens, each of our unrouged mouths a thin, strict line. On the far right, I am dressed in a pinstripe business suit—trousers, jacket, vest—a tie, a fedora on my head. My hand is clenched in a fist, my shoulders squared. Beside me stands Maya Sterling, hands on hips, pelvis forward. A black velvet shirt hangs open to the waist, baring the stripe of skin between her small breasts. In the center of this grouping, Sharon Immergluck is debonair in top hat and tails, black bow tie against a white shirt. One hand grips a pipe. Her expression bears a trace of amusement. Next to Sharon is Nancy Fried, the only one of us in a dress, but it's worn with the unyielding attitude of a dowager empress, a manner that suggests no softness. A long antique gown, armored by a broad-shouldered

353

jacket, a large floppy hat on her head. Her ample body lends the implacable air of Gertrude Stein. On the far left, Arlene Raven, founder of the LAP, leans against the wall, her long legs in black pants, black jacket snug on her lean frame.

This is our collective depiction of "butch."

In the second image, we have transformed ourselves into "femme." The picture is sunlit, a shag of palm leaves in the background. We are clustered together, two of us seated, our lips parted, smiling. We are all in dresses; many of us hold elaborate fans from Nancy's collection. My gown is chiffon; Arlene's is lace. Nancy is in satin, her cleavage visible. Maya and Sharon are in simpler dresses; Maya now sports Sharon's top hat, awry on her mass of curls. We mostly face one another, interacting; only I look directly at the camera.

Arlene had imagined the LAP as an organized effort to further her investigation of a lesbian sensibility in art. The rest of us—current and former FSW students drawn by her invitation to participate—have concocted a project far beyond Arlene's original intention to research the work of Romaine Brooks and other historical and contemporary lesbian artists. We are after nothing less than an exploration of the meaning(s) of "lesbian,"—an ambition consistent with Arlene's approach to art history—and the manifestation of a culture in which those meanings can be expressed and amplified.

We envision the LAP as a context in which our own artwork can be produced and understood; I for one am already devising a performance project about a female future that I will produce under LAP's auspices.

We imagine the LAP as a springboard from which to launch a reinvention of the lesbian community. Nancy and I concoct lavish events we will create and host. "Beautiful, elegant events," Nancy muses with a dreamy expression, conjuring the lush environments she will, with her sculptor's sensibility, fashion.

"Events that aren't boring and depressing to attend," I agree, grimacing at the memory of dark-lit lesbian bars, patrons camouflaged in flannel shirts and jeans, hard eyes and tight shoulders, the cramped and constricted body language of self-hatred.

"Events to which I could wear this!" Sharon beams, pirouetting in top hat and tails on the flagstone path of the garden. It is clear that we will not be content to merely study the aesthetics of lesbians; we are determined to wield our influence over them as well.

The Natalie Barney Collective is in the process of designing an educational program through which aspects of lesbian culture and experience can be studied. "There's not another context in which you can learn anything positive about lesbians," Arlene asserts. And in 1977, this is virtually true.

We're planning a gay/straight dialogue, at Sharon's suggestion, "So the heterosexual women in the FSW don't freak out." A therapist as well as a writer, Sharon is always attentive to group dynamics.

The Natalie Barney Collective butches up, 1977. (L to R) Maya Sterling, Sharon Immergluck, Arlene Raven, Nancy Fried, Terry Wolverton. © E.K. Waller Photography.

Femme version of the Natalie Barney Collective of the Lesbian Art Project, 1977. (Seated L to R) Nancy Fried, Arlene Raven. (Standing L to R) Maya Sterling, Sharon Immergluck, Terry Wolverton. © E.K. Waller Photography.

"And we need to network with other lesbian artists across the country and around the world," Maya's eyes glitter, anticipating an excuse to travel.

"And we have to get lots of media coverage," I remind them, "to contradict all those horrible stereotypes about lesbians."

"Right," Maya quips, "like that we're butch or femme!" We cackle with laughter until the photographer says, "Could you please hold still?" and we pose for another shot.

It is 1977, and feminist lesbians don't officially believe in butch and femme. Feminist canon has labeled role-playing as "heterosexist" and declared "androgyny" the sought-after standard. If butch and femme are talked about at all, it is in an historical context, as a quaint custom left over from the fifties, the bad old days of the closet, when lesbians didn't know any better than to mimic what men and women do together. Like every generation, we unthinkingly disrespect the generation that has come before.

The members of the Natalie Barney Collective believe we are being saucy and bold in daring to depict ourselves in these ancient roles, defying not only the conventions of heterosexual culture but also flouting the current standards of correctness within the lesbian community. In our thrift-store finery, a kind of hippie elegance, we push the butch/femme stereotypes until they warp and bend, make them into material for art. There is about this photo shoot, as with all of LAP's activities, a determined element of crackpot.[4]

It is with a fervent sense of mission that I've immersed myself in the LAP, the first time since coming to the Woman's Building that I've felt confirmed in my decision to do so, the first time I've seen a clear focus for my considerable energies. The juxtaposition of "lesbian" and "artist" makes possible the integration of two central parts of my identity, creates more ground on which to stand. Thus named, I feel less crazy, less queer.[5]

At one of our earliest LAP meetings, Arlene had observed that, as a collective, we would need to use our own lives as a basis for this investigation; our own experiences as lesbians were the foundation of our theory. We accepted this premise, already well trained as feminists that "the personal is political." In 1977, we don't yet fully realize that our theory will be limited and circumscribed by the fact that we are six white women in our twenties and thirties. And we don't fully comprehend that looking at our lesbian experience through a magnifying glass will bring us face to face with the pain of our lesbian oppression.

Are any of us equipped to undertake this? Are we sufficiently honest with ourselves, do we have enough trust in one another? Are we capable of reading the content of our interactions at the same moment we are engaging in them? And if so, how does such studied observation alter the content of our behaviors?

On this sunny July afternoon in the garden behind Nancy's house, we don't know the answers to these questions, or even that such inquiries await us. We're not thinking about butch and femme, where each of us might fit on that spectrum of identity. We leave unspoken the fact that some of us look ill at ease in our dresses, others of us appear less convincingly butch.

We are playing dress-up, posing for pictures, engaging in performativity. Laughing and mugging for the camera, we are smoking joints, enjoying the California sunshine, grooving on being outrageous lesbians. We believe that in this way—our outright rejection of second-class status for lesbians, our refusal to accept anything less than a marvelous quality of life—the Natalie Barney Collective will change the world.

Fall 1977

A single sheet of thick paper, the prototype of a poster created by graphic designer Bia Lowe to represent the LAP. Never reproduced, it's a one-of-a-kind artwork.

Across the bottom of the page, the project's acronym: LAP. Above these letters, two line drawings scissored from children's workbooks, stacked one atop the other. The illustration style suggests the early sixties, the seat of nostalgia for my generation, a time when the world seemed hopeful and prosperous.

The top cutout depicts a woman seated. The viewer is aware of the bend in her hips, the drape of her dress over her thighs, the slight concavity of the dip between her thighs, a certain inviting space. Her lap.

Beneath this image, in the other cutout, a cat tongues milk from a bowl.

Within this juxtaposition, there is tension between the simple domesticity of the scenes, which bespeak comfort, even innocence, and the inescapable erotic inference created by their apposition: the lesbian, after all, is the one who laps at the lap.

The urge to render innocence to lesbian sexuality is not only characteristic of Lowe's work of the time. The organizers and students of LAP sought out the work of lesbian artists across the country; we read these images as mirror and blueprint, a reflection of our culture as it was and a guide to what we wished it to become. Many lesbian artists in the seventies set out to remythologize lesbianism, to redeem it from the images of depravity and evil that were common in both pornographic depiction and religious interpretation, to make it "good."

Thus, the "HERSHEKISSESHER" (1977) multiple, by the artist Clsuf, duplicates the signature wrapping of a Hershey's Kiss (what could be more innocent than a candy kiss?)—the same strip of white paper, the same blue type, playing with the language of the confectionery's brand name to suggest a different kind of sweetness. Or the bread dough sculptures of Nancy Fried (such a homey, non-threatening medium!), capturing scenes of domestic lesbian life—two women in the bath, one nude woman giving another a foot massage—and painted with the exquisite detail of a Fabergé egg. Or the solarized photos of artist Tee Corinne, explicit as they are in the portrayal of lesbian sexual practice, create a rosy glow, almost a halo, around their subjects that confers a benediction on their acts.

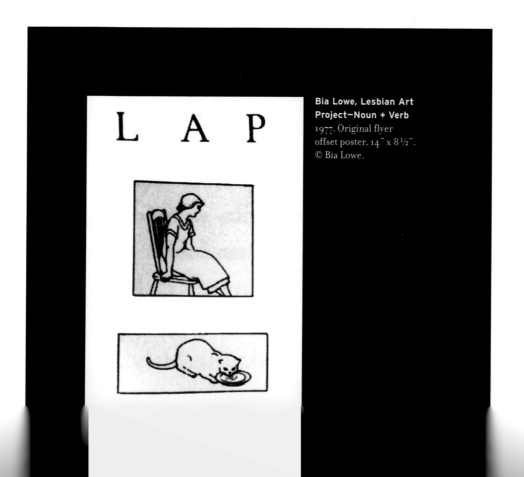

Bia Lowe, Lesbian Art Project—Noun + Verb
1977. Original flyer offset poster, 14" x 8 ½".
© Bia Lowe.

we need: jeans, t-shirts, jewelry, old postcards, tuxedos, sunglasses, birdbaths, shoes, scarves, buttons, costumes, pillows, dress dummies, leather jackets, pink flamingos...

WILL YOU HELP?

The Store at The Woman's Building   1727 North Spring Street   Los Angeles, Calif. 90012

Photo: E.A. Waller   Design & Production: Nancy Fried, Donna Farnsworth

Will You Help?, 1977. Poster soliciting donations for the Store, a thrift store organized by Nancy Fried for the Woman's Building. © E.K. Waller Photography.

What is common to all of these images is their intention to disarm the viewer, and to make the strange familiar, even soothing. In the eighties and nineties, a subsequent generation of lesbians will come to challenge this strategy, charging that it robs lesbianism of its power to shock and inflame. This generation will glorify "bad girls," bringing a punk sensibility, a calculated strategy of transgression, to the depiction of lesbian imagery. But in the seventies, to merely raise the issue of lesbianism is incendiary, and perhaps this more gentle assertion of lesbian sexuality serves to desensitize the art world, pave the way for the more confrontational work that is to come.

∞∞∞

Seven women stare out from the poster; all eyes confront the viewer. We are posed some seated, some standing—in a desolate corner of the Woman's Building: bare walls, ragged floor, poor lighting. We range in age from our twenties to our forties, our bodies tall or short, corpulent or thin, large breasted or small. We are all naked. In bold type, a headline demands, "WILL YOU HELP?" Smaller text goes on to specify, "We need: jeans, t-shirts, furniture, jewelry, plants, old postcards, toys, tuxedos, sunglasses, mirrors, birdbaths, shoes, scarves, umbrella stands, Christmas tree lights, beads, buttons, carpets or rugs, frames, dishes, dresses, costumes, pillows, dress dummies, leather jackets, pink flamingos."

It is a poster soliciting donations for a new thrift store conceived by Fried and Valerie Angers as a fundraising strategy for the Woman's Building. While not strictly a LAP endeavor, The Store is fueled by the vision and energy of many lesbians (all but one of the women in the photograph identifies as such, or did so at that time) and is launched with the outrageous spirit to which LAP is dedicated.

Over the summer of 1977, a campaign to pass the country's first anti-gay rights ordinance has been waged and won in Dade County, Florida, with Anita Bryant as its celebrity spokesperson. In the fall, conservative California state senator John Briggs introduces a bill that would ban gay teachers in public schools. Rather than retreating in the face of these threats, the gay and lesbian communities are galvanized into founding a political movement, raising millions of dollars, being vocal about our cause in the media, and demanding accountability from elected officials.

The women of the Natalie Barney Collective, too, respond with flagrant defiance of those who would deny our right to exist. More than ever we are committed to being visible as lesbians in our personal and professional lives. We channel the fear and vulnerability we feel into increasingly raucous displays of lesbian sensibility, determined to celebrate ourselves.

The Store's opening is observed with a fashion show organized by LAP. Originally conceived as an opportunity to model the wares of the thrift shop, the occasion morphs into performance art as we give vent to personas that express our gender identities. Sharon returns in top hat and tails to act as Mistress of Ceremonies; Bia sports elegant pajamas and robe; Holiday Jackson wears a glamorous fifties cocktail dress with a stuffed parrot on her shoulder. Madcap, with a ferocious undertone: *I am woman, hear me roar, dahling.*

The hostile political climate lends urgency to our Feminist/Lesbian Dialogue within the community of the FSW, the first time, according to Arlene, that this type of discussion has been formally held. Such events are always fraught: all feeling a little defensive, fearful of being made to feel like the Other, or even resentful of having to declare themselves. Lesbians historically carry this feeling of queerness and isolation from their experiences of oppression within heterosexist society, but at the Woman's Building, straight women also feel like a beleaguered minority, believing themselves judged as lesser feminists for being involved with men. LAP's dialogue does not resolve these issues, but does allow them to be aired, to become discussible, and further serves to create more visibility and presence for lesbian students in the FSW, something for which I had longed my first year there.

In addition to weekly planning meetings, LAP sponsors two additional public events that fall: one is an exhibit of Fried's bread dough sculptures. The opening reception is followed by a "Sizzling Disco" to intensify that spirit of festivity we wish to foster. The other is the first in a series of Lesbian Create·Hers Salons, highlighting significant creative work of lesbians. Our inaugural salon features architect Noel Phyllis Birkby.[6] We also launch monthly worksharing groups in which lesbian artists can present their work to others for feedback and dialogue, and consciousness-raising groups around specifically lesbian topics within the FSW. And we plan a full roster of activities for the coming winter.

The first season of the LAP is an enormous success, as lesbians flock to our events. So, too, the "WILL YOU HELP?" poster is a hit; donations pour in from across the country to establish The Store. Aside from its marketing function, though, the piece is also noteworthy as an art image: Although nude, the women portrayed are not objectified, not sexualized, not coy. Each of us stares directly at the viewer without self-consciousness or apology. Even as we appeal for help, naked to the public eye, we do so not out of vulnerability or neediness. We have stripped ourselves of the trappings of identity handed down to us; we are starting from scratch, ready to re-clothe ourselves in another guise, poised to invent ourselves anew.

Winter 1978

They might be petroglyphs or runes, an ancient language of symbols. The six crudely rendered ideograms are my attempt to articulate a new vision of lesbian community, to define the roles apparent and necessary to further the work of the group.

Arlene Raven and I sit in my light-filled apartment in the hills of Echo Park. She and I are now the sole directors of the LAP. After a summer of feverish planning and a fall of breakneck producing, the Natalie Barney Collective has imploded and burned out.

It's more than exhaustion that has caused the group's dissolution. The tasks we have set—to hold ourselves up as public icons of an idealized lesbian culture, to interrogate our own conduct and motives as they are unfolding, and to reveal our findings to one another—bring us face to face with our core fears and personal weaknesses.

When one of us sends home a coming out letter and is disowned by her family in response, we must each confront our alienation and estrangement from our families of origin. When two others end their lovers' relationship, we each find ourselves probing our own fears of trust, our reluctance to bond with another woman. When Arlene resumes her love relationship with Cheryl Swannack, from whom I have recently parted with bad feelings, we are each required to consider how community can thrive despite fissures of jealousy and resentment.

To focus on lesbianism as a state of being could not help but evoke our own internalized homophobia, the fear and hatred of our own and others' queerness. To embrace that queerness is to embrace isolation, marginalization and exile. Committed as we are to living our vision—a world in which lesbians are celebrated, luxuriant and unrestrained—we discover our insides wired for self-loathing, scorn and shame.

The tension between the world we dream and the one in which we live creates skirmishes and misunderstandings, and ruptures long-standing friendships and burgeoning intimacies. It has sorely tested everyone's commitment and accountability to the work.

Nancy has expressed her intention to stay connected to LAP as an artist, but withdrawn from all administrative work. Sharon, Maya, and Kathleen have taken greater distance from the project. I can't imagine stopping the work we have begun; my identity as a lesbian artist is central to my being at this time, and in LAP I've found both mission and purpose.

Throughout the summer and fall, the collective had focused on how the LAP might serve the community. In shifting to a partnership structure, Arlene and I have prioritized those activities that will most satisfy us. "Women always think we have to be self-sacrificing," Arlene reminds me, "but that's the same old patriarchal model—and who needs it?" And she gives her signature dismissive laugh—"Ha!"—a throaty half-cackle, one beat, as if withdrawn abruptly.

Gone are the plans for aggressive grant writing to support salaried positions. Gone is the far-reaching media campaign. Gone is anything that requires a high level of administration. The Natalie Barney Collective had, Arlene and I decide, been seduced by a male notion of institution building—the bigger the better, impact measured by numbers served. We will instead trust that our work—on whatever scale—will create a shift in consciousness that transmits itself from woman to woman, a revolution from the inside out.

In letting go of our worldly ambitions, I ask myself now, were we truly forging a female model, one that assumed our influence would be psychic, cellular, would work its way through an underground network of women's wisdom? Or were we unwittingly participating in our own marginalization, ensuring that our efforts would be buried, lost to history? Were we redefining power or giving up on it?

More than two decades later, I see a lesbian community that has more visibility and that expects much more for itself. Lesbian lives are depicted on TV, and explicit images of lesbian art hang in the collections of major museums. Young lesbian artists don't hesitate to flaunt their sexuality and politics. These circumstances exist in part because LAP existed. But few, if any, of these young artists have even heard about the LAP. Did our decision to work outside of mainstream culture ensure our erasure?

In the winter of 1978, what Arlene and I have retained of our plan for LAP are the art projects, some social and community events, Arlene's research on the life and work of painter Romaine Brooks and her contemporaries, and the planning for a Program of Sapphic Education. The program, inspired by the Greek poet's school at Mytilene, is conceptualized as a one-year, one-time-only project. Neither Arlene nor I want to create an institution for which the maintenance will be our responsibility.

We've adopted a model of seasonal education first developed by artist Jere Van Syoc and philosopher Linda Smith in the Women, World, and Wonder program at Thomas Jefferson College, wherein the activities of learning are geared to the mood or meaning of the time of year. Autumn is a time for gathering, the development of community, and for this season we've envisioned eight one-day workshops on Sunday afternoons; these are held at Arlene and Cheryl's home in order to create the atmosphere of a salon and provide a sense of safety and privacy. Arlene and I alternate or share responsibility to teach these workshops on subjects such as "Lesbian Relationships," "The Lesbian Body," and "I Dream in Female/Lesbian Consciousness as Non-Ordinary Reality."

Winter is the time for study and contemplation, focusing and conceptualizing. During these months we will offer a series of in-depth, eight-to-ten-week classes, including "Lesbian Art History," "Lesbian Writing," "Feminist Neology," "Feminist Astrology," and the workshop portion of the development of a new performance project, *An Oral Herstory of Lesbianism*.

Spring is the time for blossoming, and into this season is scheduled the performance of *An Oral Herstory of Lesbianism*, which will involve a large sampling of participants in LAP. Summer is envisioned as a time for travel, making connections with other lesbians across the country, expanding the impact of our work.

We intend our Program of Sapphic Education to not only inspire art making, but to build lesbian consciousness and community, and the six symbols are my attempt to identify the archetypal functions required to fulfill this vision.

"The Organizer" posits a small circle, perched like a human head atop a thick, broad-shouldered "T"; any resemblance to the cross of crucifixion is strictly a Freudian slip. Within the LAP, I am the organizer, the one who figures out schedules and budgets, plans events, and types the press releases. The one who worries.

Like the sun, "The Visionary" radiates from a central circle, illuminating previously unlit areas of consciousness. Arlene is the visionary, purveyor of brilliance.

"The Artist" is a pure arrow of intention, direction, and activity. Cheryl Swannack seems most like this symbol to me, in her tenacity, her will to do. Still, there are many artists in the LAP constellation. I admire the refined sophistication and philosophical thinking that graphic designer and writer Bia Lowe brings to her work. Nancy Fried is a ball of fierce energy whose sculptures will one day sell in New York galleries. When she came to the Woman's Building, the same year I did, she didn't think she was an artist, but she has blossomed with the attention and encouragement she's received. Clsuf, née Claudia Samson, is a former member of Rhode Island Feminist Theater now working in graphics and other ephemeral art, including food as art. And Jere Van Syoc is a creator of windmills and altarpieces—multimedia interactive sculpture—and mythmaker. Jere had been my instructor at Thomas Jefferson College in Grand Rapids, Michigan, and has come to Los Angeles as a LAP artist-in-residence in 1978.

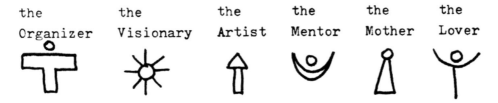

the Organizer   the Visionary   the Artist   the Mentor   the Mother   the Lover

Both visionary and artist seem like exalted positions compared to mine; I harbor a secret dread that my tombstone will read, "She was a great organizer," my own creativity buried under layers of competence and responsibility, my own brilliance unrecognized, forgotten.

Arlene is also "The Mentor," depicted as an upturned crescent cradling a smaller circle. While she acknowledges this as her role, she is adamant that the mentorship be mutual, she and I each learning from the other. It is our declared feminist lesbian principle to unseat the hierarchy that has been traditionally inherent in the mentor/student role, but I secretly worry that this egalitarianism has no basis in reality. Other than my organizing skills, my ability to manifest ideas into practical applications, I cannot see what I might bring to her, although she insists she is inspired by my decidedly alternative vision, my metaphysical bent, and my fierce commitment to lesbianism. It will be many years later, after being a teacher and mentor myself, before I will fully understand her determination to stave off the isolation of that role, to subvert the objectification and projections that one receives when one is the mentor.

None of us wants to be "The Mother," this role so despised, so disempowered under patriarchy, although in truth we all want one. The glyph is an isosceles triangle supporting a small circle at its tip. As lesbians, we all feel like motherless girls; we want to be taken care of, not tend to someone else. As teachers in the Program of Sapphic Education, Arlene and I are seen in this role, and not infrequently our students project onto us their disappointed expectations of their own mothers. We chafe against it.

And we all want to be "The Lover," consider it an expression of our destiny as lesbians. The symbol resembles a young tree, fresh branches stretching in an inviting embrace. The unwritten history of the lesbian movement reveals how much is built upon the energy of lovers, with presses and bookstores, coffee houses and theater companies, political campaigns and art projects all fueled by sexual energy between women.

And this energy, gone sour, has at times undermined those same endeavors, led to their dissolution. There is, in our core group, spoken and unspoken tension. We are lovers and former lovers; former teachers and students; friends and estranged friends; women with spoken and unspoken attractions, and spoken and unspoken enmities.

Such details are the weft of the fabric of LAP. Our activities flow from the energy of these connections, our theories born from the attempts to wrestle with our difficulties and define our relative positions. Bereft of meaningful relationships with our biological families, we attempt to create an alternative family, a utopian community, born of our visions and dreams. The symbols and the roles they illustrate are my attempt to build a structure and find my place within it.

∞∞∞∞

A heart-shaped pillow sheathed in pink lamé. One of the dozens that festoon the Woman's Building performance space for LAP's "Dyke of Your Dreams Day" dance, our own saucy retort to the rituals of Saint Valentine. Though we disdain the culture of heterosexuality, we still feel free to steal whatever seems useful and transform it as we see fit.

Nancy Fried designed those pillows and then enlisted Sue Maberry to sew them. An FSW student who was just starting her coming out process, Sue was more than glad to whip up three dozen stuffed pillow hearts if it meant getting to hang out with the women of LAP. Nancy has also corralled a group of us to join her at the Woman's Building the day before the dance to help with installation. This first meant reclining our bodies onto long strips of midnight blue photo backdrop paper onto which our outlines were traced in gold glitter. That was followed by hours spent on ladders suspending everything from the eighteen-foot ceiling—lamé hearts hung like plump moons and glittered panels with their diving female forms lined the perimeter of the dance floor. And twinkle lights blinked their tiny beams across the stretch of space. This is a far cry from the wood-paneled, darkly lit bars that are the customary habitués of lesbian socializing. We go to this effort because we believe lesbians deserve a beautiful environment for valentine courtship.

The next night, this space is filled with over three hundred women flirting with their bodies to Natalie Cole's "Sophisticated Lady," the Pointer Sisters, and Gloria Gaynor's "I Will Survive"—the most female-affirmative disco we can assemble. Clsuf

Clsuf, *OVO*, 1978. Button created for the performance *FEMINA: An IntraSpace Voyage*. © Clsuf.

serves nonalcoholic beverages under a sign that reads, "Lick·Hers," both advertisement and invitation.

And I, too, am on that dance floor, in a floor-length, black crepe dress from
the forties—wide shoulders, narrow waist. I am shaking my hips, spinning around as
flashes of glitter and pink lamé spark across my vision. Like the other women of LAP,
I am tired of lesbian oppression, and tonight I want to be fabulous, transported, to dance
homophobia into oblivion.

Spring 1978

The button has shiny silver print on a black background. "OVO," it reads in neon script.
A made-up word. Feminists of the period are always altering language; we alter the
spelling of "wimmin" to take the "men" out, we rename the study of the past "herstory,"
and some adopt new last names to subvert patrimony. The power to name is the power
to confer meaning.

The button is part of the ephemera of *FEMINA: An IntraSpace Voyage*, the collaborative performance project I have originated as part of LAP. *FEMINA* is about a
group of women who find life on Earth unbearable, and who make the decision to

journey together to another planet. Cheryl has joked that my next performance must be titled *Butchina*.

Clsuf made the buttons. The term "OVO" was invented by the play's codirector, Ann Shannon, who also defined the word's multiple meanings.

We were sitting in the brick-red Val's Cafe on the third floor of the Woman's Building early one evening before rehearsal, and she spelled it out on a scrap of notebook paper.

"OVO, see, it's used as a greeting, like 'hello.' But it's also an expression of approval, like 'Bravo!'" Ann bobbed her curly wedge of hair and gazed intently at me to see if I was following.

"So, like, 'Great rehearsal, women, OVO!'" I demonstrated, and she beamed.

"But, look," she continued, "it's a pictograph, too—see how it looks like the female reproductive system?" She turned the page around in case I might fail to catch the resemblance.

"*And*, it's also a *map* of our journey to *Femina*, see?" she pressed on. "How we start out in one space," she traces the first circle, "catapult through time and space," her pen slashes the V, "and end up in another dimension altogether!" She drew the final O, circling several times until the pen bled through the paper.

These were the years of *Star Wars* and *Close Encounters of the Third Kind*. It made me mad: Why did only men get to project their visions of future? I considered myself a witch, and believed it when Z. Budapest insisted that "thought forms become material."[7] If women didn't get busy imagining our destiny, I feared we would find ourselves stuck once more in someone else's vision of the future.

The women who were drawn to the creation of *FEMINA* were desperate to reinvent ourselves, to find a world in which our values were reflected and our strengths validated, a world wherein we did not feel crazy. The performance was a metaphor for the vision of LAP—the rejection of the world we'd been handed, the undertaking to build a new context, and to construct new selves untainted by oppression. Bonding with other women and summoning our inner power were the engines that would take us there. The scary journey from one self to another. The alchemy of transformation.

Summer 1978

The talking bead. A clay cylinder, less than an inch long, flecked with brushstrokes of black paint in an African pattern, the bisque of the clay darkened by the oils of my skin. I wear it on a strap of leather bound with a knot at my throat; I never take it off. Over the years the press of my larynx has worn an indent in its side. Arlene teases that this bead holds all my secrets, all the words I never say.

We are in my apartment for our weekly LAP meeting. Arlene sits in the bentwood rocker; I perch in a floral upholstered chair given to me by a friend. Between us is a table made from an upended wooden crate that I retrieved from the sidewalk in

Toronto's Chinatown, elegantly draped with a lace runner crocheted by my great grand-mother. The lace is spotted with dripped candle wax, scorched with roach burns, cinders fallen from the countless joints passed back and forth across this table.

One of the most critical parts of Arlene's and my work together on the LAP is the examination of our working relationship. The seventies definition of "lesbian," at least among feminist lesbians, stretched to include any bond between women; neither erotic arousal nor genital contact was required. Although Arlene and I are not lovers, by this definition we are having a "lesbian relationship," and we are determined to study its every nuance for clues to further understand such connections. What we ask of ourselves is intimacy without sexuality, a willingness to open to one another in all ways but the physical.

This exploration lends our meetings—at her house or mine—a sweaty, claustrophobic, hallucinatory quality that is further enhanced by the dope we smoke at every gathering. We brew strong coffee, light candles—we share a more than casual interest in witchcraft—pass a joint back and forth and descend into a watery underworld of the psyche.

We both gravitate to the practice of magic; many cultural feminists in the seventies embraced witchcraft as an ancient form of women's power and healing. It is common for us to begin our meetings with a tarot spread, studying the imagery of the cards for clues to our interaction. We burn candles—green for healing, red for passion, purple for inspiration—and light incense. We tell one another our dreams. The practice of magic is not so different from the practice of art, with its aim to manifest what exists only in the mind, its close reading of symbols, the insistence on a realm beyond the literal. My encounters with Arlene take place in that unmapped territory, outside the ordinary boundaries of space and time as we attempt to plumb taboo subjects—sexual abuse, madness and isolation.

The intimacy of these meetings is fervid, an exploration of secrets, of dark corners of the self we have not previously revealed, an attempt to acknowledge emotions and perceptions that the outer world neither sees nor validates. We try to push ourselves to trust enough to make this journey together, to rely on one another to lead the way into this terrain, to guide us out again.

I am terrified by these sessions, but at age twenty-four I lack the inner awareness to even recognize my own fear. When I was a child, my parents' battles drowned out the canned laughter of the television on a nightly basis, and I have spent so many years afraid that I cannot even identify it, nor all that remains closed inside me in response to it.

I can't even see, at this point in my life, how much I fear my own authenticity, even as I hunger for it. I have rejected all of the received identities—my mother's daughter, the heterosexual woman, the would-be professional striving for the middle class—in search of that authentic self. Yet there remain doors inside me I can't pry open, or that, when I try, slam shut and seal more tightly than before.

And there is much to fear between Arlene and myself. Arlene is nearly ten years older, the instructor and founder of the institution where I am a student, a credentialed professional in a mainstream art world in which I believe I can never be powerful. We are attempting to create a working partnership, which requires that I simultaneously acknowledge her mentorship and perform as her equal. Each role is challenging for me; on the one hand, I have little respect for or trust in authority, and on the other, it is a constant struggle to believe I bring qualities of equal value to our partnership.

Scarier yet, Arlene is Cheryl's lover. Cheryl is a forceful personality, and although I am well aware of her capacity for charm, the intelligence and resourcefulness that initially drew me, since our breakup, she has come to seem a kind of nemesis for me. I am still unnerved by how I allowed her to dominate our relationship, how spineless and enervated I felt by the end of it. Though I'd never admit it, I'm afraid of Cheryl. My work with Arlene pulls me closer to Cheryl's orb, makes our interaction inevitable.

I don't trust Arlene with regard to this issue. My mother never protected me from my stepfather's rage, his sexual advances, and I have no faith that Arlene will prove a more reliable shield. This issue is undiscussable between us; how can I speak badly about her lover, especially since her lover was once mine? How can I talk about trust with someone I do not trust?

At the age of twenty-four I have no foundation for the kind of honesty that Arlene and I ask of ourselves. In my family, lying and denial were the balms we used to soothe our festering wounds: no one had been hit, drinking was not a problem in the family, incest was not occurring under our roof. Where would I have learned trust?

Arlene is as afraid as I am, but I only see that in retrospect. She is taking a risk to love, to reveal herself to someone who may not be fully able to receive her. She tries to tell me about her terror, but because I won't admit my own, I can't allow hers to become real to me. Instead, we light another joint, and precariously step across the high wire of yet another topic. Today Arlene suggests we talk about the sexual energy between us. I am frozen. I think about my current girlfriend, and I think about Cheryl. If Cheryl knew about this conversation, she would be furious. And can I be certain that Arlene will not tell her?

I'm not aware of feeling any sexual energy between us, any physical desire for her. Is this something about which I'm in denial? My incest history has created some dislocation of my erotic impulses. My sexuality is often performative; I can't always identify authentic erotic desires. My draw to Arlene is profound, but has always seemed to be about her brain and her vision, the opportunity she has created for me. But I feel that she wants and expects something more, although I'm not completely clear what "more" might be. Still, I don't want to insult or disappoint her.

Does she feel more? Is she coming on to me? The room shrinks, its walls narrowing, and my vision dims.

I drink the dregs of coffee grounds, sharp and bitter on my tongue. I sputter something, "If I...uh...did feel...you know... anything, I...uh...wouldn't want to, you know, ...do anything about it...because of...uh...you know...our girlfriends...." I have stopped breathing.

She registers—what? amusement? hurt?—in her black eyes. "There are lots of reasons why this is frightening," she acknowledges. To my ears, she sounds so calm, her voice unbroken, her tone even. "Including that our lovers would be threatened. It would also be too emotionally intense."

It would? I don't know, but she is pointing a way out, and I am more than happy to concur. "And it might get in the way of our work," I add. Each reason is another step away from this nerve-racking possibility, and with every step I feel my lungs ease their constriction.

"Under patriarchy, there's so much pain around women's sexuality," Arlene continues, steering us into the safety of the theoretical. Her hands lightly rub the tops of her thighs, clad in green army surplus pants. "You were molested. I was raped. And the powerful taboo against women's intimacy, for which women have been killed."

So we construct a theory to lead us away from the source of threat. We envision a "sexual" energy abstracted from the body, consummated in our work together, expressed through the media of art and magic. And I am only too eager to embrace this theory.

There is a lull. Perhaps the meeting is over for today. Then she asks me, "Do you feel more unloved or unloving?"

I cannot know the motivation behind her question, but I assume it expresses her disappointment in me. Given my history, there is only one answer I can offer. "Unloved," I answer, and think I read in the grimace at one corner of her mouth that she believes the opposite. She wants something else from me, I understand this much, but am uncertain of what it is or how to offer it. I don't know whether I have it in me to give. Then I have an impulse that becomes action before it is even a thought. My fingers are at my neck; they grasp the rawhide band that circles there. They make a clumsy stab at loosening the knot, but sweat and time have melded the coiled strands into a solid mass. I say nothing to Arlene, but step over to my altar, pluck up the knife that rests there next to a hunk of crystal. I slip the blade between the band of leather and the delicate skin of my throat and pull. The blade slices, rawhide swings free; the bead tumbles into my palm. I feel it, light in the hollow of my hand, yet it seems to fairly pulse. I remember shoplifting it from a bead store in Ann Arbor when I was nineteen. This clay bead has nestled against my larynx for four years, absorbing the vibration of every sound that emanated from me, and every sound that I choked back.

I return to the living room, my chair across from Arlene. "I have something for you," I tell her, and place the bead in her hand. She stares at my throat, the white

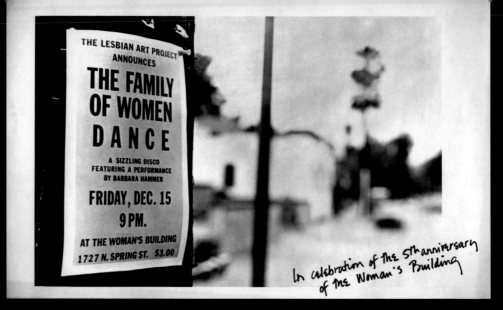

The Lesbian Art Project Announces The Family of Dance, 1979. 8½" x 11". Woman's Building Image Archive, Otis College of Art and Design.

line, untanned, that cinctures my neck, and then down at the talking bead. She smiles and is pleased.

Winter 1979

The poster is a photograph of a poster tacked to a telephone pole on a palm-lined city street. With its block typography stacked in rows, this poster mimics the style of hundreds of placards that adorn lampposts and telephone poles all over town, in bright yellow or with rainbow backgrounds announcing dances and musical events—"RAUL RUBIO Y SU COMBO."

This poster, designed by Bia Lowe, announces The Family of Women Dance, sponsored by LAP. Family is a frequent topic within the LAP. Many of us feel estranged from our families of origin, but we hunger to belong to a unit. So we declare ourselves a family of women, will into being a mythical network of friends and lovers and ex-lovers bonded with all the ferocity of blood.

But there are problems. Some of us have ties, problematic as they might be, to our biological families, and this creates a conflict of allegiances. When, for example, my girlfriend wants to spend Thanksgiving with her mom and brothers, I feel deserted; the family of women dissolves into empty words. Will the bond between us always be secondary to the ties of blood, of history?

Too, the field of psychology has not yet offered up the model of the dysfunctional family. We assume our family problems are either political—the fault of patriarchy—or personal—our parents are just fucked up. We have yet to understand the roles we play within the family dynamic—the good child or the scapegoat, the responsible one or the troublemaker or the child who disappears—or that we are doomed to replicate those dynamics within our own utopia. I don't comprehend how Arlene and Cheryl have come to represent my mother and stepfather to me, how viewing them this way makes me complicit with my own powerlessness, how this will inevitably impact our work together. And who knows whom I represent to each of them?

In the meantime, we will name ourselves family and celebrate it. The poster was at first imagined by Bia as an exact replica of those displayed on major streets in the city—Sunset, Hollywood, and Olympic boulevards. Bia wanted to print thousands and enlist a gang of lesbians to go out after dark, dressed in dark clothing and armed with industrial staples and thumbtacks. It spoke to that desire for lesbian visibility, the hunger to claim our territory in the world.

But in 1979, this visibility is still not safe; we imagine a legion of creepy men flocking to the Woman's Building, invading its safety to ogle or wreak vengeance on the lesbians. So Bia creates a single prototype, and we drive to Echo Park and staple this poster to the splintered wood of a telephone pole. We photograph it, taking pains to reveal its bold display on the street, just as careful to take it down before we go.

From this photo, Bia creates another poster, to be sent discretely through the mail to a select list. Still, the poster invites the viewer to imagine a world in which "The Family of Women Dance" would be advertised on any busy street in the city of Los Angeles, a world in which we do not yet dwell.

Spring 1979

The color Polaroid doesn't do justice to the magic of that afternoon. Half a dozen women in shorts and tank tops lounging in a sunny backyard, surrounded by dozens of strips of vibrant pink cloth spread out on the grass, draped over shrubbery, hanging from clotheslines and tree branches. The photo obscures the purpose of our activity; neither does it reveal the delirium we feel—pleasantly stoned, the afternoon light on our skin, the explosion of shocking pink against the meticulous green of the lawn, the flush of communal spirit as we come together in our task.

We've gathered to dye 180 yards of white gauze to be used for the set of *An Oral Herstory of Lesbianism*, a performance piece collaboratively created by thirteen lesbians at my inception and under my direction. Bia and cast member Cheri Gaulke conceived of the pink gauze set; they intend to completely enclose the performance space within this sheer drapery. The audience will feel like they are enclosed inside a big vagina. Viewed from the outside, the lighted interior will glow like a rosy lantern.

Neither Bia nor I have our own washing machines, and we'd already been kicked out of more than one laundromat for trying to ply our Rit dye in their Kenmores. When we'd attempted a wash after midnight at one twenty-four hour establishment, figuring that the supervision would be lax to nonexistent, we'd encountered an old man in filth-encrusted jeans who'd unzipped them and flashed his penis at us before the first rinse cycle. We squealed in disgust and grabbed our dripping, half-dyed lengths of gauze, leaving the machines full of reddish suds. With only four weeks to go before the production opened, we are beginning to despair of ever getting all that fabric pink.

It is my friend Joanne Kerr who comes to the rescue, offering her large-capacity Maytag for our use; Joanne had, until recently, been married, and still owned many of the accoutrements of an Orange County housewife. She'd come to the Woman's Building as a PhD candidate in anthropology; her dissertation had to do with gift-giving rituals across cultures, and she wanted to study the practice of making art to be given as gift that was commonplace within the feminist art community. Since her arrival, she'd "gone native," experimenting with relationships with women, and immersing herself in the life of the community she'd set out to study.

That very life is throbbing in the terraced backyard of her house in Franklin Hills this April afternoon, as women pull armloads of gauze from the washing machine and spread the impossibly pink yardage out to dry. Those in attendance today—Clsuf, Geraldine, and Paula, among others—are not all cast members in the production. The women who drape pink gauze across green grass are part of the community of artists at the Woman's Building who are always eager to support the efforts of another woman artist, knowing that they might well call on you to help with their next project.

Sister Sledge's "We Are Family" blasts from the stereo speakers into the spring air. We pass joints in a desultory fashion; sunbathe between loads of wash; feast on pita sandwiches stuffed with tuna or cheese, sprouts, tomatoes, roasted red peppers that Joanne graciously serves. Our labor seems ancient and tribal—the women of the village coming together on wash day, helping one another to hang and to fold, exchanging gossip and advice. At the same time the bright colors, sunshine, and music create a festival atmosphere. And there is too the element of pure crackpot—Rit Dyeing 180 yards of fabric in a single washing machine—certainly another entry in that long and varied list of "What I Did for Art."

It is a moment that embodies for me my aspirations for lesbian art in those days: sensual, celebratory, communal, crackpot. A conscious refutation of the depressed, oppressed, downwardly mobile or politically correct strains of lesbian life that seemed to dominate outside the realm of art. We are engaged in creating a myth of the lesbian as artist, and for that afternoon, giddy with the enormity and eccentricity and joy of our task, we are alive inside that myth.

The poster for *An Oral Herstory of Lesbianism* is a long strip, a vertical column composed of successive rows of women's faces, seven frames across. Each row is a different color of the spectrum; each depicts one of the cast members of the performance.

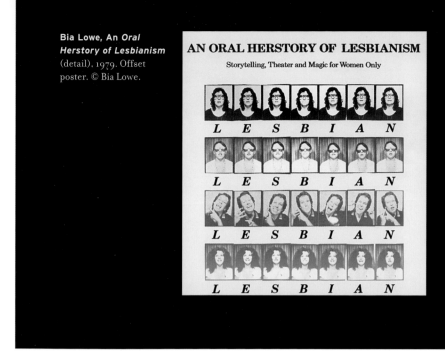

Bia Lowe, An *Oral Herstory of Lesbianism* (detail), 1979. Offset poster. © Bia Lowe.

Seven frames, and in each, the woman forms a distinct letter with her mouth. "L," the lips part, the tongue lodges behind the front teeth. "E," the open mouth stretches wide at the corners. "S," the teeth come together, while the lips still part. "B," the lips purse, almost pucker, before the "ee" sound blasts them apart. "I," the throat opens, the mouth stretches vertically. "A," a rounding of the mouth, teeth parted. "N," the tongue makes contact with the hard palate.

Hours spent in a photo booth in front of Woolworth's in Hollywood, plunking quarters into the machine, shooting strip after strip, trying to get the perfect visual representation of each letter. "L-E-S-B-I-A-N." Thirteen women articulating their identity.

The concept and design are Bia's; the offset printing is done by Cynthia Marsh—who is not a lesbian, although many a woman wishes she were—on the old printing press in the Women's Graphic Center at the Woman's Building.

Oral—as we have affectionately and lasciviously dubbed the performance, has been created through a three-month process of workshops that I conducted. These sessions utilized theater games, writing exercises, and consciousness-raising to explore our experience as lesbians.

There are the inevitable coming out stories, but one of our members, Brooke Hallock, has recounted her experience of coming out to—and being rejected by—her teenaged daughters rather than her parents. We explore community life in the bars, on the sports field, and—in a piece Arlene has written about the myriad attractions between women that often go unspoken—at a card table. We examine the challenges of relationship—finding, initiating, and maintaining an intimate connection. Chris Wong examines her identity as a Chinese lesbian, torn between the traditions of her culture and the lure of an alternative lifestyle, using the form of the Chinese Ribbon Dance. From this wealth of stories we weave the performance with the hope of creating a new tapestry that reveals and expands the meaning of "lesbian." It is clear to me that we do not represent all lesbians—we are all from approximately the same generation, and all white women, except for Chris and Brooke, who is Native American. It is, after all, *An Oral Herstory...* not *The Oral Herstory....*

Still, in seven frames, thirteen women face the camera, ready to spell out our identity, ready to offer the stories of our lives.

∞∞∞

The scarf is blue and white, a long strand of chiffon. It comes from Paris, a place this working-class twenty-four-year-old can scarcely imagine. Arlene has given it to me, a gesture with resonance I have probably chosen to overlook, or am not equipped to receive, a token of our connection. I keep it on my altar.

It is scarcely possible that the two phone calls could have come in the same day, but they have conflated in my memory, two phone calls that shifted my foundations. Perhaps the whole month leading up to the opening of *Oral* has compressed in my mind into one long, nightmarish day.

The first call is from my mother, telling me that she's decided to marry for the third time, barely a year since her divorce from my stepfather. In that year I have tried, from 2500 miles away, to support her to be on her own, inundating her with my feminist cant, finding her a therapist, encouraging her to move when my stepfather started stalking her. I feel rejected by her decision to wed again, my puny efforts no substitute for having a man on whom to lean. It's small of me, but I am disappointed by her choice; I withhold my approval.

The second call is from Cheryl. It comes in the early afternoon, catches me off-guard. She's excited, her words spit like the rat-a-tat of a machine gun, and it takes me a while to sort their meaning. "Lesbian porn...Playboy funding...Lesbian Art Project..." It's a few moments before it comes clear.

When Cheryl and I were lovers we used to joke about a scam to make a lot of money marketing fake lesbian porn videos. We'd advertise our titles in the classified sections of *Hustler* or *Penthouse* and watch the cash flow in. "Lesbians Eat It Raw," for example, would depict short-haired women eating sushi; "Black and White Pussies Lap It Up" would in fact portray our cats drinking milk. It was a perfect scheme, we thought, for "ripping off the patriarchy," exploiting men's fantasies of lesbians but actually delivering normalized portraits of lesbian life. We congratulated ourselves on the political correctness of this scheme, though we did worry that the plan might backfire if our customers—frustrated at being so misled—decided to take out their ire on some unsuspecting lesbian.

Now it appears that Cheryl wants to pursue this project in earnest. She's had the brainstorm that she might get funding from the Playboy Foundation to do it. In the seventies, the Playboy Foundation, under the direction of Christy Heffner, was eager to fund certain feminist activities, and this created bitter controversy in more than a few underfunded women's organizations. The Woman's Building board of directors has already voted decisively against going after Playboy money, and that's why Cheryl means to submit her proposal through the LAP. And to do so, she intends to become a formal partner with Arlene and me in LAP, something I imagine she has wanted for a long time.

My limbs go cold with dread. There isn't an aspect of her idea I feel inclined to support, yet I fear the consequences of opposing her. I try stalling for time. "I don't know, Cheryl, there's a lot to think about...."

She interrupts me. "There's no time to think," she snaps, her tone insistent. "I need to know right now—are you going to support me or not?"

Here's the real issue, I think then, tasting the acid of fear on my tongue. "I need to talk to Arlene," I say, as calmly as I can. Trying to push back a plummeting sensation of doom, I cling to a corner of the bookcase; my knees are in danger of collapsing.

Through the receiver I hear a muffled exchange of words between them. I stare dully out my window at the line of palm trees framed against the horizon. Eventually Arlene comes to the phone, but her voice, so strained and distant, is almost unrecognizable to me.

"Arlene," I nearly plead, "I'm concerned about this. I mean, Playboy? And do we really want to change the whole structure of LAP?" *Rescue me, stand up for me*, a little girl inside me begs, but Arlene will never go against her lover to back me up.

She speaks to me as if we are strangers, as if she has no comprehension of my concerns. I have heard this tone in my mother's voice, years before, and again today when she announced her marriage plans. "I have no problems with what Cheryl is asking," Arlene insists, "but if you do you'll just have to say so."

Despite the blaze of sunshine out the window, the chill in my body intensifies. Like a bad dream from which I can't shake myself, I see there is no escape. It is a moment toward which I've been moving ever since I first met Cheryl, inexorable as in a dream, and now it has arrived. Too much is at stake. Both Cheryl and Arlene are in the cast of *Oral*, and it is so close to opening that to lose them will be catastrophic. Maybe Cheryl is counting on this as well.

Cheryl gets back on the phone.

"I can't decide right this minute," I tell her, "We need to have a meeting..."

Again, she cuts me off. "No," she insists, "I have to know right now."

I exhale deeply. "If I have to tell you right this minute, if there can't even be any process about this, then my answer is no."

Cheryl's anger is something I have always feared; unlike many women who learned to suppress their rage and power, turn it against themselves, or deflect it into passive aggression, Cheryl allows it full expression. Now it breaks over me in a wave of furious verbiage. She has supported my efforts all of these years; how dare I withhold my support from her? She bangs the receiver into the cradle of the phone, and I am left to anticipate the aftermath.

Neither Cheryl nor Arlene quits the cast of *Oral*. Cheryl begins to woo the other members of the cast, paying them compliments, being extravagant with her attention, inviting them to parties after rehearsal, parties from which I am conspicuously excluded. She finds private funding for her video project and hires several cast members to work on it. The gossip that filters back leads me to suspect that she uses these occasions to voice doubts about the production and my competency to carry it to completion. No overt mutiny occurs; still, the cast—many of them heretofore friends and colleagues—grows unmistakably cooler toward me, less supportive of my artistic vision, more challenging of my leadership. The mutual support that characterized the workshop process has evaporated. I come to dread rehearsals, and more than once give serious thought to abandoning my own project. I take to spending the hours prior to rehearsal shaking with anxiety, pressed against my mattress to quiet my pounding heart, spinning fantasies of moving to another city and changing my name.

Then one afternoon, sitting on my bed in my apartment staring out at Echo Park Lake, an understanding stirs in me. I will never prevail, I know suddenly, by opposing Cheryl directly, scrapping to win back power in the eyes of my cast. I can only empower myself, I see with utter clarity, can only face my adversaries by becoming large enough to encompass them. The air in my apartment grows heavy, and I see myself expanding, not my body but the essence inside, swelling and widening, broadening its horizons. The animosity with which some members of the cast regard me will not threaten me if I am secure in my own authority. I can contain this dissonance, I decide; it need not define me or the art project.

In this moment something shifts in me that will never shift back. I learn a secret about power. I will be much older before I learn to apply it to my personal interactions, but it forever changes the way I approach my work with others. It will be still more years before I come to regard Cheryl with gratitude for being the agent of this lesson. It's a lesson about leadership, and also about the isolation inherent in this position.

I begin to reassert myself in rehearsal, taking the cast members' ideas and insisting that they push them further. I no longer look to the actors for validation, but become even more intently focused on the quality of the work. With just days to spare, the show takes shape and gels. It's good, and everyone knows it. The thirteen performances of *An Oral Herstory of Lesbianism* come off without incident, and each night audiences of women thrill to the tension and transcendence generated within the pink gauze performance space.

Some days after that disastrous phone call from Cheryl, I receive another. "Because you have been so horribly unsupportive of me," she declares, "I want you to give back everything I ever gave you."

I don't argue or protest or plead my case. I don't resist or refuse. I do exactly as Cheryl asks. I am scrupulous in my sweep through my apartment. The big items are a bentwood rocker she'd bought me because I had no furniture, and the original drawing of my cat Ruby she'd made to illustrate an image from one of my poems. There is a little jewelry, the odd T-shirt, some record albums, notes she'd written to me, items from my altar. Exhaustive in the extreme, I even excavate an old toothbrush, bristles splayed and curled, that she'd once loaned me, and I add it to the pile.

Somehow, whether through an overzealous sense of thoroughness or because of unexamined resentments, the scarf Arlene had given me is also included in the heap of items to be returned. The blue and white chiffon scarf that Arlene had brought me from Paris.

A friend helps me haul everything to Cheryl and Arlene's house, the last time I ever visit that property. We pull into the driveway and quietly unload the items onto the porch, then we drive away. Perhaps some spell is finally broken.

My interaction with Arlene has been strained ever since I said no to Cheryl, and now she is even colder. I'm not sure why she's angry with me; perhaps it's the tension of mediating the estrangement between Cheryl and me. We stop having meetings of the LAP without ever formally deciding to do so. We had planned to spend our third and final year of LAP working on a book about the project, but it seems mutually understood that this will no longer be possible.

We do have one last meeting, about six weeks after the completion of *Oral*, at a Mexican restaurant not far from Arlene's house. It's a dark dive, a cool refuge from July blasting on the sidewalk outside. I scoop mouthful after mouthful of blistering salsa onto corn chips as Arlene and I inter the LAP.

Just as we are getting up to leave the restaurant she asks me, "Why did you give back the scarf?" and I can see that she is wounded. I can scarcely remember doing so; certainly it wasn't in my intention to reject her. "Your argument was with Cheryl," she insists, "not with me."

How can I explain the ways I'd felt betrayed by her, that I'd seen the two of them function as a unit, how I felt she'd set me up and let me down? How the family of women had too perilously replicated my own family?

I am sorry to have hurt her, and dumbfounded that I actually could. I have felt unloved, but now she tells me I have been unloving.

"I'm sorry," I say, lamely, "it was a mistake." And this is partially true.

The rest remains unspoken, a story for the talking bead.

Spring 1980

XX chromosomes determine femaleness. The symbol XXX imagines the parthenogenic woman, she who creates from her own source— the lesbian artist.—"Great American Lesbian Art Show" poster

THE GREAT AMERICAN LESBIAN ART SHOW

What is Lesbian Art and Who are Lesbian Artists?
The Great American Lesbian Art Show (GALAS) wants to answer that question. We believe there is a uniquely lesbian sensibility that is informed by our lives, our visions and our love of women. Exploring the diversity of form and content in our creative work, we hope to more clearly reveal the nature of lesbian sensibility.

By creating a national network of lesbian art exhibits, we will be able to examine a number of factors which determine similarities and differences in our work (regional geography; urban or rural environment; age; race; feminist or non-feminist community.)

We invite you to participate in the Great American Lesbian Art Show, a national series of exhibits and events honoring lesbian creativity. beginning May 1, 1980. Co-sponsored by the Woman's Building and the Los Angeles Gay Community Services Center, the goals of GALAS are:

- to celebrate lesbian art, making it public, visible and accessible.
- to build a national network of lesbian artists and a permanent slide collection of lesbian art.
- to increase awareness of the power of lesbian vision and sensibility.

We invite you to organize exhibits of lesbian art in your own communities, in galleries and in non-traditional spaces (for example: your home; your garage; the campus of a nearby college or community college; your local women's center, bookstore, health center or bar.) These shows will occur at the same time all across the United States!

Concurrently, the Woman's Building will exhibit an invitational show curated by GALAS, which will honor eight artists whose work is visibly lesbian. Another part of this exhibit is a continuous slide presentation containing documentation of all the work exhibited nationally by you.

G A L A S

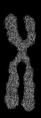  

XX chromosomes determine femaleness. The symbol XXX imagines the parthenogenic woman - she who creates from her own source, the lesbian artist.

What is lesbian art? Some definitions include: art made by lesbians; art which explores lesbian content; art which is woman-identified. There's no strict definition—if you feel your creative work is lesbian in form or content, *please join us!*

We encourage work in all media and multi-media; lesbian culture is immensely rich and diverse. We also suggest creating lesbian art events (openings, celebrations, dinner parties—in L.A. we're trying to organize bus tours to visit all the local shows!) to enhance the spirit of these occasions.

How can you become part of GALAS?
- *Give Yourself a Show! Give Your Friends a Show!* If you are interested in exhibiting your work or the work of women that you know, contact us before January 15, 1980. Be as specific as possible when you write to us. Let us know: names of artists exhibiting, where you live, where you're showing, descriptions of work, etc. We also love gossip: the reactions of your friends and/or community to the GALAS project!
- *Meet Lesbian Artists!* Would you like to be a GALAS area coordinator for your city or region? If so, contact us before December 15, 1979.
- *Contribute!* We are relying on individual donations to cover the costs of this project. If you have dollars to spare, please send them to GALAS. If you have the means to make a large donation ($100 or more, tax-deductible), contact Barbara Stopha at the project address.
- *Document!* If you're exhibiting work as part of GALAS, we'd like you to send us 3 slides of your work by April 15, 1980. Be sure to label them with your name, the title of the piece, materials used and date completed; also please indicate where you live and where the work is being shown. These slides are non-returnable. They will be shown in a presentation at the Woman's Building exhibit, and will be compiled in a permanent archive of lesbian art.

When we hear from you, we'll send you a brochure with further information on how to develop your GALAS participation, including tips on fundraising and publicity, ideas for alternative spaces, and a report on regional sponsors and coordinators.

Who we are—Tyaga, Lyricon Fire Jazzwomin, Barbara Stopha, Louise Moore, Bia Lowe, Kathleen Burg, Terry Wolverton, Betsy Irons, Elizabeth Canelake, Dara Robinson, and Linda Kahn. We are a loose collective of lesbian artists which has formed to create the GALAS project.

The Woman's Building is a public center for women's culture, whose programs include the Feminist Studio Workshop, the Community Galleries, and the Lesbian Art Project.

The Gay Community Services Center is a Los Angeles County-funded social services organization geared towards the needs of lesbians and gay men.

Write to:

GALAS
c/o GCSC
P.O. Box 38777
Hollywood, CA 90038

THE GREAT AMERICAN LESBIAN ART SHOW

Bia Lowe, *Great American Lesbian Art Show (GALAS)*, 1980. Offset poster. © Bia Lowe.

We are painting the walls red. Not an elegant burgundy, or an understated rust. Matador red, waving our sexual cape at the furious bull of homophobia.

We are painting the walls of the Woman's Building gallery for the "Great American Lesbian Art Show" (GALAS) an unapologetic scarlet.

We grip the long extension poles, spreading color from floor to eighteen-foot ceiling, straining the muscles of our shoulders and backs. Our skin is splattered with flecks of red, like bright blood or an erotic flush. The walls soak up our crimson wash; they demand coat after coat. We paint for days. At night when I close my eyes, my vision is suffused with green, red's vibratory opposite.

GALAS is not simply this exhibit, but a yearlong project to bring national recognition to lesbian art and artists. It is the brainchild of the artist Tyaga, an open-faced blonde with a crew cut. She has assembled a collective of women to plan a national exhibition of lesbian art. Inspired, without question, by the LAP, GALAS sprang up in the wake of LAP's demise. I am still in shock from its dissolution; it feels on the one hand natural to be working on this lesbian art endeavor, and yet it also feels profoundly odd.

These red walls will be graced by the work of ten artists[8] who've been visible as lesbians in their careers. We've chosen erotic line drawings by Kate Millett; wry, moody neons by Lili Lakich; an enormous wrapped sculpture—suggestive of a hungry mouth or a greedy vulva—by Harmony Hammond; the disarmingly domestic dough sculptures of Nancy Fried; and somber, brooding oils by Gloria Longval.

We've chafed under the limitations of budget and geography, and by the absence of scholarship and critical discussion about the work of contemporary lesbian artists. We can't claim to represent lesbian artists across the United States (let alone the Americas); all of the artists in the GALAS invitational reside in New York or Los Angeles.

So in addition to the Woman's Building show, we've also sent out a call—via the feminist press—urging lesbians to organize exhibits in their own communities and to send us documentation of these works. Over two hundred art shows and events are planned across the country, including nearly twenty satellite events in Los Angeles.[9] Slides of work from these shows will be on continuous view as part of the GALAS exhibition at the Woman's Building.

The working process of the GALAS collective bears no similarity to that of the LAP. We haven't probed our personal histories or dissected our feelings; we haven't formulated theory. The group is task-focused and the tasks have been multiple: research, curating, fundraising, installation, and publicity. The GALAS Collective has made no attempt to bond as a family, which, after the turbulent years of LAP, I find to be a relief. Still, it is odd to work on a lesbian project without Arlene. She is curating her own exhibit—Woman·Woman·Works—which will be installed in the first floor gallery of the Woman's Building concurrently with GALAS. There is no interaction between us about these shows.

The almost yearlong process of organizing GALAS was a phenomenon in itself, and included the organizing of several other events along the way. Dozens of local artists and writers flocked to "Amazon Ambrosia," a daylong lesbian art worksharing with featured presentations by artist Harmony Hammond and Liza Cowan, former publisher of *Dyke* magazine. An upscale crowd of politically active lesbians and gay men were drawn to the benefit reading by Kate Millett and Paul Monette (in a display of co-gender cooperation uncharacteristic of the time), hosted by our organizational cosponsor, the Los Angeles Gay and Lesbian Community Services Center. The crackpot element was in full force at "An Intimate Dinner for 150 Celebrating Eleanor Roosevelt and All Great Lesbians," a performance art dinner I created, catered by Clsuf and Twolip Art, with appearances by The Waitresses and singer Silvia Kohan.

It is the spring of 1980, and we are flushed with bravado. The red walls signal the unabashed spirit of GALAS, our determination to claim territory, be visible, and revel in unsubtle beauty. They signal the breadth of our ambition, our insistence upon being public. We are rewarded with a feature article and review in the *Los Angeles Times*, and a review in *Artweek*, the first time lesbian art has received this level of mainstream recognition. The red walls speak of our intent to mythologize; our adoption of three X chromosomes—whimsical, dancing DNA—as our logo, is a bold assertion that lesbians are, as writer and philosopher Monique Wittig posited, "a third sex."

We don't know that the world is about to change. It is May; we can't foresee the presidential election in November that will turn our revolution upside down. The disappearance of arts funding and the emergence of economic hard times will send the Woman's Building scrambling for the cover of mainstream respectability, making us think twice before using the word "feminist," let alone "lesbian," in grant proposals, brochures, or exhibitions.

In the spring of 1980, we think we've moved from the reinvention of ourselves as lesbians to taking over the planet with our mutant biology, our crackpot sensibility. We can almost taste the world we've conjured through our art: life-affirming, celebratory, erotic. So we paint the walls red, as if against the long chill we don't yet know is coming.

Postscript: Fall 1990

The banner—ten feet by eight feet—spills down the side of the three-story building on Industrial Street in the heart of the downtown arts district. Eyes gaze between open palms, and the text reads, "I feel what I want/I want what I feel." Designed by artist Susan Silton, the banner announces the exhibition "All But the Obvious," the first lesbian group show to be mounted in Los Angeles since GALAS, ten years earlier.

This exhibit takes place not at the Woman's Building, but at LACE (Los Angeles Contemporary Exhibitions); by this time the Woman's Building is no longer considered the center of contemporary feminist discourse. In fact, this next generation is not looking for a feminist center. The theoretical bases have shifted from the activism of a women's movement for social change to academy-based consideration of post-

Susan Silton, *i feel what i want i want what i feel*, 1990. Gelatin silver print. 10" x 8". © Susan Silton.

modern European philosophers—Foucault, Mann, Derrida, and women such as Julia Kristeva and Luce Irigaray. Seventies feminism has been dissected, criticized, and summarily dismissed.

The work in "All But the Obvious" is made by a new generation[10] of artists, and points up two distinct trends in lesbian art of the late eighties and early nineties: theoretically based works such as *Disturbances*, by Millie Wilson, which embeds multiple layers of theoretical references, and post-punk "Bad Girl" art, such as S/M-laced photographs—*Be My Bitch* is one title—by Della Grace.

The curator of "All But the Obvious," Pam Gregg, has no knowledge of the LAP or the "Great American Lesbian Art Show," and expresses only mild interest when I approach her to talk about it.

A few months later, I am commissioned by *The Advocate* to write a feature about this new generation of lesbian artists. This gives me an excuse to call a dozen young women in Los Angeles, New York, San Francisco, and Chicago; during my interviews I ask them what they know of lesbian art in the seventies. I am stunned that almost none of them has any idea of her predecessors. One mentions Barbara Hammer, the lesbian filmmaker who's been working since the early seventies; at least two cite the avowedly heterosexual Judy Chicago. Perhaps Judy's name comes to mind because she used vaginal imagery?

I feel profound discouragement at my findings—it seems all of our work has been entirely erased. I have no doubt that these young artists can only make the work they are creating because of the pioneering efforts of LAP and GALAS a decade earlier. In this way, we were not ineffective; in this way, I see our legacy. But the artists and theories of LAP and GALAS are unknown to these women, rendered invisible or ridiculous. I am once more thrown back on my question—in so utterly rejecting the structures of the dominant culture, did we marginalize ourselves irredeemably? Or was it only in turning our backs on those dominant structures that we were able to spawn a next generation, oblivious to us as they might be?

"I feel what I want / I want what I feel," Silton's banner proclaims. It's a resonant statement, insistent on sensation and emotion, the body and the heart. In this postmodern, theory-driven time, it's almost subversive. Yet there is a collective vision— a social intention—that is absent from the work in this show, which speaks of personal gratification or weaves intricate webs of intellectualism. The walls of the gallery remain stark white.

Notes

1. The Natalie Barney Collective was named after the expatriate writer who lived in Paris in the twenties and gathered about her a community of artistic and independent women, many of them lesbians, that was known for its celebratory and iconoclastic spirit.

2. A sixth member, Kathleen Burg, did not attend the photo shoot that day.

3. Fluxus is an international network of artists named and loosely organized by George Maciunas in 1962, and noted for blending different artistic media and disciplines.

4. A former professor of mine at Thomas Jefferson College, the feminist philosopher Linda Smith, remarked that during the process of alchemical transformation, as one substance transmutes into another, the pot cracks. The old container is insufficient to house the new substance. Thus a "crackpot" may be someone undergoing just such a transformation of the self.

5. Within LAP, we explored and reclaimed the term "queer" more than ten years in advance of the political activists who in the nineties would call themselves Queer Nation. "Queer," which had been used for decades to revile gays and lesbians, was an accurate reflection of the alienation we felt within heterosexist society, and the way we often internalized that alienation, the feeling of not belonging.

6. Later salons featured performance artist and filmmaker Barbara Hammer, witch/playwright/activist Zusanna Budapest, and artist and mythmaker Jere Van Syoc.

7. Zusanna Budapest is a former actress and practicing witch who, through her writings and public speaking, did much to popularize the notion of witchcraft as an ancient female art, the practice of which had led to great punishment of women during the Inquisition and subsequently. Interest in witchcraft was widespread within cultural feminism of the seventies, in part as an effort to redefine the notion of power and to claim it for women. This quote is from a conversation with the author.

8. The ten artists were Lula Mae Blocton, Tee Corinne, Betsy Damon, Louise Fishman, Nancy Fried, Harmony Hammond, Debbie Jones, Lili Lakich, Gloria Longval, and Kate Millett.

9. In addition to expected locations such as New York, San Francisco, Boston, and Chicago, there were also shows in Bozeman, Montana; Winter Park, Florida; Lawrence, Kansas; Alexandria, Virginia; and Anchorage, Alaska.

10. When I speak of a "generation" here, I am not strictly speaking of the artists' chronological age, but rather of the point in time at which they came to art making and the social, political, and philosophical structures with which they are aligned.

By the Hand of the Father, original theater work cowritten and directed by Theresa Chavez with writers Oscar Garza, Eric Gutierrez, and Rose Portillo. Pictured actors: Rosa Portillo and Kevin Sifuentes, premiered Plaza de la Raza's Margo Albert Theater, Los Angeles, 2000. © Theresa Chavez.

L.A. Real, original performance, Theresa Chavez, writer and director. Pictured actress Rose Portillo, premiered National Women's Theatre Festival, Los Angeles, 1992. © Theresa Chavez.

UNBURYING HISTORIES: THE FUTURE(S) OF FEMINIST ART

Theresa Chavez

1.

I am someone who is connected to and surrounded by many histories, all of which are buried, misunderstood or romanticized.

I am a Chicana and a Californiana—a seventh generation Californian/Los Angelina whose Mestiza past is buried under the surface of postindustrial Los Angeles. My history is revealed, if at all, in a reconstituted version made up of Taco Bells, romanticized *señoritas*, Zorro movies, and idealized fantasies represented in Mission Revival homes with tile roofs.

I am an interdisciplinary theater artist. A majority of my original theater work is developed, written, and created collaboratively within the context of an arts organization, About Productions, which I cofounded in 1988, and for which I serve as the artistic director. Over the past nineteen years, much of the work of this company has dealt with uncovering histories that my colleagues/collaborators and I are connected to and which, without this artistic devotion, would remain silent within the world at large and even within the framework of the art and theater worlds. Histories of Los Angeles, of California, and of the West; Chicano and Mexicano histories; Native American histories; gay and lesbian histories; histories of feminist writers; and histories of the avant-garde. Not just uncovering but illuminating them in the present tense.

My work is connected to art and theater movements whose histories have been neglected or shattered, regarded only to illuminate a particular historic era or a specific discipline, and rarely seen as a whole or as intersecting worlds. Dada, Fluxus, Bauhaus, Judson Church, Chicano art, experimental theater, performance art, feminist art—they are, in some cases, just beginning to be recognized outside the rarified world of the art historian or art aficionado. Because of their experimental, even revolutionary, nature, these histories and their related art practices tend to be ignored by the mainstream and, thus, are left to be rediscovered over and over again, each artistic generation defining them as something "new and original." And because of their transdisciplinary, interdisciplinary, or multidisciplinary natures, they also tend to fall through the cracks of the still-in-use, nineteenth-century manner of categorizing art practice into standard, singular disciplines.

One of these various histories I am specifically and directly connected to is the semi-buried history of feminist art practice at California Institute of the Arts (CalArts), which began with the founding of the Feminist Art Program by Judy Chicago and Miriam Schapiro in 1972, and its subsequent incarnation at the Woman's Building.[1] In the mid-eighties, I worked at the Woman's Building, as a very young artist. In 1987, I received an MFA from CalArts and have, as of this writing, been teaching at CalArts for the past sixteen years.

Current and past artists/faculty, academicians, and administrators at CalArts have passed on very little knowledge of or perspective on the school's relationship to feminist art and to the Woman's Building. There are no references to it in the "official history" that is available through the CalArts Office of Public Affairs. In some schools (there are six—music, dance, theater, art, film/video, and critical studies) there exists no class or requirement that would pass on this knowledge; in others there are opportunities to at least be introduced to this feminist history.

CalArts has joined the ranks of those in the field of art who, for various reasons, neglect to point out and illuminate the role of this experimental, politically motivated, socially passionate, and community-driven movement that questioned and pushed the boundaries of contemporary art making. So most students (and possibly most faculty) do not know that CalArts is directly linked to one of the most important and prominent institutions in the feminist art movement. Perhaps because the idea for the Woman's Building came from a group of renegade women who had been teaching at CalArts, rather than from the men at CalArts, we have a gaping historical hole left from an ideological and cultural split created out of necessity and survival.

The reality of having been born of and deeply influenced by cultures, histories, movements, ideologies, and practices that are at heart revolutionary is a constant for me. What is in flux is my relationship to these various genetic and sociopolitical voices and conditions. Revolutions have a peculiar life span that both requires the individual to subscribe to certain beliefs held by the movement, and later (perhaps years later) offers a renewal of those vows performed in an individualistic, self-determined manner. Who are we now that the revolution is over, pre-empted, destroyed, or reinvented? How do I now redefine myself and, in turn, redefine the revolution?

388

All images:
On earth as it is in heaven.
original theater work, cowritten by
Theresa Chavez, Laurel Ollstein, and
Rose Portillo; directed by Theresa
Chavez. Pictured actors clockwise from
top: Jesse Ramirez, Laurel Ollstein, and
Ramirez. Premiered 24th St. Theatre,
Los Angeles, 2002. © Theresa Chavez.

They Shoot Mexicans, Don't They?, original theater work, cowritten and directed by Theresa Chavez. Pictured (foreground) actor and co-writer Rose Portillo; and (background L to R) dancer Courtney Combs, actor Michael Manuel and dancer Veronica Caudillo; premiered Luckman Center Fine Arts Complex, Los Angeles, 2005. © Theresa Chavez.

And what of those younger artists who missed the big party, the one the revolution threw when it was birthing itself, staking its claim, and becoming fulfilled? What if you missed the party but received its gifts anyway? Are you obligated to the gift givers? Are the gift givers obligated to explain those gifts, where they came from, how they were chosen, and why they are wrapped in a particular way?

RE: Inventing the Wheel

I am not a historian; I am an artist. I teach classes in interdisciplinary studies at CalArts and I have made it part of my teaching practice to make my students aware of not only CalArt's feminist history but also of other intersecting histories that, due of their experimental nature, have been relegated to the corners of visual and performing art history.

Young artists tend to be ignorant of these particular histories and tend, in a vacuum, to create similar work. I find this is no less true with the art produced by my female students, whether or not their declared intentions are feminist. This is not to say that the students' goal is purely to be original, but instead that the goal should be to strive to be informed, influenced, and, in turn, interesting. Quoting work that has preceded one's can be an elegant exercise and a useful context in which to put one's work. And although each generation speaks in its own terms, the perspective of student artists can be shaped with knowledge offered as a gift from previous generations.

One of the classes I have designed and taught is called "RE: Inventing the Wheel." It is a survey that covers many of these aforementioned histories of the twentieth century and presents perspectives by multiple artists, writers, and curators who visit my classroom to represent the momentous movements from which they come and to speak of the vital work they continue to produce.

In some cases, this class is the only time students are introduced to feminist art history, especially as it relates to CalArts and the Woman's Building. I'm indebted to Nancy Buchanan and Terry Wolverton for bringing their first-hand experiences into the classroom and to Rachel Rosenthal and Barbara Smith for connecting their work with the work of the Building and the feminist art movement, and in turn enlightening my students. The efforts of these artists to directly engage these students has allowed this feminist history—to which they are connected simply by enrolling at CalArts—to become tangible and visceral and to remain at their fingertips.

2.

To further explore the students' relationships to feminism and feminist art history, I chose to engage in a form of dialogue with a group of graduate and undergraduate women who studied at CalArts from approximately 2000 to 2007. Conducted largely through e-mail, I posed a series of questions and invited their responses. Those responses reveal a group of women who have grown up within an American culture that is deeply ambivalent about the term "feminist." Our exchanges reveal a group of women who have inherited (sometimes without knowing it) a legacy that allows them to construct themselves as women artists in any way they see fit. And they reveal a group of women whose range of art making supersedes that of the generations preceding them and who only sometimes must directly address the quandary of how to negotiate the feminine perspective in one's art and one's life. These women understand that they must make a choice about their identity in relationship to their art making, but their decisions, by and large, will not be driven by the question "Am I a feminist?" but rather by "What kind of feminist am I?"

My special thanks go to the participants in this dialogue. The range of their responses partially can be attributed to the range of disciplines they represent, as some fields have a more direct link to "second-wave feminism." Visual art in particular, having been at the forefront of this movement, has made major strides. Others, still dominated by men, have not created the opportunities to match the visual art's engagement in feminist art making and dialogue, and the basic education of women. The participants are composer/vocalist Julie Adler (JA), visual artist Nicole Antebi (NA), photographer/

filmmaker Diane Arellano (DA), musician Erin Breen (EB), vocalist Nina Sun Eidsheim (NSE), theater and film director Rachel Goldberg (RG), performance artist Christine Gump (CG), multimedia artist Carole Kim (CK), artist/performer Alanna Lin (AL), visual artist Theresa Masangkay (TM), and visual artist Melissa J. Regas (MJR).

3.

What follows are the questions I posed to these students, a selection of their responses, and my own commentary in response to them.

In your own unique way/style, please describe how you think (or don't think) of yourself as a feminist OR an artist who is a feminist OR a feminist artist OR perhaps a female artist. (If none of the above use your own description.)

I think of myself as an artist who happens to be of the female gender. (MJR)

I essentially equate intelligence with feminism. I know the world doesn't abide by this equation but I'm always a bit shocked, at least initially, when an intelligent person is not a feminist. Feminism is part of who I am, how I perceive the world around me, how I move within this world. (CK)

I am an artist. I am a woman. Neither excludes the other, nor are they mutually inclusive. (RG)

I'd say "female artist" is fine with me. The title of "female" has never had me feeling alienated from anything, misrepresented or tied to anything. (CG)

I have found that contextualizing myself as a feminist artist invariably predetermines the work. To avoid hypocrisy, I subscribe to the idea of becoming both a woman and an artist. (NA)

Yes, becoming. Honoring the process of discovering what one is for oneself. Why use the term "feminist" for oneself: Is it a gift or a Girl Scout honor badge? Is it something to be earned, something to be embraced, something to be enveloped by? Is its meaning something to be understood, studied? Who will help you understand its past, present, and future? Does it need to be taught? Or in the current contemporary context, can we assume that in a young woman's journey to define her self-identity as an artist she will have the access, and the desire, to seek the tools and knowledge she needs, and therefore she should be left to her own creative devices, experiences, and discoveries?

Nicole Antebi, *Invisible Inflatable/Deflatable Monument: Russian Church, Jerusalem,* 2002.
Mixed media, dimensions variable. Photograph by Anthony Cunha. © Nicole Antebi.

Julie Adler, *Inbedded*, 1998. Still image from video/performance, Valencia, California. Photograph by Lara Bank. © Julie Adler.

I am a female artist. As time goes by, I find myself [and]...my surroundings emphasize the fact that I am a woman. The Gaze follows me. How would my days and life be carried out in its absence? Is there life outside, or is the Gaze the creator of "female life?" How has the gaze influenced me, shaped me as an artist?... Much of the Western Classical repertoire sustains the myth of the lethargic woman, the witch/crazy woman in its opera literature.... The stereo-type of the "soprano" is imbedded in the opera literature. The voice category "soprano" is used in roles such as the naïve young girl subject to an old pig's desire (Susanna), and the temptress who leads the male astray from his socially sanctioned principles (Carmen)....As a woman and a performer, I am performing for a gaze that has been engrained by socialization. And now, actively playing around and working with this issue, I find that going too far away from the roles the carrier of the gaze offers, one finds oneself erased. (NSE)

I worked with what was a sense of woman caged, silenced, struggling to make sound or com-municate, a woman on a pedestal, or stuck in a bed, hidden, alien, full of desire for speech and to be heard. That it can be labeled "feminist" because it represents the position of a woman struggling for her "rights"; that these social and political implications are evident in my work is absolutely fine by me. I think that to be feminist is to advance the "cause" of women in general, to continue to expose and then root out all the inequalities and inequities that still exist in the world between men and women. As long as there are women still covered from head to toe in burkas or beaten down by rules and social platitudes, feminism should exist. (JA)

394

How did you grow up with the term "feminist?" Who influenced how you respond to that term? How American is your response to the term? And as you grow as an artist, how will your perspective change, especially as you meet other woman from other worlds, other cultures?

I have never considered myself a feminist, which I imagine comes from growing up in the late eighties, when all the hard work seemed to have been completed. I must have taken feminism for granted, imagining that it related to women's suffrage or wearing pants. "Feminism" to me suggested something far short of "equality"; the feminists we heard of were full of hatred, raging male bashers loudly seeking the disempowerment of men. The concept sounded whiny and somehow weak.... I loathed the generalizations that were associated with the expression and avoided it accordingly until this survey. I am realizing now that feminist art denotes something much farther reaching than feminism and that it absolutely applies to me as a musician and will continue to apply to me in a still fairly male-dominated field. (EB)

I do identify as a feminist artist. I feel [gaining] ownership of my feminist artist identity has and continues to be a complex journey. I began to consider the idea that perhaps women weren't quite "equal" during my undergraduate experience. In a film lighting class consisting of about fifteen students, I was one of two female students. Our male instructor often used the other female student and myself as the film subjects. The problem with always being the subject is that we could not see our instructor explain lighting, since we were often the diagram he pointed out to the male students. [C]onsequently, the education of our male peers resulted at the expense of our own.... Prior to this experience, I never really believed women had reached full or true equality but I didn't think I would ever have such blatant gender discrimination experiences. I feel lucky that in time I was able to process these experiences and emerge as person committed to gender equality and social justice. I look back on my baptism by fire experience as necessary to becoming a critical thinker. (DA)

Since starting at CalArts, in 2005, in the MFA in Art program, I have been asking myself about my relationship with the word "Feminist." I'm constantly questioning the word, whether or not I need it, or belong to it. And my thoughts about it are changing every day. (TM)

A young Muslim student of mine was living inside what I would consider to be the contradiction of becoming an independent, university-educated woman and continuing to practice a religion that, in my opinion, not only separates men and women but also regards her role in that practice to be less important than her male counterpart. Her commitment to both worlds was so complete that she could seamlessly move from one to the other and stunningly fully integrate these two spheres within her own mind and body. For the time being, she had learned to negotiate the complex territory that allowed her to become fully realized academically but that simultaneously demanded her acquiescence to a religious system that defines participation according to gender.

395

The majority of women whom I know from college and graduate school settings generally identify themselves with what I now distinguish as "secular-feminism." As an adult convert to Catholicism, I have often been assumed to be outside of self-respecting feminist woman-hood.... It has been my good fortune to fall upon a community of Trappist, feminist nuns who have led me to a lexicon for which I have been searching a very long time. I am a feminist in that I believe in the inherent mutuality and equality of the sexes as metaphorical resources in the depiction of God's image in the world. Humanity—all men, all women—are together the sacred likeness of God in the world and should be respected and cherished. (AL)

As we witness the seemingly contradictory complications our students and colleagues experience, we must work to reconsider what it means to be a feminist. If one of feminism's goals is to free women to become truly who they are and to act in any way they feel or see fit (and as long as their individual and collective choices do not erode or undermine historical feminist achievements) then we must accept those woman and those acts in the spirit of those goals. The power of this acceptance will be a gift that embraces any and all versions of intelligently self-defined womanhood as acted upon by current and future generations of women—American and otherwise.

Please describe the general attitude towards feminism of your fellow artists, students, etc.

This question is tricky because quite honestly it is not brought up. I have never worked on any projects with someone who was vocal about being feminist. The strong women I have encountered in my travels certainly frowned upon feminism as a movement, preferring to do their own art in their best capacity, completely unconcerned with labeling it or themselves. If I had to generalize, most young men and women recoil at the term, anticipating the quality of an overtly feminist artistic work to be more like a pamphlet or tirade. (EB)

I find my more successful artist friends are very aware of gender, race, and class social dynamics and often utilize these issues within their respective art practices. On the other hand, my friends who have a superficial understanding...seem more confused and even bitter. I think they don't have the necessary tools to process their experiences, and personalize instead of analyzing or questioning. I really do think it's critical that women artists are educated on our/their history. I believe this education should encompass women of all racial, economic, and sexual preference backgrounds. It's critical that young women artists are exposed to the process of owning and accepting our collective experiences and narratives; otherwise we risk needlessly struggling to conform to fields or disciplines that have their own particular histories of embracing or rejecting women artists. (DA)

Above: **Alanna Lin, *Mindy Chiu with Hairbrush*.** 2006. Digital print. © Alanna Lin

Left: **Erin Breen, performance artist, Paul Kirby and Nans Kelder, set designers, *Vanishing Currents*.** 2005. Image includes partial view of set design on tall ship Amara Zee. Lafitte, LA . See video at www.caravanstage.org. Photograph by Erin Breen.

It seems that three-fourths of the people I meet think that "Feminism" was a temporary wave during the seventies and that the activism led to full equality between men and women. The remaining one-fourth is a greatly varied group ranging from feminist activists to "patriarchic leaning" men. (NSE)

Generally, my peers are either apathetic or displeased with the seventies feminist model for action. The criticism seems to be located in the vulnerability facing the author of a personal work and the alienation of men. However, there is a firm acknowledgement of the [women's] movement's impact on the positions that women occupy today. (NA)

There are a lot of women around now who are consistently outside of any discrimination for their sex… their work is empowered in both feminine and masculine ways… women aren't as afraid to use masculinity in work…it's sexy, and stimulating…the confidence it instills has become stunning to the senses of both men and women.[2] (CT)

Actually, I came to CalArts not knowing how conceptual the direction of the visual arts department was. My art practice had been evolving very "organically" and "intuitively," words associated with the "female." I use these words deliberately because they were verboten in class critiques. Teachers would actually cringe at hearing these two words spoken. I was making art without having the concept/idea come first in any logical form. And I was very interested in not being "mental" about it. I write all this because my attitude in conjunction with my body/ self in the art made me "feminist" but apparently stuck in the seventies. It was as if the faculty (my mentors) had positioned me in the past, that we were now beyond the self-absorbed, sexually tinged, expressionistic, and potentially "essentialist" work of the seventies, and it was up to me to transcend this "platform" and move forward into the postmodern, deconstructed view of feminism. No definitions were actually given for what that was supposed to be. (JA)

What I am trying to get at is that there is a "generalized feminism," which has generalized notions of equality and what women deserve, that often seems myopically self-centered and not tied into the greater implications of feminism that have been recently and explicitly articulated to me. Feminism, like religion, is easily flattened by a literalization of its symbols. Is Feminism about womyn's will to power? The right to unlimited minutes with cell phone and dildo and other metonyms for liberated womanhood? Is it about defeating false notions of "otherness"? Is it about social justice, human justice? I think there is a cacophony under the umbrella of feminism, and while most of us benefit from the real political achievements of feminism, plenty of us are divorced from an intimate consideration of what it's all about. (AL)

I feel that we all have different ideas about what Feminism is. Sometimes I like to call it "Feminisms." But through organizing/curating the symposium and exhibition at CalArts (Exquisite Acts & Everyday Rebellions: 2007 CalArts Feminist Art Project), I find my fellow artists (alumni, faculty, and students) are willing and excited to have a discourse about their own idea of Feminism. (TM)

The term "feminism" still proves to be much more problematic than one would hope. I find that my peers, students, and friends are either hesitant to align themselves as feminists and/or feel the need to qualify their relationship to the term.... I don't know whether coining a new term would be effective. Certainly, persisting to educate and inform is necessary. (CK)

Perhaps what's lacking today is the opportunity to reinvent, redefine, and even possibly reassert the right to reconsider the term "feminist" in a group and/or collaborative process in order to create work that lives within the context of feminist art practice but also intersects with, is in dialogue with, and is enlivened by other movements, histories, and practices.

We can collectively look back, but can we collectively look forward? Feminist art as a term has ridden a slippery slope as it has moved from generation to generation. It has been left to the individual artist to define the term for herself. Furthermore, the splintering of our contemporary lives into infinitesimal interests and the pursuit of these interests as individual acts do not support an entire generation of artists collectively redefining what feminism means. I only ask then that young women be given the opportunity to study its permutations and as a contemporary artist choose wisely how you would like to use it in relationship to either yourself or your art making or both.

Have you been educated about the seventies feminist art movement in any way, shape, or form? If yes, how has that history influenced you and your work? What parts of the legacy of this movement are useful to you as a contemporary artist, and which are not?

Yes, I have been educated in this art movement. In some ways it feels like a blip on the landscape. And yet it was very much connected to other events/happenings/artistry.... I feel camaraderie with what the women did then. It's nice to have the lineage behind me. But, unfortunately, I don't feel the community these women may have felt back then. To me, that communal spirit is gone in the art world, in terms of women's work specifically. If I work from emotion and impulse, in alignment with those of the past, I am happy to follow that legacy. (JA)

Did the Woman's Building serve its purpose (for its time) and then allow its shockwaves to spread out and affect whoever is in the path of the aftershocks? Culture-specific institutions within the art world have sustained themselves much better than feminist institutions, yet this doesn't mean than institutions that are built on a feminist or feminine network of ideas, visions, and concepts should not be envisioned and built.

Theresa Masangkay, still of right channel of *Pop*, 2006. Two-channel video, Super 8 transferred to digital video, 11 minutes. © Theresa Masangkay.

Rachel Goldberg, director, *Salome*, 2001. Interdisciplinary production using film, puppetry, masks, and music, Raven Theatre, Los Angeles. Photographs by Sean Higgins. © Rachel Goldberg.

There's no question for me that my predecessors have helped pave the way to my being able to be the person I am today. (CK)

I have not been educated about the seventies feminist art movement in any way, shape, or form. I'm interested, but have never read about it on my own. (RG)

While attending CalArts, I was told first-hand accounts of Judy Chicago and Miriam Schapiro's legacy there. They introduced fiber arts and crafts as legitimate materials for producing art objects. This is integral to my practice. Parts of the movement that are not useful to me are the claims about gender distinctions. (NA)

I have absolutely not been educated about the feminist art movement. The most I have heard about this genre of art is within my first semester of graduate school at CalArts. (EB)

My most formal education in the seventies feminist movement has been at CalArts, in Theresa Chavez's "RE: Inventing the Wheel" class, through lecturers and visiting artists. My contact with feminist works has been from photos documenting performances or exhibitions, video documentaries, manifestos, articles, and books. Being in a dialogue with other women's work is pertinent to feeling a sense of creative and critical community. (NSE)

I find having a sense of history and a sense of [what] my artistic predecessors accomplished or how they were hindered by their gender useful and inspirational. I make it a point to keep in mind that the most successful women were often viewed as the most outrageous, indecent, and audacious women within what is considered their most productive periods. I can't recount anything I learned about women artists that isn't useful. (DA)

I have been educated about the seventies feminist art movement, especially through my study of Judy Chicago. Through reading her autobiography, I learned about discrimination towards female artists in college as well as the art world of galleries and art magazines. I admire and am thankful for the influence of the Woman's Building. It was a place that provided a voice of confidence, inspiration, and courage for female artists. (MJR)

I took a critical studies class with Christine Wertheim (Fall 2006) titled "Womanhouse: CalArts, Feminism, and the Arts." We read articles from The Power of Feminist Art,[3] *discussed feminist theory, and had conscious-raising groups. What influenced me the most, other than the intimate conversations we had, was reading an essay by Yolanda M. Lopez and Moira Roth.[4] I really appreciate that they were aware of their own personal connection with Feminism, questioned its history, and decided to write an essay that focused on what they thought needed to be included. (TM)*

Is it the legacy of the Woman's Building that feminist art is a living, breathing, evolving form reshaped by each generation of women who choose to make art? Young artists who are feminists or feminist art makers have evolved in such different environments from their predecessors that they are almost like two different animals. In the present tense, feminism has become a fluctuating act of redefinition within the context of one's personal and professional circumstance, geography, culture, etc. In the past tense, we can locate feminism and discuss it through the act of stopping time and focusing on a specific historical moment. In the future tense, in order to further its evolution we must be in dialogue with third-wave *feministas*.

If you had a "room of your own" what would it ideally look like? Describe how it would be a part of a larger space (building, network, community) or be its own independent space.

In a rural setting, perhaps a large converted barn or warehouse-type building, but set in a very beautiful, natural location, away from any big city environment. This space would have a baby grand piano (my grandmother's, actually), and a recording room, complete with computer, audio equipment, and sound-proof booth. Another part of the space would be made into a visual arts work/studio space, complete with walls for drawings, paintings, and a large work-table and shelves for objects and collected items.

This building would be linked to my main residence and there would also be a yoga room, and a meditation room, perhaps to accommodate groups of people. As well as envisioning my own residence and art/work space, I would like to be able to create an arts residence center (on the same property?) where people could come on retreat to make their own artworks but have opportunities to sit in meditation twice daily, eat together at meals, and come to evening dharma (Buddhist teachings) talks. So, built into the arts residency would be development of community, dialogue, and spiritual practice. (JA)

A space similar to Judy Chicago and Miriam Schapiro's vision of Womanhouse. *However, each room would be in a constant state of flux or reinvention. The space would realize an ever-expanding, rhizomatic site similar to that of the Winchester Mystery House or the Internet.[5] (NA)*

I will be Dominatrix. In the space there'll be paper figures true-to-life size, including Beethoven, Stravinsky, Boulez, and Elvis Presley. This can presented as a film, or on a stage level with the audience. Maybe taped text (my voice) talking about my relationship to them. Maybe taped voices talking about them, or musical or written quotes by them. I will do funny things to the paper-men, return the Gaze—not really the gaze, but play with them like chess bricks. I think the space/film should be saturated with really funky music while I perform these actions, a series of performances. (NSE)

Christine Gump, *Gumplestiltskin*, 2005. Performance at American Circus, International Cultural Tourism Festival, Beijing, China. © Christine Gump.

I am not sure if "room of your own" is in reference to the feminist movement. I am not familiar with the term. I believe it means if I could have my own ideal space, what would it be. Ideally, I would like my room to be part of a larger space, in terms of network and community. I would love to create a space open to artists of all disciplines, where artists could pursue their mediums for free (i.e., darkrooms for photographers, stages for theater artists, easels and studios for painters, recording studios for musicians, etc.). In exchange, they would teach classes to local children for free and be active in community outreach and schools. Hopefully, the space would foster collaboration between different art forms, the community at large with the artists, students, and teachers, adults and children. It would have a gallery, stages, and screening rooms. It would invite artists from all over the world and from all sensibilities to share their work and create in this space. It would be difficult to find such a space and develop the funding to support it, but this would be a "room of my own" which would hopefully be a room for all. (RG)

Envisioning an ideal room of my own would be more a conceptual space than an actual, physical, architectural space. It would mean a shift in scale and access to people (and the time people would be able to devote to any given project), resources, equipment, and materials. The same issues of interaction and collaboration would come into play. (CK)

My dream room would be a wide-open space in the midst of a public park. The four inside walls would be covered with a mural of a digital image facing each other of me swimming in a sunset. My room is a pathway where people walk through into another environment filled with the aspiration that anything is possible with an open heart and imagination. Then when people leave the room, they will see their original environment in a new light. Using my room as a place where others can feel at home and inspired to live their dreams would fulfill my goal as an artist. (MJR)

A room of unlimited technical expertise and tools…state of the art…a place to explore myself and my work inside the possibilities of the future….(CG)

I would like to see a community-based space working towards developing young women filmmakers, screenwriters, and playwrights of color. I feel these disciplines continue to be male dominated and often exclude the voices of women of color. Particularly in film, the perspectives of women of color continue to be severely underrepresented. I think developing young, female filmmakers and screenwriters is a step toward achieving mainstream representation (portrayals of Latina, African-American, Asian, and Native American women in film) through a variety of perspectives. (DA)

A stage on one end, not too high...maybe the floor is just a few inches higher and it is acoustically engineered. There ARE windows, but they can be blacked out quickly and easily. There are couches and rearrange-able chairs to seat seventy to one hundred people. Everything is moveable so we can have dance lessons or art exhibits. We are in the middle of a medium-sized town, active members of the community. There are education programs in loads of disciplines and writing workshops and book releases and a big kitchen and an outdoor amphitheater and visiting artists and photography and a million adventures! (EB)

Inside my Broad Studio [at CalArts]. And the larger space would be the campus. I often feel very comfortable here. It's a place that I can often be myself and at the same time constantly question who that person is. (TM)

Nancy Pelosi has just become the first woman Speaker of the House of Representatives of the U.S. Congress. An extraordinary feat. We as women are impressed and pleased. Yet despite its standing as an democratic institution, congress still exists within a

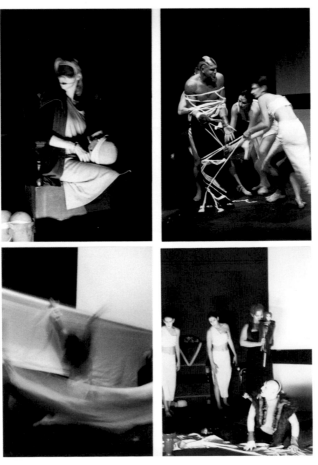

Carole Kim, *Chasing the Pools*, 2005. Still from live-feed performance-based installation in the pine tree grove at Barnsdall Art Park, Hollywood, CA (dancer: Shuriu Lo, live camera: Maile Colbert, live mix: Pablo Molina). © 2005, Carole Kim.

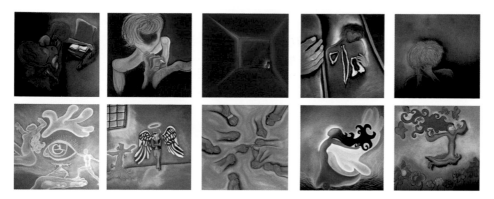

Melissa J. Regas, *Why Happy, Why Sad*, 2008. Painting series, collection of 10 paintings, mixed media on canvas, 4' x 4' each. © Melissa Regas.

monolithic, masculine framework and one could make the case that it has become corrupted by this particular framework. Pelosi has become part of it. It has already been created, and no matter how many women are elected to serve in it, the institution itself will always be primarily defined by its framers. This is why it is extremely important that institutions created by woman that forward a feminist framework exist and be preserved either as institutions or within the public historical archive and dialogue. These institutions have and will approach the great questions of humanity and the environment in their own unique manner. And they will provide solutions that represent an entirely different set of assumptions and strategies.

4.

Dear Julie, Nicole, Diane, Erin, Nina, Rachel, Christine, Carole, Alanna, Theresa, and Melissa,

The basic fact that all of you are still practicing the act of making art, still voicing an artistic point of view, and still envisioning a self that moves through the world as an agile spirit seeking the freedom to express yourself creatively is a minor miracle. For the most part, you have no internal questions about whether you have the right to practice, voice, envision, move, seek, and express within yourself and within the institutions you must negotiate in order to be an artist in the United States. There are only the external questions raised by the cultures of which we are part, collectively and individually, that in some antiquated way continue to seek to control our right to express and create and be recognized for the artistic work we do.

The different historical contexts of our lives cannot help but influence who we are and how we see ourselves. I can only offer you my story of how I got here and you can impart yours to me. This act of exchange does not cancel out our experience, it only broadens our sense of who we are as women, as human beings, as artists.

I consider myself lucky to have grown up in a turbulent time when the Civil Rights Movement was forcing a reconsideration of the entire structure of American society.

I am a Chicana. I can say that without equivocation. I was able to add this to my identity because I grew up during the time "Chicano" was first defined. It was revolutionary and its worldview struck a chord that continues to resonate throughout my body.

I am a feminist. I can say that without equivocation. I was able to add this to my identity because I grew up during the time "feminist," as in "second-wave feminist," was first defined. It was revolutionary and its worldview struck a chord that continues to resonate throughout my body.

But I realize that the social contract for the mutually agreed upon definition of certain terms such as "feminist" has expired. So I pass it onto you to redefine and use as you may. But use or don't use it thoughtfully, with a mix of bold political stance, conscious social context, informed historical reference, and enlightened personal choice.

I consider it a measure of our accomplishment that women of your generation have such choices.

In Sisterhood (as we once would have said),

Theresa

5.

As of this writing, in 2007, many of the CalArts students quoted in this essay are now CalArts alumnae. Their thoughts here are in response to their experience as CalArts students. As they've evolved as artists and as women, their relationship to feminism and/or to a feminist art practice continues to evolve. As CalArts continues to question its own racial and gender inequities, I find their responses still timely and pertinent.

CalArts generally does not promote its relationship to feminist art history, but it doesn't shy away from it either. In March of 2007, the institute supported a student-organized symposium and exhibition titled Exquisite Acts & Everyday Rebellions: 2007 CalArts Feminist Art Project. The project is primarily supported by the School of Art (along with the Office of the President and the Student Council). Greatly due to its faculty, the School of Art has offered its students many opportunities to discover the feminist history hidden beneath the official record and has encouraged its students to explore how it is relevant to them in the present tense.

Exquisite Acts & Everyday Rebellions was conceived in response to the spring 2007 exhibition *WACK! Art and the Feminist Revolution*, at the Museum of Contemporary Art, Los Angeles. It is in some respects a watershed year for the recognition by American museums of the influence feminist art has now had on several generations of artists, both in the United States and abroad. Along with MOCA's major show, New York's Museum of Modern Art (MoMA) and the Brooklyn Museum are organizing symposiums and exhibitions that, in their own important yet parochial way, will surely illuminate the primary brand of American "second-wave feminism" generated mostly by a revolutionary band of white, middle- and upper-class women. As economics allow, a major and more diverse set of women is emerging to study and professionally create contemporary art. This national shift, which is a true reflection of demographics in the United States, will continue to produce an evolution of feminist art practice that I greatly look forward to experiencing.

Inevitably, as young female artists do not have to confront their disciplinary headmasters in regards to whether they have the right to simply pursue a creative practice, their need to self-define as feminists has been diluted. As to whether their work should be defined as feminist has in some ways become a separate and perhaps more crucial matter. Some of the responses published here give reason to assume that young artists have to some degree assimilated a point of view that is derived from "second-wave feminism" but that is also intriguingly and uniquely informed by their own state of being. They have much to teach us.

Biographies of the Respondents

JULIE ADLER is an artist working in the mediums of music (voice and composition), painting, drawing, and writing. She is a graduate of Cooper Union and w222q. In the past, she was coproducer of EARJAM, a new music festival; Vocal Lounge; and Call & Response, a concert featuring new music works and Tibetan monks. Recent activities include travel to India, China, and Eastern Tibet and working on projects related to Tibet and Tibetan Buddhism, including as coproducer of *Living Wisdom with His Holiness the Dalai Lama* (Sounds True, 2006) and contributing assistant to *Portraits of Tibetan Buddhist Masters* (UC Press, 2005). She is now associate producer on "The Tibet Connection," a monthly radio program on KPFK (Radio Pacifica) (http://www.thetibetconnection.org). Examples of past music work can be found on http://-www.my space.com/julieadler.

NICOLE ANTEBI is a Los Angeles-based visual artist. Her work about the Salton Sea was exhibited at Kristi Engle Gallery and the Dallas Contemporary in 2007. Additional collaborative projects include *Failure! Experiments in Aesthetic and Social Practices* (co-edited with Colin Dickey and Robby Herbst) and the exhibition *Failure Ridiculous Terrible Wonderful at Park Projects* (co-organized with Robby Herbst and Irene Tsatsos); http://registry.whitecolumns.org/view_artist.php?artist=2613 and/or www.hausgallery.com

ERIN BREEN completed her BFA in clarinet performance at Carnegie Mellon University in 2003. She spent two years working with a circus theater company, performing as an actress and multi-instrumentalist with aerialists, actors, and videographers. The shows are performed on the deck of a ship and the audience watches from shore. At the time of writing, Erin is in her first year of the master's program at CalArts, focusing her studies on the collaborative process in performance art while studying clarinet, saxophone, and flute.

DIANE ARELLANO received her bachelor's degree from CalArts in 2005. Diane's work investigates the social dynamics that arise from nuanced yet fundamentally blanket generalizations of race, class, and gender that persist in mainstream cultures. Diane's carefully woven narratives of a transforming, illusive, and oftentimes indefinable Latino identity are most frequently contextualized within the boundaries of Los Angeles County.

RACHEL GOLDBERG earned her MFA in Directing for Film and Theatre from CalArts and her BA in Theatre and Psychology from the University of Pennsylvania. She recently taught Acting Technique and Scene Study at the University of Pennsylvania's Summer Academy, attended the Lincoln Center's Directors Lab as an invited playwright, and had the great pleasure of working with Quentin Tarantino in the editing department of *Kill Bill Vol. 2*. Rachel was also the assistant director on a staged production of The Resistible Rise of Arturo Ui, starring Jason Alexander, Noah Wyle, and Harry Hamlin. As a member of Film Outreach LA, Rachel was a key player in the inception of a program dedicated to providing at-risk youth in the Los Angeles area with film-making skills and mentors. Her original scripts for both stage and film have won or reached finalist status in many festivals around the country.

CHRISTINE GUMP performs as Kitty Gump in Trash Band (http://www.trashband.net) and works on stilts in Gumplestiltskin, which is devoted to eccentric and one-of-a-kind performances (http://www.gumplestiltskin.com); she cofounded both groups with her husband. She is in her final year of a Master's in Traditional Chinese Medicine. She believes this is a direct progression from her work as a performance artist, with Chinese medicine being a deeper level of human integration and experience utilizing the emotional and spiritual body to express a message of healing.

CAROLE KIM is an interdisciplinary artist with a focus on performance-based video installation combining digital/new media technologies and the sensitivity of the improvisational live performer/participant. Her work emphasizes video's capacity as a live medium and the illusory architecture of layered video projection in space. More recent works have introduced the live presence of dancers into this layered landscape, mediating the body while preserving the dynamic edge of the live performer. The performances are immersive environments that often explore a decentralized performance space that supports an integrated reciprocal exchange between sound, image, movement, and space.

ALANNA LIN is a writer/performer-at-large on the Internet and Los Angeles and vicinity, operating under the project moniker "Fascinoma," a.k.a. "Mindy Chiu." She loosely runs LTBB (Little Tokyo Bed and Breakfast), an artist's rehearsal/recording workshop out of Downtown Los Angeles, and between 10:00 a.m. and 3:00 p.m. daily, she can be found at Michael Mangia's foundation for innovation in the arts and promotion of the arts, Orphan Records. Her website is defunct, her MySpace page hosts "improvised musics," and her blog can be found all too easily—Google: Mindy Chiu. She doesn't sleep, eats too much bacon, and has been diagnosed as being in love.

THERESA MASANGKAY is a Los Angeles-born artist who works primarily in painting and video. Her work investigates time, memory, language, and power. She is currently an MFA candidate at the CalArts, where she is the co-organizer and cocurator of Exquisite Acts & Everyday Rebellions: 2007 CalArts Feminist Art Project. Theresa has also received a post-baccalaureate in painting and drawing from the School of the Art Institute of Chicago, and her BA from the University of California, Irvine.

MELISSA J. REGAS obtained her BFA from CalArts in December 2001 and received subsequent training in media arts and animation at the Art Institute of California, San Diego. Currently, she is a freelance graphic and fine artist. Her recent group show at Script Memorial Hospital, *Artful Healing Program: Series II*, was presented by Studio Vivace. Melissa is also teaching art to children ages three to five at the San Diego State University Children's Center. Melissa has a severe to profound bilateral hearing loss and lives between the Deaf/Hard-of-Hearing and Hearing cultures. As a user of sign language, the historical clichés of gender and culture signs became increasingly disturbing to her. This inspired her to search for an unbiased approach that evolved into a new model: Peoples' Sign Language (PSL). As an artist/performer and advocate for PSL, she has created a video series that address various proposals to invite dialogue and suggest new options (http://www.mjrhoneybeecreations.com).

NINA SUN EIDSHEIM is a scholar, performer, and assistant professor in the UCLA Department of Musicology. She is particularly interested in the performative aspects of the production, reception, and perception of vocal timbre; her research examines aspects of the voice and its inferred meaning in opera, popular music, and music technology through the lenses of American and African-American studies, performance, culture, gender, and race. Currently she is preparing a book manuscript tentatively titled *Musicology in the Flesh: An Essay on Voice, Body and Affect*. Inspired in part by her work as a genre-crossing singer working within contemporary classical repertoire, improvisation, and live electronic performance, Eidsheim is dedicated to an interdisciplinary and multi-modular approach to the study of musical cultures. As part of this effort, she composes, commissions, and produces music with her electro-acoustic ensemble, soNu. The ensemble's most recent large-scale collaborative work was an opera written by composer Anne Lebaron and librettist Douglas Kearney, which was premiered at REDCAT in Los Angeles (http://adagio.calarts.edu/virtualcage/?page_id=1424).

Notes

1. The Woman's Building was founded in 1973 by Chicago and two other CalArts faculty, Arlene Raven and Sheila Levrant de Bretteville, partly due to the sexism they and their female students encountered at CalArts.

2. Ellipses are in original text.

3. Norma Broude and Mary D. Garrard, eds., *The Power of Feminist Art: The American Movement of the 1970s, History and Impact* (New York: Harry N. Abrams, Inc. 1994).

4. Yolanda M. Lopez and Moira Roth, "Social Protest: Racism and Sexism," in *The Power of Feminist Art*.

5. The Winchester Mystery House, located in San Jose, California, was built by Sarah Winchester, the heiress to the Winchester Rifle fortune, and was under continuous construction from 1884 to 1922. Winchester believed the house was haunted by the ghosts of those who'd been killed by Winchester rifles, and that only continuous construction would appease them. The mansion has 160 rooms and includes inexplicable features such as doorways and staircases that lead to nowhere. It is currently a tourist attraction.

Betty Ann Brown is an art historian, critic, and curator. She received her Doctor of Philosophy in Latin American art history in 1977. In the late seventies, her interest shifted from Aztec art to Chicano art and, ultimately, to all contemporary art. Her books include *Exposures, Women & Their Art*, coauthored with critic Arlene Raven and photographer Kenna Love; the edited *Expanding Circles: Women, Surrealism & Art History*; and the electronic format textbook, *Art & Mass Media*, coauthored with Robert Pelfrey. Her current research examines how artists are portrayed in the mass media. Brown is a Professor of Art History at California State University, Northridge, where she has taught since 1986.

Theresa Chavez is an interdisciplinary theater artist based in Los Angeles. She is cofounder and artistic director of About Productions (www.aboutpd.org). Under her direction, the company has engaged with numerous communities and cultural, educational, and artistic institutions in the greater Los Angeles area, as well as nationally, in the production and presentation of innovative performance/theater works and educational programs. Chavez has directed, co-written, and produced numerous original theater and performance works, including the critically acclaimed *By the Hand of the Father*, which was broadcast nationally on PBS television. A published playwright, she was included in *Women Playwrights of Diversity*, a book that describes the work of ninety women identified by professional theaters or scholars as significant voices in theater. From 1991 to 2007, she directed and taught in the California Institute of the Arts Interdisciplinary Studies program.

Sheila Levrant de Bretteville develops site-specific, permanent public projects that have become increasingly participatory and open ended. Her earliest public art projects, *Biddy Mason: Time & Place* and *Omoide noShotokyo*, in Los Angeles, deliver some of the hidden history and everyday lives of people at each site. Most recently . . . , her interactive LED project in Hong Kong, and *Step(pe)*, in Yekaterinburg, Russia, extend an invitation to their local populations to participate through the inclusion of open-ended, changeable parts. Participation as part of the work itself informed many seventies print projects, such as *Pink*, and it reemerges in her public art projects, for example in the "lazy Susan" table in *Take a break . . . Out to lunch . . . Back to work*, at the Rhode Island Department of Labor and Training, and in the sparkling ellipses throughout *At the start . . . At long last . . .* , at New York's A train terminus. In 1990, de Bretteville became the first woman to be tenured at the Yale School of Art; in 2010, she was honored by being given an endowed chair, aptly named Caroline M. Street Professor of Art.

Cecilia Dougherty is an artist working in video, photography, and web applications. Areas of interest include women's rights, feminist theory, and woman's place in the new global (dis)order; queer identities and sexualities; spaces, architecture, everyday life, and globalization; and social networking, digital activism, and new media. She has had numerous shows, screenings, and retrospectives. She is also a writer who has published essays, reviews, artist's pages, poetry, and fiction in anthologies and journals including *Radical Light: Alternative Film and Video in the San Francisco Bay Area, 1945–2000*, *Felix XXX*, *Nest*, *Millennium Film Journal*, *Afterimage*, *Swingset*, *Film Comment*, *Artbyte*, *New Art Examiner*, *Blocnotes*, and *Framework*. Her work has been written about and cited in books including *Lesbian Art in America*, by

Harmony Hammond; *Chick Flicks*, by B. Ruby Rich; and *Time Binds: Queer Temporalities, Queer Histories*, by Elizabeth Freeman. Additional book and journal citations include *Contemporary Quilt Art*, by Kate Lenkowsky, *Art in America*, *The Village Voice*, *Gay and Lesbian Quarterly*, *Artweek*, *Film Comment*, and *High Performance* magazine, among others. Currently, Dougherty is Core Faculty at the Milton Avery Graduate School of the Arts, Bard College, and faculty at the International Center of Photography, New York. She lives in Brooklyn, New York.

Sondra Hale is Professor of Anthropological and Women's Studies at University of California, Los Angeles. When she is not doing research on women's movements in the Middle East and Africa, she works on critical art theories within feminist, postcolonial, and cultural studies. She has curated multicultural art exhibitions, written numerous catalog essays, and taught African criticism at California Institute of the Arts. In 1985, she edited *The House of Women: Art and Culture in the Eighties*. Hale, a Vesta Award winner, was an active figure at the Woman's Building in the eighties, serving on the board of directors, teaching seminars on art critical theories, and co-organizing a Woman's Building national conference, The Way We Look, the Way We See: Art Criticism for Women in the '90s. She is currently writing a book on Sudanese modernist artists in exile.

Jennie Klein is an associate professor at Ohio University, where she teaches contemporary art history and feminist art theory. She has published in *n. paradoxa*, *PAJ*, *Art Papers*, *Genders*, *Feminist Studies*, *Journal of Lesbian Studies*, and *New Art Examiner*. She is presently completing a coedited book on performance art, and is the editor of *Letters from Linda M. Montano* (Routledge, 2005) and coeditor with Myrel Chernick of *The M Word: Real Mothers in Contemporary Art* (Demeter Press, 2011). She has presented her work nationally and internationally, most recently in Kuopio, Finland.

Michele Kort is senior editor of *Ms.* magazine. A longtime journalist in Los Angeles, she is also the author of three books, including the biography *Soul Picnic: The Music and Passion of Laura Nyro*. She is coauthor of the forthcoming anthology *Here Come the Brides: The Brave New World of Lesbian Marriage*. Way back in the mid-seventies, she was the comanager of the Woman's Building for a year and a half, and remained connected with the Building for many years after that as an extension program teacher and advisory board member.

Lucy R. Lippard is a writer, activist, and author of twenty-one books (including one novel) on contemporary art and cultural criticism. She is the cofounder of a number of activist artists' groups, including Ad Hoc Women Artists' Committee, Heresies collective and *Heresies* journal, Political Art Documentation/Distribution (PAD/D), and Artists Call Against U.S. Intervention in Central America. She is also cofounder of the New York artists' bookstore, Printed Matter. Her books include *From the Center*, *The Pink Glass Swan: Selected Feminist Essays on Art*, *Mixed Blessings*, and *On the Beaten Track: Tourism, Art, and Place*. She lives in Galisteo, New Mexico, where for fifteen years she has edited the community newsletter.

Bia Lowe is the author of *Splendored Thing: Love, Roses & Other Thorny Treasures*, a memoir about falling in love. Her first book, *Wild Ride*, won the QPB New Directions Award for creative nonfiction. Her essays have appeared in many publications, including *Salmagundi*, *The Kenyon Review*, and *Harper's*, and have been selected by Robert Atwan for *Notable Essays of 2003* and *1995*, in the Best American Essays series. Lowe was poetry editor at *Ms.* magazine (2003–05).

Laura Meyer, Associate Professor of Art History at California State University, Fresno, has written widely on the feminist art movement in California. Her essays and book chapters appear in *Sexual Politics: Judy Chicago's "Dinner Party" in Feminist Art History*; *Art/Women/California: Parallels and Intersections, 1950–2000*; *The Sons and Daughters of Los: Culture and Community in LA*; *A Companion to Art Since 1945*; and *n.paradoxa*. In 2009, she produced the exhibition and catalog *A Studio of Their Own: The Legacy of the Fresno Feminist Experiment*, documenting the Fresno Feminist Art Program, which lay the groundwork for subsequent feminist programs at the California Institute of the Arts and the Los Angeles Woman's Building.

Michelle Moravec is Associate Professor of History at Rosemont College. A historian with a focus on the intersections of feminism, culture, and activism, she received her PhD in Women's History from the University of California, Los Angeles. She is the recipient of fellowships from the Getty Research Institute, the Archives of American Art, the Sallie Bingham Center for Women's History and Culture, and the Southern California Historical Society. In addition to conducting over fifty oral history interviews with participants in the feminist art movement, she has authored numerous essays about artists associated with the Woman's Building. Her current project investigates the overlapping concepts of women's culture in both feminist activist and academic communities during the 1970s and 1980s.

Kathleen Walkup is Professor of Book Art and Director of the Book Art Program at Mills College, where she teaches typography, letterpress printing, and artists' bookmaking to undergraduate and graduate students. Her earliest teaching included letterpress workshops at the Woman's Building. Her interests include the history of women in print culture and conceptual practice in artists' books; she has lectured and written widely on these areas. Her most recent curatorial project is *Hand, Voice & Vision: Artists' Books from Women's Studio Workshop* (Grolier Club, New York, 2010, plus several other venues). She is cofounder and was the first executive vice president of College Book Art Association. She is a consultant for the PBS program *Craft in America*, and writes a seasonal blog, *New Irish Journal*.

Terry Wolverton is author of eight books: *Embers*, a novel-in-poems; *Insurgent Muse: Art and Life at the Woman's Building*, a memoir; *The Labrys Reunion* and *Bailey's Beads*, novels; *Breath*, a self-published collection of short stories; and three collections of poetry: *Black Slip*, *Mystery Bruise*, and *Shadow and Praise*. A new novel, *Stealing Angel*, will be published in 2011. She has also edited fourteen literary anthologies, including the award-winning, six-volume series *His: Brilliant New Fiction by Gay Men* and *Hers: Brilliant New Fiction by Lesbians*. She spent thirteen years at the Woman's Building as an artist, student, teacher, and administrator, eventually serving as Executive Director. She is the founder of Writers At Work, a creative writing center in Los Angeles, where she teaches fiction, creative nonfiction, and poetry. She is also Associate Faculty Mentor in the Master of Fine Art Writing Program at Antioch University Los Angeles.

From Site to Vision: the Woman's Building in Contemporary Culture

From Site to Vision was originally published as an (e)book in 2007 by the Woman's Building and edited by Sondra Hale and Terry Wolverton. In developing and researching all the components (exhibition, website, oral histories and publications) for *Doin' It in Public: Feminism and Art at the Woman's Building*, we felt it was important to bring these insightful books together into a two-volume set. This is one effort, of which we hope there will be many, to provide an in-depth view of the significance of the Woman's Building in the development of feminist art and women's culture in Los Angeles.

Pacific Standard Time

Doin' It in Public: Feminism and Art at the Woman's Building has been organized by Otis College of Art and Design as part of Pacific Standard Time: Art in L.A. 1945–1980. This unprecedented collaboration brings together more than sixty cultural institutions from across Southern California for six months beginning October 2011 to tell the story of the birth of the L.A. art scene. Pacific Standard Time is an initiative of the Getty. The presenting sponsor is Bank of America.

Doin' It in Public: Feminism and Art at the Woman's Building is made possible by a generous grant from the Getty Foundation with additional funding provided by the Andy Warhol Foundation for the Visual Arts, Henry Luce Foundation, Department of Cultural Affairs of the City of Los Angeles, the Barbara Lee Family Foundation, and Supporters of the Woman's Building.

Project Directors and Curators
Meg Linton
Sue Maberry

Project Advisors and Consultants
Jerri Allyn
Nancy Angelo
Cheri Gaulke
Vivien Green Fryd
Sondra Hale
Alexandra Juhasz
Jennie Klein
Michelle Moravec
Elizabeth Pulsinelli
Jenni Sorkin
Susan Silton
Terry Wolverton

Project Research Assistants
Jenay Meraz
Joanne Mitchell
Kayleigh Perkov
Julia Paoli
Paige Tighe